Thomas Henry Farrer

# Free Trade versus Fair Trade

Thomas Henry Farrer

**Free Trade versus Fair Trade**

ISBN/EAN: 9783744733922

Printed in Europe, USA, Canada, Australia, Japan

Cover: Foto ©ninafisch / pixelio.de

More available books at **www.hansebooks.com**

# FREE TRADE

*versus*

# FAIR TRADE.

BY

SIR T. H. FARRER, BART.

CASSELL & COMPANY, LIMITED:

LONDON, PARIS, NEW YORK & MELBOURNE.

1885.

# PREFACE TO FIRST EDITION.

For the following pages I am alone responsible. They contain an attempt to illustrate established truths, and to expose exploded though not obsolete fallacies; but they trench so closely on the politics of the day that I should have scarcely felt justified in writing them for publication without the encouragement of the President of the Board of Trade.

For the Tables appended. I am indebted to Mr. E. J. Pearson and Mr. G. H. Simmonds, of the Statistical Department of the Board of Trade. They will be found to contain useful and interesting information, whatever may be thought of the inferences I have drawn from them. Those who have had much to do with statistics will know how difficult it is to use them properly, and how easy and how mischievous it is to use them carelessly and improperly.

T. H. FARRER.

*Board of Trade,*
*December,* 1881.

# PREFACE TO SECOND EDITION.

In revising this work and the annexed Tables, I have carried the figures down to date, excepting in Tables VIII., IX., X., and XI., which relate to a temporary and special subject; in Tables XIII. and XIV., which give the rates of Import duties levied abroad on our principal manufactures; and in Tables XVIII., XIX., and XX., which contain an analysis of the Exports of France, Germany, and the United States into food, raw material, and manufactures. These five Tables involve great labour, and to complete them to the present time would not be worth while.

I have added two Tables to the Appendix, the one, XXI., relating to the Trade of the Australian Colonies and Canada during the last decade; and another, XXII., containing an epitome of the various statistics of the United Kingdom, which are generally appealed to as evidence of the condition of its population and industries. Such an epitome I have often wanted myself, and hope that it may be found generally useful. For these Tables, and for the figures and statistics generally, I am indebted to Mr. Bateman, Mr. Simmonds, and Mr. Stanley, of the Commercial Department of the Board of Trade.

I have also added observations on various topics, suggested by recent circumstances; among which may be mentioned Chapter XX., on the question, Whether English taxes on our own industries can be compensated by duties on foreign goods ; Chapter XXII., on Investment of Capital abroad; Chapter XXXII., on present depression in England ; Chapter XXXIII., on present depression in America ; various illustrations of the diverse effects of Freedom and Protection in particular cases in Chapter XXXV ; and a Chapter on Sugar, XXXVI.

I have also tried to eliminate everything of a personal or party character. There has been much Fair Trade literature since the date of my first Edition, but it has not essentially altered the position. I have read it to the best of my ability, and it must not be thought that I have neglected its contents because I have not attempted to criticise them in detail. A straightforward statement of the reasons which make me think the Fair Trade proposals inadmissible is more likely to be readable and effective than a detailed exposure of arguments which seem to me fallacious, or of statements which seem to me incomplete or inaccurate.

T. H. FARRER.

*1st June*, 1885.

# CONTENTS.

## CHAPTER V.



## CHAPTER VI.



## CHAPTER VII.



## CHAPTER VIII.

## Part II.—Retaliation.

## CHAPTER XXIX.



Trade of Canada since new Canadian tariff—Comparison of growth of trade, &c., in Victoria and New South Wales.

## CHAPTER XXX.



Losses of Farmers due to four causes : 1, Rise of rents ; 2, Rise of wages ; 3, Lowered prices ; 4, Deficient production—First three a loss to the landed interest, not to the whole community—What is the effect of deficient harvests on entire community ?

## CHAPTER XXXI.



Burden of proof lies on those who call for change of our policy—Commercial depression subsequent to 1873—Exaggeration of prosperity of 1872-73—Statistics founded on price misleading—Prices of raw material—Temporary causes of inflation—Large exports and high prices not necessarily tests of prosperity—Appreciation of gold—Change in mode of doing business.

## CHAPTER XXXII.



Since 1880 there has been revival and subsequent depression—Causes : 1, Agricultural depression continued ; 2, Boom and subsequent collapse in shipping ; 3, Boom and collapse in United States' railways ; 4, Consequent revival and subsequent depression in iron trade ; 5, Glut of corn ; 6, Wars and Protective tariffs—Extent of depression : Statistics for 1879 to 1884 of Shipping—Railways—Production of coal and iron—Cotton—Wool—Consumption of sugar, tea, &c.—Pauperism—Savings Banks.

## CHAPTER XXXIII.



Depression in the United States—Mr. Forwood—Mr. Mc.Culloch's Report on the glut in manufactures in the United States—Agriculture in the United States—Railways in the United States—Bankruptcies in the United States—And in England—Clearing House business in the United States and in England—Emigration to the United States—Employment of labour in United States—*Bradstreet's* inquiry and report—General reduction in wages—Employment of labour—Protected industries have suffered most—Steel and iron have suffered most of all—These facts illustrate the effect of Protection.

## CHAPTER XXXIV.



Shipping of the United Kingdom—French shipping—United States shipping—Early promise of United States shipping—De Tocqueville's prophecy—Present state of American as compared with British shipping—Shipping as compared with railway interest—Present depression.

## CHAPTER XXXV.



Leather, increase of manufactures of—Free importation of foreign hides—Leather, tanning and manufactures of—Salt, French duty on—Silk; French duty on cotton yarns—Clocks in England and United States—Woollens in United States—Steel rails in United States—Copper in United States—Biscuits—Wire.

## CHAPTER XXXVI.



Importance of sugar politically and economically—Enormous and increasing supply—The supply is both of cane and beet sugar—Raised in all countries and climates—England's share as compared with other countries—Share of the United States, France, and Germany—It is food—It gives employment—It is also raw material—These results obtained by free importation—Taxation on sugar—Drawback on exportation—Difficulties of European Governments—Reduction and final repeal in England of sugar duties—Results—German tax and drawback—Austro-Hungary—France—Belgium—Holland—United States—Brazil—New Zealand—General action of Foreign Governments—Imports of sugar from, and exports of manufactures to Germany, Holland, and Belgium—Importunities of sugar refiners and West Indian planters—Refiners' case—Case of West Indian planters—Causes of growth of beet sugar—Restriction of the market impossible—Is cane being supplanted by beet?—Planter's interest and colonial interest not identical—West Indian sugar a comparatively small interest—They have no case for change of our fiscal system—Remedies suggested—What are bounties?—What are the retaliatory duties to be?—"Most-favoured-Nation" clause—Bad effect of retaliation abroad—Effect of duty on price—Conclusion as to sugar.

## CHAPTER XXXVII.



Englishmen must buy dearer and worse goods—Sale of English goods would be diminished—Materials would be scarcer

# FREE TRADE *v.* FAIR TRADE.

## Preliminary.

### CHAPTER I.

#### DIFFICULTY OF KNOWING WHAT TO ANSWER.

WHEN I was asked in 1880 by the president of the Cobden  Club to write something in defence of Free Trade, it seemed to me—recollecting as I did the instruction in politics which I had received from the Corn Law Controversy—as if I had been asked to prove Euclid, or give a reason for the rules of Grammar. That governments can by protective or prohibitory duties prevent and diminish, but cannot create or increase trade; that every tax on trade is a diminution of the produce of industry, felt most certainly and probably most severely by the country which imposes it; that it is just as unwise and unrighteous to prevent the number of men who make up a nation from buying their food and their clothes where they can get them best and cheapest as it would be to compel me to buy my bread from the nearest farmer or my coat from the nearest tailor; that a law which prevents the people of England from buying in France or America is in no essential respect different from a law which prevents the people of Middlesex from buying in Surrey or Lancashire; that every innocent operation of trade is necessarily an advantage to both parties concerned in it, and that to stop it by law is necessarily an evil to both;—all these, with the numerous consequences derived from them, appeared to me to be such elementary truths that I did not know where to begin.

Nor did I find much help when I looked into the public  speeches and articles of Protectionists, Fair Traders, and Reciprocitarians. Loud assertions that the British workman is disgusted with Free Trade, and a convert to Protection;

B

Attacks on Free Trade principles.

appeals to the prejudices and self-interest of special classes; allegations of national ruin, which every one knows to be false; misstatements of historical facts which have happened within my own recollection; suggestions of the superior wisdom of Prince Bismarck or M. Thiers; imaginations of the grand imperial policy which Mr. Pitt or Mr. Huskisson would have followed had they been in the place of Sir R. Peel and Mr. Cobden; attacks on Cosmopolitanism and praise of Imperialism; denunciations of political economy, in which the ignorance of the writers was as conspicuous as the violence of their language; and general philippics against Radicals, Philosophers, and members of the Cobden Club;—in all this I could find little to answer, though much to grieve at.

Allegations of National decay.

As to evidence of facts, I could find little or none. Appeals indeed there have been—*e.g.*, in the *Quarterly* *—from the general experience which is conveyed by the National statistics, to special cases, and appeals of this kind have latterly gained strength from the depression which undoubtedly exists at this† moment in many important branches of trade. To this depression and its causes I shall refer in subsequent chapters.

Recent Protectionist utterances.

There has also, since the date of my first edition, been an abundance of writing and speaking—to be found partly in the publications of the Fair Trade League, partly in newspapers and periodicals—in support of Fair Trade principles. One thing is clear from them, viz., that Fair Trade and Protection are the same thing, and that the policy and arguments of Fair Traders are those which we fondly hoped had been silenced for ever in 1846. I find in these papers abundant attempts to show in one form or another that Governments can divert trade without restricting it; that they can forcibly transfer purchases from one country to another without raising prices; and that they can raise the price paid to the seller without raising the price paid by the buyer. I find, also, a constant use of statistics, which, from one cause or another, is insufficient, incomplete, or misleading. To quote or reply to all these statements in detail would be tedious, if practicable; but I trust that I shall be found to have omitted no argument which is of real or general importance.

Let me refer, however, to one allegation which has been made in this controversy to the effect that " it is the race for

---

* *Quarterly*, 7th October, 1881.      † See Chapter XXXII. below.

cheapness caused by foreign competition which has demoralised so many of our own industries, and brought English goods into disrepute in once valuable markets." I need scarcely say that proof or facts to substantiate this charge are, as usual, wholly wanting. Nor will I pause to ask whether the evil, if it exists, is to be remedied by making English goods dear, which would be the inevitable effect of Protection here, as it is now the effect of Protection in foreign countries; but I will quote a passage I have come across in a letter from Josiah Wedgwood, dated 21st April, 1771, more than a hundred years ago :— *[Demoralisation of Manufacture by Foreign Competition.]*

"The potters seem sensible of their situation, and are quite in a panic for their trade, and indeed with great reason, for low prices must beget a low quality in the manufacture, which will beget contempt, which will beget neglect and disuse, and there is an end of the trade. But if any one warehouse distinguished from the rest will continue to keep up the quality of the manufacture, or improve it, that house may perhaps keep up its prices, and the general evil will work a particular good, and they may continue to sell ware at the usual prices when the rest of the trade can scarcely give it away." *[Josiah Wedgwood.]*

We may see from this that the apprehension of competition begetting cheapness, of cheapness begetting badness, and badness destruction of our trade, is not confined to the present generation, and existed when there was no foreign competition and abundant protection. We may also see what the clearheaded, stout-hearted Josiah Wedgwood thought to be the true way of meeting such competition; and we may judge from the subsequent history of the potteries what the ultimate effects of his mode of meeting it have been—results wider, probably, than he ever contemplated.

Let me support this view by an extract from a more modern authority.

"We ought, I think, to put legislative remedies last, instead of first, in our system of inquiry. *Of course, the great thing is to get the correct facts ; then to ask whether the depression in any particular industry is temporary or chronic ; and, if chronic, whether it is due to causes within our control. Sometimes we find ourselves face to face with impediments which are absolutely insuperable, and which it is but waste of time and strength to contend against. But more commonly I think there are remedies to be found in the exercise of greater skill, the employment of more capital, the opening up of new fields of enterprise.* *[Sir Stafford Northcote.]*

*Anything seems to me better than endeavouring to get out of a difficulty by inferior work, which is what we are always tempted to try. If a farmer starves his land, if a manufacturer puts shoddy for cloth, and so on, he increases the permanent difficulties of his case, for the land becomes less productive, and the cloth loses its character, and so loses its market. Foreign competition is, of course, one of the difficulties our working classes have to contend with ; but that is a condition of our existence, and we must meet it in the best way we can."**

Reaction against Free Trade principles.

But since the time of the Corn Law controversy there has no doubt arisen a new generation, to whom much that was burnt into the minds of their fathers by a mortal struggle has become merely an accepted tradition. There have been downs as well as ups in trade, and these have—not without fault on the part of Free Trade advocates—been attributed to our Free Trade policy. There has been a wave of National, as opposed to Cosmopolitan, sentiment passing over the world ; which, if it has produced its good effects in the consolidation of a Free American Union, and in the unification of Italy and Germany (effects, it must be remembered, odious to many of our own Imperialists), has also produced its bad effects in the Franco-German war, in the Pan-Slavonic movement against Turkey, in the tide of Imperialism which has been sweeping over ourselves, and which is not yet exhausted, in the French troubles in Africa, in the adoption of a protective policy by the United States, and in the partial relapse into a similar policy evinced by some of the nations of Europe and by some of our own colonies.

Pious Opinions.

It is not amiss, under such circumstances, that we should be reminded that there is no such thing in politics as an "infallible dogma ;" that every one has a right to a "pious opinion ;" that a great political party and its leaders have a perfect right to advocate Retaliation or Reciprocity or Fair Trade, or whatever other name or form a reversal of our existing policy may assume ; and that that policy cannot exist, and ought not to exist, unless it is able to justify itself.

Questions deserving an Answer.

There are, moreover, certain questions emerging out of the chaos of wild assertions, to which sensible and disinterested people, even though they may be resolute Free Traders, may justly require an answer, and which, perhaps, have

* Extract from a letter written by Sir Stafford Northcote to Mr. George Potter, dated 30th November, 1884, and published in the *Times*.

not been as completely answered as they ought to be; such, Questions deserving an answer. for instance, as the following, viz. :—

How is it that a period of excessive export, such as 1870–1875, is a period of undoubted prosperity; whilst a period of excessive import, like the subsequent period, has been a period of comparative depression?

If the French Treaty was right, and was followed by enormous increase of trade, is it not right to put ourselves in a position to make similar bargains by putting on duties which we can afterwards take off?

How is it that the trade of Protectionist or half-Protectionist nations, such as America and France, has advanced as quickly as or more quickly than that of Free Trade England?

Does not the present attitude of the world towards Free Trade prove that the anticipations, and consequently the reasoning, of the Free Traders was wrong?

Can we do anything to promote trade with our colonies?

Questions such as these, taken by themselves, form detached parts of a great subject, and do not afford a satisfactory opportunity of dealing with the merits of Free Trade or of the objections which have been made to it. I was, therefore, very glad when an association was formed, comprising most of the persons who have been putting forward such objections, and when that association placed before the world a programme in which its authors not only professed to state in short terms their reasons for departing from Free Trade, but placed before the world an outline of the new policy which they would have us substitute for the commercial policy of the last 40 years. Such a programme, however worthless in itself, affords a definite sub- Programme of Fair Trade League ject for discussion, in the course of which we have the great advantage of considering not only whether our present policy is absolutely good, a question which in this incomplete world it is seldom possible to answer with perfect satisfaction, but whether it is, or is not, better than other possible policies. I propose, then, first to state the effect of the programme of the Fair Trade League; to point out shortly the assumptions on which their proposal for a change of policy is founded; to show the groundlessness of those assumptions; and then to criticise at some greater length the two main propositions contained in their programme. In doing this, we shall have the opportunity of treating the incidental questions which I have mentioned above.

## CHAPTER II.

### PROPOSALS OF THE FAIR TRADE LEAGUE.

Programme of League. THE programme of the Fair Trade League is not definite in its particulars, but its principal features are as follows :—

1. Raw materials of manufacture to be admitted free.
2. Food to be taxed when coming from foreign countries ; to be admitted free when coming from our colonies and possessions. This taxation to be maintained for a considerable term, in order to give the colonies time to develop their products.
3. Tea, coffee, fruit, tobacco, wine, and spirits to be taxed 10 per cent. higher when coming from foreign countries than from our own colonies. It is not clear whether it is intended that they or some of them are to be free from taxation altogether, when coming from the colonies.
4. Import duties to be levied upon the manufactures of foreign countries which now impose prohibitory or protective duties on our manufactures ; such duties are to be removed in the case of any nation which will agree to take our manufactures duty free.

I am not aware that this programme has been altered since the date of my first edition. The subsequent publications of the League support, but do not materially vary, these proposals.

Mr. Sampson Lloyd's letters. Mr. Sampson Lloyd, in his letters published in 1882, would have us impose a differential tax on all foreign products in favour of all our colonies, with the threat that if any one of them will not reduce their duties on our goods, we will withdraw the privilege from that colony, and tax their products as foreign.

Mr. Farrer Ecroyd's resolution. Mr. Farrer Ecroyd has embodied his proposals in the following resolution, which has at any rate the merit of being more definite :—

"That, in view of the growing injury inflicted upon our industries by foreign tariffs, and the consequent importance of more rapidly developing the resources of India and the colonies, it is expedient to free ourselves as early as possible from the restraints of commercial treaties; to abolish duties upon tea, coffee, cocoa, and dried fruits imported from British possessions; to levy specific duties (in no case equal to more than ten per cent. upon ordinary average values) upon the like articles, as well as upon wheat, flour, and sugar imported from foreign countries; and also to impose an import duty upon foreign manufactures, with the notification that it should cease to operate, as against each nation, from the day on which such nation should admit British manufactures duty free."

The recent agitation on the subject of the Colonies and Colonial Federation has given emphasis to the Colonial Policy of the Fair Trade League, and we hear in various quarters proposals embodying certain features of that policy.

Before dealing with the Fair Trade programme as a practical proposal, several questions would have to be asked and answered, e.g.— *The vagueness of these proposals.*

1. What is meant by *raw materials*, and what is meant by *manufactures*, and what is the economical distinction between the two? This is a question which has not always received the attention it deserves, even at the hands of economists.

2. What would be the effect on the revenue of the practical abolition of the duties on tea, and coffee, and fruit? As a measure of economical and social reform, it would, of course, if the revenue admits of it, be welcome to every Free Trader.

3. Is it intended that food shall be admitted free from all our colonies, even where they levy protective or prohibitory duties on the produce and manufactures of the United Kingdom? And if not, is there to be a tariff bargain in each case?

4. Are the manufactures of the colonies to be admitted free, even where they place a protective or prohibitive duty on the manufactures of the United Kingdom?

These questions raise serious questions of principle and practice, the discussion of which might prove awkward to the Fair Traders, and which in general are, probably from this reason, purposely left obscure. But there is sufficient intimation of two general principles, viz. :— *Two great Principles.*

First, that we should depart from our present principle of neutrality, and that our trade with our own colonies and *1. Encouragement of Colonial Trade.*

possessions should be artificially encouraged by means of an artificial discouragement of our trade with foreign nations.

*2. Retaliation on Foreigners.*

Secondly, that we should place retaliatory duties on the manufactures of all countries which place duties on our manufactures.

These principles I propose to discuss.

*Assumed National decay.*

There is one preliminary difficulty : The advocates of this new policy, like the other writers and speakers to whom I have referred above, instead of prefacing and supporting their proposals for so great a change by an appeal to evidence which it might be possible to sift, content themselves with general assumptions, which may be denied by those who disbelieve them, but which it is difficult to disprove without a wearisome array of facts and figures. Thus it is assumed that our industries are permanently depressed and decaying ; that the excess of imports above exports is a sign of this decay; and that we are losing our position as manufacturers in the markets of

*These Assumptions answered already.*

the world. These assumptions have been dealt with already in speeches by Mr. Gladstone, Mr. Chamberlain, Mr. Cross, and Mr. Slagg ; in Mr. Whittaker's article in the October number of the *Nineteenth Century* of 1880 ; in Mr. Mundella's speech on Mr. Mac Iver's motion on the 1st of November, 1884 ; in Lord Granville's reply to Lord Dunraven on the 7th of November, 1884 ; in Mr. Williamson's article in the January number of the *Fortnightly*, 1884 ; in the publications of the Cobden Club ; in Mr. Giffen's published papers ; in many articles of the *Times*, in the *Statist*, *Economist*, and other newspapers ; and have been conclusively disproved.

It has been shown that, taking all the usual tests of national prosperity—the returns of trade, of shipping, of the income tax, of banking, of pauperism, of crime, of the general consumption of articles of food and luxury—the progress of the country as a whole is, beyond doubt, great and continuous, and that any recent depressions and fluctuations are such as have taken place at all times, and as can be easily explained by special causes, to some of which I shall have to recur below. No answer has been given to these figures, except statements concerning the well-known depressions in certain businesses, and appeals from general experience to the particular evidence of special observers in particular cases.

For convenience of reference, I have added in the Appendix a table, No. XXII., containing a summary of the statistics of the population of the United Kingdom, and of facts relating to their condition, so far as the same can be obtained, from 1840 to the present time. It comprises the following items, viz. :—Number of population, national revenue, national debt, local taxation, income tax, education, emigration, pauperism, crime, foreign trade, shipping, railways, clearing house and Bank of England returns, savings banks, production of coal and iron, price of wheat, consumption per head of spirits, tea, sugar, and imported flour, and letters delivered. It is scarcely necessary to observe that such statistics are always more or less incomplete; that they must be read with care; and that particular conclusions must be drawn with caution. But they present a synoptic view which is sufficiently accurate for general purposes, and which leads with certainty to the general conclusion that the industries of our people are not failing, that their condition is not deteriorating, and that the nation is not in a state of decay.

Beyond this I will not attempt to enter upon any general examination of the state of the country, and we may proceed at once to examine on their merits the two leading principles of the Fair Traders, viz., a new Colonial Policy, and Retaliation upon Foreign Nations. In doing so I shall have occasion to touch again on some of the above topics. In discussing these principles, I shall not confine myself to the actual proposals of the Fair Trade League, but shall endeavour to see whether the principles they advocate, which are not devoid of a certain superficial plausibility, are capable of any practical application, even though that application is not contained in the Fair Trade programme.

Table XXII. Statistics of condition of England since 1840.

# Part I.

## NEW COLONIAL POLICY.

———◦———

### CHAPTER III.

#### GENERAL CHARACTER OF THIS POLICY.

A great
National
policy.

THE Fair Trade League propose their new policy not only as a measure of economical reform, by which, as they say, Freedom of Trade would be in substance promoted, and our production and wealth increased, but as a " Great national policy which, while stimulating trade at home and promoting the prosperity of all classes, would bind together more closely by the ties of a common interest, the mother country and her scattered populations, strengthening the foundations and consolidating the power and greatness of the empire."

Imperial-
ism.

To some of us these words may appear not a little suspicious. They are not ill calculated to attract those who think that the glory of England consists in the extent of territory subject to her imperial sway, in domination over subject peoples, in superiority of strength, and in her power to inspire fear in the other nations of the world. But they are capable of a more innocent construction ; they may mean only that whilst free and peaceful intercourse is to be desired amongst all mankind, it is especially to be desired and promoted amongst those who have sprung from the same origin, who have the same history, who speak the same language, whose lives are ordered by the same laws and customs, and who are subject to the same form of government. If this is their true meaning, it is not for the Cobden Club, whose motto is " Free Trade, peace, good-will amongst nations," to object to such a policy, nor would I say one word against it. To improve and render more cordial the relations between the United Kingdom and our great English-speaking and self-governing colonies would, indeed, be a labour worthy of a statesman, or of a generation of states-men. But the British Empire is made up of very different elements. To deal with Canada or Australia, on the one hand, and with India or Ceylon on the other, as united with us by the same relation, and capable of being dealt with in the same manner, is to confound things which are really distinct. Even in our purely commercial relations with these different countries, there are, as will be seen below, great differences; and in all the political relations by and through which the proposed new commercial policy is to be carried out, the differences are still greater. There is, therefore, great reason to view with suspicion any plan which proposes to apply one and the same policy, and that an entirely new and experimental policy, to all these different communities, and it is, at any rate, necessary to subject it to the strictest examination. If, upon such examination, it can be shown that the policy in question is founded on a misapprehension of existing facts, that its economical consequences to the colonists and to the mother country will not only not be what its advo-cates anticipate, but will be injurious to them both, and that, so far from strengthening the friendly relations of the colonies to the mother country, such a policy is calculated to cause ill-will and to precipitate disruption, then we may, without hesitation, discard this latest product of Protection and Im-perialism, as we have discarded other follies of the kind.

Suspicious Character of this Policy.

---

# CHAPTER IV.

## ASSUMPTION THAT OUR COLONIAL TRADE IS MORE STEADILY INCREASING AND LESS FLUCTUATING THAN OUR TRADE WITH FOREIGN COUNTRIES.

At the bottom of the new Colonial Policy lie two assumptions, which, though stated with the vagueness which characterises all the Fair Trade arguments, are no doubt to be implied from their programme. These are, first, that whilst our profitable trade with foreign countries is both unsteady and declining,

Superior Growth and steadiness of Colonial Trade assumed.

our profitable trade with our own colonies is steadily increasing ; and, secondly, that our own colonies are more and more ready and willing to receive our goods, whilst foreign nations are more and more disposed to reject them.

I propose to deal with these two assumptions successively, and shall be able to show that neither of them can be accepted as true. Those who are satisfied already that these assumptions are unfounded ; that our trade with foreign countries is as valuable to us as our trade with our colonies ; and that the trade of all countries is so bound up together that to limit one branch is to limit others also, may pass over the long array of facts and figures contained in this and the two following chapters, and go on to Chapter VII.

Fair Trade allegations of superior growth and profit of Colonial Trade.

Let us see what the Fair Trade League say in favour of the first of these assumptions. They give, in this programme, as the chief reason for the proposal to tax foreign food, and admit colonial food free, that it will " transfer the great food-growing industries we employ from Protective foreign nations, who refuse to give us their custom in return, to our own colonies and dependencies, where our goods will be taken, if not duty free, yet subject only to revenue duties almost unavoidable in newly-settled countries, and probably not equal to one-third of the Protective duties levied by the United States, Spain, Russia, &c. ;" and to this is appended the following amazing note :—" Even at the present time every quarter of wheat imported from Australia affords us in return sixteen times as much trade and employment as a quarter of wheat imported from the United States, and every quarter of wheat imported from Canada thirty-five times as much as one imported from Russia " ! !

Mr. Farrer Ecroyd, again, who, in his article in the October number of the *Nineteenth Century*, 1881, made himself the expositor of the Fair Trade programme, says :—" Had it (viz., the £30,000,000 of produce which he assumes to have been lost by our bad harvests) been purchased from our own colonists, the money would have come round again, and have given employment to all our industries, as an immensely-increased export of our manufactures would have paid the bill ;" and again—" Our experience teaches us that in buying food from our colonies, we enjoy a return trade in our manufactures at least twenty times larger per head than with the Americans and Russians ;" and again—" Assuming that we shall purchase food produced in our own dominions *as cheaply* as it now is purchased in the United States or in Russia, experience assures us that we shall obtain in exchange for the purchase of it a dozen or twenty times more employment for home industries than we now do."

It is really difficult to get at what is in the brains of men who make such statements. It would seem that they think that the simple export of British goods without payment is *per se* a good to this country; that Australia gets (say) sixteen or twenty times as much of our manufactures in payment for a quarter of wheat as Russia or the United States get; and that, therefore, it is of the utmost importance to us to transfer our custom from Russia and the United States, to whom we pay so little, to Australia, to whom we pay so much. But it is the facts, not the reasoning, of these passages with which I have now to do. Mr. Farrer Ecroyd continues:—" In connection with this subject, let any one carefully study not only the very large value of British manufactures purchased annually per head by the inhabitants of our colonies as compared with the Americans, but also the remarkable steadiness of the colonial demand as compared with the violent fluctuations in that of the United States. And, further, let him examine the expansion during the past twenty-five years of the outlet for our manufactures in India and our colonies, compared with the stunted growth, or positive decline, of the trade to foreign high-tariff markets. He will then be able to form some idea of the demand upon our industries that would accompany the gradual transference to India and the colonies of the growing of fifty million pounds' worth of food, now annually imported from the United States and Russia ; and, bearing in mind that the economic gain from that increase of employment, however great, would probably be of far less value than the moral and social results of its superior steadiness, he will begin to appreciate more fully the importance of this great question to our labouring population."

These statements are very vague ; but the impression which they convey concerning the facts of the colonial trade is shared by many persons who are not members of the Fair Trade League, and there is some evidence which may be fairly quoted in favour of it. There is, especially, one passage much quoted and relied on, which is both specific and accurate, and which, therefore, it is worth while to give at length. It is from an official report of the Board of Customs,* and is as follows :—

"EXPORTS."

"*Produce and Manufactures of the United Kingdom.*"



"The value of the produce and manufactures of the United Kingdom exported to foreign countries and British possessions in the year 1880 was as follows, namely :—

| | £ |
|---|---:|
| Foreign Countries | 147,806,267 |
| British Possessions | 75,254,179 |
| Total | 223,060,446 |

showing an increase of £31,528,688 upon the value of similar exports in the year 1879, or 16½ per cent., and by assigning to each of those divisions its proportion of the increase, we find that the value of the goods exported to foreign countries exceeded that of 1879 by £17,276,620, or 13¼ per cent., and that the value of goods sent to our colonies and dependencies was greater by £14,252,068, or 23½ per cent., than in 1879.

"The following table shows the percentage of difference in a series of ten years between the value of the export trade in goods of home manufacture to foreign countries and British possessions respectively, on a comparison of the figures of a given year, with those of the year preceding, namely :—

| Year. | Total Value of Exports. | Value of Exports to Foreign Countries. | Value of Exports to British Possessions. | Proportion of Foreign Countries to Total. | Proportion of British Possessions to Total. |
|---|---|---|---|---|---|
| | £ | £ | £ | Per Cent. | Per Cent. |
| 1871 | 223,066,162 | 171,815,949 | 51,250,213 | 77·0 | 23·0 |
| 1872 | 256,257,347 | 195,701,350 | 60,555,997 | 76·4 | 23·6 |
| 1873 | 255,164,603 | 188,836,132 | 66,328,471 | 74·0 | 26·0 |
| 1874 | 239,558,121 | 167,278,029 | 72,280,092 | 69·8 | 30·2 |
| 1875 | 223,465,963 | 152,373,800 | 71,092,163 | 68·2 | 31·8 |
| 1876 | 200,639,204 | 135,779,980 | 64,859,224 | 67·7 | 32·3 |
| 1877 | 198,893,065 | 128,969,715 | 69,923,350 | 64·8 | 35·2 |
| 1878 | 192,848,914 | 126,611,428 | 66,237,486 | 65·7 | 34·3 |
| 1879 | 191,531,758 | 130,529,647 | 61,002,111 | 68·2 | 31·8 |
| 1880 | 223,060,446 | 147,806,267 | 75,254,179 | 66·3 | 33·7 |

"Taking the extreme limits embraced by the table, we find that

* Parliamentary Paper, No. 2953, 1881, p. 19. Observations having a similar tendency occur in the Reports of the Customs for subsequent years, but I will not occupy space by quoting them.

in 1871, when the total export value was almost identical with that of 1880, the proportion of the goods that found their way to our colonies was represented in value by £51,250,213, or 23 per cent. of the total sum of £223,066,162, whilst in 1880 the proportion was £75,254,179, out of a total of £223,060,446, or 33·7 per cent." Customs Report of 1881.

### "*Exports to British Colonies.*"

" We give below a list of the principal articles, with their values, that make up the aggregate of our trade with the colonies, with the view of showing in what respect the increase of 24 millions, which has accrued in the same period of ten years, is chiefly exhibited."

| Articles. | Value in the Year 1871. | Value in the Year 1880. | Increase in 1880 as compared with 1871. |
|---|---|---|---|
|  | £ | £ | £ |
| Apparel and slops | 1,538,370 | 2,675,766 | 1,137,396 |
| Arms, ammunition, and military stores | 356,845 | 565,904 | 209,059 |
| Beer and ale | 1,195,663 | 1,209,733 | 14,070 |
| Coals, cinders, and patent fuel | 881,418 | 1,224,315 | 342,897 |
| Copper, unwrought and wrought | 817,063 | 1,206,888 | 389,825 |
| Cotton yarn | 2,258,368 | 3,789,685 | 1,531,317 |
| Cotton manufactures | 19,166,944 | 27,349,975 | 8,183,031 |
| Iron and steel, unwrought and wrought | 4,591,917 | 8,222,146 | 3,630,229 |
| Leather, unwrought and wrought | 1,133,988 | 1,362,581 | 228,593 |
| Machinery and mill work | 999,401 | 2,065,995 | 1,066,594 |
| Paper of all kinds | 486,084 | 959,378 | 473,294 |
| Silk manufactures | 320,787 | 878,089 | 557,302 |
| Woollen manufactures | 3,172,110 | 4,414,763 | 1,242,653 |
| Other articles | 14,331,255 | 19,328,961 | 4,997,706 |
| Total | 51,250,213 | 75,254,179 | 24,003,966 |

" The above-mentioned twenty-four millions represent an increase of nearly 47 per cent. in ten years in regard to our trade with the colonies, but, on the other hand, the value of our trade with foreign countries has decreased in the same period from £171,815,949 to £147,806,267, or 14 per cent., the total export trade for 1871 and 1880 being, as we have said, almost identical in amount, although showing such wide differences when classified under 'Foreign Countries' and ' British Possessions ' respectively."

Customs
Statement
as to Colo-
nial Trade
ncom-
plete
and mis-
used.

Now, this passage is, as I have said, perfectly accurate as regards the facts to which it is confined; the misfortune is that it does not contain all the facts, or give a complete account of the case; that it consequently conveys a wrong impression, and that it is capable of being misused, and has been misused accordingly.

In the first place, ten years is far too short a time by which to measure the progress and value of different branches of trade.

In the second place, this table only professes to give the exports of British produce from the United Kingdom; it does not give the imports, and without this it is useless as an index to the comparative values of the foreign and colonial trades, except, indeed, in the opinion of those who think that the value of our trade depends solely on what we give, and not also on what we get.

In the third place, by lumping all foreign countries on the one side, and all the different British possessions on the other, an impression is produced that there is some general law governing each class, which produces results differing for the two classes, but identical for all the cases within each class; and this impression is made use of with great effect by those who contend that the whole object of Trade is to export, and that, since the colonies take a growing proportion of our exports, it is our business to encourage trade with our colonies, at the expense of our trade with foreign countries. I have already pointed out how different are the circumstances of the different parts of the British Empire, and how much our relations to our self-governing colonies differ from our relations to India. Now, it is not a little remarkable that if we analyse the above comparison of 1880 with 1871 we shall find that the greatest increase in exports to the colonies, on which the Customs report lays stress, is due to India. Our exports of British produce to India were—

In 1871 .  . £18,053,478, or   8·1 per cent. of the total.
 ,, 1880 .  .  30,451,314, or 13·7      ,,          ,,

The exports to the Australian colonies were :—

In 1871 .  . £10,051,982, or   4·5 per cent. of the total.
 ,, 1880 .  .  16,930,935, or  7·6      ,,          ,,

The exports to British North America were :—

In 1871 .  . £8,257,126, or   3·7 per cent. of the total.
 ,, 1880 .  .  7,708,870, or  3·5      ,,          ,,

Further, in 1880 the exports to British India were Customs report as to Colonial Trade incomplete and misused. £9,000,000 more than in 1879, thus accounting for three-fifths of the increased colonial export for that year; so that, whilst the exports to India and to Australia very largely increased in the decade, those to British North America diminished.

Similar differences might be pointed out in the exports to foreign countries. When investigated, they are often very instructive, as I hope to show below. I mention this now only to prove, even within the narrow limits of the Customs table, how fallacious it is to draw from figures of this description any such general results as the Fair Traders have done.

It would be useless to quote or answer all the erroneous statistics, or erroneous conclusions from statistics, which have appeared on this subject; but when so great an authority as Mr. W. E. Forster, in advocating Imperial Federation, is said to have quoted figures concerning the comparative value of our foreign and colonial trade, some of which are inaccurate and others incomplete, it is worth while to call attention to the fact. I need not say that Mr. Forster has never indorsed the views of the Fair Traders: but, on the contrary, if I remember right, he expressly repudiates them.

In his recent speech at Bradford, as reported in the *Times* Mr. Forster's speech on Colonial Trade. of February 26th, 1885, are the following statements:—

"The annual trade of the British dominions beyond the seas with the United Kingdom was—exports and imports, £190,000,000; and with other countries £170,000,000; a total of £360,000,000, or six times what it was at the beginning of this century."

These figures of the trade are, after deducting bullion, and deducting also Malta trade, in accordance with the official returns of the trade for 1882; but as regards the trade at the beginning of the century, I cannot find that there are any figures which can be quoted with confidence.

Mr. Forster's speech, as reported, goes on to state that "the trade of the United Kingdom with foreign countries in 1872 was more than £248,000,000, and in 1882 was £214,000,000: a decrease in 10 years of £34,000,000; and that the trade of the United Kingdom with British possessions, which in 1872 was £66,000,000, had increased in 1882 to £99,000,000."

The figures no doubt relate to the export trade only; and, if so, they are not quite correct. The actual figures are:

C

<table>
<tr><td rowspan="6">Mr. Forster's speech on Colonial Trade.</td><td colspan="2" align="center">1872.</td></tr>
<tr><td>To Foreign Countries   ..   ..   ..</td><td>£249,000,000</td></tr>
<tr><td>To British Possessions   ..   ..   ..</td><td>£66,000,000</td></tr>
<tr><td colspan="2" align="center">1882.</td></tr>
<tr><td>To Foreign Countries   ..   ..   ..</td><td>£214,000,000</td></tr>
<tr><td>To British Possessions   ..   ..   ..</td><td>£92,000,000</td></tr>
</table>

But to take any single year as the test of the course of trade, without examining the circumstances, is very apt to mislead, and does so in this instance. It so happens that 1872 was a year in which our exports to the Continent were much swollen by the results of the Franco-German war, and the payment of the French indemnity,* and, probably, also swollen by errors in our own export figures.

It is also, for reasons given at length elsewhere,† misleading to take our exports alone, or our exports to particular countries, as tests of the value of trade. Imports are as valuable as exports, and exports to a colony may be, and probably are, only one link in a chain in a circuitous trade which binds England, the colonies, and foreign countries together. The figures which I have given below and in the Appendix embrace the whole of our trade for many years; and it is to these taken as a whole, and not to the reports for a particular year, that we must look if we mean to draw accurate conclusions.

Mr. Forster is further reported to have said that the "total trade of imports and exports of the United Kingdom with the world outside British possessions had increased from 1854 to 1882 more than 77 per cent., but that the total trade, import and export, of the United Kingdom with British possessions had increased more than 170 per cent." If Mr. Forster said this, he must have been grossly misled. The official figures are as follows :—

| | Foreign Countries. | British Possessions. | Total. |
|---|---|---|---|
| 1854   ..   .. | £197,000,000 | £71,000,000 | £268,000,000 |
| 1882   ..   .. | £528,000,000 | £192,000,000 | £720,000,000 |
| Increase   ..   .. | £331,000,000 | £121,000,000 | £452,000,000 |
| Increase per cent... | 168 | 170 | 169 |

So that our trade with the colonies, instead of increasing more than twice as fast as our trade with foreign countries,

---

* See below, pp. 26 and 27.     † See below, pp. 30—36.

has in fact just kept pace with it. More complete figures on this point will be found below.

It is no doubt difficult to give, except in figures so long and minute as to be unreadable, any general view of the comparative results of our trade with the different countries of the world, but I will try to do so as briefly as I can, relegating the more cumbrous tables to an Appendix.

First, assuming the position held by the Fair Traders, that what we give, and not what we get, is the standard by which to judge of the profits of trade, let us see what our exports of British produce have been since 1840.

Exports to Colonies and Foreign Countries since 1840.

*Statement showing the* Total Exports of British and Irish Produce from the United Kingdom to the undermentioned Countries in each of the Years 1840, 1860, 1872, 1880, *and* 1883.

|  | 1840. | 1860. | 1872. | 1880. | 1883. |
|---|---|---|---|---|---|
|  | £ | £ | £ | £ | £ |
| To Colonies ...... | 11,886 167 | 26,699,543 | 42,084,663 | 44,802,865 | 51,603,468 |
| ,, British India .. | 5,212,839 | 16,965,292 | 18,471,394 | 30,451,314 | 31,874,084 |
| ,, Europe : |  |  |  |  |  |
| Russia ...... | 1,602,742 | 3,269,079 | 6,609,224 | 7,952,226 | 5,036,614 |
| Germany .... | 5,579,669 | 13,491,513 | 31,618,749 | 16,943,700 | 18,787,635 |
| Holland .... | 3,416,190 | 6,114,862 | 16,211,775 | 9,246,682 | 9,506,246 |
| Belgium .... | 880,286 | 1,610,144 | 6,499,062 | 5,796,024 | 8,327,941 |
| France ...... | 2,378,149 | 5,249,980 | 17,268,839 | 15,594,499 | 17,567,512 |
| Spain ...... | 404,252 | 2,471,447 | 3,614,448 | 3,222,022 | 3,785,034 |
| Italy ........ | 2,162,931 | 4,514,287 | 6,557,538 | 5,432,968 | 7,121,948 |
| Turkey ...... | 1,387,416* | 5,064,233 | 7,639,143 | 6,765,966 | 6,689,775 |
| Otr Countries in Europe .. | 2,006,555 | 4,964,956 | 10,987,309 | 9,727,887 | 11,695,989 |
| ,, United States of America .. | 5,283,020 | 21,667,065 | 40,736,597 | 30,855,871 | 27,372,968 |
| Total...... | 25 101,210 | 68,437,566 | 147,742,684 | 111,537,785 | 115,891,662 |
| ,, Other Countries | 9,108,524 | 23,788,826 | 47,958,666 | 36,268,482 | 40,430,259 |
| Total Foreign | 34,209,734 | 92,226,392 | 195,701,350 | 147,806,267 | 156,321,921 |
| Total...... | 51,308,740 | 135,891,227 | 256,257,347 | 223,000,446 | 239,799,473 |

* Including Greece, Wallachia, and Moldavia in 1840.

Putting these figures in the form of percentages, they are as follows :—

|  | To Colonies. | To India. | To Foreign Countries. |  |
|---|---|---|---|---|
| 1840 | 23 | 10 | 67 | 100 |
| 1860 | 19½ | 12½ | 68 | 100 |
| 1872 | 16½ | 7 | 76½ | 100 |
| 1880 | 20 | 13½ | 66½ | 100 |
| 1883 | 21½ | 13¼ | 65¼ | 100 |

C 2

There is here no symptom of any permanent increase in the percentage of the colonial exports, but rather the reverse. The percentage of the foreign exports, which rose rapidly with the loans and inflation of 1872, has otherwise remained steady, and there have been great fluctuations in the percentage of the Indian trade. There is certainly nothing in these figures to lead one to suppose that we should sacrifice the trade with foreign countries in order to nurse the colonial trade.

Trade with Colonies and Foreign Countries in each of the last 25 years, as a whole.

But no view of trade is complete which deals with exports alone, nor is a comparison of one single year at one period with another single year at another sufficient to show the general course of trade. I have therefore annexed* four tables, showing for each of the last twenty-eight years the amount and proportions of our trade with foreign countries and with our own colonies and possessions respectively. The first of these tables gives the exports of produce of the United Kingdom; the second gives the total exports, including re-exports of foreign and colonial produce; the third gives the total imports; and the fourth gives the total of the imports and exports. For each year is given the percentage of the foreign and colonial trades respectively. From these tables it is clear that whether we take, as the Fair Traders do, the exports of British produce only, or the total exports, or the total imports, or, which is the fairest test, the whole of the trade exports and imports together, there is not the least ground for the assertion that the whole of our trade with our own possessions has grown faster than our trade with foreign nations, or that it is subject to fewer fluctuations. Taking the exports of the produce of the United Kingdom, the exports to the colonies were 33 millions in 1856, rose to nearly 54 millions in 1866, sank to 48 millions in 1869, rose to 72 millions in 1874, fell to 61 millions in 1879, rose to nearly 85 millions in 1882, and fell to 83½ millions in 1883. Of the imports, the colonial share is smaller, but equally fluctuating. It was 43 millions in 1856, 38 millions in 1858, 93 millions in 1864, since which time it declined, being as low as 73 millions in 1871, and 78 millions in 1878, rising again to 92 millions in 1880, and to 99 millions in 1882. Taking the whole of the trade of the United Kingdom—imports and exports

---

* See Tables I., II., III., and IV., in Appendix.

together—which is by far the fairest test, the colonial share of the trade was 80 millions in 1856, 149 millions in 1864, 114 millions in 1867, 165 millions in 1877, 145 millions in 1879, 174 millions in 1880, and 191 millions in 1882. If we turn to the tables, we shall see that these fluctuations are as great as those which have taken place in the trade with foreign countries. The proportion which our colonial trade bears to our whole trade has varied between 31·3 per cent., at which it stood in 1863, to 20·9 per cent., at which it stood in 1871; it stood at 25·6 per cent. in 1856, at 24·9 per cent. in 1880, at 26·7 per cent. in 1882, and at 25·8 per cent. in 1883. It has kept pace with our foreign trade, and forms about a quarter of it. But it fluctuates as much as our foreign trade, and forms a smaller proportion of it now than it did twenty years ago.

But even these figures, whilst amply sufficient to show that there is no ground whatever for supposing that our foreign trade, as a whole, is either more precarious or less profitable than our colonial trade, lump all foreign countries and all colonies together, and fail to show how different has been the course of trade with different colonies and different countries, and how fallacious it is to include in one and the same class either the one or the other. I have therefore added to the Appendix some tables,* showing what has been the course of trade with each foreign country and with each colony or group of colonies for the last eighteen years, giving for each country and for each year the exports and imports separately, and the percentage which they constitute of the aggregate imports and exports. I have also added a table† giving a summary of the whole, showing, in the form of percentages, what has been the proportion which our trade with each country and each colony in each year, and in each completed period of five years, has borne to our whole trade.

The following summary shows at a glance what proportion of our whole trade has been carried on with each foreign country and each colony for each of the three periods of five years, ending with 1880, and for the subsequent three years.

Trade with each Foreign Country and each Colony for each of last 18 years.

* See Tables V. and VI., in Appendix.
† See Table VII., in Appendix.

## FOREIGN COUNTRIES.

*Statement of the proportion Per Cent. of our whole Foreign Trade carried on with each Foreign Country.*

| | Russia | Germany | Holland | Belgium | France | Italy | Turkey | Egypt |
|---|---|---|---|---|---|---|---|---|
| | Pr. Ct. | Pr. Ct. | Pr. Ct. | Pr. Ct. | Pr. Ct. | Pr. Ct. | Pr. Ct. | Pr. Ct. |
| 5 Years ending 1870. | 5·3 | 9·0 | 5·4 | 3·2 | 11·2 | 1·9 | 2·6 | 4·5 |
| 5 Years ending 1875. | 5·0 | 8·8 | 5·5 | 4·1 | 10·8 | 1·8 | 2·1 | 2·9 |
| 5 Years ending 1880. | 4·2 | 8·2 | 5·8 | 3·8 | 10·9 | 1·6 | 1·9 | 1·9 |
| 1881 | 3·3 | 7·6 | 5·5 | 3·6 | 10·1 | 1·6 | 1·7 | 1·8 |
| 1882 | 4·1 | 7.8 | 5·8 | 4·2 | 9·6 | 1·5 | 1·6 | 1·5 |
| 1883 | 3·9 | 8·2 | 5·6 | 4·2 | 9·3 | 1·6 | 1·8 | 1·8 |
| Average for whole Period. | 4·6 | 8·5 | 5·6 | 3·8 | 10·7 | 1·8 | 2·1 | 2·8 |

## FOREIGN COUNTRIES (*continued*).

| | United States | Brazil | Chili | Peru | China | Japan | Other C'ntries | Total |
|---|---|---|---|---|---|---|---|---|
| | Pr. Ct. | Pr. Ct. | Pr. Ct. | Pr. Ct. | Pr. Ct. | Pr. Ct. | Pr. Ct. | Pr. Ct. |
| 5 Years ending 1870. | 13·7 | 2·5 | 1·2 | 1·0 | 3·0 | 0·3 | 12·2 | 77·0 |
| 5 Years ending 1875. | 15·5 | 2·3 | 1·1 | 1·1 | 2·8 | 0·4 | 13·1 | 77·3 |
| 5 Years ending 1880. | 17·6 | 1·8 | 0·8 | 0·8 | 2·8 | 0·5 | 12·8 | 75·4 |
| 1881 | 20·2 | 1·9 | 0·8 | 0·5 | 2·4 | 0·5 | 12·8 | 74·3 |
| 1882 | 17·7 | 1·9 | 0·9 | 0·5 | 2·1 | 0·4 | 13·8 | 73·4 |
| 1883 | 18·6 | 1·8 | 0·8 | 0·4 | 2·0 | 0·4 | 13·8 | 74·2 |
| Average for whole Period. | 16·3 | 2·1 | 1·0 | 0·9 | 2·7 | 0·4 | 12·8 | 76·1 |

COLONIES AND BRITISH POSSESSIONS.

*Statement of the proportion Per Cent. of our whole Foreign Trade carried on with each Colony.*

| | British North America | British West Indies | Australian Colonies | India | South Africa | Other British Possessions | Total |
|---|---|---|---|---|---|---|---|
| | Pr. Ct. | Pr. Ct. | Per Cent. | Pr. Ct. | Pr. Ct. | Per Cent. | Per Cent. |
| 5 Years ending 1870. | 2·7 | 1·7 | 4·8 | 9·7 | 0·9 | 3·2 | 23·0 |
| 5 Years ending 1875. | 3·1 | 1·5 | 5·3 | 8·1 | 1·2 | 3·5 | 22·7 |
| 5 Years ending 1880. | 2·9 | 1·5 | 6·6 | 8·5 | 1·6 | 3·5 | 24·6 |
| 1881 | 3·0 | 1·2 | 7·3 | 9·2 | 1·9 | 3·1 | 25·7 |
| 1882 | 2·9 | 1·4 | 7·4 | 9·8 | 2·0 | 3·1 | 26·6 |
| 1883 | 3·0 | 1·2 | 7·2 | 9·9 | 1·5 | 3·0 | 25·8 |
| Average for whole Period. | 2·9 | 1·5 | 5·9 | 8·9 | 1·4 | 3·3 | 23·9 |

In order that I may not appear to overlook the facts relied on by the Fair Traders, I give the following summary, in a similar form, of the course of our export trade to each country. The following percentages are the percentages of the total exports, including re-exports of foreign and colonial produce. But the percentages are much the same as they would be if the exports of the produce of the United Kingdom alone were included, and in the tables appended the figures for both kinds of export are given fully. But, whilst I give these figures in deference to the weaknesses of the Fair Traders, I protest against the notion that exports are more important than imports, and also against the notion that the direct trade to or from each country and colony shows the whole character of the transaction. Trade is circuitous, and the debt which accrues to us in consequence of an export to a colony is often repaid to us by our imports from some foreign country. Moreover, as we shall see below, temporary causes have an immense effect both on our exports and imports ; and although in the long run trade balances itself, the exports to any one country for any given year, or short term of years, or even the exports

Exports to each Foreign Country and each Colony for 18 years.

and imports together, are often a most imperfect index of the nature of our whole trade with that country.

### EXPORTS TO FOREIGN COUNTRIES.

*Statement of the proportion Per Cent. of Exports from United Kingdom, including Re-exports, to each of the undermentioned Foreign Countries.*

|  | Russia. | Germany | Holland | Belgium | France | Italy | Turkey | Egypt |
|---|---|---|---|---|---|---|---|---|
|  | Pr. Ct. | Pr. Ct. | Pr. Ct. | Pr. Ct. | Pr. Ct. | Pr. Ct. | Pr. Ct. | Pr. Ct. |
| 5 Years ending 1870. | 3·5 | 12·6 | 6·9 | 3·4 | 10·1 | 2·8 | 3·2 | 3·3 |
| 5 Years ending 1875. | 3·6 | 12·6 | 7·6 | 4·5 | 10·0 | 2·7 | 2·5 | 1·8 |
| 5 Years ending 1880. | 3·6 | 11·4 | 6·2 | 4·7 | 10·5 | 2·7 | 2·8 | 1·0 |
| 1881 | 3·1 | 9·9 | 5·1 | 4·6 | 10·1 | 2·5 | 2·5 | 1·1 |
| 1882 | 2·8 | 10·0 | 5·3 | 4·9 | 9·7 | 2·4 | 2·3 | 0·9 |
| 1883 | 2·5 | 10·4 | 5·2 | 4·8 | 9·6 | 2·7 | 2·4 | 1·2 |
| Average for whole Period. | 3·4 | 11·8 | 6·6 | 4·4 | 10·1 | 2·7 | 2·7 | 1·8 |

### EXPORTS TO FOREIGN COUNTRIES (*continued*).

|  | United States | Brazil | Chili | Peru | China | Japan | Other Foreign Countries | Total |
|---|---|---|---|---|---|---|---|---|
|  | Pr. Ct. | Pr. Ct. | Pr. Ct. | Pr. Ct. | Pr. Ct. | Pr. Ct. | Per Cent. | Pr. Ct. |
| 5 Years ending 1870. | 11·7 | 2·7 | 1·0 | 0·6 | 2·6 | 0·7 | 11·8 | 76·9 |
| 5 Years ending 1875. | 12·0 | 2·5 | 0·9 | 0·8 | 1·9 | 0·7 | 12·6 | 76·7 |
| 5 Years ending 1880. | 9·4 | 2·5 | 0·6 | 0·4 | 1·9 | 1·1 | 12·8 | 71·6 |
| 1881 | 12·4 | 2·3 | 0·9 | 0·3 | 2·1 | 1·1 | 12·8 | 70·8 |
| 1882 | 12·6 | 2·4 | 1·0 | 0·4 | 1·6 | 0·8 | 12·8 | 69·9 |
| 1883 | 12·0 | 2·3 | 0·7 | 0·3 | 1·5 | 0·9 | 13·9 | 70·4 |
| Av. for whole Period. | 11·3 | 2·5 | 0·9 | 0·6 | 2·0 | 0·8 | 12·6 | 74·2 |

COLONIES AND BRITISH POSSESSIONS.

*Statement of the proportion Per Cent. of Exports from United Kingdom, including Re-exports, to each of the undermentioned Colonies.*



| | British North America | West Indies | Australia | India | South Africa | Others | Total |
|---|---|---|---|---|---|---|---|
| | Pr. Ct. | Pr. Ct. | Per Cent. | Pr. Ct. | Pr. Ct. | Pr. Ct. | Per Cent. |
| 5 Years ending 1870. | 2·9 | 1·2 | 5·4 | 8·9 | 0·7 | 4·0 | 23·1 |
| 5 Years ending 1875. | 3·3 | 1·2 | 5·9 | 7·5 | 1·4 | 4·0 | 23·3 |
| 5 Years ending 1880. | 2·9 | 1·2 | 7·7 | 10·1 | 2·2 | 4·3 | 28·4 |
| 1881 | 3·1 | 1·0 | 8·1 | 10·4 | 2·6 | 4·0 | 29·2 |
| 1882 | 3·5 | 1·1 | 9·3 | 10·0 | 2·6 | 3·6 | 30·1 |
| 1883 | 3·3 | 1·2 | 8·8 | 10·9 | 1·7 | 3·7 | 29·6 |
| Average for whole Period. | 3·1 | 1·2 | 6·8 | 9·1 | 1·6 | 4·0 | 25·8 |

It would take more time and more knowledge than I possess to explain in detail the figures contained in the appended tables. Each foreign country and each colony shows its own fluctuations, both of imports and exports, and these fluctuations have been as great in the colonial as in the foreign trade. It would be most instructive to trace these fluctuations to their real causes. Protectionist tariffs have, no doubt, in some cases, and to some extent, been causes of these fluctuations; but other causes, such as the cotton famine, the Franco-German war, the French indemnity, English investments abroad, bad harvests in Europe and good ones in America, the wars in South Africa and in Egypt, have probably been still more potent factors. To trace the effect of these causes would throw light on many a delusion, and it is to be wished that some competent person would undertake to do this completely. At present I can only call attention to one or two facts connected with the different trades.

### *Our Trade with Germany and Holland.*

Germany and Hol'and.

These two countries may be taken together, since much German trade goes through Holland. Their proportion of our whole trade, including imports and exports, has remained steady during the last eighteen years. The exports increased in the five years ending 1875, especially in the years 1871 and 1872, and decreased in the five years ending with 1880, and have since slightly increased. The exports of British produce to Germany were, in 1870, 20 millions; in 1872, $31\frac{1}{2}$ millions; of which considerably more than one-half consisted of cotton and woollen manufactures; in 1880, 17 millions, and in 1883, nearly 19 millions. The German tariff may have been one cause of the diminution in 1880, and a real decline in the demand for English woollen manufactures may have been another. But in comparing the figures of cotton and woollen manufactures of different periods, there are several circumstances to be taken into consideration. There were probably considerable errors in our Trade statistics up to 1872–73, making the value of woollen exports appear larger than it really was. Further, the price of the raw material constitutes a large part of the price of the manufactured article; the whole of the raw cotton and much of the raw wool come to us from abroad, and have to be paid for; and the prices of both have fallen since 1872, that of raw cotton more than 30 per cent. The apparent loss on exports has, therefore, to be diminished by the difference. But there was another temporary cause, independent of tariffs and of prices, which, no doubt, increased our exports to Germany in 1871 and 1872.

Effects of French Indemnity.

The French indemnity of 200 millions was paid to Germany partly in French cash, partly in French exports, but partly also through England, so that a part, and probably no inconsiderable part, of the large English exports of merchandise to Germany in the period from 1871 to 1875 consisted, in fact, of advances to Germany on French account, to be repaid to England by France. This is confirmed by finding that the imports into Germany from the principal European countries, viz., France, Belgium, United Kingdom and India, Italy, and also from the United States, during the five years 1871 to 1875, exceeded her exports to those countries by 23 millions a year, an excess which was reduced to eight millions in

1877.* It is also confirmed by the French statistics,† which, after showing a large excess of imports in 1871, probably to make up losses caused by the war and the defective imports of 1870, show a large excess of exports, especially to Germany, Belgium, England, and Switzerland, amounting to not less than 24 millions a year during the years 1872 to 1875. In short, France borrowed to pay the indemnity; England and other countries made advances in the shape of goods, and France has since been repaying these advances, or the interest upon them. There are, therefore, good reasons to explain the increase of German trade in 1872–75, and its subsequent decrease, without supposing that English industry is on the decline, or that the demand for English manufactures, even in Germany, is failing. On the contrary, it appears that it is now again on the increase.

The trade with Belgium is also increasing, as mentioned below. Taking Germany, Holland, and Belgium together, there is a point in our recent trade with them which deserves special notice.

The increase in the exports of British produce to Germany, Holland, and Belgium has been four millions and a half between 1880 and 1883. The increase in the value of the imports of sugar from these countries in the same years was about three millions. As these are the countries which are accused of injuring our workmen by giving a bounty on sugar, it may be some consolation to learn that they are not only providing us with cheap sugar at their own expense, but are also taking our goods in return, and employing our other industries to a larger extent than they ever did before.‡

Sugar, and how it is paid for.

### Our Trade with Belgium.

Our whole trade with Belgium is steady. Our export trade to Belgium is, on the whole, increasing; but the export of British produce was rather more in the years 1871–75 than in the years 1876 to 1880, probably for the same reasons as have been shown to apply in the case of Germany. The total

Belgium.

---

* See Table VIII., giving the Exports and Imports of Germany from 1868 to 1877. These figures are taken from the statistics of the several countries. If taken from German statistics, the figures for the imports into Germany would, no doubt, be increased, and those of exports from Germany diminished.

† See Tables IX. and X., French Imports and Exports, 1868 to 1877.

‡ See Chapter on Sugar below, p. 186

export trade to Belgium is now again increasing, and amounts to fifteen millions.

## Our Trade with France.

France.

The proportion which our trade with France bears to our whole trade has varied very little. It was rather less in nominal value in the five years ending 1880 than in the previous five years, but has been increasing since 1879. Our exports to her increased very largely in 1871, and have maintained a high average since. They were 33 millions in 1871, 25½ millions in 1877, and 29½ millions in 1883. But in 1871, out of the 33 millions, 15 were re-exports; in 1877, out of the 25½, 11 were re-exports; whilst in 1883, less than 12 were re-exports. This is probably due to the effect of the Suez Canal in bringing Oriental goods direct to French ports On the other hand, the exports of British and Irish produce to France were 18 millions in 1871, 14 millions in 1877, and nearly 17½ millions in 1882 and 1883: so that France is now taking more of our own produce than she did a few years ago. Her exports to England, in common with her exports to other European countries, increased still more largely, giving, as above stated, a surplus of exports over imports to these countries for the five years ending 1875 of 18 millions a year, a surplus probably due to the payment of the German indemnity. Since then French imports into the United Kingdom have diminished from 46 millions in 1875, to 38½ millions in 1883.

## Our Trade with Italy.

Italy.

There has not been much change in the amount or proportion of our trade with Italy. But one thing is remarkable. Italy is one of the few countries where our exports exceed our imports. This they have done for the last eighteen years, at the rate of two millions a year and upwards. During the last three years the excess has been from four to five millions. Now it is impossible to believe that we are doing trade with Italy at a loss. Is it not more than probable that Italy pays her balance to us in a circuitous way? Looking to the French statistics (see Table X.), we find that the imports from Italy into France exceed the exports from France to Italy by an amount averaging in the last ten years five millions sterling a year; and we hear, *usque ad nauseam,* that France sends us many millions more than she takes from us. It is, therefore, most likely the case that Italy sends us goods through France, and thus pays her balance to us, and increases the apparent French exports to England at the same time.

### Our Trade with Turkey.

Our imports from Turkey decreased largely between 1877 and 1879, for reasons too obvious to dwell upon. It has since increased by two millions.

Turkey.

### Our Trade with Egypt.

There has been a large diminution in our trade with Egypt, but some of it is nominal, because since the opening of the Suez Canal many cargoes to and from the East, formerly entered as to and from Egypt, have been entered as to and from the countries of destination and of shipment in the East. They may thus possibly swell the apparent increase of our Indian and Colonial trade. In the comparative cessation of the import of raw cotton from the East since the American market has been re-opened, and in the cessation of loans to Egypt after 1873, are to be found other reasons for the diminution of our trade with Egypt.

Egypt.

### Our Trade with the United States.

It is our trade with the United States which is the *pons asinorum* of our Fair Traders, and I shall have occasion to refer to it again.* Our whole trade with them has increased very largely, both absolutely and proportionately. It constituted 13·7 per cent. of our whole trade in the five years ending 1870, and 17·6 per cent. of our whole trade in the five years ending 1880. For the last three years it has ranged from 17·7 to 20·2 per cent. Our exports to the United States were 11·7 per cent. of our whole exports in the period 1866 to 1870, and only 9·4 per cent. in the period 1875 to 1880. Since 1880 they have ranged from 12·6 to 12 per cent. This diminution, together with a considerable addition to the aggregate trade, is made up by an increase of imports. The exports to the United States, which had risen very largely in 1880, have maintained themselves at about 37 millions, being by far the largest amount exported to any one country, whether foreign or

United States.

* See Chapters XXVIII., XXXIII., XXXIV., and XXXV.

United
States

British. The imports from the United States, which were 107 millions in 1880, were 99 millions in 1883. It would be idle to repeat what has been said so often already of our loans to the United States made in the earlier period, and of the payment of interest upon these loans which now appear in our imports. Nor is this the place in which to attempt to disprove the assumption made without the shadow of an argument, and, as I believe, without the shadow of foundation, by some of the Fair Traders, that we are now calling back capital from the United States. This point is referred to below in the chapter on exports and imports (Chap. XXI.); here I will only notice that, in speaking of the reasons for the excess of imports, I have given some figures which, if they approach the truth, show that we are increasing and not diminishing our foreign investments; that we are still lending rather than recalling capital; and, if this is so, the United States is certainly one of the countries to which we are lending most. One or two important facts I may point out which are shown by these tables—viz., first, that our exports to the United States increased from $17\frac{1}{2}$ millions, at which they stood in 1878, to 38 millions in 1880; and, secondly, that there are circumstances mentioned below, under the head of Indian trade, which make it in the highest degree probable that we pay for imports of corn from America by exporting manufactures to our own possessions in the East. As an illustration of the way in which this may take place, I may quote a passage from the *Economist* in the second week of October, 1881 :—" Last week the steamer *Australia*, from Sydney, landed over a million dollars in gold at San Francisco. Australia, of course, pays this gold on English account."

### *Our Trade with Brazil.*

Brazil.

Our trade with Brazil has declined, but the imports have decreased more, and are now less, than the exports. As we have lent money to Brazil and do much of the carrying trade for her, it is clear that our imports from her ought very largely to exceed our exports to her; and as her exports to the United States very largely exceed her imports from the United States, there can be little doubt that we pay some of our debts to the United States for corn and cotton, by exporting our manufactures to Brazil.

### *Our Trade with Chili and Peru.*

Both our aggregate trade and our exports to Chili and Peru considerably decreased in the five years ending with 1880, and for this the cessation of our loans to Peru, and the subsequent Peruvian collapse, and afterwards the war between Chili and Peru, are sufficient reasons. They now show symptoms of revival. *Chili and Peru.*

### *Our Trade with China.*

Our imports from China maintained their comparative position until 1880; since then they have decreased a little both absolutely and comparatively, possibly in consequence of a larger quantity of Chinese goods going direct to Continental ports through the Suez Canal. Our exports to China averaged six millions in the five years ending 1870; nearly six millions in the five years ending 1875; and something less than five millions in the years ending 1880. During the three years ending 1883 the exports have maintained about the same position as in the previous five years. This, however, is a case where nominal values conceal the real facts. Three-fourths and more of our exports to China consist of cotton and woollen manufactures. Now the quantity of cotton goods exported to China during the latter period was 2·6 per cent. more than during the previous five years, and of woollen goods 18 per cent. At the same time the price of raw cotton, which forms a large proportion of the cost of cotton goods, was 23 per cent. less in the latter than in the former period, and the cost of raw wool also much less. Consequently the real value of the exports of the produce of British labour was considerably greater in the latter than in the former period. Yet this increasing export trade is what the Fair Traders desire to check, by placing a differential duty on Chinese teas. It must also be remembered that Hong Kong, the trade with which swells the lists of colonial imports and exports, is really a depôt for China, and that in order to do justice to the trade of China, a great part of our trade with Hong Kong should be added. *China.*

### *Our Trade with Japan.*

The aggregate trade and the exports have both increased. *Japan.*

*Our Trade with British North America.*

British North America.

British North America is certainly one of the colonies to which our Fair Traders would wish to show special favour. It is Canada which is to profit by their new policy, especially by a tax on United States corn. Now, according to our own statistics, our annual imports from British North America have averaged $9\frac{1}{4}$ millions in the five years ending 1870, $10\frac{1}{2}$ millions in the five years ending 1875, $11\frac{1}{4}$ millions in the eight years ending 1883. Our annual exports have averaged $6\frac{3}{4}$ millions in the five years ending 1870, 10 millions in the five years ending 1875, and $8\frac{1}{2}$ millions in the eight years ending 1883. So that whilst the imports from Canada have gone on increasing, our exports to Canada under her Protectionist tariff have not only not increased in proportion, but are less than they were at an earlier period. These are figures from our own statistics. I have not the most recent Canadian figures, but the following is an extract from the speech made in the Canadian House of Commons by Sir Richard Cartwright on the 3rd March, 1885, in answer to Sir Leonard Tilley's Protectionist budget speech.

"Of our own produce, we sold to Great Britain in 1873, 31,876,000 dollars; in 1884, 37,410,000 dollars worth. We sold 6,000,000 dollars more of our own produce to Great Britain in 1884 than we did in 1873, and from the people of Great Britain, with whom the Minister (Sir L. Tilley) desires to favour our trade we bought in 1873, 68,360,000 dollars, and in 1884 we imported 41,826,000 dollars. We sold them 6,000,000 dollars more than we did eleven years ago, and we bought from them 26,000,000 dollars less, and the honourable gentleman considers that a proof, I suppose, of how favourable his tariff has been to the interests of our trade with Great Britain. I apply the same rule to our exports to the United States. In 1873, deducting bullion and short returns, we sold to the people of the United States 33,416,000 dollars worth of goods. In 1884 we sold them 31,632,000 dollars worth. We sold them about 2,000,000 dollars more than in 1873, deducting the goods in transit, with which the honourable gentleman has no right to complicate the account. In 1873 we bought from the people of the United States 38,147,000 dollars, and in 1884 we bought 49,785,000 dollars; and that is the year in which we improved our trade with Great Britain, and in which we diminished our trade with the United States. Our trade with Great Britain is

26,000,000 dollars less than it was eleven years ago, and our trade with the United States is 12,000,000 dollars more to the United States than it was eleven years ago. And, sir, that is not all. Our trade with Great Britain was based on a much smaller population in 1873, and our trade with the United States in 1873 was much more in our favour than appears on the trade returns.

"Then, it was we who did the smuggling; now, it is the Americans who do the smuggling into this happy country."

Sir R. Cartwright is borne out by the account given at the late meeting of the British Association at Montreal by the well-known statistician, Mr. Stephen Bourne, of the state of our trade with Canada. It is the more remarkable because the conclusion he comes to is, that we ought to refuse to trade at all with Foreign Protectionist countries in order to encourage our trade with Canada and other colonies! He says :—

"Turning to the table which sets forth the imports into Canada, it will be observed that the value has of late years exceeded that of the exports, both in the trade with the United Kingdom and the whole world, an indication that she is absorbing more than she is parting with. There is this great distinction between the two, that whereas the exports are of the raw materials for food or manufacture by the purchasers, the bulk of the imports are of manufactured goods to be used or consumed by the customers. Even those shown as animal and agricultural products are mostly in a state for use; whilst the manufactures and miscellaneous so greatly preponderate over the other classes as to altogether dwarf those in the comparison. In these, too, the proportion drawn from the United Kingdom is smaller than in the exports and less in value than those supplied by the United States. In both cases they range over every description of articles required for daily use, either for consumption or as instruments in carrying on the several industries. Like as with the exports, it is surprising to find that increase of population has brought no addition in value to the trade of recent years; indeed, that of 1883 is less than it was in 1873. This is more marked in the drafts upon the mother country which are in fact 40 per cent. less now than they were ten years ago. Lower prices may have in some degree caused this diminution, but if so as regards the exports from England, it enhances the increase

D

Our trade with Canada.

of volume in the trade with the United States, where the difference between the highest year, 1883, and the lowest one, 1880, is as much as 90 per cent. upon the smaller amount. No doubt these conditions will be greatly altered when through railway communication exists, but at present it would seem that the colony does not respond in the degree which might be looked for to the investments of capital from the mother country or the additional people she is sending over. Increased consumption must be going on; the inference therefore is that more is manufactured within the Dominion than there was formerly. The contiguity of the United States is doubtless a powerful reason for resorting to her stores, though not an encouraging feature in her relations to the mother country."

It is to be remembered that Canada largely increased her duties by her Tariff of 1879, that she is still increasing them under the high-sounding title of a " National Policy," and the above figures show the results of this policy on her trade with the mother country. This subject is further referred to below, pp. 47, 48.

### *Our Trade with the West Indies.*

West Indies.

The British West Indian trade has been nearly stationary; but our exports to the West Indies have been slightly less in nominal amount for the five years ending 1880, than for the five years ending 1875.

### *Our Trade with the Australian Colonies.*

Australia.

The imports from the Australian colonies have risen from £11,423,268 in 1866, to £25,663,334 in 1880, and to nearly £27,000,000 in 1881, and the rise has been steady, except in the case of a great jump in 1880. Since 1881 they have declined by £1,000,000. But our exports have not risen in nearly the same proportions, nor so steadily; they were £14,620,779 in 1866, and only £18,748,092 in 1880. In 1874-78 they averaged about 21 millions annually; since 1880 they have risen, amounting to 28 millions in 1882, and to nearly 27 millions in 1883.

Australia is, however, the one group of self-governing colonies to which the Fair Trader will point as showing a steady progressive increase in the whole trade, and a comparatively large recent increase in the exports they take from this country. But I am not sure that the Fair Trader will be much comforted when he learns that one great reason for the increase of exports is the larger amount of the loans which England has been making to Australia. The amount of her public debt has increased from $27\frac{1}{2}$ millions in 1867, to 78 millions in 1879, and to 109 millions in 1883.* It was estimated † that our loans made to Australia in 1880 amounted to 10 millions, and that her aggregate debt to us, including investments of all kinds, was not less than 120 millions. It is probably now much more. In the *Standard* of the 30th December, 1884, the Colonial loans for the past year are estimated at £31,000,000, most of which probably went to the Australian group. The advance of the principal probably accounts for a large part of the increase of our exports. But I fear that the Fair Traders, who are so much alarmed at the imports which the United States send us in payment of the interest on their debt to us, will at no distant time have to groan over a similar excess of imports from Australia, arising from a similar cause. And if the authority to whom I have referred is right in supposing that Australia becomes indebted to us every year for freight earned by our shipowners to the extent of many millions, they will have an additional source of alarm, for we shall get that amount of imports from them without giving them any visible exports whatever in return.

Another thing to be remarked concerning Australia, as concerning India, is that she exports to the United States more than she imports from them. I have already mentioned an instance of the way in which she makes payment to the United States on English account, and there are probably many more; if we check our imports from the United States, we shall check our exports to Australia as well as to India.

## Our Trade with South Africa.

The imports from South Africa rose steadily in the fifteen years ending with 1880 from £2,700,000 to £5,640,000, and have continued at about the same amount since. In our exports there was a rise till 1876, when there was a drop of nearly a million, viz., from £5,350,412 in 1875 to £4,502,739

---

* See Table XXI. in Appendix.    † See the *Economist*, Aug. 27, 1881.

in 1877. In 1879 and 1880, owing probably to the war, and not to legitimate trade, there was a great rise, and in 1880 they amounted to £7,206,000. In 1882 they rose to £8,000,000, but fell in 1883 to £5,000,000.

### Our Trade with India.

India.

The imports from India on the whole decreased during the fifteen years ending with 1880. The aggregate for the five years ending 1870, was 150 millions; for the five years ending 1880, 143 millions. The highest year was 1866, 37 millions; and the lowest 1879, 24½ millions. Since 1880 they have increased and amounted to about 39 millions in 1882 and 1883.

Our exports to India have been steady, ranging from 18 to 25 millions, and increasing slightly in each succeeding period of five years. But in 1880 there was a great jump from £22,714,682 to £32,028,055, and this increase has been maintained in subsequent years.

Circuitous Trade of England, the East, America, and other Foreign Countries.

But there is something further to be learnt from the Indian trade. Whilst in 1880 the exports to India, including bullion, were 37 millions, the imports from India were only 30 millions; a very remarkable fact in itself when we remember that in addition to the freight, charges, and profits, which we ought to receive over and above the value of our exports, India has to pay us about 20 millions annually in the form of tribute, for which she gets no return in goods. If this fact stood alone, it might warm the heart of a Fair Trader, but it would be an embarrassment to the political economist. Let us see if it is capable of explanation. Omitting the year 1880, we find that for the ten years ending 1879, according to the English statistics, our exports to India, including bullion, were 286 millions, and our imports from India 303 millions, or an annual average of over 28 millions of exports to 30 millions of imports. This, though more intelligible than the figures for 1880, still leaves much to be explained. Two millions a year is far short of what India ought to send us. Turning to the Indian statistics, we find that for the same ten years, the imports into India from the United Kingdom, were 351 million pounds, or an average of 35 million pounds a year; and that her exports to the United Kingdom were 295 million pounds, or an average of 29 million pounds a year; leaving an aggregate surplus of imports of 56 million pounds, and an annual average Circuitous surplus of imports of more than five million pounds. The Trade. difference between these statistics and our own is accounted for partly by the fact that though the rupee has fallen in value it is converted in the Indian statistics at the rate of 2s., and partly by the difference between the value of goods at the port of shipment, and their value at the port of arrival, but the Indian figures make it still more difficult to understand how India manages to pay her tribute to us, more especially since in the case of India there cannot be the transfer of securities by which in many other cases the balance of trade is settled. The exports of railway material to India, which were in fact loans to India, will account for a part, but only a small part, of the difference. But if we turn to another page of Indian statistics we shall find the explanation. There are many countries to which India, according to her own statistics, exports much more than she receives from them, viz. : France, Austria, Italy, the United States, China, and Ceylon. Appended is a table* giving her trade with these countries for the same years—1870 to 1879. From this table it appears that the aggregate imports into India from these countries during that period was 57 millions, and the annual average nearly six millions ; whilst the aggregate export to them from India was 243 millions, and the annual average above 24 millions ; leaving an aggregate surplus export of 186 millions, and an average annual surplus export of nearly 19 millions; which, curiously enough, is about the amount of the English tribute. This coincidence is, no doubt, accidental, and the real value of the exported goods when they reach the place of exportation must, of course, be much higher.

Now all these countries, except Italy, to which I have referred before, are countries to which, according to our own statistics, England exports much less than she receives from them, to the great sorrow of the Fair Traders. Perhaps they will be comforted when they see that the balance is redressed by means of that Indian trade which they are so desirous to encourage. England buys what she needs from America, from France, and from other countries ; India buys from England ; and America, France, &c., in their turn buy from India and the East. The process may be more circuitous still. For instance,

---

* See Table XII., in Appendix.

Circuitous Trade.

India exports to China much more than she receives from China, averaging for the ten years ending 1880, nearly 10 millions a year; China sends to America, as well as to England, more than she receives from them; England no doubt sends manufactures to India; India sends opium, &c., to China; China sends tea to America; America sends corn to England, and thus the accounts are balanced. But however numerous the steps of the process, and however circuitous the channels, trade will find its way and its level.

I have dwelt on this case because it is a good illustration of the folly of supposing that the statistics of the direct trade between any two countries give a complete account of their respective dealings, and of the consequent difficulty of foreseeing the ultimate effect of anything which promotes or impedes a particular branch of trade. In this case it is quite possible that the European demand on America for corn may have stimulated the export trade of India, which, as we have seen, has largely increased in the last few years. And it is also possible that if our Fair Traders could have their way in checking the supply of American corn to England they might be injuring that Indian trade which they are so anxious to promote.

Effect of Suez Canal

There is another observation to be made on the above figures. The proportion of our trade with France and some other Continental nations has slightly declined; so has our trade with all British colonies and possessions, excepting Australia and India. May this not be in part due to the Suez Canal, which on the one hand brings those possessions in closer communication with England, and on the other hand transfers the *entrepôt* trade of the East from England to Mediterranean ports?

Colonial Trade fluctuations.

With such figures as given above, it is nonsense to say that our colonial trade is free from fluctuations; that the demand for our exports is steadily and constantly on the increase, or that it bears in each case a fixed proportion to our imports.

Tables of Colonial Imports and Exports.

I have added to the Appendix a table (No. XXI.), showing the total imports and exports of each of the Australian colonies, and of Canada, during the last ten years. One remarkable fact is that Canadian trade is small in proportion to her population, when compared with the other colonies, and stationary; and another, that of all our colonies, New South

Wales, the Free Trade colony, is the one in which trade has progressed the most rapidly.*

From all the above figures it is clear that our direct trade with the colonies, considered in the aggregate, maintains about the same proportion to our whole trade which it did twenty years ago. It was 24 per cent. in 1866, and 25 per cent. in 1883. In the case of some colonies it is increasing, in others diminishing. With Canada and the West Indies it is nearly stationary; with Australia and India it is increasing. It is also clear that it fluctuates as much as our direct trade with other countries.

Some other things are also made obvious by them; for instance—

The direct trade with our different colonies and possessions has no uniform character making it to differ from the direct trade with foreign countries.

The direct trade either with foreign countries or with the colonies is no complete or real indication of the whole character of the trade. It is often circuitous, and the flow and return of our trade with any given country is often only completed by a roundabout route through one or more other countries. To restrict our trade with a foreign country may be to restrict the trade of a colony, and *vice versa*.

The amount of our exports to and imports from each foreign country and colony is at different times influenced by a large number of causes altogether independent of the permanent demand for our manufactures in that country, *e.g.* by such things as the Franco-German war, the French indemnity, the cotton famine, the Indian tribute, the opening of the Suez Canal, the war in South Africa, or in Egypt, and, perhaps, above all, by the character and quantity of British investments abroad. Statisticians have estimated these at £2,000,000,000. of which between three and four hundred millions are probably lent to our English-speaking colonies, and between six and seven hundred millions to the whole of the British Empire abroad, all of which tend to cause exports as the capital is lent, and imports as the interest is paid.†

*Marginal note:* Conclusions. Colonial Trade does not increase more or fluctuate less than Foreign Trade: the two are intimately connected: are similar: and are similarly influenced by many local and temporary causes.

---

* See Chapter XXIX., below:
† See *Economist* of Feb. 9th and 16th, 1885.

# CHAPTER V.



I PROCEED to consider another assumption ot the Fair Trade League—the assumption, namely, that the colonies will receive our goods on better terms than foreign countries; that they are, so far at any rate as we are concerned, less commercially hostile and less Protectionist.

It is not easy to follow the history in the changes of any one tariff, to compare specific with *ad valorem* duties, and to ascertain their several effects on our principal manufactures. Still less easy is it to compare the history of the tariffs of different countries and their several effects on our trade. But before any assumption such as I have mentioned was made, this ought to have been done. That it has not been done I need not say.

In the programme ot the Fair Trade League it is simply asserted that in our own colonies "our goods will be taken if not duty free, yet subject only to revenue duties almost unavoidable in newly-settled countries, and probably not equal to one-third the Protective duties levied by the United States, Spain, Russia, &c."

From this and similar expressions it might be supposed that the tendency of foreign countries generally was to increase their Protective duties, and the tendency of our colonies to diminish them. It is desirable to see what the facts really are. In 1879 two returns* were obtained by Mr. Talbot, giving the duties levied on the principal English manufactures in the colonies and in foreign countries in 1859 and in 1879 respectively; and a return was subsequently moved for by Lord Sandon, giving the duties levied on the principal English manufactures in all foreign countries and in each of the colonies.†

---

* See Parl. Papers Nos. 200 and 218, of 1879.
† See Parl. Paper No. 333, of 1881.

There are also appended to this paper two tables,* the one giving the actual rates of duty levied on our manufactures in the different countries and colonies at the time of these returns, the other giving the same reduced, so far as possible, into *ad valorem* duties, for the purpose of comparison. The figures in both are probably accurate enough for the purpose of the present argument, but it must be borne in mind that every statement of an *ad valorem* duty is necessarily uncertain. The price of the article at the time, the place at which the value is taken, the modes of estimating it, are all varying and uncertain factors, so that in comparing *ad valorem* duties with one another, and in reducing specific duties into *ad valorem* duties, there is always large room for doubt and inaccuracy. Since these tables were prepared, further changes have been made, generally in a Protectionist direction; and to the most important of these I have called attention in the text. Taking the different countries in succession, the general features, as shown in the above returns, and taking also into consideration subsequent alterations, seem to be as follows :—

Rates of Duty in Foreign Countries and Colonies.

### Russia.

Russia made large diminutions in her heavy duties between 1859 and 1879. From the 1st January, 1881, they have been raised 10 per cent.; but not to the extent by which they had previously been diminished. As, however, the duties are now paid in gold, the difference in value between paper and gold made the duties in many cases as high as or higher than in 1860. From the $\frac{1}{13}$th July, 1882, a new tariff and revised classification came into operation, affecting the greater number of imported articles adversely. Several articles were removed from the free list and subjected to duty, and increased duties were imposed on a great number of others. In all cases those duties, which were previously charged *ad valorem*, were changed for specific. In July, 1884, coal and coke, hitherto admitted free, were subjected to duty, and the duty on cast iron raised.

Russia.

* See Tables XIII. and XIV. For these and other tables and information I am indebted to Mr. E. J. Pearson, late of the Statistical Department of the Board of Trade. The labour of preparing them is so great that I have not had them altered so as to show changes in foreign and colonial tariffs, which have been made since 1881; but I have in this and the following chapter called attention to the most important of these changes; for this information I am indebted to Mr. Bateman.

Tariffs of Foreign Countries.

On Jan. 20/Feb. 1, 1885, the duties on various articles were again considerably raised. There has recently been imposed in the customs duties a new duty on the importation of agricultural machinery and an increased duty on herrings.

### *Germany.*

Germany.

In Germany there were very great reductions between 1860 and 1870, so that the tariff previous to the late increase was a very moderate one. In 1879 came Prince Bismarck's well-known Protectionist measures, and the duties on many articles of manufacture, as well as on food and raw materials, were largely increased. On some few articles the German duties are now higher than in 1860, but in most instances they are much lower; and, high as they are, they are not now on the whole so high as the duties imposed at the same time by Canada. On the 21st of March, 1885, a Bill was passed, provisionally raising the duties on cereals, malt, wine, and millers' products. The Reichstag has been considering for some months a proposal to raise the duties on many other articles of import, and the Bill has just passed.

### *Holland.*

Holland.

In Holland there has never been an increase, and the reductions have been frequent and steady. Her tariff is now one of the lowest in the world, as low in fact as the tariffs of our Free Trading colonies. No change since 1881.

### *Belgium.*

Belgium.

In Belgium, again, with the exception of sugar, mentioned below, there has been no increase, but many reductions. Her tariff, though not so low as that of Holland, is on the whole lower than that of France. It will compare favourably with that of Canada, if not with that of Victoria. A recent increase has been made in the excise duty on sugar, and the surtax on foreign sugars was increased at the same time.

### *France.*

France.

In France there were several diminutions of duty between 1860 and 1881. The duty on woollen yarns had been increased. Except in the case of iron, the duties were far lower than those of Canada. But a new conventional tariff came into force in May, 1882, and extended to the United Kingdom in virtue of the law of February 27th, 1882. The differences are numerous, and consist in many cases in the substitution of specific for *ad valorem* rates. On many articles the specific duties hitherto enforced were considerably raised, but on the other hand many important reductions were made. On the 28th of April two decrees were issued, signed by the President, putting in force the laws relating to increased Customs duties on cattle and cereals. From time to time changes have been effected in the construction of the tariff, and the tariff itself appears to have been in some cases harshly applied—certainly as regards imports from this country.



## Denmark.

The duties are, with a few exceptions, the same as or lower than in 1860. No alteration since 1881.



## Sweden and Norway.

Sweden.—The duties have been generally reduced since 1860, and in no case increased, except on spirits and sugar. There has been no alteration of importance since 1881 in the Swedish tariff.



Norway.—In 1882 the existing tariff was revised, some duties being increased and others decreased, but in the majority of cases the increases considerably preponderated over the decreases. In July, 1884, a new tariff was introduced, and certain changes effected in duties on articles of export from this country, there being a tendency to a slight increase.



## Italy.

Between 1859 and 1879 there were large reductions. The duties were subsequently increased, but not to the extent of the previous reductions. A treaty of commerce was established between Italy and France in November, 1881, and put into force on the 16th May, 1882, and under this treaty some important reductions were effected and extended to the United Kingdom, and a law was passed on the 6th July, 1883, further modifying the Customs duties, slightly decreasing them in a few cases. They are, on the whole, lower now than in 1860

Tariffs of Foreign Countries.

but on some important articles of British produce they are higher. The tariff is now less favourable than that of France, but much more favourable than that of Canada.

## *Austro-Hungary.*

Austro-Hungary.

The reductions between 1860 and 1870 were very large indeed. A considerable increase has since been made on silk, cotton and woollen goods, and on leather, but the recent increases are nothing like the previous reductions. A new general tariff involving a considerable augmentation of duties, came into force on June 1st, 1882. As to articles included in the Conventional tariff conceded to Italy in 1878, the augmentation did not take effect on British goods; but other articles not so included are numerous. It has been for some time in contemplation to considerably increase the duties on many articles, and a notification has recently been received to the effect that the consideration of the proposed changes is to be postponed till the autumn. The Austrian tariff is, on the whole, except in the matter of iron, considerably more favourable than that of Canada.

## *Spain.*

Spain.

Spain reduced her enormous duties between 1859 and 1879, but has since placed differential charges on English goods in return for what she considers our differential duties on Spanish wines. A new tariff came into force on August 1st, 1882, but reductions which were made applied, almost exclusively, to imports from other countries enjoying most favoured nation treatment, and therefore did not benefit British trade. On July 13th, 1883, the duties on certain raw materials imported into Spain were modified. Negotiations for a commercial treaty with this country have been proceeding, but are broken off. It is to be hoped that in reforming her tariff, the abuses of her Custom House system will also be reformed, for they are quite as great impediments to trade as her tariff.

## *Portugal.*

Portugal.

Portugal also made some reductions in her heavy duties between 1859 and 1879. A new Conventional tariff, which considerably modified the old tariff, was conceded to France and extended to other countries by the law of June 7th, 1882, Tariffs of<br>Foreign<br>Countries. and the duties then established were of a more favourable character, many reductions being made, and in several cases *ad valorem* duties were substituted for specific rates. Some slight addition has since been made.

## *United States.*

The United States are, among foreign countries, the one United<br>States. great exception to the rule that duties are, on the whole, lower than before 1860. Their present tariff, varying from 35 to 100 per cent. *ad valorem*, is not only much higher than it had ever been in previous years, but is much higher than any other of the tariffs I have referred to, and is probably as near prohibition as a working tariff can be ; and yet such are the beneficent laws of Providence, that, in spite of the folly of man, the United States do an enormous trade with us and with other countries, and have, no doubt at an immense and needless cost to themselves, the use of a large share of the good things of other countries. It has been altered from time to time, and considerable changes were made in 1883. But its general character and effect are unaltered.

On the whole the tendency of foreign countries since 1881 has been to increase their protective duties.

## CHAPTER VI.

### PROTECTION IN THE COLONIES.

LET us now consider the case of our own colonies. The Protection<br>in the<br>Colonies. following appear to be the facts :—

## *New South Wales.*

The tariff here always has been and still remains very low— New South<br>Wales. lower, except in one or two particulars, than any European tariff. New South Wales is, *par excellence*, a Free Trading colony. There has been no change of importance since 1881.

Tariffs in
Colonies.

## *Victoria.*

Victoria.

Victoria, which had in 1859 a tariff as low as New South Wales, had raised her duties considerably in 1879, and has raised them still more since. They are now considerable, and are, on many important articles, as high as those of France, Italy, or Austria, and higher than those of Holland or Norway. No change of importance since 1881.

## *South Australia.*

South
Australia.

There were no import duties in 1859; in 1879 she had imposed considerable duties on various articles of British manufacture, and these still remain. No change of importance since 1881.

## *Western Australia*

Western
Australia.

Had duties of about 7 per cent. *ad valorem* in 1859; many of them were increased to 10 per cent. by 1879, and they have since been still further raised. They are now as high as, or higher than, those of Victoria. No change of importance since 1881.

## *Tasmania.*

Tasmania.

There were no import duties in 1859; in 1879 considerable duties had been imposed, which have since been raised. They are now, on the whole, higher than those of Victoria. The general effect of the tariff remains unaltered.

## *New Zealand.*

New
Zealand.

There were no import duties in 1859; in 1879 duties amounting to 10 per cent. had been imposed on many English products. These duties have since been raised, and the tariff is now as high, on the whole, as those of other Australian colonies. In 1881 her duty of 15 per cent. on cottons was taken off. There has been no important change since.

## *Queensland.*

Queens-
land.

There were no import duties in 1859; since then duties have been imposed, which, however, are not as high as those of the last-named colonies, though higher than those of New South Wales. There has been no important change since 1881.

### *Canada*



Has, as is well known, largely increased her duties by her tariff of 1879, and has since made minor alterations, which however, have not changed the Protective character of her tariff. Some of these alterations certainly strike our industries. Her tariff is now considerably higher than those of France, Italy or Austria, and of course much higher than those of Holland or Belgium. It is thoroughly Protective, whatever Mr. Goldwin Smith may say to the contrary. It was expressly so intended by its authors, and bids fair, if the spirit in which it was proposed continues to prevail in Canada, to rival the monstrous tariff of the United States. Nor is there any tendency to improvement. Sir L. Tilley, on the 3rd of March last, 1885, introduced his budget in an elaborate speech. He is an economist who would gladden the heart of the Fair Trader. He apparently thinks that he can perform the feat of making goods dear to the buyer and cheap to the seller at the same time. He is shocked at the excess of imports into Canada ; he apologises for their increase in 1883-4. He prides himself on redressing the balance of trade, and on making his country pay to foreign countries more than she receives from them. He quotes certain figures, not undisputed, to show that in consequence of what he calls his "national policy" (which, it must be remembered, is a policy of Protection against foreign, including English, goods), Canadian manufactures have increased in the number of hands employed by 50,000, in wages paid annually by £3,000,000, and in annual value of products by £16,000,000. He seems to think that this is a pure addition to the wealth of Canada, which, but for his policy, would have gone to foreigners or to Englishmen, instead of being, as it really is, a compulsory and artificial transfer of the labour and capital of Canadians from the industries in which they can produce more to industries in which they can produce less, and a consequent diminution of the aggregate wealth of Canada and of employment for its labour—a wrong not only to the Canadian consumer, who has to pay more than he would have to pay if he bought in the open market, but a still greater wrong to the Canadian labourer and emigrant, who is prevented from producing what would give him the largest result and employ the largest quantity of labour at the highest wages. At the same time,

Sir L. Tilley does not challenge the fact that in 1878, before his Protectionist tariff, Canada sold abroad 4,127,000 dollars worth of her own manufactures, and in 1884 only 3,500,000 dollars worth ; and that—whilst the population and resources of Canada have greatly increased in the interval ; whilst Prince Edward's Island and Manitoba have been added to the Dominion ; whilst, above all, there have been enormous and exceptional demands in Europe for the natural products of Canada—the whole exports of Canada, including food and timber, which stood at 73 millions of dollars in 1873, only stood at 77 millions in 1884. He admits also that Protection has had its usual effect, viz., that of fostering unnatural production and causing a glut in the protected industries. He congratulates himself on having transferred from Great Britain to Canada the industry of sugar refining ; but admits that Canada has a refinery too much. He congratulates himself on having ousted the foreign cotton manufactures, but admits that the protected Canadian industry has over-stocked its own market, whilst at the same time it cannot relieve itself by exportation. Does he look at this national policy as temporary ? Quite the contrary. He contemplates a duty of 1·50 dollars on iron ; he increased the duty on printed cotton goods last year. At the present moment he is revising his tariff. On woollen goods, on pickles, on cutlery, on mouldings, on picture frames, on imitation precious stones, on manilla hoods, on umbrellas, on china and earthenware, on hardware for furnishing, on chains, on acetic acid, on tissue paper, on glucose, on carpets, on labels, on sheet iron, on asbestos, on axle grease, on cotton quilts, on extract of beef, on foreign tobacco, the Customs duties are to be increased on the sole and simple ground that these articles can be made in Canada. Nothing is too big and nothing too little ; his meshes catch everything. In short, a Canadian has only to say that he is making something, and Sir L. Tilley is ready to prevent his fellow citizens from buying of any one else. I need hardly point out how many articles made in England are included in the above list, nor need I again refer to the fact mentioned by Sir R. Cartwright, that the imports of British goods into Canada, which were of the value of 68 millions of dollars (about £14.000,000) in 1873, were 42 millions (about £9.000,000) in 1884 ; or to the further fact, that our own exports to the United States amount to £38,000,000 a year. But I would ask my Fair Trade and Imperialist friends whether, looking to the matter from their favourite point of view of exports alone, they are ready to give up an export trade of nearly £40,000,000 in order to encourage one of less than a quarter of that sum? and also whether the policy openly avowed by the successful minister of Canada is such as to invite England to restrict her own production and consumption in order to encourage that of Canada? Surely if there is to be a *rapprochement* it should be from the Canadian side.

*Tariffs in Colonies. Canada.*

### *Cape of Good Hope.*

In 1859 the duties were $7\frac{1}{2}$ per cent. In 1879 they had been raised to 10 per cent. An additional 15 per cent. on the then existing duties was imposed in 1884. The duty on many articles has since been raised to 15 per cent. *ad valorem*, and other considerable increases made.

*Cape.*

### *West Indies.*

In Jamaica there are duties of $12\frac{1}{2}$ per cent., which have not been altered since 1859.

In Barbadoes duties of 3 per cent. have been raised to 4 per cent. No substantial change since 1881.

*West Indies.*

### *Mauritius.*

Moderate duties exist, about $6\frac{3}{4}$ per cent., which have been very slightly raised since 1859. No substantial change since 1881.

*Mauritius.*

### *Ceylon.*

In Ceylon there are moderate duties, about 5 per cent., which have been raised to $6\frac{1}{2}$ per cent. since 1881.

*Ceylon.*

### *India.*

In India the duties are moderate and few, and, as is well known, have been recently lowered; and in 1882 the cotton duties were taken off altogether; but this has been done not by the people, or even by the Government of India, but by English influence.

*India.*

From the figures given in this and the preceding chapter it is clear—

E

Conclu-<br>sion that<br>Protective<br>tendencies<br>are as<br>strong in<br>Colonies as<br>in Foreign<br>Countries.

First. That with the important exception of the United States no foreign country has since 1859 raised its duties to a point as high as that at which they then stood.

Secondly. That several European countries have, till recently, gone on continually reducing their duties, although the tendency at the present moment is to increase them.

Thirdly. That there is no one of the self-governing English-speaking colonies, except New South Wales, which has not increased its duties since 1859, and that some of them, and those the most important, have increased them largely.

Fourthly. That the tariffs of several of the Australian colonies are as high as, and that of Canada higher, than the tariffs of France, Italy, Austria, or Germany, and much higher than the tariffs of Holland, Belgium, or Norway.

Consequently, the assertion of the Fair Traders, that whilst foreign nations are refusing our goods our colonies are ready to take them duty free, or subject to moderate duties, is not only not correct but is the contrary of the fact. If tendencies are to be judged by experience, there is as great a tendency to Protection in our colonies as in foreign countries.

---

# CHAPTER VII.

## IS A CUSTOMS UNION OF THE BRITISH EMPIRE POSSIBLE?

Assump-<br>tions of<br>Fair<br>Traders no<br>ground for<br>New<br>Colonial<br>Policy.

I THINK that it has been satisfactorily proved that the special assumptions on which the Fair Trade League have based their demand for a differential treatment of the colonies are unfounded.

The direct trade with our colonies is about one quarter of our trade with the world.

The direct trade with our colonies, and especially our export trade generally, has not, taking a long series of years, increased faster than our trade with foreign countries. At the present moment the direct trade with our Australian colonies and with India is increasing, probably on account of our large investments in these countries. This is a natural, and therefore healthy development of our relations with them.

Even where our exports to our colonies appear large, and those to foreign countries appear small, in comparison to our imports from them, there is good reason to believe that the exports to the colonies depend upon, and are often caused by, the imports from foreign countries.

Our trade with our colonies is subject to fluctuations no less than that from foreign countries.

The colonies, or at any rate those with whom we must treat as independent and self-governing communities, show at least as great a tendency to Protection as foreign countries.

There is, therefore, nothing in the existing facts to call for a reversal of our settled policy of non-interference with trade; nothing to justify an attempt to check trade with foreign countries in order to divert it to our colonies. On the contrary, the trade of the mother country with the colonies, and her trade with foreign countries, are both progressing, and they are so mingled that any attempt to check foreign trade, whilst it would undoubtedly diminish the whole bulk of our trade, would very probably interfere with and diminish that very colonial trade which it was intended to encourage.

But is it possible to do anything by legislation to encourage our trade with the colonies? If so, by all means let it be done. The motto of the Cobden Club, "Free Trade amongst all Nations," is entirely consistent with the earliest and utmost possible development of Free Trade with our own fellow citizens. If there is to be choice amongst those with whom we are to do business, let us choose in the first instance to do it with those with whom in other ways we have the closest relations. Only let us be sure that we do not injure ourselves or them in so doing, and that in seeking for a closer relation than that which already exists, we do not strain the bonds which at present keep us together. The Free Trader will not yield to the Fair Trader or to the Imperialist in national pride, in jealousy for British greatness, and in all that constitutes the glory of the British name and character; nay, he would be willing, where greater interests are at stake, to sacrifice to them some portion of material prosperity; but when restrictions on commercial liberty are proposed in the interests of material prosperity, he requires to have it proved that they will really promote that prosperity; and when they are proposed in the interests of imperial relations with our colonies, he desires to be assured that they will not strain and weaken those relations.

E 2

Customs Union of the British Empire a dream.

It would, indeed, be an object worthy of the ambition of any statesman or generation of statesmen to form a perfect Customs Union, embracing the whole British Empire. If it were possible to have no duties whatever in any part of that Empire on goods brought from any other part of it; if, for purposes of trade, India, Canada, Australia, the Cape, and the West Indies were as much one country as Yorkshire and Lancashire, it would be a consummation at least as welcome to the members of the Cobden Club as to the most devoted Imperialist. But such a consummation is a dream. It involves the same fiscal system in countries differing widely as the poles in climate, in government, in habits, and in political opinions. It is contrary to the very principles of self-government. It would prevent any change in taxation in one of the countries constituting the British Empire, unless the same change were made in all. Desirable as it is, it may be dismissed at once from practical discussion.

Self-Government involves freedom, and therefore diversity of taxation.

It has, indeed, been said that such a thing was at one time possible, and that it has been lost by want of statesmanship; that in giving our colonies self-government, we missed the opportunity of requiring them to adopt our tariff; and that what would now be impracticable as an Imperial interference with their liberties, would then have been willingly adopted as a condition upon which those liberties might have been granted. Such an assertion raises no practical question; but it is, I believe, a complete mistake. Self-taxation is of the very essence of self-government. To have required such colonies as Canada and Australia to adopt our system of external taxation, and to model their own internal taxation accordingly, and to continue to insist on that requirement, whatever their own change of opinion or condition might be, would have been to clog the grant of self-government with a condition which would have destroyed its value. Free Trade is of extreme importance, but Freedom is still more important; and to force Free Trade on a free country is a breach of the fundamental principle which includes Free Trade.

# CHAPTER VIII.

## PROPOSALS OF THE FAIR TRADERS FOR ENCOURAGING COLONIAL TRADE ARE PROPOSALS TO RESTRICT TRADE.

DISMISSING the notion of an Imperial Customs Union to the limbo of impracticable ideals, is it possible for anything to be done by the British Parliament to promote commercial intercourse with the colonies? 

The course proposed by the Fair Traders is to place a differential tax on articles of food which come from foreign countries, and to admit food from the colonies free ; to charge more on articles of luxury, such as tea and coffee, tobacco, wine and spirits, coming from foreign countries than is charged on the same articles coming from the colonies ; and to charge adequate import duties on the manufactures of foreign countries which do not admit our manufactures free of duty, whilst allowing colonial manufactures to be admitted free of duty.

I presume this to be the meaning of the Fair Trade manifesto; but I must admit that the original document is hazy upon the question whether the duty on colonial tea and other luxuries is to be remitted altogether, and also upon the question whether colonial manufactures are to be admitted free unconditionally, or only on the condition that our manufactures are admitted free into the colonies. Nor have subsequent publications cleared up these doubts.

Now, the first observation on these proposals is that they have for their object to divert trade by interrupting one of its natural channels, and therefore their effect must be to diminish the whole volume of trade. They are, consequently, open to the fatal objection which makes all Protection odious to Free Traders—viz., that they hinder people from buying and selling where they find it to their interest to buy and sell—that they limit production by preventing people from using their natural capacity to the utmost in making and selling the things which they can make better than others. They are restraints on trade and manufacture. And when it is alleged that there will be no ultimate loss, because with due encouragement 

Fair Traders propose to diminish Trade.

the new market will be as productive as the old one, the answer is that the burden of proof lies with those who make such an improbable assertion. Take Canada as an instance, since Canada is the colony to which the Fair Traders point as able to supply us with corn. Now, so far as Protective duties are concerned, Canada is, as I have shown, fast following the Protectionist example of the United States, though she has a good way to go before her tariff is so obstructive to her export trade as that of her great neighbour. Still, in spite of the advantage Canada thus reaps from her lower tariff, she now sends us only 2·9 per cent. of our imported wheat, whilst the United States send us 42·6 per cent. Of flour British North America sends us 3·0 per cent. whilst the United States send us 66·7 per cent. British North America in 1883 sent us 3·2 per cent. of our total food supply, whilst the United States sent us 28·9. Is it conceivable, with the known advantages of people, soil, and climate which the United States possess, that any restriction on free production which the most audacious of Fair Traders might advocate, would so far change the natural condition of things as to enable Canada to displace her gigantic rival, without diminution of the aggregate produce, and without loss to the British customer?

It is needless to follow this point any further. To shut out or obstruct our Foreign Trade must restrict production. Leaving this general objection, let us consider the proposals of the Fair Traders in detail.

# CHAPTER IX.

## PROPOSED TAX ON FOOD.

Differential Tax on Food the keystone of the Fair Trade proposals.

Of all the proposals of the Fair Traders, by far the most important is that which contemplates a tax on foreign food.

This proposal has been scouted by the working classes, and is rejected by the Conservative leaders,* and it seems superfluous to discuss it. Nevertheless, it is perhaps more defensible than any other part of the scheme. It is the keystone of the edifice

---

* It has been recently emphatically repudiated by Sir Stafford Northcote and by Lord Salisbury.

of Fair Trade. It is the only bribe which offers a real temptation to the colonist: it is the only threat which has any terror for the United States. And if there is any interest in this country which demands protection from the legislature, it is that interest which is at once suffering from bad seasons and from low prices, and which is deprived by foreign competition of the compensation for bad seasons formerly found in high prices.

It is, therefore, difficult to discuss the scheme at all without discussing the proposal to place a differential tax on foreign articles of food.

The big loaf and the little loaf are good electioneering answers, but they do not exhaust or explain the question, and they do not convey the whole truth.

It may be interesting, in the first instance, to see where our supplies of food come from; and I annex tables* which have been prepared, showing the proportions in which the different countries of the world supply us with each of our principal articles of food, and a summary showing what proportion of the whole each country sends. The following are the general results :—

Foreign countries send us 141 millions' worth, or 82·7 per cent. of the whole; and our own possessions send us 29½ millions' worth, or 17·3 per cent. The United States send us 28·9 per cent. France sends us 6·8 per cent., and Germany, 9·9 per cent.; whilst British North America only sends us 3·2 per cent., and Australia only 1·4 per cent.; Russia sends us 6·7 per cent.; India sends as much as 8·2 per cent.; China sends 4·5 per cent. But India, which is of all our own possessions far the largest purveyor, is beyond our present purpose, since we already arrange her tariff as we think best. The above figures include so-called luxuries, such as tea, tobacco, coffee, wines and spirits. But if we exclude these, and confine our attention to articles of food which are not stimulants, the results will be similar. Of wheat, British possessions send us 24.0 per cent., and of flour 3·4 per cent.; and foreign countries, 76·0 per cent. and 96·6 per cent. respectively. Of meat, British possessions send 17·0 and foreign countries, 83·0 per cent. Of animals for the butcher, British possessions send us 13·0, and foreign countries, 87·0 per cent. France sends us 24·0 per cent., and Holland 35·7 per

Tax on Food.

Where does our Food come from?

Four-fifths from Foreign Countries and one-fifth from Colonies.

---

* See Tables XV. and XVI., in Appendix.

cent., of our aggregate importation of butter—whilst British North America only sends us 2·2 per cent. Of bacon and hams, the United States send us 78·7 per cent., and of cheese, 55·1 per cent., whilst British North America—the only colony which sends us any of these articles worth mentioning—sends 4·9 per cent. of bacon, and 25·9 per cent. of cheese. Eggs come to us in large quantities from Germany, France, and Belgium, but only in very small quantities from the colonies. Potatoes come to us in great abundance from France, and in still greater quantities from Germany, but none from British America or Australia. Rice, sugar, tea and coffee are almost the only articles of first-rate importance of which large proportions come from our own colonies ; and these come not from Canada or Australia, with whom it is proposed to make tariff bargains, but from India, Ceylon, Mauritius, and the West Indies, in all of which there are at present moderate tariffs, and in which—India, perhaps, excepted—the power of production, and consequent market for our manufactures, is extremely limited.

Looking, then, to the amount of food we get from foreigners, as compared with what we get from the colonies, it is clear that to legislate with the view of changing our source of supply from the one to the other is a task not to be undertaken lightly or without a clear view of the results. Let us see, therefore, what are the objections to it.

---

# CHAPTER X.

## WHY IS A TAX ON FOOD OBJECTIONABLE?


THE reason why it is not desirable to divert the purchase of food from the cheaper to the dearer market is not simply that it raises the price of food. It will probably do this, and the result would be most serious. According to Sir J. Caird's calculations, made in 1878, our whole consumption of agricultural produce was then worth about 370 millions ; of which 260 were home produce and 110 foreign. The increase of population requires an addition of about 4 millions annually ;

and the proportion of foreign produce consumed has increased considerably since 1877. Assuming the consumption to be now 400 millions, and assuming that two-thirds of this is home produce and one-third foreign, the effect of a general rise in price of 10 per cent. would be that our population would have to pay 40 millions for their food more than they now pay. And supposing that this rise in price were caused by a tax on food produced in foreign countries, 26 millions out of this 40 would go to our own landed interest at home; and of the remaining 14 millions part would go to the Colonial food grower, and the remainder only into the public exchequer. This is by itself a startling conclusion. But it is far from being all the evil which would result from a compulsory change of market. An equally important, if not more important, result would be that it would prevent both the purchaser and seller from getting the most they can with the means which Providence has given them.

The buyer will have less to buy with, and the seller will have less to sell. If the English people are compelled to buy their food at home, they will spend on the production of food an amount of energy and capital which, if employed in making something else, would buy a much larger quantity of food from America; and they will compel the Americans to divert the capital and energy they now spend in producing food to making things which can be made much better and cheaper in England.

The result will be just the same if our Parliament compels English people to buy their food in Canada. If they are to be deterred by a differential tax from buying the cheapest food in the United States, and to be compelled to buy dearer food from Canada, the result will be not only that England will pay more for her food, but that the Canadian producer of her food, having to spend more labour and energy in producing it than the United States farmer now spends on it, will have less to spend on English manufactures than the United States farmer has.

To this the Fair Trader makes two answers. First, that the price of food would not be raised, because America has a surplus which she must export, tax or no tax; secondly, that a rise in the price of food in this country would be a cheap price for the additional market for English goods which would be acquired in the colonies by buying our food there.

It is obvious that these answers are inconsistent with each other. If the price of corn is not raised in this country, and if America is still to supply our market at present prices, there will be no transfer of English purchases to the colonial market, and the whole of the Fair Trade proposal will fail. It is only by giving a higher price that we can encourage a greater growth of Canadian corn. If the Fair Traders are consistent, and really wish to effect their object; if they wish to confine our custom to those nations which buy freely from us, they must absolutely prohibit all goods, food included, from those nations which do not do so. To say we are to stop their selling, and still to receive from them what we now get from them, is blowing hot and cold. But, in fact, the notion that the price of corn would not be raised by a tax is absurd. The United States farmers are not under any spell to produce a certain fixed quantity of corn. They may, in a given year, under the stimulus of exceptional demands, produce more corn than can be sold at a remunerative price, but they will not continue to do so. They produce corn because we want it, and will pay them a remunerative price for it. If we check that demand by a tax, they will reduce their supply. The Western farmer is able to send wheat to Liverpool and London because, after paying cost of cultivation and of transport, the price leaves him a profit. If we increase these costs by adding a tax, it will reduce his market, and in many cases destroy his profit. He consequently will no longer produce, and will leave his farm for something else, as we know too well that many emigrants have done. The result of any tax on American corn, which is to transfer our custom to the Canadian market, *must* be to raise the price of corn in this country. But, say the Fair Traders, " Even if this is the case, it is no great harm. Food is not a raw material of manufacture; to raise the price of food will not necessarily raise wages, for, as Cobden said, wages do not rise and fall with the price of food. Our manufacturers, whatever happens to our workmen, will be able to produce as cheaply as before ; and they will be able to sell much more, because the colony will, in return for the corn, receive their manufactures duty free ; whereas the United States, by placing prohibitive duties on them, do their utmost to refuse them." " Even at the present time," so runs this precious argument, " every quarter of wheat imported from Australia affords us in return sixteen times as much trade and employment as a

quarter of wheat imported from the United States, and every Tax on
quarter of wheat imported from Canada thirty-five times as Food
much as one imported from Russia."

One really does not know where to begin in dealing with
such an argument as this !

"Food is not a raw material of manufacture; for Cobden
said that wages did not rise and fall with the price of food."
It is difficult not to feel indignant at such a use of Cobden's
name. What was it that Cobden really did say? The Protectionists had accused him of wishing to lower wages for the manufacturers' benefit. They said, "You are doing no good to the
workmen by lowering the price of corn, for wages will be
lowered as the price of corn falls, and that is your real object."
To this Cobden replied, "You are utterly wrong : wrong in
your imputations, wrong in your facts. Wages do not fall with
the price of food ; wages have been highest when corn has been
lowest. Nor am I seeking, nor shall I get, low wages. Low
wages do not mean cheap labour. Let us buy foreign corn
untaxed. The price of food will probably fall, but the demand
for our manufactures at home and abroad will certainly increase,
and the workmen's wages and the manufacturers' profits will
both rise." Cobden was right, as the workmen well know :
and they will no doubt understand the difference between
him and his mis-quoters. Cobden said, " Leave corn untaxed,
let food fall, and let wages rise." The Fair Traders say, " Tax
corn, let food rise, and let wages fall." And they quote
Cobden as their authority !

But let us consider a little what the effect of raising the Effect of
price of food to the workman himself really is, and let us raising
omit for the present all consideration of the market for our Food on
manufactures caused by the purchase of food abroad. The our
workman's wages will go less far than they did, and the Workmen,
comforts of his life will be reduced ; if the labour-market and on their
admits of an increase in wages, he will demand and get it, Expendi-
and the cost of production will be increased accordingly to ture.
the manufacturer ; if it does not, the workman will be reduced
to the alternative of either living in less comfort than he has
done hitherto, or of emigrating. If he does the former, not
only will he and his family suffer, but he will be obliged to
spend more upon food and less upon clothing, and this in
itself will reduce the market for manufactures. If he emigrates,
so much productive labour is lost to the country. To the

Tax on
Food.

manufacturer, employer, and workman alike, any artificial increase in the price of food is *per se* an unmixed evil, even without considering its effect upon the Foreign market for our manufactures. Much more is it an evil to them when it is remembered that the same measure which increases the price of their food also prevents them from getting the full return for their own expenditure of skill, capital, and labour.

# CHAPTER XI.

## FALLACY OF SUPPOSING THAT COLONIAL MARKETS WILL COMPENSATE US.

Dealings
with Colo-
nists are
not more
profitable
than deal-
ings with
Foreigners.

BUT then, say the Fair Traders, this evil is to be compensated, and more than compensated, by the additional market for our manufactures which will be opened to us in the colonies. Now, in the first place, I have shown that the tendency of the colonies is to close, and not to open, their markets, and that in Canada the duties recently imposed on our manufactures, though not yet equal to the enormous duties of the United States, are approaching them, and are higher than those of many foreign States. But let us assume that the colonial duties on our goods are and continue much lower than the foreign duties, where is the new market to come from? Does the Fair Trader think that the United States farmer sends us a shipload of corn for nothing, and that if we get it instead from the colonial farmer, we shall still give to the United States what we now give, and also give to the colonial farmer, in exchange for his shipload of corn, many shiploads of manufactures which we now turn to some other beneficial use? If he does think this, does he think that the second transaction is much better for us than the first? And if he does not think this absurdity, what can be the meaning of the astonishing state-ment I have quoted above from the Fair Trade League circular? He apparently takes from the statistics of trade the quantity of corn imported from Australia and the United States, and the quantity of our manufactures exported to those countries respectively, and, finding that for every quarter of Australian wheat we export to Australia sixteen times as much of our manufactures as we export to the United States for every quarter of United States wheat, comes to the conclusion that for each quarter of Australian wheat we pay sixteen times as much of our cotton and cloth as for an equal quantity of United States wheat, and that the transaction is consequently sixteen times as profitable, not to Australia which receives, but to England which pays, this wonderful price! These are the new prophets who are to subvert the doctrines of Cobden and Peel! The fact, of course, is that for every quarter we import, whether from Australia, from Canada, from Russia, or from the United States, we pay the market value—no less and no more. Whether it is paid for by the export of an equal value of English manufactures to the United States, or by the export of English manufactures to India, or to some foreign country, and by a further export from that country to the United States, or even by some route more circuitous still, or by the remittance of bullion, or by a cancellation of interest upon debt, it must be paid for by this country, and the price paid for it will be the value of a quarter of wheat in the English market. The United States farmer does not give us his wheat for nothing; he takes from us whatever the competition of the English farmer, the Canadian farmer, and the Russian farmer allows him to take. The Canadian farmer does precisely the same. If they compete on equal terms they obtain equal prices, and set going an equal quantity of English labour to provide a return. If the United States farmer is able to produce wheat more cheaply and abundantly than the Canadian farmer, he can give us a larger quantity in return for the same quantity of our labour; in other words, both his labour and our labour go farther; there is more production, and both benefit. If under these circumstances we forcibly transfer the business from the United States farmer to the Canadian farmer, we do not thereby get a new purchaser for our goods, we only substitute a worse for a better purchaser—a worse for a better supply.

But then, it is said, Canada, Protectionist as her tariff is, is less Protectionist than the United States, and does less to keep our goods out of the market. If this is the case, she and we both get the benefit of it now. The Canadian farmer is so much the better off, and so is our manufacturer. All the good we

Tax on Food.

can get by the lower tariff of Canada we are now getting. We shall not increase that benefit one jot by adding to the obstruction now caused by the United States tariff a new obstruction of our own. The United States tariff is doing serious injury both to the English manufacturer and consumer of corn, and to the American farmer and consumer of English goods ; to the former probably less harm than to the latter, because the Englishman has the rest of the world to go to, whilst the American cannot escape from his own tariff. But the injury thus caused will not be diminished, but aggravated, by interposing another obstruction of our own.

In short, if, under the existing Protectionist American tariff, the American farmer can compete with all the world in the English market, it is because what England has to pay him with goes farther in the American market and produces a greater return than it does elsewhere. To transfer the custom forcibly to the Canadian market is to make what England has to pay with worth less than it now is.

Confusion between individual commercial dealings and International Treaties or arrangements.

I sometimes think that there is a fatal confusion in the minds of Fair Traders and Protectionists between a commercial treaty, or arrangement between nations, and the individual dealings of commerce. The Commercial Treaty assumes the mischievous and delusive form of a bargain, in which we, as a Free-trading nation, appear to give much and receive little. Hence people are misled into a hazy conclusion that the individual bargains made under such a treaty, or under what is called one-sided Free Trade, are in themselves one-sided and unfair, and that in the dealings between the merchants of a Free-trading nation like ourselves and those of a Protectionist or semi-Protectionist nation like the United States or France, the Protectionist tariff causes our merchants to have the worst of the bargain. But this is pure delusion, and confusion of thought. The American farmer is not enabled to drive a better bargain with the English manufacturer by reason of the Protectionist tariff ; on the contrary, of the two he is the one more hampered by it. The relaxation of that tariff would be an immense boon to the Englishman, but it would be a still greater boon to the American. The evil of Protection is not that it benefits one party to a trade bargain at the expense of the other, but that it injures both, and prevents trade bargains from being made.

## CHAPTER XII.

### EFFECTS OF AN ENGLISH TAX ON AMERICAN CORN ON AMERICAN COMPETITION WITH ENGLISH MANUFACTURES.

BUT let us follow the consequences of a tax on American food a little farther. America has an abundant supply of the most energetic and versatile labour in the world, and also an abundant supply of capital. At present this labour and capital are largely employed in providing Europe, and England especially, with food, because that is the most profitable way in which American labour and capital can be employed. But we are asked to make this employment less profitable for her, and to deprive her of her present market for her enormous agricultural produce. What would be the natural result of such a step? Why, to divert her energy and capital from providing the food we want to buy from her, and to drive it into providing the manufactures which we want to sell to her. At present, in spite of, possibly in consequence of, her system of Protection, the sale of her highly forced and highly priced manufactures is in a great measure confined, or nearly confined, to her own subjects, and she is no rival to England in our own markets, or in the markets of the world; whilst even in her own markets our manufacturers compete with hers. In 1880 we exported to her $24\frac{1}{2}$ millions of manufactures, and imported from her $2\frac{1}{2}$ millions. Out of her total exports about 10 per cent. are manufactures, and 90 per cent. food and raw materials, chiefly agricultural produce.[*] But if we deprive her of her market for agricultural produce, we shall drive her into manufacture, and there is no saying how formidable a rival she may become.

At the time of the repeal of the Navigation Laws, all the best judges thought that the carrying trade of the world must pass into the hands of the Americans. It has passed into our own, as is shown fully below (Chapter XXXIV.). There are probably several causes for this; but the most important to my mind is, that America has found in her internal

*Tax on American Agriculture would drive America into Manufacturing competition.*

---

[*] The proportion of manufactured articles has slightly increased since 1880.

development, and especially in her farming, and in the railways which farming creates and sustains, an industry more profitable to herself and to the world than the ocean carrying trade. To us the ocean carrying trade has been the more profitable employment. She has done the farming, and we have done the ocean carrying, to the great advantage of both. If we cripple her farming, there is no saying that she may not take from us our ocean carrying.

## CHAPTER XIII.

### OBJECTION THAT WE ARE PAYING FOR AMERICAN CORN BY RECEIVING BACK PRINCIPAL OF INVESTMENTS.

*If America owes us money she must repay, or pay interest, whether we buy her corn or not.*

"But," say the Fair Traders, "granting that America must be paid in some way for the food she sends us, she is paid, not in goods, but by setting against it the loans we have made her. In this way she is not only paying interest upon them, but is repaying to us our capital, upon which consequently we are living." The latter assumption, viz., that America is sending back capital to us, is utterly without proof, and is probably false.* The statement that she sends us food in payment of interest on what we have lent her is to a great extent true. But I am not concerned at present with the truth or falsehood of these statements ; I only mention them for the purpose of showing that they are *nihil ad rem.* If America owes us money, which, or the interest on which, she is now repaying in corn, she will equally owe us this money if we transfer our custom for corn to Canada, and if she does not repay us in corn, she must repay us in something else. That something else will be something which, *ex hypothesi*, we want less than corn ; it may, as I have pointed out, be manufactures or freight, which will compete with our own.

*Absurdity of supposing that interest on Foreign In-*

And here I have to notice a so-called argument, which I was at first disposed to pass over as too absurd to be refuted, but which has been so often repeated that it calls for a passing notice. It has been stated in the following terms :—

---

* See below, Chapter XXI.

" But even if it could be proved, as it certainly cannot, that all this enormous disproportion of imports has been paid for out of our income, and without any diminution of our investments, that would still do nothing to reassure our working classes as regards the interests of labour. They are concerned in the acquisition of imports of food in exchange for the production of their industry, rather than in payment of income due to us from our foreign investments. For, suppose such investments to be increased fivefold ; suppose England to contain multitudes of well-to-do people who owned them, and lived upon the income paid to them, let us say in the shape of food from America, and clothing, furniture, and luxuries from France ; is it not evident that the balance of trade might be satisfactorily accounted for by financiers, while our agriculture and manufactures were alike languishing, and every year affording less employment, and at lower wages, to fewer workmen ? English land might be forced out of cultivation by American competition, or turned from arable to grass to such an extent as to more than half depopulate our rural districts and country towns, and drive the people into the larger cities and manufacturing districts, or to emigration. The demand for manufactures in the agricultural districts would thus be seriously reduced, whilst the free import of French manufactures and luxuries—preferred by the ever-increasing class who lived on foreign incomes—would curtail the employment of our artisans, whose wages would be still further reduced by the competition of the displaced agricultural labourers.

"In one word, our imports would be acquired more and more in payment of interest or rents due from abroad to owners of foreign investments living in this country, and less and less in exchange for the handiwork of our industrial classes, and so the former would increase whilst the latter would be driven first to lower wages and diminished comforts, then to destitution, and finally to emigration without resources and under the most painful conditions."

I find it really difficult to understand this. What is it that we are importing as interest on our investments, especially from America? Food and raw materials constitute nine-tenths of our imports. How do the Fair Traders suppose that these are consumed? How much of them do they think the wealthy and the idle put into their own stomachs or on their own backs? And of the manufactures imported, how many are used by the

F

Interest.
Foreign In-
vestments
comes
home as
Food and
Raw
Material.

working classes? Let any one cast his eye down the list of British imports, and he will see that there is not one of the articles mentioned in the list which is not either an article to be used in our own industries, or an article to be used by those employed in our industries. Silk, woollen and cotton manufactures, gloves, dressed skins, and wine are almost the only articles in our list of imports which are not simple articles of food or materials of manufacture. Assuming, which is a preposterous assumption, that the whole of these are articles of luxury, neither used by nor giving employment to the working class, how much do they amount to? To about 25 millions out of 410 millions of imports. The question thus raised by the Fair Traders is not, it must be remembered, a question of whether these imports are spent on reproductive employment, but a question of whether they are used by workers or by idlers. If the Fair Traders are right, they are used by idlers; and our workers are to be driven to destitution and emigration by the loss of wages and employment. Now, even if employed in unproductive labour, they will not be employed in support of idleness. But can it be doubted that the great bulk of these enormous imports is employed in supporting reproductive labour? Every pound of raw material, every article which requires further labour to complete it, is imported for the purpose of employing labour upon it. The food, the clothing, the common luxuries, tea, coffee, tobacco, sugar, are consumed in supporting and making tolerable the lives of millions of artisans in our factories, of labourers in our fields, of workmen who are erecting, extending, and improving our railways, our docks, our mines, our ships, our dwellings, our shops, our schools, our churches, our towns. They are employed in extending our reproductive powers, and in making life comparatively healthy and pleasant, not for the wealthy few, but for the toiling many. The contrast between wealth and poverty is sad enough, and the excesses of luxury are lamentable. But the proportion of our national income or of our imports which is consumed in luxuries is a mere trifle compared with that which goes to support useful labour. The fear that the payments which foreign countries are now making us as a reward for former labour will make us poorer and render future labour unproductive, is the wildest of many wild chimeras.

The very contrary is notoriously the case. The recent

depression in business has been markedly distinguished from earlier commercial depressions by the fact that it has affected profits far more, and more quickly, than it has affected employment, wages, or the well-being of the working classes. Millowners, coalowners, ironmasters, landowners, and farmers have suffered more or less severely. But the mill-hand, the miner, the workman, the labourer, until a very recent period, suffered, and are even now suffering comparatively little, as is shown by a comparison of the state of the country with its state at former periods of depression, and by the infallible tests of pauperism and of consumption. Capital has borne the brunt of the blow. By the simple expedient of leaving things alone, and repealing the wicked and pernicious laws which made scarce the food of man, and curtailed the rights of labour, we have advanced one step towards the millennium of the economist, the politician, and the Christian philanthropist, viz., the more equal distribution of good things. The workmen are better off than they were, and, as the action of the Trades Unions shows, they know the reason why.

But even if investments abroad were the evil the Fair Traders imagine them to be, the transfer of our custom from foreign countries to the colonies would do little to remove it. For we are now *wasting* (as the Fair Traders would say) our surplus earnings largely in the colonies; we are lending to Australia and Canada as we have in former years lent to the United States. Our investments in Canada and the Australian colonies are said to amount to between 300 and 400 millions; and our investments in Australia are said to be increasing at the rate of more than 10 millions a year, a fact which accounts for the increase of exports to those colonies. Our loans to the colonies in 1884 are said to have amounted to upwards of 30 millions.* But the time must soon come when those colonies will be doing as much to ruin us by paying us interest in the shape of imports, as, in the opinion of the Fair Traders, the United States are now doing, and then what is to become of us? If such a conclusion drives the Fair Traders to despair, it is some consolation to think that it will carry comfort to the heart of another great Imperialist, Sir Julius Vogel, who also

The recent depression has hit the rich and spared the poor.

Transfer of Trade to Colonies will not prevent Investments abroad.

---

* *Standard*, 30th December, 1884.

F 2

would like to see us exercise a large control over the colonies, but who wishes us to do so in order, *inter alia*, to encourage those investments of English capital in them which are the terror of the Fair Traders.

The precise effect of foreign investments on our own industries I have dealt with more fully below. See Chapter XXII.

---

# CHAPTER XIV.

## TARIFF BARGAINS WITH THE COLONIES.　ARE THEY POSSIBLE?

To do so
we must
first impose
duties on
ourselves,
which is
out of the
question.

WE have hitherto considered the effect of a differential tax on foreign articles of food pure and simple, and without reference to any reciprocal benefit to be derived from action to be taken by the colonies. But it is possible, for the language of the Fair Traders is very vague, that they mean colonial articles of food to be admitted free only from those colonies and possessions which admit our manufactures free, and that they mean to make the differential duty a means for driving a tariff bargain with the colonies. If so, an important question of principle arises, viz., whether it can be worth our while at any time, or under any circumstances, to impose a duty on imports, which will do us an immediate injury, in order that we may have a weapon wherewith to fight foreign countries or British colonies in making tariff bargains. This question is raised explicitly by the further proposal of the Fair Traders to tax foreign manufactures, and I propose to consider it when dealing with that proposal in the Second Part of this work. If it is to be answered in the negative, as I am sure that it is, the proposal to drive a tariff bargain with the colonies by the bribe of a differential duty on their competitors must fail at once. But I do not propose to argue this large question here, and will assume that it may be answered in the affirmative. Making this assumption, let us consider what sort of bargains we can possibly drive with the colonies, and let us consider, first, what we must give them and what we can get from them ; and then, secondly, what they must give to us and what they can get from us by such a bargain.

First of all, then, as our foreign food supply is to be trans-ferred to the colonies, and as they now only supply us with one-sixth of it, we must cut off five-sixths of our present sources of supply, and trust to their being made up by countries which now only furnish one-sixth of it. What the effect of this may be on the quantity and price of food and the welfare of the people it is frightful to consider.

Secondly, we shall lose the whole of the custom for our own produce arising out of purchases of food in foreign coun-tries, and, as they amount to more than 140 millions a year, this is a scarcely less serious consideration.

Thirdly, we shall cripple our powers of production by making food dear, and be less able to compete for custom in neutral markets.

Fourthly, we shall run a very serious risk of retaliation by foreign countries. If we say to France, or to America, "We will not buy corn, or meat, or butter, or cheese, or eggs from you," they will retort by refusing to buy cotton, wool, silk, and iron from us ; not only shall we ourselves cut off a very large pro-portion of our foreign exports, but we shall tempt foreign nations to cut off the remainder.

Taking the average of the last eighteen years, our trade with foreign countries has been about three-fourths of our whole trade, and our trade with British colonies and possessions has been about one-fourth of it. Our whole trade, imports and exports included, is 700 millions a year. We are, therefore, asked to cripple and endanger three-fourths of this, or a trade of more than 500 millions a year.

What are we to get in exchange ?

First, we shall get so much custom for our goods in the colonies as arises from the additional purchases of food we make in the colonies. But, as the colonial supply of food will be much less than that which we now get from foreign countries, and as its price will be much higher, this market must be much less valuable than that which we give up. So far, therefore, we are large and pure losers. But we shall get, in addition, what-ever advantage is to be gained by the reduction our colonies may make in their tariffs in return for what we do for them.

What will this amount to ?

Now, in the first place, we may eliminate India. The Indian tariff we practically make ourselves. We have deter-mined, rightly or wrongly, that she shall not levy duties on our manufactures. Her consent is not asked ; we need no bargain for the purpose. We may, for similar reasons, eliminate all the Crown colonies. In short, the only colonies with which we can make bargains are the self-governing colonies in British North America, in Australasia, South Africa, and some of those in the West Indies. But of these there are many which now levy very small duties on our manufactures, and those by way of Revenue rather than of Protective duties. With regard to these, all that we can expect to get by way of a bargain is that their duties shall not be raised, and this is a prospective and contingent, not a present and certain, benefit. In fact, the only colonies in which any large reduction of duties is possible are Canada, Victoria, Western and South Australia, Queensland, Tasmania, and New Zealand. New South Wales, one of the most important of the Australian group, is free, or nearly so, already. But let us take the whole of our colonies in British North America, in Australia, and in South Africa, and suppose that throughout them all it were possible to get a reduction of duties, what would this advantage amount to? The trade of the United Kingdom with the whole of these colonies, taking, as before, an average of eighteen years, is about 10 per cent. of our whole external trade ; not much more than our trade with Germany ; not so much as our trade with France ; little more than half as much as our trade with the United States ; about one-eighth of our whole trade with foreign countries. If we take those colonies alone which now levy considerable duties, the trade with them will not be more than one-half this amount. Consequently, it is only about 5 per cent. of our whole trade for which we can expect any substantial benefit by a tariff bargain with our colonies, whilst the trade which we shall injure and cripple by such a bargain is 75 per cent. of that trade.

I think we may, then, draw two conclusions, that it is not worth our while to make any such bargains; and, secondly, that if we were to make any such bargains, it would be madness to adhere to them, if foreign countries were to offer to reduce their tariffs on condition of our repealing the differential dues on their produce which such a bargain implies.



This is not, however, the view of some of our colonial reformers. For instance, a writer, signing himself "Imperialist," in the April number of the *National Review* for 1885, urges that a leading feature of the Conservative policy of the future

should be "to tax foreign imports, while granting free admis- Tariff bargains with Colonies. Proposals of Imperialist Reformers.
sion to colonial products of all kinds;" and a similar proposal
is advocated by Mr. Thomas Gibson Bowles in the May number of the *Fortnightly Review*.  Mr. Stephen Bourne, the well-
known statistician of the Customs, in his address at Montreal,
goes much further, for, after showing how Canada declines the
business of the mother country, he proposes that we shall
deprive ourselves altogether of trade with Protectionist countries
in order to encourage colonies which discourage us, and that
Canada shall in like manner deprive herself of trade with her
nearest neighbour !

The writer of the article "England and her Colonies," in
the April number of the *Quarterly* for 1885 is more alive to the
difficulties of this question ; but even he, after dismissing as
impracticable Mr. Forster's notion of an  "Imperial Zollverein
on the basis of this abolition of all customs or excise except
upon intoxicating liquors or tobacco," because the colonies
would not agree to it, suggests that Lord George Bentinck's
plan of "taxing foreign produce while admitting colonial wool
and other materials duty free" is the only basis on which we
can build any reasonable expectation of constructing an Imperial Zollverein.

In the last century we alienated our colonies from the Their absurdity.
mother country by taxing them.  In this century our colonial
reformers wish to alienate the mother country by making her
tax herself.  They seek to bind our colonies to us by leaving
them free to tax our products, whilst we are not only to abstain
from taxing theirs, but are to burden ourselves with the worst of
taxes in order to give them an exclusive monopoly of our
markets.  Surely, if there is a policy which could make the
mother country hate her colonies it is this !

Now let us look at such a bargain as I have described above What would the Colonies get?
from the colonial point of view.  What would they gain and what
would they lose ?  I think we must admit that if England gave
them the monopoly of her market for food they would gain considerably.  Canada, Australia, and India would send us much
more corn if United States and Russian corn were excluded
from our ports.  India would send us more tea if China were out
of the market, and the Cape and Australia would send us more
second-class wine if we could not get good wine from France
or Spain.  Even this would not be an unqualified advantage
to them.  The production of the world would be diminished,

Tariff bargains with Colonies. What would they get?

and they would bear some share of the loss; their people would be diverted from doing what they can do best, to the providing of those things which the English market demands, and India certainly would lose some of the trade which, as we have seen, she now does directly or indirectly with the United States. But it is idle to talk of such proposals as these. England certainly will not contract her sources of supply to such an extent. Nor will she make a sacrifice at all where she gets nothing in return. She can only get a return from those colonies which now impose restrictions on the import of English goods. We may, therefore, as before, eliminate India and other colonies or possessions which are governed from home. The only colonies which can make a bargain are the self-governing colonies, and amongst them those only which now levy duties on English goods. That they might gain something immediately by the bargain, I have admitted. What will they have

What would they give?

to give up? First of all, there are those colonies which only levy a small duty, say 5 to 10 per cent., with the *bond fide* object of raising revenue, and without any thought of Protection. To these colonies, with but little realised property, and with an organisation very different from those of an old country, it would probably be a very serious financial difficulty to raise a revenue in any other way—a difficulty which might in itself counterbalance any gain they might derive from our differential tariff. Those colonies, again, such as Canada and Victoria, which levy heavier duties, and which levy them avowedly for purposes of Protection, would have to make a serious surrender. They would, in the opinion of Free Traders, be really benefiting themselves by reducing their tariff in our favour; but in their own opinion, and in the opinion of the Fair Traders, they would be doing themselves harm. They might be tempted to do it, but in doing it they would feel they had made a concession to us, and we should be obliged to accept it as a concession.

What would be the position of the Colonies when the bargain is made?

But suppose the concession made and the bargain completed. Suppose that we have excluded the United States corn from our market, and that Canada has admitted English goods freely to her market, what will be the condition of things? The United States may leave things alone. In that case, as I have shown above, England will find herself suffering from insufficient supplies, from a contracted market for her goods, and from the new competition in manufactures which she will have forced upon the United States. She will be discontented and disgusted with her bargain, and with the other party to it. Or the United States may retaliate by prohibiting English goods. In that case England will be still more discontented and disgusted. Or the United States may do that which it must be the desire and object of every honest Fair Trader and Reciprocitarian to make them do—they may offer to throw open their market to English goods on condition that England will again throw open her market to United States corn. In that case England will be more than ever disgusted if her bargain with Canada prevents her from accepting their offer. Indeed, it is scarcely within the limits of possibility that such a bargain could under such circumstances be kept. That England, which now does a trade of 140 millions a year with the United States, even under the present Protectionist tariff, and of 21 millions with Canada, should refuse the proffered trade of a country which has between 50 and 60 millions of people and the finest soils and climates in the world, for the purpose of nursing a trade with a country which has between 4 and 5 millions of people and a far inferior soil and climate, is too much to expect of human nature. And if the bargain is not kept, or if the terms of the bargain with Canada are such as to allow England to accept the United States' offer, what will be the position of Canada when she is thrown over, and the United States are again admitted to free competition in the English market? She will have been misled into an unnatural course of industry and expenditure, and she will be left to her own resources when it suits the convenience of England so to leave her. The Fair Traders have some hazy inkling of this difficulty, for they propose that the fixed duties on foreign food are to be steadily maintained for a term long enough to develop our own instead of foreign territories. But do they really think that this is possible; that our own people would submit to years of privation in order to develop a possible future in Canada or Australia when that privation might be at once changed into plenty by admitting foreign produce? Are any such arrangements as these likely to stand? Are they desirable in the true interests of Imperial union not to mention the commercial interests of the parties concerned? Are they likely in the end to promote that good feeling between England and Canada which it is the professed object of all of us to encourage? Are they not much

Tariff bargains with Colonies. Any forced attempt at Union must lead to Disunion.

more likely to cause estrangement, recalcitration, and disruption? To such questions there can be but one answer. We may be quite certain that any forced attempt at unnatural union, any unbusiness-like sacrifice of interest to sentiment, will only destroy those feelings of kindness which it is the object of all to promote.

I have taken the case of Canada as the most striking illustration of the fatal difficulties which would attend any such tariff bargain as we have been considering. Similar arguments apply to the other self-governing colonies, and it is unnecessary to repeat them. It seems to me abundantly clear that no tariff bargain with any colony which has for its condition a differential tax on foreign produce imported into England is for a moment to be thought of.

---

# CHAPTER XV.

## COMMERCIAL TREATIES WITH THE COLONIES, ARE THEY POSSIBLE?

Can we make Commercial Treaties with Colonies, such as the French Treaty?

A CUSTOMS union of the empire is then impracticable. An attempt at a closer connection with the colonies, to be effected by imposing differential taxes on foreign produce, is not to the real interest either of England or, in the end, of the colonies, and it is much more likely to lead to separation than to union. There is yet a third method of improving commercial relations with the colonies, which is scarcely suggested in the Fair Trade programme, but which may deserve a few moments consideration. It is that of a commercial treaty such as we have made with France and other foreign nations; a treaty in which we impose no differential duties, but only reduce our own duties, and reduce them for all equally.

Narrow limits within which such Treaties would be applicable.

Here, again, we may at once dismiss from consideration all the colonies or possessions which are practically governed from home; and these, including India, will, so far as trade is concerned, amount to one-half of the whole.

Our whole trade with our colonies is, as I have shown

above, about one-fourth of our whole trade, and it is therefore only one-eighth of our whole trade that can possibly be affected by such a treaty. Practically it is much less; because we do not want commercial treaties, or, indeed, alterations of any kind, except with those colonies which levy sensible duties on our goods. The whole affair is, therefore, of less moment to us than it might at first sight appear.

Now, with respect to the self-governing colonies, we have, in giving them self-government, left them free to impose what duties they please, with one restriction, viz., that they shall not make their duties differential; that they shall, if they place Customs duties on the produce of one country, place the same duties on the produce of all. But even this restriction has been surrendered on two special occasions. Canada, or rather the British colonies in North America, were in 1854 allowed to make a Reciprocity treaty with the United States,* by which a large number of articles, the produce of Canada and of the United States respectively, were admitted duty free into each of those countries, although the same goods remained subject to duty when imported into those colonies from the United Kingdom, or from foreign countries other than the United States. The denunciation of this treaty by the United States was one of the causes that led to the present Protectionist tariff in Canada; and the resumption by the United States of the policy which dictated that treaty would, no doubt, lead to the resumption of a similar policy by Canada. Another case, rather less striking, because it was between different colonies, and not between a colony and a foreign nation, was that of an arrangement between New South Wales and Victoria concerning the Customs duties levied on the boundary between the two colonies in the basin of the river Murray. In these cases, the principle of equal treatment gave way to the still more important principle of self-government, and to the demands for freedom caused by local contiguity. And, no doubt, a similar course must and will be followed when similar cases occur again, as they are sure to do. Even at this moment, proposals having this tendency are being discussed in Australia, and in the case of the British West Indies. It may be all very well to say, as a matter of theory, that when nations are divided by great natural barriers, such as hundreds of leagues

*Treaty ratified 9th September, 1854.

of sea or mountain, there is all the more reason for abolishing artificial barriers. But this is not the way in which the facts present themselves to the ordinary mind. I feel the need of dealing freely with my neighbour across the street long before I understand that the same need exists for freedom in my dealings with an alien in China. It was by the obvious absurdity of an artificial barrier between Surrey and Middlesex that Cobden brought home to men's minds the much less obvious absurdity of an artificial barrier between England and France. If, therefore, any strong case arises again, such as an approach to commercial union between Canada and the United States, or between any of the Australian colonies and their neighbours, we may take it for granted that the one principle of equal treatment, which we have hitherto maintained, will give way, and that in this, as in other matters of taxation, the colonies will exercise and enjoy complete self-government.

In short, the colonies in question are, so far as tariffs are concerned, in as free and independent a position as foreign nations ; and if we are to make commercial treaties with foreign nations, there seems to be no *primâ facie* reason why we should not make similar commercial treaties with our self-governing colonies. In making such treaties we should, of course, be governed by the same rules as have governed us in making treaties with foreign countries. We should give no such differential treatment as is suggested by the Fair Traders, and we should make no reductions of duties which we do not consider to be for our own advantage.



The question then arises, whether there are any duties which we now levy on colonial produce which we could reduce ; remembering that if we reduce them for the colonies we must reduce them for other countries also. Now, what are the products of the self-governing colonies which we tax? The only articles of this description in our tariff are cocoa, coffee, chicory, dried fruit, tea, tobacco, wine, beer and spirits. The exports of these articles from the colonies, according to the latest returns, are as shown on the following pages, 77, 78.

*Quantities and Value of certain Articles of Domestic Produce, exported from the principal Colonial and other Possessions of the United Kingdom, according to the latest Returns.*

| — | COCOA AND CHOCOLATE. | | COFFEE. | | CHICORY. | | DRIED FRUIT. | |
|---|---|---|---|---|---|---|---|---|
| | Quantities. | Value. | Quantities. | Value. | Quantities. | Value. | Quantities. | Value. |
| | Lbs. | £ | Lbs. | £ | Cwt. | £ | Lbs. | £ |
| India . . . . . | — | — | 38,082,800 | 1,438,863 | — | — | 12,577,600* | 32,828* |
| Ceylon . . . . | 378,216 | 14,246 | 34,411,369 | 1,273,628 | — | — | — | — |
| Mauritius . . . | — | — | 438 | 11 | — | — | — | — |
| New South Wales . . . | — | — | — | — | — | — | — | — |
| Victoria . . . . | 17,889 | 1,016 | 304,122 | 15,411 | 12,457 | 2,916 | — | — |
| South Australia . . . | — | — | — | — | — | — | 15,317 | 370 |
| New Zealand . . | — | — | 311 | 20 | — | — | — | — |
| Queensland . . . | — | — | — | — | — | — | — | — |
| Natal . . . . | — | — | 224 | 6 | — | — | 21 | 1 |
| Cape of Good Hope . . | — | — | — | — | — | — | 248,012 | 3,665 |
| Canada . . . . | — | — | 100 | 4 | — | — | — | 127 |
| Newfoundland . . . | — | — | — | — | — | — | — | — |
| Jamaica . . . . | 267,347 | 5,080 | 9,448,100 | 160,618 | — | — | — | — |
| Barbadoes . . . | — | — | — | — | — | — | — | — |
| Trinidad . . . | 11,649,785 | 372,629 | 40,822 | 1,024 | — | — | — | — |
| British Guiana . . . | — | — | 3,779 | 147 | — | — | — | — |

* Including vegetables.

*Quantities and Value of certain Articles of Domestic Produce, exported from the principal Colonial and other Possessions of the United Kingdom, according to the latest Returns (continued).*

| | TEA. | | TOBACCO. | | WINE. | | BEER. | | SPIRITS. | |
|---|---|---|---|---|---|---|---|---|---|---|
| | Quantities. | Value. | Quantities. | Value. | Quantities. | Value. | Quantities. | Value. | Quantities. | Value. |
| | Lbs. | £ | Lbs. | £ | Gall's. | £ | Galls. | £ | Galls. | £ |
| India | 59,911,703 | 4,083,880 | 19,085,543 | 167,650 | — | — | — | — | 93,324 | 45,499 |
| Ceylon | 1,665,768 | 85,891 | 4,306,273 | 86,837 | — | — | — | — | 129,827 | 20,859 |
| Mauritius | — | — | — | — | — | — | — | — | 551,894 | 51,298 |
| New South Wales | — | — | — | — | 43,288 | 14,430 | 21,951 | 1,835 | 48,802 | 5,565 |
| Victoria | — | — | — | — | 30,638 | 11,493 | 19,982 | 1,764 | 12,055 | 10,321 |
| South Australia | — | — | 3,231 | 525 | 90,242 | 23,743 | 17,755 | 1,508 | — | — |
| New Zealand | — | — | — | — | — | — | 552 | 63 | — | — |
| Queensland | — | — | — | — | 190 | 71 | — | — | 13,085 | 2,252 |
| Natal | — | — | 748 | 31 | — | — | — | — | 91,217 | 3,824 |
| Cape of Good Hope | 250 | 4 | 519 | 30 | 121,852 | 23,845 | 360 | 45 | 4,648 | 1,624 |
| Canada | — | — | 684,732 | 16,772 | 277 | 91 | 18,641 | 1,595 | 16,604 | 3,077 |
| Newfoundland | — | — | 1,250 | 52 | — | — | — | — | — | — |
| Jamaica | — | — | 27,831 | 3,435 | 2,546 | 445 | — | — | 2,013,683 | 226,862 |
| Barbadoes | — | — | — | — | — | — | — | — | 1,002 | 93 |
| Trinidad | — | — | — | — | — | — | — | — | 1,909 | 260 |
| British Guiana | — | — | — | — | — | — | — | — | 2,517,975 | 264,902 |

India and Ceylon may be excluded, for the reasons above given. I may also remark that there are large re-exports of tea from New South Wales and Victoria, which are, no doubt, re-exports of Chinese or Indian imports, furnishing additional evidence of the circuitous nature of the trade of the East, to which I have adverted above. On spirits, England is not likely to make any reduction. Omitting these, the striking feature in this scanty list is the total absence of any article imported from those colonies with whom we might wish and be able to make a tariff bargain. viz., the North American and Australian group. Indeed, the only article in the list which affords any scope for an alteration, which the colonies would accept as a boon, is wine. We know from the evidence before the Wine Duties Committee that, both at the Cape and in Australia, the high duty of 2s. 6d. per gallon on wines containing 26 degrees of spirit, when compared with the duty of one shilling on French wines, is felt as a grievance. The quantity of wine now imported from them is very small; and whether much more would be imported if the duty were reduced is, to say the least, very doubtful, considering the cost of labour in the colonies, and the preference in this country for French, Spanish and Portuguese wine. Under these circumstances, whilst admitting fully the expediency of removing any grievances which these colonies may have in the matter of the wine duties, we may conclude that these duties are not of sufficient importance to afford the means of making tariff bargains with them.

Putting aside wine, which is at this moment unimportant, and likely to continue so, it is quite obvious, then, that we cannot with our present tariff offer any reduction to the self-governing colonies which they would accept as a boon, and that we are unable, therefore, to make tariff bargains of any kind with them.

But there is another consideration of some importance, since it illustrates the peculiarity of our commercial relations with our colonies.

It is not to be expected that we should conclude any such tariff bargain with Canada without a most favoured nation clause. That clause is the Alpha and Omega of all our commercial treaties. It is the one point which we retain when all others fail; the feature on which their upholders mainly rely; the feature which redeems them in the eyes of those who otherwise dislike them. To make a tariff bargain with Canada without stipulating that we shall treat one another as well as we treat the rest of the world, would be an admission that we are, or are likely to be, on less intimate terms with our own colony than with any foreign nation. And yet such a clause might give rise—nay, would be almost sure to give rise—to dangerous differences. Canada and England are separated by the Atlantic; Canada and the United States are distinguished rather than separated by a bridged and navigable river or by an imaginary line. Trade between England and Canada has to overcome natural difficulties; trade between Canada and the United States would be unchecked but for artificial difficulties. Even now the Canadian trade with the United States increases more rapidly than her trade with the United Kingdom. The people of Canada and of the United States are similar in race, in language, and in habits, and are becoming more so daily. Temporary and accidental circumstances have made Canada and the United States assume a hostile commercial attitude; but their disputes are the quarrels of lovers, and it is pretty certain that sooner or later the people of the two countries will desire to trade freely with one another, to the infinite advantage of both. It has happened before, and it will happen again. When it happened before, Canada made a treaty by which United States goods were admitted into Canada on better terms than English goods, and England allowed—indeed, could not help allowing—the treaty. There is nothing to prevent such a thing happening again. Indeed, it is of all things the most probable. What, then, would be the feelings excited in Canada if a clause in her tariff bargain with England prevented her from making with the United States a bargain of ten times more importance to her real interests than any bargain she could make with England? Would not such a clause go far to make her seek for complete separation?

Similar difficulties might well arise in Australia, if we were to attempt to get any one of her colonies to make a separate bargain with us. Their closest natural commercial relations are with one another, and these they will probably prefer to relations with the mother country. Nay, there have been suggestions of special treaties between some of these colonies and countries in America.

I have dwelt upon these points, not because I wish to exaggerate or anticipate difficulties which may never arise, but to show how easy it may be, in trying to draw bonds closer, to strain them to snapping. Let us by all means have the utmost possible commercial connection with our colonies, but no such tie as may be felt by either party as a grievance.

## CONCLUSIONS OF PART I. AS TO A NEW COLONIAL POLICY.

THE general conclusion to which these considerations lead us is that there is little to be done by legislation or treaty to bring us into closer commercial relations with the colonies. Except, perhaps, in the trifling matter of the wine duties, we have already done all that we can to clear the way on our side. It is for the colonies to play their part. Many of them are doing so fairly enough. The others will do so when they feel it to be their interest, without being specially bribed. It is not in our power to do more. Nor is this to be wondered at, when we consider that all which a Government can really do for trade and manufacture is not to impede it.

The English Government can do little or nothing to extend Colonial Trade.

All that Fair Traders and Protectionists are urging as to the duty of Governments in providing markets for their people, and other nonsense of a like kind, really means, when it comes to be sifted, that Governments are to check and prevent trade under pretence of guiding it ; that they are not to allow merchants and manufacturers to do that which is their interest to do. Such a course it is contrary to our commercial interests to enter upon, and it is much more likely to weaken than to strengthen the political connections of the different parts of the empire.

Governments can check but cannot create Trade.

G

# Part II.

## RETALIATION.

────◆◆◆────

## CHAPTER XVI.

### RETALIATION ON MANUFACTURED GOODS ABSURD.

English
Retaliation
on Foreign
Manufac-
tures
Impotent
and
Suicidal.

THE second of the two great principles of the Fair Traders is Retaliation. They desire to impose retaliatory duties on the goods of foreign countries which do not admit our goods duty free.

These duties are not to apply to our food imports, which have been dealt with already, nor to imports of raw material, but to manufactures only. It is a sufficient practical answer to a proposal of this kind that the weapon is in our hands absolutely inefficacious. Of our imports, ninety per cent. are estimated to be raw materials or food, and ten per cent. only what are called manufactured articles. If we take particular nations, the case is stronger. Our trade with the United States is one-sixth of our whole trade, and their tariff is the most hostile of any; whilst the interest which is affected by their competition is our most suffering interest. But out of their imports into the United Kingdom, which exceeded 100 millions in 1880, about 2½ millions only were manufactures; whilst out of our exports to them 24½ millions were manufactures. Will they not laugh at us? or, if not disposed to laugh, will they not treat us as they have treated the Canadians, and place still further obstacles on our imports?

To France we exported in 1880 upwards of 12 millions' worth of manufactured and half-manufactured goods; 2½ millions' worth of raw material; and one million's worth of food. From France we imported 23 millions' worth of manufactured and half-manufactured goods, 3 millions' worth of raw materials, and nearly 15½ millions' worth of food. Here there is more to retaliate upon than in the case of the United States, but the proportion of manufactures which we send to France is greater than the proportion which she sends to us. We send her little but manufactures, whilst she supplies us largely with food. To Germany we exported in 1880 nearly 14 millions' worth of manufactured and half-manufactured goods, less than 2 millions' worth of raw materials, and less than 1½ million's worth of food. From Germany we imported in 1880 a little over 4½ millions' worth of manufactured goods; 3½ millions' worth of raw materials, and 16¼ millions' worth of food. If we are to play a game at who can do most to stop each other's manufactures, it is clear that Germany will have the best of the match. What is true of these countries is true of others. We are *par excellence* the manufacturing country, and for us to play the game of who can best destroy manufacturing industry is simple suicide.

# CHAPTER XVII.

### PROPOSAL TO TAX MANUFACTURES AND LEAVE "RAW MATERIAL" FREE—DIFFICULTY OF THE DISTINCTION.

BUT when we are told that raw material must be admitted free, and that manufactures are to be taxed, I should like to ask what distinction can be drawn between these two classes of goods which would justify a different treatment? When I look down the list of so-called raw materials, I see nothing which is not both the produce of some previous labour and the means or material of some further labour; and when I look down the list of so-called manufactured articles, I find the same thing. I am unable to draw any line between the two, or to find any principle by which to distinguish them.



If the quantity of labour employed in producing the article is to be the test, the labour employed to produce so-called raw materials may, and often does, far exceed the labour necessary to turn that raw material into a manufactured article. There may be more labour in getting coal, or in growing wool, than in spinning or weaving. If we are to be guided by the operation of the article as a means or a stimulus towards further

G 2

production, I am unable to see how the raw produce of the soil operates for this purpose more directly or more effectually than the article into which it is subsequently converted by human labour. I do not see why the alkali out of which glass or chemicals are made is not as efficient a means of production as the salt out of which the alkali is made. Let us take any list in which an attempt is made to distinguish between raw products and manufactures. We get into difficulties at once. The alkali, for instance, to which I have referred, heads one list of manufactured articles, but it is chiefly useful as a material to be employed in subsequent manufactures. "Apparel and haberdashery," which come next, are, no doubt, manufactures as complete as it is possible to conceive ; but even here the boots of the navvy, the shirt and apron of the operative, the blouse of the French labourer, the jersey of the sailor, or even the neat cloth coat and shirt of the clerk or manager, are as much the means and essential conditions of further production as the stone, the iron, or the wool which these persons are employed in manipulating or disposing of. Horses come first in one list of "raw produce ;" but a farm horse is at once the final product of skill in breeding for generations, and is a direct instrument in further production. "Clocks" come first in another list of manufactured articles, and there is certainly no more finished article of human ingenuity than a clock ; but is not a clock the *sine quâ non* of every place where productive labour is at work ?  Is it not the great economist of time, which is the principal of all factors in production?  I might go through the list in the same way, pointing out how each article of large or general use is, on the one hand, the result of previous labour, and the means for further labour. Nay, the same thing is true of food also. Food is the means of keeping the human machine going, without which there can be no productive labour ; it is the most obvious, if not the most important, of raw materials ; it is to the man and woman what the coals are to the steam engine. We admit this when we class food and raw materials together as articles which are not to be taxed, or which are to be taxed more sparingly and cautiously than other things. But, like other raw materials, food is not really more necessary to further production than other articles of general human use. The house in which the artisan lives, the clothes which he wears, the tools which he uses, are no less means and instruments in making the articles which he produces for sale than the food which forms his blood and muscles, the coal which drives his steam-engine, or the material of fibre, of wood, or of metal which he is converting into use. We may go farther, and say that the so-called luxuries, the tea, sugar, and tobacco, which make life tolerable to himself and his children, are also instruments by which his powers of production are increased. Nay, we may assert, with the most exact truth, that the wine which refreshes the brain of the man of science, the statesman, or the physician, is in the highest degree conducive to the production of wealth. All active and useful human life is one cycle of unintermitted and contemporaneous production and consumption—of production, in order to procure articles of consumption ; of consumption, in order the more effectually to produce. There may, of course, be useless and even mischievous consumption of excessive or pernicious luxuries, but these are, economically speaking, a trifle in the vast mass of human consumption ; and there may also be foolish and ill-directed production. But, generally speaking, all human consumption is a direct means of production ; and this makes me doubt whether there is any real sense in the commonly-received doctrine that it is better, on economical grounds, to tax articles of consumption—that is, articles which are in a fit state to be at once eaten, worn, or otherwise used by man—than articles which he has to do something more to before he can use them. But this is, I am glad to say, a controversy on which I need not enter ; from the Fair Traders, or from some of them, I am too glad to accept the admission that raw material is not to be subject to a retaliatory duty ; and only mention the point now, because, if we admit that manufactures are to be taxed, we may find it difficult to stop there.

I have said, "or from some of them," because they are not consistent with themselves. Mr. Farrer Ecroyd, for instance, in a letter published by their League, considers the free admission of raw materials necessary, and he is a man who does not juggle with words. But in a later manifesto of the Fair Trade League, published in 1884, consisting of letters by Mr. Sampson Lloyd and notes in illustration of them, I find that the writers are impressed with the above arguments concerning the difficulty of distinguishing raw material from manufactures. What is the conclusion they draw ? Not, as one might expect, the natural conclusion, that we cannot exclude manufactures whilst

terial as an article which cannot be produced at home !

admitting "raw materials;" but that "raw materials" must be defined afresh, by excluding from the term "raw materials" articles used in manufacture *which can be produced at home.* "Raw material" thus acquires, in the language of these writers, a meaning which will puzzle economists; and the Fair Trader, whilst professing in terms to give our manufacturer the free import of materials, refuses to allow him to use, under that designation, any foreign article used in manufacture which is produced abroad and which can also be produced at home! This, of course, is Protection pure and simple, and helps to show, what really needs no proof—that Fair Trade and Protection are the same thing.

# CHAPTER XVII.

## OTHER PROPOSALS FOR RETALIATION.

Arguments in favour of Retaliation.

THE Retaliation of the Fair Trade League is, as we have seen, ridiculous from its impotency; but this does not show that all Retaliation would be inefficient, or, if efficient, undesirable. Proposals for Retaliation, if once adopted, will not stop where the Fair Traders leave them, and there are arguments in favour of the principle of Retaliation which require a more complete answer than is to be found in the impracticability of a given plan. I do not know that these arguments have ever been more fairly, clearly, and vigorously stated than by Lord Salisbury, in his speech at Newcastle, on the 12th October, 1881. He said :—

Lord Salisbury at Newcastle in 1881.

"I now only wish to say a word with respect to a matter which, perhaps, through being exciting, occupies some considerable portion of public attention at the present moment. It has been said that we of the Conservative active party are anxious to return to the state of things existing before 1840 in respect to fiscal matters, and sundry terrible consequences have been deduced from the assertion. I, for one, do not possess the desire, nor do I think that such a return would be for the public welfare; but it does not do for the Government to ignore the commercial difficulties under which the country labours by the simple device of accusing their opponents of a desire to return to the state of things to which I have referred. Whenever the evil of the present state of things is pointed out to them, they, instead of replying, call us lunatics, or beat the great tom-tom of Free Trade in order to drown our voices. It is undoubtedly the fact, and I do not think that any one can traverse the statement, that in one respect the apostles of Free Trade thirty-five years ago made a gigantic miscalculation when they said that if the country adopted their principles the rest of the nations of the world would follow their example. (Cheers.) It was repeatedly held out, both by Mr. Cobden and Sir Robert Peel, and undoubtedly it influenced many minds at the time. I am very far from stating that as their only reason. I do not mean to say that their policy would have been different if they had had a different belief; but they had the belief, and took every opportunity of communicating it to others, that our example would be followed by other nations of the world. That, I take it, is an undoubted fact in history. Well, that has not been the case. The third of a century has passed by, and all the nations by which we are surrounded have not only not become more Free Trade, but on the whole have become more Protectionist. America, I believe, is more Protectionist; the Protectionist feeling is rising in France. Both of them, mind you, are complete democracies, so there is no pretence for saying that this particular form of opinion has been imposed by the ruling classes. They are countries where it is undoubtedly the sentiment of the people, and nothing else, which governs the conduct of the Government; and in both these countries the feeling of Protection has increased, and is increasing. In Russia, on the other hand, a despotism of the closest type, still you have the same phenomenon. A feeling of Protection is increasing, and the measures of Protection are multiplying. In a kingdom like Germany, with certain constitutional liberties, but ruled undoubtedly by the acutest brain that this century has seen in Europe, you still see this remarkable phenomenon —that the tendency towards Protection is increasing. In our own colonies, where, if anywhere, we ought to have some influence, there, too, unfortunately, the Protectionist feeling is strong, and our own productions are shut out from the markets of our own children. Now, that is a fact which I say it is idle to ignore. It is childish to imagine that our example now,

Arguments for Retaliation. Lord Salisbury.

after so many years, will alone have any effect upon these nations. They have their own experience; they have their own philosophers to teach them. Many of them are, and certainly believe themselves to be, as far advanced in intellectual culture as ourselves. What is there to induce them to defer to our judgment, and to follow our example in this respect? If we intend to act upon them, we must find other motives; and I think we have a right to ask, without pledging ourselves to any opinion until the facts are known, that there should be a thorough investigation into the question whether we are now pursuing the right course for the purpose of inducing those other Governments in some degree to lower the terrible wall of tariffs which is shutting out the productions of our industry from the markets of the world. There is no reason that we should pledge ourselves to any particular course until the facts are known. But if you make a suggestion of this kind, you are immediately told, 'This is Reciprocity and Retaliation, and behind it lurks the shadow of Protection.' Reciprocity and Retaliation! But what are these commercial treaties, if they do not involve the principle of Reciprocity? Sir Charles Dilke will very soon meet the French Minister of Commerce, and they will be talking over the respective products of their respective tariffs, and practically Sir Charles Dilke will say to the French Minister of Commerce, 'If you will give me this relaxation of duty upon cotton, I will give you this relaxation of duty upon wine.' But what is that but Reciprocity? And when Sir Charles Dilke finds that the French Minister of Commerce is difficult to deal with, he will say, 'Well, but if you do not give us this duty, if you do not give us this relaxation upon cotton, I will not give you a relaxation of duty upon wine.' What is that but Retaliation?

"Therefore I say, ever since you adopted the principle of commercial treaties, ever since that memorable date, 1860, the principle of what they are pleased in their own language to term 'Reciprocity and Retaliation,' is conceded.

" It is merely a question of policy, arising upon the state of facts in each particular case, whether you have the means of any alteration of your tariff which you can with due consideration for your own interests adopt, whether you can so do it in the case of the tariff of your neighbour; and it seems to me that that is a sensible course of conduct to adopt. There is no doubt that by abandoning duties which are useful to you for revenue purposes you confer a great benefit upon foreign countries. Why should you not ask for a price in exchange for that benefit? Why should you not obtain for your own industries a benefit corresponding to that which you are conferring upon them? *Arguments for Retaliation. Lord Salisbury.*

"I do not know, until inquiry has been made and opportunities gained of ascertaining, whether it presses either upon the food of our people, or the raw material of our industry, both of which must be held sacred. I do not know what opportunities we may have of exercising this salutary influence upon foreign Powers; but in spite of any formula, in spite of any cry of Free Trade, if I saw that by raising a duty upon luxuries, or by threatening to raise it, I could exercise a pressure upon foreign Powers, and induce them to lower their tariffs, I should pitch orthodoxy and formulas to the winds and exercise the pressure."

Now, if I wished to find a strong argument against all tariff bargains, I should point to this speech of Lord Salisbury's. He may exaggerate the sanguine views entertained by Sir R. Peel and Mr. Cobden of the prospects of universal Free Trade; he may also exaggerate the present tendencies of other countries to Protection; and the Retaliation he suggests—viz., upon that inappreciable part of our imports which consists of luxuries— is, unless he means to include amongst luxuries the tea, sugar, and tobacco which are the comforts of our working people—as impotent as that of the Fair Traders. *This argument derives its strength from Commercial Treaties.*

But, unlike many of the Fair Traders, he states his case fairly, and he puts in very clear terms the impression which our commercial treaties have made, and are making, on many minds besides his own—an impression from which it is very difficult to escape, especially for a diplomatist. Our minister at a foreign court will tell you, "Don't trouble me with your arguments; tell me with what force you will back them." If the Foreign Secretary is to make a bargain, he must have something to bargain with.

Lord Salisbury may, however, be thought by some Free Traders to be a poor economist, and a diplomatist of a very suspicious type; but he has support where one would least expect it. I have seen arguments not very different in character in a perfectly unsuspicious quarter. In the *Pall Mall Gazette* of the 8th and 12th August, 1881, were some letters signed X., by an ardent advocate of commercial treaties, in which, after pointing out, first, that such a treaty as Cobden's, which only reduced duties and gave no preferences, differs *toto cælo* from such treaties as *"X." in the Pall Mall Gazette.*

Arguments for Retaliation.

the Methuen Treaty, which gave a distinct preference and stipulated for the maintenance of differential duties ; and, secondly, that exports are as important a factor in trade as imports—two facts which no sound Free Trader would for a moment deny—the writer proceeded to draw the conclusion that it is the business of the Government of this, and of every other country, to do as much for its exports as for its imports, and, after dismissing the notion of differential duties of a protective character, suggested a differential duty on wines as a legitimate means of compelling France to admit our exports. A large part of his letters consists in the exposure of the fallacy which he supposes the school of Ricardo to commit when they say, "Take care of the imports and the exports will take care of themselves." He points out with perfect truth that a limitation on our exports is as much a limitation on our trade as a limitation on our imports, and he implies that however free our ports may be to foreign imports it will do us little or no good if the hostile tariffs of foreign countries continue to limit our exports.

More reckless Advocates of Retaliation

A notion similar in substance, but much more recklessly expressed, finds its utterance in the constant misrepresentations we have lately heard of the views and objects of the authors of our present policy. We are told that what Mr. Ricardo, Mr. Cobden, Sir Robert Peel, and others had in view, as the principal object and result of their Free Trade policy, was the abolition of foreign restrictions on our exports ; that they believed themselves, and prophesied to the people, that if we in England would take off our duties, foreign nations would certainly take off theirs ; that in this they deceived and were deceived ; that foreign nations have not followed our example ; and that these short-sighted politicians, were they now with us, would at once admit their mistake and revise their policy.

Misrepresentation of the Origin of the Policy of fighting hostile Tariffs by Free Imports.

We have been told, for instance, that Mr. Bright, having raised a formidable agitation against the Corn Laws, Sir Robert Peel, rightly or wrongly, was of opinion that it was necessary for the interest of the country that that agitation should be closed, and that on this account, without waiting for any negotiations with foreign Powers, he introduced the system of Free Trade which Mr. Gladstone has carried further. Now, what were the real facts? The first step taken by Sir Robert Peel was his first reform of the Tariff in 1842, and in his cautious fashion he based it rather upon financial necessities than upon Free Trade principles. In doing this he had postponed certain further reductions of duties, on account, amongst other reasons, of commercial negotiations then in progress. Thereupon Mr. Ricardo, in two successive years, 1843 and 1844,* brought forward a motion urging the immediate remission of our own duties without waiting to see what other nations would do. In the very interesting debates upon these motions, some members, amongst others Mr. Disraeli, defended the principle of Reciprocity. Sir R. Peel and Mr. Gladstone clearly agreed with Mr. Ricardo in the principle he advocated—a principle on which they subsequently acted—but objected to its immediate application, and to the abstract form in which his motion was couched. Mr. Ricardo himself, Lord Grey (then Lord Howick), Mr. Ewart, Mr. C. Villiers, and Mr. Cobden, supported the motion on the ground, which was admitted on all hands to be true, viz., that for 25 years we had been struggling by means of our own duties to obtain reciprocal reductions from other nations, and had failed entirely, a fact which is constantly and conveniently ignored by the present advocates of Reciprocity. They said, further, that if the great object of this country were to obtain reductions in foreign tariffs, the best way to effect it would be to reduce our own, to show foreign nations that we believed in our own principles, and to convince them by our own consequent prosperity that our policy was the true one. In their anticipations of the wisdom of foreign nations, and in their under-estimate of the strength of protected interests, they were perhaps too sanguine. But this was not the only ground, or indeed the real ground, on which they supported the motion. That ground was the principle, true then as now, that whether foreign nations maintain their own duties or not, it is for our interest to abolish ours, and that if we would but do this in our own interest our own trade must prosper, let foreign nations do what they will. As regards Sir Robert Peel, he has himself stated his reasons for adopting a free trade policy in one of the finest speeches he ever made.† Mr. Disraeli had asserted that —"We can only encounter the hostile tariffs of foreign countries by countervailing duties;" and Sir Robert Peel's speech was an emphatic refutation of this doctrine, and an uncompromising defence of the opposite principle—viz., that you can

Arguments for Retaliation. Debates of 1843 and 1844.

Our interest is to abolish our own Protective duties, whether other nations reduce theirs or not.

---

* See "Hansard," vols. 68 of 1843, and 73 of 1844.

† "Hansard," 1849, vol. 106, p. 1429.

Arguments for Retaliation.
Origin of our present policy.

best fight hostile tariffs by free imports—a principle upon which his great tariff reforms were really founded. The immediate suspension of the Corn Laws was due, he said, to the temporary scarcity of food; but the ultimate repeal of that, as well as of other Protection laws, he founded on principles of free trade—a principle which he asserted as positively, and defended as powerfully, as Mr. Bright, Mr. Cobden, or Mr. Ricardo. These great economists were right. Their policy was adopted, and our trade did prosper. No one of these distinguished men doubted, as X. seems to suppose, that foreign protective tariffs are a great impediment to our trade, or that it is most desirable that they should be reduced or repealed. What they said was—"A foreign tariff is one impediment: over that you have no power. Your own high tariff is another and a separate impediment, with an additional and cumulative effect; over this you have power. Remove the impediment over which you have power, and do not wait for the removal of the further impediment over which you have no power. You will gain much if you do not gain all. Half a loaf is better than no bread." But the consideration of this fundamental question deserves a new chapter.

## CHAPTER XIX.

### HOSTILE TARIFFS MUST BE MET BY FREE IMPORTS. STATEMENT OF THE PRINCIPLE.

Fallacies in the arguments of Lord Salisbury and others.

THE fallacy by which X. and Lord Salisbury and many others are misled consists in thinking of a high tariff as a complete barrier, a solid wall, a watertight sluice which allows of no passage. If this were the case, it would be quite true that one high tariff is just as great an impediment to trade as two, and that there is no use in removing one unless you can remove both. If every foreign country were to build an impervious wall round itself, so that no trade could enter, it would not signify how much or how little of a wall there may be round England; no trade could pass either one way or the other. But even in the pre-Huskisson days of absolute legal prohibition, the wall was broken through by the smuggler; and, in the present day, no nation practises absolute prohibition, even on paper. The metaphor of a barrier-wall misleads, as metaphors constantly do. If we are to have a metaphor, Lord Palmerston's metaphor of two turnpikes, one at each end of a bridge, each of which offers some obstacle to the traffic, is a much better one. At the present time every nation, however protective in its tendencies, does what it thinks best calculated to promote its own exports, and therefore cannot destroy but only check, its imports, which are the necessary concomitants of exports. No existing tariff is such as to keep out foreign goods altogether ; each tariff has its weakest point, its lower and less protective duties. Moreover, as a matter of fact, all nations are not protectionist. In many tariffs protection is a secondary or partial object ; and in other countries importation is altogether free. There are, therefore, abundant means of export ; there are even abundant channels, often direct, often circuitous and indirect, by which, so long as a protectionist country exports at all, the exports of a free country can reach, and in the nature of things must reach it. Trade will go on, and does go on, in spite of hostile tariffs, although the number of transactions is, in consequence of such tariffs, less than it otherwise might be ; and each trade transaction is, from its very nature, profitable to both parties engaged in it.

*Principle of Free Imports.*

*Protective Tariffs impediments not barriers.*

Let us, however, consider a little more carefully what the position of a nation is which opens its ports whilst other nations are shutting theirs ; what our position would be, on the hypothesis (which is untrue) that, whilst we retain a Free Trade tariff, all other nations put heavy duties on our goods. I think it can be proved that, though we shall not have as much trade absolutely as we should have if other nations were free like ourselves, we shall be better off relatively ; the trade and the production of the world will be less, but we shall have a larger share of it.

*Position of a Free Trade country in the midst of Protectionist countries.*

The point, though elementary, is so important that it is worth while to consider it attentively. Let us first take the simplest case, that of barter between two merchants living in two different countries, and let us think what would be the effect on their dealings of a tax, imposed in either country on the importation of the commodities in which they deal. Suppose that A, a Frenchman, makes 100 yards of silk in France, and B, an Englishman, makes 100 yards of cloth in England. They exchange these one for the other. Suppose that the French Government puts on the English cloth a duty equal to the value of the cloth ; suppose, further,

*Effect of Protective Duties as between two Countries only.*

that the cloth is a necessity to the Frenchman, and that it is only to be got from England. The effect of the French duty upon the Frenchman will be, that he will have to pay twice as much for the same quantity of cloth as before ; in other words, he will have to pay 200 yards of silk for his 100 yards of cloth. Then suppose that the English Government puts on the French silk a duty equal to the value of the silk, and suppose, as before, that the silk is a necessity to the Englishman, and can only be got from France. The effect on the Englishman will be that he will have to pay 200 yards of cloth for his 100 yards of silk. The effect of the two duties combined will be that the Frenchman will have to give 200 yards of silk for 100 yards of cloth, and the Englishman will have to give 200 yards of cloth for 100 yards of silk—the extra 100 yards of silk and 100 yards of cloth going into the pockets of the respective governments.

Of course, the real thing will be entirely different ; the goods will not be either necessaries or monopolies ; and the effect of the duties will be to transfer the industries, and, in so doing, to reduce both consumption and production. The effect of the French duty on the Frenchman will be to make the Frenchman buy less English cloth, to make him pay more for it, to make him buy inferior cloth from a French maker, and to make him sell his silk to the French cloth-maker for less than the Englishman would give for it. Its effect on the Englishman will be to deprive him of the best market for a part of his cloth, to make him buy less French silk, and to make him buy something with the rest of his cloth which is of less value to him than the French silk.

The further consequence of the English duty on silk to the Englishman will be to make him buy less French silk, to make him pay more for it, to make him buy inferior English silk instead, and to make him sell his cloth to the English silk manufacturer at a less price than the Frenchman would give for it. Its effect on the Frenchman will be to deprive him of his best market for a part of his silk, to make him buy less English cloth, and to make him buy French cloth instead at a higher price.

The effect of one duty, supposing the duties still to be equal, will be as great as that of the other ; they will act cumulatively in transferring English and French industries from what they do best to what they can do less well ; the French industry from silk-making to cloth-making, the English in-dustry from cloth-making to silk-making.

The aggregate production of the two parties will be diminished equally by both duties; and if one duty is taken off, the mischief to both parties will be just one-half what it would be whilst both duties are continued.

Let us now take the case of two nations who exchange goods with one another; and let us, after the manner of Bastiat, call one of them Libera and the other Vincta.

Libera determines to put no duties on the goods of Vincta —Vincta puts a duty of 20 per cent. *ad valorem* on the goods of Libera. The result will be damaging alike to Libera and Vincta; Libera will be able to sell less to Vincta, and to buy less from Vincta in return; Vincta will be able to buy less from Libera, and will be able to sell less to Libera in return. Now, suppose that Libera, irritated by Vincta's conduct, determines to retaliate, and to impose in her turn a tax of 20 per cent. on the goods of Vincta. What will be the result? Precisely the same as before, only that it will be double and cumulative. Vincta will be able to sell still less to Libera, and to buy less from Libera in return; Libera will be able to buy still less from Vincta, and to sell still less to Vincta in return. Both duties have had an equal effect in diminishing the buying and selling on both sides. But their action has been cumulative; the duties imposed by Libera have doubled the loss to each originally caused by the duties imposed by Vincta. Libera has done herself no good, but has done equal mischief to herself and her rival by retaliation. It will even, in this case, clearly be her interest to cease following the example of Vincta, to revert to her original policy, and become Libera again; and it will not be the less her interest to do so because she is at the same time doing good to Vincta.

But now let us consider the case of three countries, which we will call Libera and Vincta No. 1 and Vincta No. 2. Suppose that they have a triangular trade with one another, and that these three trades (that of Libera with Vincta 1, that of Libera with Vincta 2, and that of Vincta 1 with Vincta 2) are each equal in amount, and that each of them is represented by 6. Then 18 will represent the aggregate trade of all three, and each will possess an equal share of it, which will be repre-sented by 6. Now suppose that Vincta 1 and Vincta 2 each put equally heavy duties on their respective imports. Libera

Principle
of Free
Imports.
Abstract
illustration.

remaining free as before. The trade between Libera and each of the others will be subject to one set of duties, but the trade of Vincta 1 and Vincta 2 with each other will be subject to two sets of duties. The aggregate exchange, and with the exchange the production of all three countries, will be diminished, but not in equal proportions. The trade between Vincta No. 1 and Vincta No. 2 will be diminished in a larger proportion than the trade of each with Libera. If we suppose that each set of duties has the effect of diminishing the trade on which it is charged by an amount represented by 1, the whole diminution will be equal to 4, and the aggregate trade of the three countries will now be represented by 14 instead of 18. Of this diminution, 1 will fall on the trade between Libera and Vincta No. 1, which will now be 5 instead of 6 ; 1 on the trade between Libera and Vincta No. 2, which will also be 5 ; and two on the trade between Vincta No. 1 and Vincta No. 2, which will now be 4. Each country will, of course, have half the trade between itself and each of its neighbours, and the whole trade will now be divided as follows :—Libera will have 5 instead of 6 ; Vincta No. 1 and Vincta No. 2 will each have 4½ instead of 6. The following diagram will make this clear :—

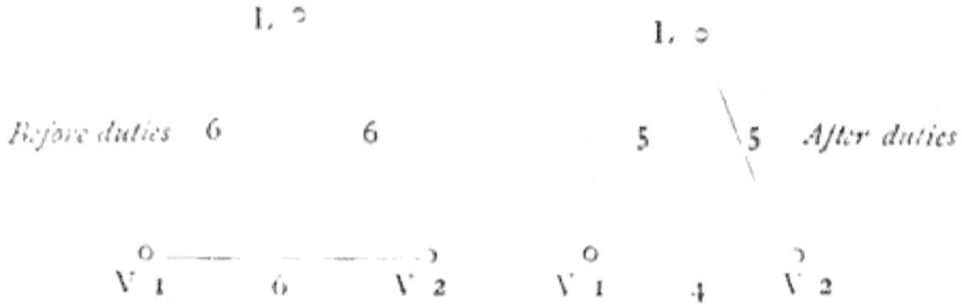


In the same way it may be shown that if of three countries trading with one another under three tariffs equally protective, one does away with Protection, the production and trade of all will be increased, but the largest share of the increased trade will fall to the one which opens its ports. When she opens her ports she must do good to her neighbours as well as to herself, though not so much good—a thing which it is important to remember in examining the consequences of adopting a Free Trade policy. Its adoption by one country is followed by an increase of the trade of other countries as well as of her own, though her own trade reaps the greatest benefit.

I am not very fond of illustrations of this kind. They are apt to appear to be mathematical demonstrations, when they are really only rude and abstract illustrations of one of the many elements which go to make up the infinitely complex and delicate conditions of human business. But taken merely as an illustration, I believe the above formula represents a general truth. Perhaps a more homely illustration will make the matter clearer. Suppose a large village or small town with three general shops in which everything is sold, from lollipops to hardware. Two of the shops are rented from the squire, who also owns nearly all the land in the parish. He says to the tenants of these two shops—"I want to do good to my estate and those who live on it, and therefore I shall require you, in buying for your stock-in-trade such articles as the estate produces, to buy these articles from your neighbours in preference to buying them from strangers. The parish produces corn, wood, vegetables, fruit. There is a local pottery, a local flour mill, a local forge for tools and hardware. All your stock of these things you shall buy from the producers in the parish ; or, if you buy them from strangers, you shall pay me a percentage on your purchases, to be used for the good of the estate." The third shop, happening to be on a bit of land not belonging to the squire, is not subject to his patriarchal theories, and buys all its stock of goods, whether of a kind produced in the parish or not, wherever it can buy them cheapest and best. I think we can tell which of these three shops will sell the best articles, will sell them at the lowest prices, and will have the largest and most profitable custom. The case runs on all fours with those countries of which two compel their producing classes to buy their goods at home, and of which the third leaves them free to buy where and how they best can.

To carry our homely illustration a little farther, let us suppose that our squire, alarmed at the success of the independent shop, and the decay of the two which belong to him, says to the rest of the tenants on his estate, " I have compelled my shops, for your sakes, to buy their stock of you. It is not fair, it is not tolerable under such circumstances, that you should take your custom to that odious free shop, or to the neighbouring town. You shall buy as well as sell at the shops belonging to the estate, and we will all support one another against these horrid strangers." I think our squire would soon find, in his flitting tenants and diminished rents, ample reason for regretting that he had meddled with their buying and selling.

So far, then, as artificial restrictions are concerned, and it is only with these we are now dealing, the country which keeps its own ports open whilst the ports of other countries are shut will not do as much trade as if the ports of all were open, but of the reduced trade which is left by the restrictions it will do a larger share. If England keeps her ports open whilst the United States, France, Germany, Italy, and other countries shut theirs, the aggregate trade of all of them, and even the actual amount of England's share, will be less than if all of them were open: but her share of what is left will be greater than that of the others, and it will be proportionately greater than it was when the ports were open. It is to her open markets rather than to those of the closed countries that each foreign country will prefer to export, and return trade is apt to follow in the same channel. To her will come raw materials, half-manufactured goods, food, clothing, everything which aids production directly or indirectly. No market is likely to be so closed against her but that she will be able to get something into it, and in doing so she will, by her command of the materials and instruments of production, be better able to compete than her rivals, who have made the materials and instruments of production dear. To all open neutral markets, and they are many, she will have full access. In all neutral markets, open or closed by duties, she will have an advantage. Her open market will attract imports; her command of all that is needed for production will give comparative cheapness to her exports. She will lose absolutely some of the direct trade with her Protectionist rivals which she might have had if it were not for their duties, but they will lose that trade also, and she will have advantages in competing with them in other markets which they will not have.

# CHAPTER XX.

## FIRST OBJECTION TO THE PRINCIPLE—HOME TAXATION.

THE preceding chapter contains a statement of the general argument for fighting hostile tariffs by free imports. Let us now consider some of the Protectionist's objections to this principle.

*Are our producers to be compensated for the taxes they pay?*

One of his favourite arguments is, that the produce of home labour, and especially of agricultural labour, is taxed, whilst foreign produce comes in free ; and he proposes to put a tax on foreign produce in order to redress the injustice.

Thus the chairman of the Fair Trade League says, in his letter to Lord Derby, p. 6 : " I will cite as an illustration the case of a bullock bred for the home market. During the two and a half years it is being reared, an acre of land must be told off for its support. The State claims on that land amount to from twelve shillings to fifteen shillings per cent. per annum depending on the county in which it is raised. Thus the English bullock costs its breeder from thirty shillings to forty shillings per head taxation, independently of the further indirect taxation incurred in the keep of its caretaker. The agriculturist asks, therefore, fairly enough, 'Why should my beast, which has contributed so much to local and imperial taxation have to compete in the same market-place with animals on which not a penny taxation has been paid ?' "

*Mr. Sampson Lloyd's taxed bullock.*

Now I will not stop to inquire into Mr. Sampson Lloyd's figures ; I will not inquire whether the sum is correct ; I will not ask on whom the taxation falls, viz., whether upon the agriculturist or upon rent ; or whether these taxes, if remitted, would go into the pocket of the landlord, or help to facilitate the production of beef. Let us assume that the tax is a tax on productive industry, and that it is to be looked at in precisely the same light as the income tax, and the rates which the manufacturer pays on his business or his factory ; and let us ask, on these very improbable assumptions, whether any such taxation affords the slightest ground for a countervailing Customs Duty on an American bullock

H 2

Objections to the principle. Taxation should be fair as between different classes.

If the Fair Traders meant that English taxation was not fair as between different classes of Englishmen, and that local rates might be more fairly apportioned than they are ; if they wished that accumulated personalty should bear its fair share of local and imperial burdens ; above all, if they meant that the incidence of taxation as between rich and poor should be fully inquired into, and the injustices, if any, be redressed, the demand would be a fair one, though it might, perhaps, land them in unexpected conclusions. But this is obviously not what they mean. If they have any intelligible meaning, it is that we shall take into consideration the taxation which falls—directly or indirectly—on every branch of productive industry ; and shall then put upon the corresponding foreign produce a Customs duty equivalent to the taxation which the home produce bears.

But Foreign producer pays direct taxes no less than ours, and is burdened with heavier charges of other kinds.

Now, in the first place, the assumption that foreign production is untaxed, or is taxed more lightly than English production, is certainly not true, and is probably the reverse of the truth. In actual direct taxation per head, England compares not unfavourably with other similar countries, whilst their taxation per head is growing much faster than ours. Supposing that, instead of simple taxation per head, we take the proportion which wealth bears to taxation, or, in other words, the capacity to pay, as our standard of comparison, England is one of the most lightly taxed nations in the world. If, again, we do not confine ourselves to direct taxation, the case in her favour becomes much stronger. Suppose, for instance, that we take military conscription into account, European nations will be found to have laid on their national industries an immense additional burden, which England does not lay on hers. And if, in addition, we take into account the loss which foreign countries by their Protective systems inflict on their industries, we shall find that the burden thrown on their productive powers becomes out of all proportion greater than that which is imposed on English industry by English taxation.

Thus Germany, France, Italy, Russia, not only rob industry of a large part of its most effective labour by conscription, but also make their productive industries less efficient by heavy protective duties. As regards our greatest agricultural provider and competitor, the United States, it has been calculated that their Fiscal system imposed on the American farmer an annual burden of some 400 millions of dollars, or £80,000,000 sterling, in the shape of increased price of manufactures excluded by their Protective tariff; and that of this 400 millions, only 60 millions found their way into the State Exchequer.* 

To burdens such as these foreign produce is subject, and in addition to the cost of transit—often over many thousand miles of sea and land—before it can reach English markets.

In the second place the financial problem involved in any proposal to counterbalance Home Taxation by Customs duties is an insoluble one. It is difficult enough to ascertain the exact incidence and effect of any tax or Fiscal burden at home. But if we are to attempt to ascertain the effect of the taxation of each foreign country on each article it produces, to compare it with our own taxation of the same article, and then to impose a Customs duty on each article which will make home and foreign taxation equivalent, we shall introduce a system of finance and of taxation more preposterously absurd and complicated than has ever yet been dreamed of. 

But the whole proposal is a delusion. We cannot get rid of our Fiscal burdens. Each country requires to raise a certain amount of money by taxation for public purposes. One country requires more and another less. This burden it must bear. It cannot by any hocus pocus throw it on foreign countries. It may shift the burden from one class to another of its own citizens: it may arrange the burden so as to do as little harm or as much harm as possible, but, assuming the purposes for which it is raised to be necessary, it can no more get rid of the necessity of paying for them than it can get rid of its soil or climate. To compensate the English farmer, at the expense of his fellow citizens, for the supposed excess, or assumed excess, of taxation in England, is much the same thing as to attempt to compensate him for his inferior soil or sunshine; and any attempt to do so can only result in limiting the productive powers of the country as a whole. 

It would indeed be a charming discovery if Governments could relieve their own countrymen from taxation by simply taxing the produce of other nations. Chancellors of the Ex-

---

* See Mongredien's "Western Farmers of America." Cassell & Co. The burden of these increased prices is less now. But this is because Protection has stimulated an unhealthy growth of manufacture, and a consequent glut and depression which have depressed prices, and brought ruin on the industries which the system was intended to protect. See below, Chapter XXXIII.

Objections to the principle. Taxation.

chequer would revel in their budgets, which would become, if not small, yet delightfully easy ; and Jingoes would triumph in the simultaneous impoverishment of their neighbours and enrichment of themselves. Fortunately, or unfortunately, no Chancellor of the Exchequer can do anything of the kind. He cannot draw his taxes from any country but his own. He can injure other nations, but not without injuring his own still more. Regarded from his own point of view, Protection, in proportion as it succeeds in its primary object, will destroy his revenue. It will kill the goose which lays his golden eggs.

Take two neighbouring parishes, the inhabitants of which are accustomed to buy and sell from one another. One of them has to go to great expense for drainage works and water supply, and the parochial rates rise. Would any one be silly enough to suggest that this rise of rates could be compensated by imposing a duty or restriction on the purchase by its inhabitants of goods sold by the other? And yet this is not more absurd than to suppose that we can make the Americans pay our income tax or our poor rate by laying a duty on American bullocks.

———

# CHAPTER XXI.

### SECOND OBJECTION TO THE PRINCIPLE—EXCESS OF IMPORTS.

Alleged effect of Imports

ANOTHER objection which the Fair Traders make to our principle of Free Imports is that Imports displace British production, and that consequently, the excess of Imports, which is apparent in our recent Trade Returns, is a fatal sign of the decadence of English industry. Imports are their great bugbear, and to them excess of imports means ruin. There is, perhaps, no subject on which so much nonsense has been talked. It is nonsense which reappears under a great variety of forms.

Fair Trade ploughs gratis!

For instance, I find in one of the Fair Trade tracts a long and graphic description of the making of a plough in England, and of all the English people employed in preparing the materials and putting them together. The whole culminates in the sale of the English made plough to a farmer for £12, whilst a similar article might be imported from abroad for

£11 10s. All this is for the sake of the following precious piece of political wisdom :—

"I must deal with the question in its practical bearing, and tell you that the dogma, 'buy in the cheapest market,' is a great delusion, for, in the case of the plough which produced £12 to the whole nation, if it could be bought from the the foreigner *for £11 10s.* the whole nation would certainly gain 10s. *but would lose the £12 by the collapse of that special industry*, the *nation, from the Government down to the candle-stick maker, being poorer by £11 10s. in distributive wealth.*"

Astounding conclusion ! How do the Fair Traders think the imported foreign plough is to be paid for? With nothing? If so, then the nation will be richer not by 10s., but by £12. If with something, then with what? Why, of course, with something which English workmen can make better and cheaper than they can make ploughs, and which will have to be sent abroad, and there sold to pay for the plough.

Again, in another of their leaflets I find a long story about the producer and consumer, and a long and tedious attempt to show that in consulting the interest of the consumer by encouraging imports we are damaging the producer, and discouraging exports.

In this there is a double fallacy. In the first place, producers and consumers are really the same people. The distinction between producer and consumer is of use and of interest in arguing questions of political economy, where the different capacities in which men act, and the different motives which impel them to action, have to be taken into account ; but producers and consumers are, in real life, the same persons. Every producer is a consumer, and every consumer (except the purely idle, whom we need not now consider) is a producer. The workman who produces steel rails consumes bread, meat, tobacco, clothing, and a number of other things. The learned classes—the engineer, the lawyer, the doctor, the statesman— whilst consuming whatever is necessary for life and health, assist in production no less than the workman. We are all— if we are doing anything useful—producing as well as consuming. There is really no interest of producers separate from that of consumers. We are all interested in buying what we want wherever we can get it best and cheapest.

Secondly, if we look to production alone, and put consumption out of the question, it is the largest amount of free

Objections to the principle. Effect of Imports.

Fair Trade notion, that Imports injure Englishmen as Producers.

Fallacy of distinction between producer and consumer.

Largest imports cause

largest production.

imports which will cause the largest amount of production. Not, no doubt, of the same articles, but of articles which we can produce better and with more advantage to ourselves and to the country than we could produce the articles which we import. The moment we cease to produce such articles we shall cease to import. So long as we import we may be sure that we have bought those imports with our labour, and either have paid, or are paying for them, with our exports. We can pay for them in no other way.

The fear of growing Imports.

But it is the growing excess of imports which fills our Fair Trade friends with their most terrible alarms.

The absurdity of these terrors has been so often and so fully exposed that it is unnecessary to repeat in detail the many arguments which show that our imports are large, because they include the profits of our present trade, and of our past savings. But it may be desirable to state the outlines of the case shortly, premising that the incompleteness of our statistical records makes error easy and exactness impossible;

Imperfection of Statistics as statement of Balance of Trade.

for, not only do our statistics of exports omit much which is really produced and sent out of the country, but all attempts to strike an exact balance of imports and exports are confused and baffled by investments, and by the traffic in securities. We know that all exports of goods are made either in exchange for the imports of other goods or bullion, or by way of loan to be repaid hereafter by imports—and we know that imports are made either in exchange for goods or bullion, with the necessary additions for freight and profit, or by way of repayment of the principal or interest of loans which we have formerly made. But we do not know how much is due to each of these causes, and we cannot, therefore, strike an accurate balance. We do not know the exact state of our debtor and creditor account with foreign countries. The difficulty is increased by the fact that securities are now used as a sort of international cash, and are transferred from country to country, not as permanent investments, but in place of bullion to settle the balance of accounts. In consequence there is large room for speculation and for error.

But all economists agree that we are a largely lending country, and that we have enormous investments abroad, of which the interest and profit are daily returning to us in the shape of imports. The case may be put shortly as follows :—

The excess of imports over exports in 1880 was

Objections to the principle. Excess of Imports.

| | |
|---|---|
| Imports . . . . . . . | £411,229,000 |
| Exports . . . . . . | 286,414,000 |
| | £124,815,000 |

and in 1883 it was

| | |
|---|---|
| Imports . . . . . . | £426,892,000 |
| Exports . . . . . . | 305,437,000 |
| | £121,455,000 |

Estimate of Foreign Investments.

The amount of English capital constantly employed abroad in private trade and in permanent investments, including Stock Exchange securities, private advances, property owned abroad by Englishmen, British shipping, British owned cargoes, and other British earnings abroad, has been estimated by competent statisticians as being in 1880 from 1,500 to 2,000 millions, and it is constantly increasing. Taking the lower figure, the interest or profit upon it, at 5 per cent., would be 75 millions, and at the higher figure, 100 millions. But a large proportion of this amount being employed in active business, would bring in more than 5 per cent. profit, probably not less than 10 per cent. Supposing one-quarter to bring in that interest, we should have, as the income of 1,500 millions capital, 94 millions; for the income of 2,000 millions capital, 125 millions. The former amount is about three-fourths of, and the latter equals, the excess of imports over exports. But besides this, there is the question of freights. A very large proportion of the trade of the United Kingdom is carried in English ships, and these ships also carry a large proportion of the trade of the world which does not come to England. This is, in fact, an export of highly-skilled English labour and capital which does not appear in the export returns, and considering that it includes not only the interest on the capital invested in the ships, but wages, provisions, coals, port expenses, repairs, depreciation, and insurance; and that the value of English shipping employed in the foreign trade is estimated at considerably more than 100 millions sterling, the amount to be added to our exports on this account must be very large. Add to this the ships built for foreigners, amounting in 1880 to 70,000 tons—chiefly steam ships—the ships repaired for foreigners and the ships sold to foreigners,

Outgoings on Ships.

Objections to the principle. Excess of Imports.

amounting in 1880 to 75,000 of sailing and 36,000 of steam tonnage, worth altogether several millions, which do not appear in our list of exports. All these outgoings, except the small part spent abroad, with the profits, must either return to this country in the shape of imports, or be invested abroad. From all I can learn, I believe that 50 millions is too low an estimate of the amount of unseen exports, which should be added on this account to the total of exports visible in our statistical returns. In addition, there are the commissions and other charges to agents in this country, connected with the carriage of goods from country to country, which are analogous in their nature to the charges of the ship-owners for conveying goods, all of which appear in our accounts of imports, but none of which appear in the list of exports. If there is any truth in the above figures, not only is the excess of imports over exports accounted for, but there is really a large surplus of imports due to us, which can only be accounted for by supposing that we are still investing large amounts of our savings in foreign countries and in the colonies.

We need not, therefore, be afraid either that we are consuming the realised earnings of past generations, or that we are ceasing to be able to earn. Though receiving more, we are still earning; and we may consume in confidence, because we produce in abundance.

I cannot finish this chapter better than with Cobden's own words :— *

Cobden's Illustration of Excess of Imports and Drain of Gold.

" Now, we are met by the monopolists with this objection : —If you have a Free Trade in corn, foreigners will send you their wheat here, but they will take nothing in return. The argument employed, in fact, amounts to this, if it amounts to anything—that they will give us their corn for nothing. I know not what can exceed the absurdity of these men if they be honest, or their shallow and transparent knavery if they be dishonest, in putting forward such an argument as that. If there be a child here, I will give him a lesson which will make him able to go home and laugh to scorn those who talk about Reciprocity, and induce him to make fools' caps and bonfires of the articles in the *Morning Post* or *Herald*. Now, I will illustrate that point. I will take the case of a tailor living in one of your streets, and a provision dealer living in another, and this

---

* See " Cobden's Speeches," p. 63. Speech in London, 8th February, 1844.

busybody of a Reciprocity man living somewhere between the two. He sees this tailor going every Saturday night empty-handed to the provision dealer, and bringing home upon his shoulder a side of bacon, under one arm a cheese, and under the other a keg of butter. Well, this Reciprocity man, being always a busybody, takes the alarm, and says : ' There is a one-sided trade going on there, I must look after it.' He calls on the tailor, and says, ' This is a strange trade you are doing ! You are importing largely from that provision dealer, but I do not find that you are exporting any cloths, or coats, or waist-coats in return ? The tailor answers him, ' If you feel any alarm about this, ask the provision dealer about it ; I am all right, at all events.' Away goes the Reciprocity gentleman to the provision shop, and says, ' I see you are doing a very strange business with that tailor ; you are exporting largely pro-visions, but I do not see that you import any clothes from him : how do you get paid ? ' ' Why, man, how should I ?' replies the provision dealer, ' in gold and silver, to be sure !' Then the Reciprocity man is seized with another crotchet, and forthwith begins to talk about the ' drain of bullion.' Away he flies to the tailor, and says, ' Why, you will be ruined entirely ! What a drain of the precious metals is going on from your till ! That provision dealer takes no clothes from you ; he will have nothing but gold and silver for his goods.' ' Ay, man,' replies the tailor, ' and where do you think I get the gold and silver from ? Why, I sell my clothes to the grocer, the hatter, the bookseller, and cabinet maker, and one hundred others, and they pay me in gold and silver. And pray, Mr. Busybody, what would you have me do with it ? Do you think my wife and family would grow fat on gold and silver?' Now, if there is any little boy or girl in this assembly, I hope they will go home, and for exercise write out that illustration of Reciprocity, and show it to any of their friends who may be seized with this crotchet respecting Reciprocity and the drain of gold, and see if they cannot laugh them easily out of their delusions."

## CHAPTER XXII.

### THIRD OBJECTION—INVESTMENT OF ENGLISH CAPITAL ABROAD.

Fair Trade objections to our foreign investments.

IN the last chapter, and elsewhere, I have spoken of our foreign investments as matters which have great influence on our foreign trade ; and our Fair Trade friends have a good deal to say about and against them. It is true that they are, as usual, absolutely inconsistent with each other and with themselves. When we point to the indebtedness of foreign countries to England as one reason for the excess of imports, they tell us that we have been paying for our imports by the return to us of foreign securities ; and at the same time they complain bitterly that, instead of spending our money at home, our rich men are constantly investing their money abroad, and thus robbing English labour of its rights here. Here is one of their appeals to working men of England :—

"Free Traders tell you that these imports are the consequence of our foreign investments. Is it any compensation to the working men of England to know that work which is their birthright is being done by foreigners for the advantage and benefit of a few rich people who have invested their capital out of their own country?"* And, again, Mr. Sampson Lloyd says: "By the virtue of foreign investments, by the power of utilising capital to equal if not greater advantage in the employment of labour on foreign soil, monied interests thrive and flourish, and home industry is handicapped by the very sources of their prosperity."† Similar quotations might be multiplied if it were worth while.

Interest of working men.
(1) In the imports which are the returns from their investments.

With one part of this subject, viz., the notion that the excess imports due to foreign investments go to swell the fortune or increase the business of the rich man and fail to reach the working classes, I have dealt above in Chapter XIII., where 1 have shown that our excess of imports being for the most part

---

* Fair Trade Tracts, No. 15.
† Letter from Mr. Sampson Lloyd to Lord Derby of 14th July, 1882

either raw material for manufactures, or common food, must go to provide workmen with the means of industry or the means of living. But it is worth while to consider more carefully the operation of an investment made by an Englishman in a foreign industry, and to see what is its effect on English industry compared with investments made at home. I speak now not of the case of absentees who spend their winters on the Riviera or in Paris, and their summers in Switzerland, and who consume in those countries the monies they derive from their investments, whether at home or abroad. I speak of the Englishman who has his home and employment in England, who invests larger or smaller sums of money in American, Australian, or other foreign securities, and who draws from them an annual income. What is his object in making the investment? Why does he put his money into foreign railways or foreign land companies rather than into farms, or manufactures, or railways in England? Simply and solely because he makes more by so doing. In general he will prefer an English security, under the protection of his own laws and government, unless the foreign security offers him some advantage in the shape of higher interest. Does he do his own country any harm in yielding to the temptation? Let us take an individual case, and see how it works.

An Englishman, whom we will call Johnson, is the owner of a farm in England, of (say) 300 acres, much of it arable, which he cultivates himself.

It costs him in labour £500 a year, and he employs (say) 16 labourers at an average of 12s. a week. At present prices of agricultural produce the farm is a dead loss to him, or does not pay more than its expenses. If he throws the whole or the greater part of it into grass he will largely reduce his expenses. He will save (say) one half of his labour bill (£250), and as much more in horses, carts, machinery, seeds, and manure, making altogether £500 a year to the good.

Now, let us suppose that, not wishing to increase his expenditure on himself, his house, or his family, Johnson is anxious to invest this money. If it had been profitable to him, he would have kept it and invested it, as before, on his farm. As it is, he looks out for what will be more profitable, and he finds that in consequence of the demand for corn in Europe, and the increasing cultivation of corn in America and India, there is no investment more profitable than an American or an

Objections to the principle. Foreign investments.

Indian railway. He buys shares in such a railway to the extent of the £500 which he has saved from his farm. How does his £500 get out there? Not certainly in gold. We import into England more gold than we export. Unless it is exchanged for capital returning home, which is unlikely, for we are constantly making fresh investments abroad, it goes out in the shape of English goods, possibly in the form of iron rails or machinery which are required for the purpose of the railway in which Johnson has invested his £500.

Certain advantages to working men

This £500, therefore, sets to work English labour as much as if it were wages on Johnson's farm. It sets to work the workmen who make the iron, the shipbuilders who make the ship which carries the goods, and the sailors who navigate her.

When it has reached America or India, what does it do there? First of all it facilitates the carriage of corn, and makes corn cheaper in this country. Then, as regards Johnson himself, it creates an obligation on the part of the American or Indian railway company to pay him interest upon it—say, at the rate of £5 per cent., by which he gets £25 a year, which he would never have had if he had continued to invest his money on his English farm in growing corn, which he could not sell at a profit. This £25 he can spend as he pleases. Possibly, being richer than he was, he may choose to spend it unproductively on his farm; possibly on his garden, his house, or on other luxuries ; possibly he may invest it again in the same way in which he invested the £500 from which it was derived. But in any of these cases it will set to work English labour ; and there will be £25 employed in setting to work English labour, which would not have existed if Johnson had continued to grow unprofitable corn. If the £25 is productively invested, it will again produce interest, to be again employed in labour, and so on. Each year the same process will be continued —each year Johnson will be diverting the unprofitable labour from his farm to profitable labour in the mine, the foundry, the shipbuilding yard, and the ship ; and the amount of capital to be returned to this country to be there employed in labour will constantly accumulate. On the whole, therefore, not only will Johnson be better off, but the money used in employing labour in this country will be increased ; and that labour will be of a better kind—because more productive—than the labour on Johnson's farm.

But now, in order to be fair, let us look at the other side

of the question. Johnson formerly employed 16 labourers on his farm—he now employs only half the number. He formerly bought seeds and manures and horses, which he no longer buys; and to this extent English labour is displaced. But this labour is *ex hypothesi* less valuable labour to the country than the English labour which his foreign investment has set to work, and it would not produce the additional interest for the future employment of English labour which the foreign invest-ment does. The displacement and transfer may, nevertheless, cause inconvenience and loss to the farm labourers concerned. Such inconvenience and loss are little, if at all, felt where the process is gradual and the labour is absorbed elsewhere; but they may be so sudden as to cause considerable suffering. For instance, the process I have thus illustrated has for many years been going on throughout Western England, as is shown by the decrease of arable land in the agricultural returns, and this change being gradual, has, down to the past year, been effected without loss to the agricultural labourer, as is shown by the maintenance or rise of his wages. It may be that quite recently things have changed; that the long continued agricul-tural depression has had a cumulative effect; that the depres-sion of prices following bad seasons has caused the change to go on more rapidly, and that it is causing some suffering at the present time.

*Objections to the principle. Foreign investments. Possible disadvan-tages to working men.*

But whether this is so or not, it remains true that on the whole the transfer of English capital from an English industry which does not pay to a foreign or colonial industry which does pay, is no loss to England generally, and causes no diminution in the employment of English labour.

*Balance of advantage.*

There are, however, two drawbacks to these foreign and colonial investments of a totally different kind, to which it is well to call attention. The one is that in case of a war with a maritime power, the returns from them would be open to greater risk than investments in this country; the other that they can more easily evade taxation by the English Govern-ment. If the Fair Traders would devote their attention to the best mode of securing safety to our immense foreign invest-ments, and of making this form of personal property pay a certain and a fair contribution to the national expenses, they might deserve public gratitude.

*Drawbacks to foreign invest-ments.*

It will be remembered that in this chapter I have been arguing with those who would treat the transfer of capital from

English estates or manufactures to foreign railways or other
foreign enterprises as an economical evil to be discouraged by
the legislature.  But the desire to make profitable investments,
however valuable economically, is not the only motive which
governs rich men ; and the love of natural beauty ; interest in
farming and outdoor life ; personal and local attachments ; are
quite sure to maintain a much larger expenditure on English
land and on English labour than would be dictated by a desire
for gain.  By all means let all such motives have their way ; but
do not let us, in the supposed interest of national wealth, be
persuaded to deprecate or discourage the foreign investments
which have done so much to increase that wealth, and to improve the condition of the toilers and spinners who produce it.

## CHAPTER XXIII.

### ILLUSTRATION OF PRINCIPLE—ENGLISH TRADE BEFORE 1860.



HAVING, in Chapter XIX., stated the general principle of Free
Traders, and having, in the three following chapters, dealt with
some of the Protectionist objections to it, I will now try to
illustrate its operation.  But it is not an easy thing to prove
any truth of this kind from statistics of actual facts, for it is
very difficult to find a test-case in which all the facts are known,
and from which all foreign elements can be eliminated, but in
the facts which have been so often cited by Free Traders we
find an approach to an illustration if not to a proof.

From the time of the end of the great war in 1815 to the
time of Sir R. Peel's tariff reforms, England was first a Prohibitive and afterwards a Protectionist country.  In 1842 the first
great reductions of duty were made.  In 1845 followed a great
further reduction.  In 1846 the Corn-law Bill was passed, and
the corn duties came to an end in 1849.  In the same year the
navigation laws were repealed.  In 1853 Mr. Gladstone's first
budget made large additional reductions, which were continued
more or less in each successive year until 1860, when the
reductions incidental to the French treaty brought our tariff to
its present simple condition, with the exception of the repeal
of the sugar duty, which took place in 1874.

If, therefore, we can compare the period of Protection in England with the period of Free Trade which immediately followed Sir R. Peel's reforms, and if we find that after these reforms had taken effect, and before 1860, when the French treaty was made, there was a great burst of activity in England, we have some evidence that reduction of Protective duties in England alone, and without reduction on the part of other nations, resulted in a great increase of English trade, the effects of which are seen in the statistics of our exports.

Our statistics of exports of domestic produce, which are the only statistics on which we can rely for the earlier years of the century, afford such a test. These averaged per annum from

| | | | | | | |
|---|---|---|---|---|---|---|
| 1821 to 1825 | · | · | · | · | about 37 | millions. |
| 1826 to 1830 | · | · | · | · | ,, 36 | ,, |
| 1831 to 1835 | · | · | · | · | ,, 40 | ,, |
| 1836 to 1840 | · | · | · | · | ,, 50 | ,, |
| 1841 to 1845 | · | · | · | · | ,, 54 | ,, |
| 1846 to 1850 | · | · | · | · | ,, 61 | ,, |
| 1851 to 1855 | · | · | · | · | ,, 89 | ,, |
| 1856 to 1860 | · | · | · | · | ,, 124 | ,, |

thus showing a large and continuous increase as the successive instalments of Free Trade came into full operation. I am aware that there were other factors at work during this period, and those who wish to see what can be said about them should turn to Mr. Gladstone's article in the *Nineteenth Century* of February, 1880. But the above figures show conclusively that an outburst of successful exportation was concurrent with the installation of a Free Trade policy in England, and with the maintenance of restrictive tariffs abroad.

---

# CHAPTER XXIV.

### ENGLISH TRADE SINCE 1860.

But it will be said in reply, " All this happened long ago, and many things have happened since then. Foreign nations have learned from us to manufacture and to rival us not only in their own markets but in the markets of the world. Protective tariffs

I

English Trade since 1860.

in this state of things will be more dangerous to us than they ever were before, for we have not only the barriers of hostile tariffs to cross, but shall find within them rivals whom we cannot expect to beat. As a matter of fact, the trade of other nations has progressed as fast or faster than our own. The United States have the most Protective tariff in the world; but their trade, as measured by their exports and imports, and their general prosperity, has grown faster than our own. France, with her tariff less Protectionist than the United States, but still Protective in a high degree, is the marvel of the world in the way she has recovered from the crushing blows of the German war. Germany has not found her Protective tariff destroy her trade. The imports and exports of Canada have not diminished since she adopted her high duties, and Protectionist Victoria runs a fair race with Free-trade New South Wales. Above all, are not our exports diminishing while our imports are increasing? Have we not had the longest period of commercial depression ever known? and is there any reason for supposing that we shall so far recover from it as to attain again our former prosperity?"

The World not so Protective as it was.

To this I propose to reply at length in the following chapters. But in the first instance I wish to observe that it is a mistake to suppose that the world is, on the whole, more protective than or even as protective as it was. In the earlier part of this century, nations were prohibitive where they are now Protectionist. Prohibition pure and simple, common enough before 1860, scarcely exists now. Many countries—*e.g.*, Holland, Belgium, Norway and Sweden—have since 1860 adopted a policy approaching our own. Scarcely anywhere in Europe are tariffs now as high as they were before 1860. Many neutral markets are free. But, secondly, be the tariffs what they may, our freedom still gives us an advantage. We can and do export, even to the most Protectionist countries, manufactures which they are trying to keep out, and we must do so as long as they burden their own industries by a Protective system, and seek at the same time to sell their raw produce to us. In neutral markets, of which there must always be many, we have enormous advantages in our free tariff. Our materials come to us free, and our people live on untaxed food.

Human laws only one factor

Let us also bear in mind that these human laws which we make so much of are but trifles in face of the great changes which are extending the borders of the nations, and bringing them together. Steam and electricity, the steamship, the railway, and the telegraph, the improvement of every art of production, including agriculture, the specialisation of these arts, and their distribution among different classes and peoples, the system of credit—all these things make the inter-dependence of different countries both more practicable and more necessary day by day; and the stream of international commerce flows on, ever widening and deepening, in spite of the puny barriers by which the folly of man tries to check and impede its course. Mischief they can do, but it is small compared with the magnificent results of the beneficent laws of Nature.

*(margin: in the great result.)*

## CHAPTER XXV.

### WHAT FREE TRADE MEANS, AND WHAT IT CANNOT DO.

AT the same time it must be remembered what Free Trade is, and what are its limits. It is merely the unshackling of powers which have an independent existence. It can produce nothing; it can create no material substance in Nature; it can beget no positive qualities in man. All it can do, and that all is much, is to leave the powers of Nature and of man to produce whatever it is in them to produce unchecked by human restrictions. Free Trade cannot make the maize and the vine grow in England; it cannot make our sands and clays yield wheat as freely as the virgin soil of the prairies; it cannot endow the negro and the Hindoo with the ingenuity and thrift of the Frenchman, or the brain and arm of the Anglo-Saxon; but it can insure that each shall be allowed to yield and do whatever it is best fitted for yielding and doing. Free Traders have been much to blame for attributing to Free Trade consequences which have probably arisen from many causes, and they are now paying the penalty of their exaggerations. It is idle to expect that England shall produce everything, or even that she shall have a monopoly of manufactures. Other countries have their own special advantages of soil, of climate, and character, which will enable them to do many things better than England. The true test of the value of

*(margin: Free Trade cannot create; it can only leave Nature and Man free.)*

I 2

True test of Free Trade.

Free Trade to England, or to any other country, is not whether she is progressing faster, or even doing a larger trade than another, but whether she is doing better herself with Free Trade than she would do without it ; and whether, in her relation to other nations which are not Free Traders, she or they derive the greater benefit from their respective commercial systems. Tried by these tests, we need not fear the comparison.

## CHAPTER XXVI.

### RELATION OF THE PROSPERITY OF OTHER NATIONS TO OUR OWN.

Our Trade can only grow by making the Trade of other Nations grow too.

BEFORE attempting to prove anything by facts and figures, let us be on our guard against a mistake, by which our Protectionist friends are constantly leading us into pitfalls. It is a very important and a very dangerous mistake, for it involves the very principle which lies at the bottom of the Free Trade controversy. To read Protectionist literature, one would imagine that no nation could thrive except at the expense of another ; that trade, at any rate between nations, is a sort of betting or gambling game, where the gain of one is the loss of another. If the list of French exports grows as ours grows, still more if it increases by a percentage faster than our own, we are in danger. If the American export account appears to exceed our own, we are lost, and so on. Unless our sale list keeps far ahead of and grows faster than that of all other nations, we are losing our position, and dwindling among the races of mankind. But the truth is, that trade is reciprocal : our trade cannot grow without making the trade of other nations grow too. Every act of trade is a sale by one man and a purchase by another, and every such a sale and purchase involves a second purchase by the first man and sale by the last. Every act of trade is an act of barter—or, rather, one-half of an act of barter. Except in the case of transfers of goods made to pay existing debts, every sale by an Englishman to a Frenchman involves a sale direct or indirect by a Frenchman to an Englishman. Every English export to France involves a French import from England, a French export on account of England and an English import on account of France. And the whole transaction is a gain to both traders and to both countries. An increase in the English export list, arising from the removal of our own restrictions, necessitates an equal and corresponding increase in the French export list; and the increase in the French exports, which follows the removal of our restrictions, is the proof and consequence of an increase in English trade. We cannot do good to ourselves without doing good to our neighbour. Nay, if we are doing much the larger trade of the two, it may very well happen that by removing some artificial restrictions which we have placed on our trade with him, we may arrive at the result of increasing our neighbour's trade by a percentage on his trade greater than the percentage by which we increase our own—a catastrophe which excites the liveliest alarm in the minds of those who think the infant of two years lives faster than the youth of twenty, because in one year the infant has doubled his age, whilst the youth has added only one-twentieth to his.

It would be seen to be the height of absurdity if a manufacturer, a merchant, a farmer were to look on the prosperity of his customers as signs of his own decay. Conceive the village baker saying to the shoemaker, "You are making too much by my custom; you have enlarged your shop, you are taking an apprentice: you eat more of my bread, it is true, but I cannot bear to see you so rich. I shall do without shoes, and go barefoot, in order that your balance may be less at the end of the year." And yet this is the spirit in which we often look at foreign statistics. The very growth in them which we envy is often the necessary result of the increase of our own trade, which, again, is the result of our own free policy. When we reduced our tariff between 1840 and 1860, we increased our own exports and imports; but we increased those of America and Germany and France at the same time.

*Folly of supposing our wealth to consist in the poverty of others.*

Consequently, in comparing national statistics, the question is not whether we increase faster than or as fast as other nations, though this question may often be answered in the affirmative, but does our Free system enable us to do trade with other nations which we should not do without it, and does it enable us to do trade from which they cut themselves off by a system of Protection?

Competi-
tion.

In saying that trade is necessarily a mutual benefit, I do not forget Competition, or the partial and local suffering which it occasionally causes. Competition becomes wider, if not more severe, as communication extends. But competition is one form of a higher law, of which in this case we can see the beneficent results, and which neither men nor nations can disregard with impunity. Free Trade cheerfully obeys this law ; *it has regard to sellers who want to sell what other people want to buy, and to buyers who want to buy what other people want to sell.* Protection discourages such buyers and sellers, and encourages instead of them, and at their expense, *the sellers who want to sell what nobody wants to buy.* If in the race of competition we were entirely thrown out ; if, whilst other nations were prospering, our forges were extinguished, our looms idle, our pauperism on the increase, and our consumption seriously diminishing, it would be time, not to reverse our policy, but to reconsider our position. But whilst the very opposite of this is the case, it is the height of folly to look with jealousy on the growing wealth of other nations who can sell what we want to buy, and buy what we want to sell.

## CHAPTER XXVII.

### STATISTICS OF ENGLISH TRADE COMPARED WITH TRADE OF OTHER NATIONS.

Compar-
son with
other
Nations.

LET us now take the case of one or two foreign countries, and see whether what we know of their trade is such as to make us fear that we are losing our hold on the markets of the world. In making any such comparison, two or three points must be remembered.

Increase of
our Trade
means
increase of
Foreigner's
Trade.

First, as I have already pointed out, the increase of our own trade necessarily involves the increase of the trade of foreign countries. This must be so, whether they open their ports or not. If they reduce their duties contemporaneously with our reduction, their trade will increase by so much the more ; if not, it will increase, but not so much. It is therefore to be expected and desired that the trade of foreign nations should increase when our own increases, and such an increase is not so much taken from us, but so much in our favour.

Secondly, in comparing our own trade with that of other countries, it is common to take the whole exports of domestic produce as the test. But this is *nihil ad rem*, so far as our manufactures are concerned. *Manufactures the thing for us to compare.*

We export little or no food, and little or no raw produce of the soil. If we wish to see whether other nations are progressing faster than ourselves, or, which is the more material point, beating us out of the market, we ought to confine our attention to what we produce ourselves. I have, therefore, in the following figures endeavoured to do this in a rough way.

Thirdly, it must be remembered that the following figures, taken from our statistics of exports, do not include the unseen exports which we make in the shape of ships and freight. These are as much the produce of English skill and labour as our cottons or our woollens, and probably amount annually, as above stated, to more than 50 millions, one-sixth of our whole exports. *Our Statistics of Export do not include Freight.*

Fourthly, even as regards manufactures, it ought to be no surprise to us that some nations are progressing faster than ourselves, or even competing with us in some articles in our own markets, if we hold our own as a whole. *We cannot keep all Manufactures.*

To hear people talk, one would think sometimes that we entertain the notion that we are to have a monopoly of manufacture, and are frightened if we see that any article which we make is successfully made in another country. Nothing can be more absurd. Providence has given us no monopoly of natural gifts, and the very essence of the Free Trade doctrine is that each country shall do what it can do best. It is not a loss, but a great gain to us, if France sends to the world, and to us among the rest, her tasteful stuffs, and if America provides us with her ingenious labour-saving machines. We have been the first in the field with the great metal and textile manufactures, and we are still first in general mechanical skill. But the probability is that other countries will by degrees follow us successfully in the older manufactures and in the coarser productions ; and that we shall still continue to invent and to supply the world with the newer products of scientific manufacture. As some evidence that this is actually the case, I may quote the following passage from Mr. Newmarch's exhaustive address to the Statistical Society, contained *We supplement Trade which we lose by new Inventions.*

English Trade compared with that of other nations.

in the Society's *Journal* of June, 1878, p. 211. "Between 1856 and 1877 supplemental exports (viz., those not included under the great heads of Textiles; Sewed; Metals, Ceramics, &c.), increase threefold, viz., from 13 to 37 millions, and the proportion to the total exports rises from 11 to 19. The progression of the figures is rapid and large, and strongly suggestive of a vigorous and inventive trade in which the rapid appearance of new commodities is proportionally pressing open and enlarging the previous classifications and vocabularies." The supplemental list thus referred to contains, amongst a multitude of articles, such as biscuits, medicines, chemicals, painters' colours, musical instruments, telegraph materials, india-rubber and jute manufactures, &c., &c. To find that France, Germany and America are making cotton and woollen goods for themselves and exporting them is what we must expect. The question we have to consider is, what is our manufacturing position compared with the manufacturing position of countries which have Protective systems, and whether such success as they have has accrued to them in consequence of their Protective systems, or in spite of them.

Distinction between food, raw materials, and manufactures. Its necessary inaccuracy.

In the tables appended, I have taken the exports of England, France, Germany and the United States at two different periods, and have divided them roughly into food, raw materials, and manufactures, and have endeavoured to see—first, what is the amount of manufactures exported by each country; secondly, what proportion that amount bears to its total exports; and thirdly, how these proportions are progressing. I have said above, that I do not myself rely on the distinctions commonly drawn between raw materials and manufactures, and that there is a great difficulty in drawing any satisfactory line of distinction between them. The distinctions contained in these tables do not therefore pretend to accuracy. No two persons would distribute the items in the same manner. Moreover, the statistical returns of each country are often classified according to its tariff, rather than according to more natural principles, and this causes additional confusion. I may mention as an instance of the difficulty the case of pig iron. It is here classed as a raw material, but it is the product of one of our most important manufactures, is one of our chief exports, and is highly protected in many foreign countries. However, I have taken the distinctions as made in tables which are already before the public; and, generally speaking, it may be said that what are here included under manufactures are special objects of protection in Protectionist countries.

As regards foreign countries, I have not carried the distinction between food, raw materials, and manufactures, later than 1880. To work out the distinction on the same principles on which the English analysis is worked out is a laborious task, and it is, after all, as mentioned above, not satisfactory. To make it on any other principle, or to accept the distinction as made in foreign returns, would, for purposes of comparison, be useless and delusive.

The case of England, as shown in these tables, is as follows:

EXPORTS OF DOMESTIC PRODUCE FROM ENGLAND.*

| | Amount, in Thousands of Pounds. | | | Percentage of Total. | | |
|---|---|---|---|---|---|---|
| | 1870. | 1880. | 1883. | 1870. | 1880. | 1883. |
| Food . . . . . | £ 7,607 | £ 8,825 | £ 9,575 | 4 | 4 | 4 |
| Raw Materials . | 13,744 | 23,272 | 23,531 | 7 | 10 | 10 |
| Manufactures . . | 178,236 | 190,963 | 206,693 | 89 | 86 | 86 |
| Total . . . . | 199,587 | 223,060 | 239,799 | 100 | 100 | 100 |

Exports of the United Kingdom in 1870, 1880, and 1883.

# CHAPTER XXVIII.

## STATISTICS OF FRENCH, GERMAN, AND UNITED STATES TRADE IN RECENT YEARS.

### *Trade of France.*

OUR direct imports from France, as is well known, exceed our direct exports to France, and they do this by an amount which exceeds anything due to us for freight and profit. But whatever the explanation of this excess may be, the proportion borne by exported English produce to French imports has

Imports & Exports from and to France before and since Treaty.

* See Table XVII., in Appendix, for the details.

increased rather than diminished since the French Treaty, whilst the actual amount of English produce exported has tripled, thus showing that the excess of imports is not due to the character of the Treaty tariffs.  The figures are as follows:—

| Average of Three Years. | Imports from France. | British Produce exported. | Re-exports to France. | Total Exports to France. |
|---|---|---|---|---|
| 1857—1859 . | 14 millions. | 5 millions. | 5 millions. | 10 millions. |
| 1878—1880 . | 40   ,, | 15   ,, | 12   ,, | 27   ,, |
| 1881—1883 . | 39   ,, | 17   ,, | 12   ,, | 29   ,, |
| In 1883 . | 39   ,, | 18   ,, | 12   ,, | 30   ,, |

The total exports from France, according to the French statistics for 1869, the year before the war, and for 1879, are as follows :—



EXPORTS OF DOMESTIC PRODUCE FROM FRANCE.*

| | Amount, in Thousands of Pounds. | | Percentage. | |
|---|---|---|---|---|
| | 1869. | 1879. | 1869. | 1879. |
| | £ | £ | | |
| Food    . | 34,017 | 33,159 | 27·0 | 26·0 |
| Raw Material | 21,482 | 25,210 | 17·0 | 19·8 |
| Manufactures | 70,504 | 69,515 | 56·0 | 54·2 |
| Total | 126,003 | 127,884 | 100 | 100 |

The value of manufactures exported from France therefore actually decreased in the decade ending with 1879, and its proportion to the value of food and raw materials exported decreased also, whilst the whole exports remained about the same.  In fact, the trade has been stationary, whilst the English trade has largely increased, as shown above.  If to the above list of exports we were to add shipping and freights, we should find that the exports of England have increased much faster than those of France.



Half the articles on which duties are imposed by the French tariff are articles to be used solely or principally

* See Table XVIII., in Appendix, for the details.

in further manufacture, *e.g.*, yarns of all kinds, cotton, silk used in and woollen, unbleached cloths, combed wool, iron and Manufacture. steel of all kinds, copper sheets and wire, coal, alkali, salt, tiles and bricks, and leather; whilst amongst all the rest are articles which conduce not less materially if less directly to production, by improving the condition of the workman, or by facilitating the conduct of business. I believe I might go through most of them, and show how France manages by imposing a protective duty to countervail her own natural advantages of soil, climate and human character, or to enhance her natural difficulties; whilst freedom from the weight of duties in our case enables us to take advantage of her deficiencies. The special cases of leather, silk, sugar and shipping, I have noticed more particularly below.

## *Trade of Germany.*

THE exports from Germany for the same years are as follows :— Exports from Germany in 1869 and 1879.

EXPORTS OF DOMESTIC PRODUCE FROM GERMANY.*

|  | Amount, in Thousands of Pounds. | | Percentage. | |
|---|---|---|---|---|
|  | †1869. | 1879. | 1869. | 1879. |
|  | £ | £ |  |  |
| Food | 28,356 | 37,948 | 25·6 | 27·3 |
| Raw Material | 38,383 | 47,283 | 34·7 | 34·0 |
| Manufactures | 43,864 | 53,551 | 39·7 | 38·7 |
| Total | 110,603 | 138,782 | 100 | 100 |

German trade has increased largely; her political triumph, and above all, the thrift and patient skill and energy of her people, have given her great advantages. How far the retrograde steps she has taken in the direction of a return to Protection may check her progress I have no means of determining. The Reports of the Chambers of Commerce in Germany, towards the end of 1880, were unfavourable to this course. They stated that the trade of the country was depressed; that the internal demand for manufactures was slack; that the price of

* See Table XIX., in Appendix, for the details.
† The values for 1869 are estimated only.

raw material was high; that food was dear; and that the working classes were worse off than they had previously been. I am not aware that any similar reports from Chambers of Commerce have been published in later years, nor have I any more recent evidence as to the condition of German Trade, except the notorious bankruptcies and distress in the German sugar trade, and the distress among German agriculturists, which has been made the ground for the protective duties lately imposed on food.

## Trade of the United States.

LET us next take the case of the United States. They levy, as is well known, enormous duties, ranging up to 50 per cent., and even 100 per cent., on almost everything that is made with hands. With all this, they have been in a state of great prosperity, and though now suffering under temporary depression, will no doubt be so again. But they suffer from fluctuations at least as much as other nations, and probably more, since their Protection system causes a glut, and at the same time prevents them from finding a market abroad. It is not long ago that we heard of depression in the towns of the United States far more acute than any which our workmen have laboured under; and their distress in the present year is probably far greater than any which we are suffering from, as will be seen below (Chap. XXXIII). But on the whole the recent growth of their trade is very remarkable.

The following is an analysis of their export trade in 1870 and 1880, excluding bullion and specie:—

Exports of United States in 1870 and 1880

EXPORTS OF DOMESTIC PRODUCE FROM THE UNITED STATES.[*]

| | Amount in Thousands of Pounds. | | Percentage. | |
|---|---|---|---|---|
| | 1870. | 1880. | 1870. | 1880. |
| | £ | £ | | |
| Food | 21,660 | 96,694 | 28·6 | 56·3 |
| Raw Material | 45,600 | 57,199 | 60·1 | 33·3 |
| Manufactures | 8,609 | 17,763 | 11·3 | 10·4 |
| Total | 75,869 | 171,656 | 100 | 100 |

[*] See Table XX., in Appendix, for details.

But it is desirable to go a little further back, and for this purpose I take the figures from a very interesting article on United States' trade in the *Times* of the 7th November, 1881. If the figures do not correspond exactly with those given above, it is because the following figures include bullion and specie ; and because, in the figures for 1880, the dollar is taken at 4s. in the *Times* article, and at 4s. 2d. in the figures given above.

The following are the exports of the United States and United Kingdom respectively, since 1840 :—

EXPORTS* OF DOMESTIC PRODUCE, IN THOUSANDS OF POUNDS.

| | United States. | United Kingdom. |
|---|---|---|
| 1840 | £22,779 | £51,309 |
| 1850 | 27,389 | 71,367 |
| 1860 | 74,637 | 135,891 |
| 1870 | 84,100 | 199,586 |
| 1880 | 166,658 | 223,060 |

Exports of United States and United Kingdom in each decade since 1840.

If to these figures were added the figures representing those exports which each country makes in the form of its shipping, the comparative growth of the trade of the United Kingdom would appear to be very much larger, especially in later years, during which the shipping of the United States has been diminishing, and that of the United Kingdom largely increasing.

It will be observed in the above figures that the trade of the United States increased little between 1860 and 1870, no doubt in consequence of the exhaustion caused by the civil war ; and that this leeway was made up in the subsequent decade. The most important observation, however, is that during the whole of the periods above mentioned the population of the United States grew much faster than that of the United Kingdom ; and that, if we take the amount of trade per head of each country in each decade, the trade of the United Kingdom has grown much faster than that of the United States. The following are the figures :—

Growth of Population in the two Countries.

EXPORTS PER HEAD OF THE TWO COUNTRIES.

| | United States. | | | United Kingdom. | | |
|---|---|---|---|---|---|---|
| 1840 | £1 | 11 | 1 | £1 | 18 | 9 |
| 1850 | 1 | 6 | 2 | 2 | 11 | 10 |
| 1860 | 2 | 10 | 11 | 4 | 14 | 7 |
| 1870 | 2 | 6 | 11 | 6 | 7 | 11 |
| 1880 | 3 | 8 | 1 | 6 | 9 | 5 |

Comparison of Exports per head.

* The exports from the United States include bullion and specie. Those from the United Kingdom do not. But this will make very little difference.

United
States'
trade.

These are not figures to alarm us. It is idle to expect that 30 million of people shall produce as much as 50 million of the same people.

The United States are probably, however, at this moment, in spite of temporary depression, one of the most prosperous nations in the world.

Causes of
United
States'
Prosperity.

The source of their prosperity is not far to seek. It is not to be found in those industries which they try to cherish by Protection, but in the raw productions of the fertile soil and climate of their immense territory. They have 50 millions of the most industrious and energetic people in the world; they have a country as large as Europe, with every variety of good climate, and with an unlimited area of unexhausted soil. They have excellent communication throughout all the parts of this immense area. Besides this, though shut off by their tariffs from the rest of the world, they have absolute Free Trade within their own borders. It is as if there were no custom houses within the limits of Europe. Besides this, they have the Old World wanting food, and affected by bad harvests. No wonder, then, that they supply the world with food and agricultural produce. Only a tenth of their population is concerned in trade. The export of manufactures from the United States in 1880 was $17\frac{3}{4}$ millions sterling, whilst our own export of manufactures in the same year was 190 millions. Even in their own highly protected market, our manufactures are sold to the extent of $24\frac{1}{2}$ millions a year; whilst in our open market theirs are only sold to the extent of $2\frac{1}{2}$ millions. With great facilities for producing iron and steel, and with a considerable native production, prices were so high in 1880 that, in spite of the duty of 40 per cent. imposed on foreign iron, we were able to send them £10,000,000 worth, whilst what they sent us was worth £200,000.

Their exports were very large in 1880, and have increased enormously in the decade; but of what do they consist?

Nature
of their
Exports.

Ninety per cent. are food and raw materials, whilst the manufactures which they try so hard to foster and protect do not amount to more than 10 per cent. Their shipping, as we shall see below, is not one-fourth—or, if we count one ton of steam as equal to four of sailing, not one-seventh of our own. Of their whole trade they carried 75 per cent. in their own vessels in 1850, and only 16 per cent. in 1880. Food constituted $28\frac{1}{2}$ per cent. of their exports in 1870, and the

amount of food which they export increased more than
fourfold between 1870 and 1880. The things which they have
not protected they provide the world with ; in the things which
they protect, and we leave free, they are nowhere in the race.
So much stronger is Nature than human law—so great are the
advantages which Freedom has over Protection.

The real moral to be drawn from American trade is the
Free Trade moral, viz., that the free development of natural
advantages, and the free exchange of natural products, are the
true sources of commercial prosperity.

----

## CHAPTER XXIX.

### TRADE OF CANADA AND AUSTRALIA.

IT is, perhaps, even now, too soon to trace the effect of the
Canadian tariff of 1879 on her trade, and it is especially
difficult to eliminate other causes which have affected it.
It would have been very strange if Canada had not, tariff
or no tariff, participated in the revival which has taken place
in the trade of the American continent ; it would be
doubly strange if, with her natural capacity for producing corn,
and with the recent scarcity in Europe, she had not very largely
increased her exports. For those exports she must be paid, and
we should therefore also expect to see her imports increase
very largely, and with them her customs revenue. We do find
an increase, but by no means so large a one as we should
expect. In 1880, after the new tariff, the amount received
as customs revenue had increased over that received in 1878,
the year before the new tariff, by a little more than a million
of dollars. The duties in 1880 amounted to about 20 per cent.
in value of the whole imports of the country. In 1874 and 1875,
before the new tariff, the duties constituted only from eleven to
thirteen per cent. of the value of the imports, and in those
years the customs revenue was larger than it was in 1880.

Comparing the trade of 1878, the year before the new tariff,
with 1880, we find that the imports were 90 millions of dollars
in the former year, and 86½ millions in the latter year ; whilst

Trade of<br>Canada<br>since new<br>Canadian<br>Tariff.

the exports were 79 millions in the former, and 88 millions in the latter. In 1873–74 the imports had been 128 millions, and the exports 89 millions of dollars. In 1883 the imports had risen to 132 millions, but the exports to 98 millions only, little more than they had been ten years before. The increased imports are probably due here, as in Australia, to the investment of foreign capital in railway and other enterprises, whilst the Protectionist tariff has had in Canada, as in the United States, the effect of restricting her foreign markets, and checking the sale of Canadian produce abroad. Considering the increase of population and of cultivated area, and considering also the immense demand of Europe for corn, it is surprising that even with the check on her industry imposed by the new tariff, the increase of exports should have been so small as it is. Canada has, probably, succeeded in calling into existence some weak manufacturing interests which will prove a thorn in her side, but she has done so in the expense of her natural industries, and has checked the flow of capital and labour from Europe, of which she stands at so much need. We have heard whispers in this country of a desire for bargains with England, under which England should either advance money to her, or give some preferential treatment to Canada as the price for a reduction of her duties on English goods. Whether such proposals have ever been entertained or made by men of influence in Canada, I do not know. But the chilling reception all such notions have met with in this country ought to be a lesson to Canada, and to other Protectionists, that if you want to win the favours of your mistress, it is a very bad plan to put on a fit of sulks in order to make your return to good-humour the price for her smiles. The Protectionist policy of Canada is deeply to be regretted by all her well-wishers here, not because it injures the trade of England, for to that trade it is a comparative trifle, but because it tends to cripple the industry of Canada, and to create a bad feeling between the two countries.



The case of Victoria and New South Wales is particularly interesting, because the two colonies are in many respects similarly situated ; and whilst the one, Victoria, has embraced Protection, the other (New South Wales) has remained steadfast to Free Trade. Both have progressed, but New South Wales has made by far the greater progress of the two.

It appears, on comparing the progress of the two colonies

for the decade ending with 1880, that the following are the Australian Trade Victoria and New South Wales. general results:—

|  | Victoria. | New South Wales. |
| --- | --- | --- |
| Population | increased from 726,000 to 860,000, or 18 per cent. | increased from 502,000 to 770,000, or 53 per cent. |
| Excess of Immigrants over Emigrants | stationary . | increased from 4,000 to 19,000. |
| The Value of Rateable Property | increased by less than one-half | more than doubled. |
| Customs Revenue | stationary . | increased by nearly one-half; and is, with a less population and low tariff, nearly as great as that of Victoria, with a large population and high tariff. |
| Imports | increased from 12½ millions to 14½ millions, or 17 per cent. | increased from 7¾ millions to 14 millions, or 80 per cent. |
| Exports | increased from 12½ millions to 16 millions, or 28 per cent. | increased from 8 millions to 15½ millions, or 94 per cent. |

Since 1880 things have pursued a similar course. I annex a table (No. XXI. in the Appendix), giving the population, public debt, and imports and exports of each of the Australian colonies from 1873 to 1883, extracted from the Victoria Year Book, from which it will be seen that New South Wales, the Free Trade colony, has increased its imports from 14 millions in 1880 to 21 millions in 1883, and its exports from 15½ millions in 1880 to 20 millions in 1883; whilst Protectionist Victoria has only increased its imports from 14½ millions to 17¾ millions, and its exports from 16 millions to 16½ millions in the same time. This table also shows that New South Wales has increased its exports in these three years far more than any of the other Australian colonies, all of which are far more Protectionist. It is exports which our Fair Traders are particularly anxious about, and it must be some disappointment to them to find that among a number of British societies starting on similar and equal terms, the one which has constantly admitted free imports has actually increased its exports far more than those which have endeavoured to promote their

J

production and their power of export by Protective **duties, thus
giving** an excellent illustration of the Free Trade maxim,
" Leave the imports free, **and the exports** will take care of
themselves."

---

## CHAPTER XXX.

### AGRICULTURAL DEPRESSION; EFFECT OF BAD HARVESTS.

Losses of Farmers due to four causes: 1, Rise of Rents; 2, Rise of Wages; 3, Lowered Prices; 4, Deficient Production.

BUT there has been a long and continuous depression of agriculture, the largest of all our productive industries; and
this, it may be said, brings with it depression of all. Now,
that the farmers have suffered severely during the last eight
or nine years, there can be no doubt. The amount of their
losses it is not easy to estimate; but competent observers calculated in 1880, that, if their then condition, arising from the
losses of the previous six years, were compared with their condition ten years before, they must have been the worse by a
sum approaching 200 millions, or, taking it by the year, 30
millions a year. As is well known, their condition has not
improved since then. The comparatively good harvest of 1884
failed to relieve them; and there is reason to believe that
landlords have recently had to make great reductions in the
rent of arable land. Whatever be the sum thus lost by the
agricultural class, it is due to several factors, of which bad
harvests is only one. A rise in rents—which had been going on
long before the beginning of the decade, and which continued
until 1872–73—an increase in the cost of labour, and a heavy
fall in the price of agricultural produce, owing to foreign competition, are other factors. Of these four factors, the rise of rents, and
the rise in the cost of labour—a most uncertain item—were
estimated in 1880 to account for something less than one-third
of the whole loss, leaving more than two-thirds of the whole loss
to the two factors of bad harvests and lowered prices. In what
proportion it should be divided between these two factors is a
matter of controversy. Some persons would attribute the larger
proportion to the bad harvests; others think that this has had a
much smaller effect than lowered prices; but that both factors
have had a great effect in causing loss to the farmers, all agree.

Upon the questions of what is the total amount of loss, and in what proportions it is to be attributed to each of these factors, I will not enter; the important point for our present purpose is that it is only that portion of the farmer's loss which is due to bad harvests which is a pure economical loss to the country. The rise of rent goes into the landlord's pocket; the rise of wages to the labourer; and if the farmer loses by the substitution of cheaper food from abroad, the consumers of that food gain in lowered prices. The present agricultural depression has, consequently, been confined, to a great extent, to the farming and landowning classes. Farmers have suffered much, rents have been remitted or lowered, but the population generally have been little affected, and trade revived for a while during the worst times of agriculture. For the first time since the repeal of the Corn Laws, foreign competition, in supplying food to our people, has been unaccompanied by such a rise in demand as to compensate, and more than compensate, the English agriculturist. Even now it is doubtful whether the recent fall in prices will have as great an effect in lowering the letting value of land as the increased demand for food, consequent on Free Trade, has had in raising it in former years.

So far, therefore, as lower prices are concerned, the nation is not a loser. The loss of the farmer and landowner is the gain of the rest of the people. But it is worth while to consider what, under a system of Free Trade, is the effect on the welfare of the entire community of so much of the farmer's loss as is really due to a bad harvest. That it is a loss to the agricultural interests, and consequently to the community, which includes those interests, there is no doubt; but to what extent does it affect the large majority of the population, who are neither farmers nor landowners? The loss which they suffer has, I believe, been both exaggerated and understated. In one of our anti-free-trade journals I find the following passage :—

"Mr. Bright explains the depression of trade by the loss of millions through the insufficiency of harvests, and the inability of all persons interested in agriculture to make their accustomed purchases.

"But the Free Traders denied this. They said that foreign corn would pour in, and must be paid for, and would bring about a profitable exportation of non-agricultural products."

J 2

Agricultu-
ral depres-
sion ; effect
of bad
harvests.

Whether the Free Traders said this or not, I do not know. But the real state of the case seems to be as follows :—

Suppose that there is a deficiency of 10 million quarters—worth, say, 20 million pounds. The agricultural interest will lose this sum, and will be actually so much the poorer. They will be unable to exchange their corn for non-agricultural products, and, so far, trade will be injured. The argument above referred to as the argument of the Free Traders, assumes that the same quantity of corn must be purchased abroad at the same price as would have been paid for the corn produced at home, and that the same quantity of non-agricultural produce must be exported to pay for it ; and that, if so, manufacture and trade will not suffer on the whole. But the above assumption is not strictly accurate, as the following considerations will show :—

1. Supposing the conditions of production abroad to remain the same, the corn brought from abroad will necessarily cost rather more than the home-grown corn would have cost, and the goods sent to pay for it will have to pay freight and expenses. This loss will fall on the whole community. If, indeed, as has been recently the case with ourselves, the importers of corn are also the carriers, the freight will return into the pocket of the nation.

2. The course of trade will be deranged, and this will be a loss to the manufacturer as well as to the agriculturist.

3. The foreign purchaser will not want so much of the same things as the home purchaser, and will probably have to be tempted by a lower price. He may want some things very much, as the United States wanted iron for railways in 1880. In that case, the price of iron would go up in England, but the price of other manufactures would go down.

4. The demand for corn will be large and immediate. Bills of America on England will be at a discount. Bills of England on America will be at a premium. The former will be in excess. There will be an immediate profit to America on the business, till the balance is redressed by the exports to America.

Consequently, in their different ways, the trading and manufacturing interests of England, as well as the agricultural interest, must suffer from our bad harvests ; but their suffering is comparatively small ; and under present circumstances is largely compensated, if not more than compensated, by the low prices of Foreign food. What their suffering would be if

Foreign food were excluded, or raised in price by high duties, it is, in the present state of our population and of their employment, frightful to contemplate.

---

# CHAPTER XXXI.

## COMMERCIAL DEPRESSION BETWEEN 1872 AND 1880.

WE have already seen, in Chapter XXIII., what an impetus our trade received in the period between 1840 and 1860. We know also how much the trade of France, as well as of England, grew after the treaty of 1860 ; and we may fairly ask our opponents, who are calling for a reversal of the policy which produced those benefits, to show not only that we have since that time been deprived of them, but that we should not have suffered that loss if we had not been Free Traders. We have a right to call upon them to define the specific evil of which they complain, and then to prove that it is due to Free Trade. I need not say that no such definition, no such proof, is forthcoming, and we are left with nothing but a vague shadow to fight with.

Let us, however, take such facts as we can lay hold of, and see how far they bear out the notion that we are losing our markets in the world.

Let us admit that our exports, as measured in nominal values, considerably diminished since those roaring years of prosperity, 1872 and 1873. They were 256 and 255 millions in those years, and 191 and 223 millions in 1879 and 1880. In 1882 they were 241 millions, and in 1883 240 millions. Let us admit, too, that this decrease of exports has been the sign and result of a real depression, and that both profits and wages have decreased since those so-called prosperous years. This in itself has nothing to do with the question at issue, unless it can be shown to arise from a permanent loss of market for our manufactures. Nothing whatever of the kind has been shown, or can be shown. But it can be shown that the prosperity of the earlier years of the decade is exaggerated ; that the depression is exaggerated also; and that there are ample causes to account both for one and the other without

**Depression since 1873.** assuming any falling off in the general demand for or supply of English goods.

**Exaggeration of Prosperity of 1872-73.** The prosperity of 1872 and 1873 has been immensely exaggerated. All persons engaged in producing coal and iron made, no doubt, enormous profits, but they were led by those profits into an extravagant expenditure, partly on personal expenses and luxuries, but still more on plant and machinery for increasing the output, which has flooded the market with excessive supply, and from which no adequate return has yet been received. This expenditure of capital in fixed and, at first, unremunerative investments, is one cause of subsequent depression. But whilst coal and iron masters made fortunes in those years, manufacturers and others who had to use coal and iron had to bear heavy outgoings, and their profits were reduced accordingly. Prices being high all round, people with fixed incomes suffered accordingly. Even the high wages of the time went less far than lower wages do when prices are lower. A great deal of the prosperity was apparent rather than real.

**Statistics founded on Price misleading.** The statistics made the exports appear larger than they really were, because prices were so high. The quantities of goods exported, and the labour necessary to produce them, were as large in the subsequent years of depression as they had been in the years of inflation, but appear to be less because prices are so much lower. The exports of British produce were 255 millions in 1873, and 223 millions in 1880. If the exports of 1880 were valued at the prices of 1873 they would be 311 millions, or larger than those of any previous year.

**Prices of Raw Material.** Imported raw material, *e.g.*, cotton and wool, was much dearer in the period of inflation than in the subsequent period of depression, and consequently that portion of the exports which is due to British labour and capital differed in the two periods much less than appears at first sight by the figures of the total exports. For instance, the raw cotton imported in 1873 was about the same in quantity as the raw cotton imported in 1879. But the raw cotton used in our manufactures exported cost us 14 millions more in 1873 than the same quantity cost us in 1879.

**Temporary Causes of Inflation.** The prices and exports of the inflated years were due to causes which were temporary and accidental, and brought with them a necessary reaction. Amongst other causes may be mentioned—

Expenditure of capital in this country on plant and ma- Depression since 1873. chinery, not even yet fully reproductive.

Investments of English capital abroad, some of which were wholly unproductive—*e.g.*, the bad foreign loans ; and some of which were not immediately productive—*e.g.*, American railways, but which are now in various ways bringing us a large return of imports.

Advances made to assist France in paying the German indemnity, which caused a large export from France and England to Germany at the time, and large exports from France to England and to Germany at a later time. I have given the figures which illustrate this process in the Tables VIII., IX., and X. in the Appendix.

All these causes have little to do with the permanent demand for goods ; all of them largely increased our exports at the time ; some of them proved in the end losses, whilst others have helped that increase in our subsequent imports which Fair Traders seem to dread even more than losses. The inflation, as well as the depression, is, therefore, fully accounted for without any reference to closed markets or decrease in permanent demand.

It is a complete mistake to suppose that extraordinarily Large Exports and HighPrices not necessarily Tests of Prosperity. large exports, very high prices, and a great demand for labour are necessarily signs of great and permanent prosperity ; they are only signs of great activity. They may be caused by a continuous demand, and by good and reproductive investments of capital, in which case they are elements of permanent prosperity. But they may be caused by bad investments, by payment of debt, or by unproductive expenditure on war, or by other causes which may lead to absolute loss. If I employ a thousand men to dig a hole and fill it up again, I shall cause high wages, high prices, and great prosperity in my neighbourhood for a time ; but my capital will be lost, and when the work is at an end there will be a sad reaction and relapse. These are very elementary truths, but they seem to be forgotten by many popular expounders of statistics.

In addition, there is another cause for a chronic and perma- Appreciation of Gold. nent diminution in the values of both exports and imports, to which I can only advert very shortly. Good statisticians are of opinion that the value of gold, as compared with commodities, is steadily on the rise, and that it has been so since the effect of the gold discoveries was exhausted. The question is too long

Depression since 1873. Appreciation of Gold. and difficult to be discussed here.*　But if the statisticians are right, as they probably are, the rise in the value of gold will account not only for some diminution in the figures of value by which we estimate our trade, but for a general fall of prices, and also of wages, which are too frequently and hastily attributed to commercial depression and to a decline in the producing and consuming powers of mankind.

The effect of the appreciation of gold must be slow and gradual, and is often concealed by the greater immediate effect of fluctuations due to other causes.　But its result in producing a feeling of depression is probably out of proportion to its real effect.　Upon the real wealth of the country as a whole it has not necessarily any effect at all.　If, as Hume has said, every one had to-morrow half as many sovereigns in his pocket as he has to-day, he would be neither richer or poorer.　He would buy or sell for half-a sovereign what he has to buy or sell for a sovereign to-day.　But a time of falling prices is notoriously a period of depression.　It is a bad time for the larger merchants who carry on the great trades of the country.　When they have to borrow money to complete their purchases, and it rises in value before they have to repay it, whilst the commodities which they buy fall in money value at the same time, they suffer actual loss : and this loss probably operates on their expectations and makes them less daring in business.　Other classes gain what the merchant loses.　The retail dealer, who can generally postpone a proportionate reduction of his retail prices, and the consumer who ultimately gets the benefit of the fall in price, share the gain between them.　But it is the wholesale trader who carries on the large speculative business of the country, and who is listened to as its representative, and he is out of pocket and out of heart at a time of falling prices.

Change in Mode of Doing Business There is another cause for chronic depression, or rather for a feeling of chronic depression, to which it is worth while to advert.　We are told that a great change is taking place in the mode in which foreign trade is conducted.　Before the times of steam and telegraph there was a long interval of time and space between the commencement and the end of a transaction ; between the original purchase and the final sale.　This afforded great scope for the merchant or middleman ; and his profits

---

* See Articles by Mr. W. Fowler in the April number, and by Mr. Giffen in the June number of the *Contemporary*, 1885.

depended upon the judgment and skill with which he could Depression since 1873. Appreciation of Gold. forecast distant and future markets. At the present time the state of markets is known everywhere at once by telegraph, and the period of transport is abridged by steam. The original vendor and final purchaser are brought nearer together, and the opportunities for the skill and judgment of the middleman are curtailed. The world gains on the whole by the change, but the old-fashioned merchants, who have done so much to make England what she is, suffer or are extinguished, and from that powerful and important class we have the natural cry that trade is bad, although at the same time the bulk of transactions is greater than ever.

Both these causes, viz., an appreciation of gold, and a change in the methods of trade, affect the same class, a class which is naturally influential in expressing its feelings of depression. That such a class should suffer is to be lamented. But the losses of this class are the gains of other classes, and it would be wrong to suppose that they constitute any real diminution in the wealth or prosperity of the country as a whole.

---

# CHAPTER XXXII.

## DEPRESSION AT THE PRESENT MOMENT AT HOME.

I HAVE left the two former chapters as they stood in the first Since 1880 there has been revival and subsequent depression. edition, as written in 1880, with a few additions. Since that time there has been a short revival of trade followed by a depression which undoubtedly exists at the present moment. The causes are not hard to understand.

### 1. *Agricultural Depression has continued.*

Bad seasons for the farmer continued until 1884; and the Causes: 1. Agricultural depression continued. fair average crops of that year brought him little benefit in consequence of the low prices caused by the glut of foreign corn. Agricultural wages continued to rise until quite recently; and though they are apparently now falling, they are high as compared with former years. Rents have been largely reduced. The

Causes of depression at present moment.<br>1. Agricultural.

conversion of arable land into pasture has continued in the last two years at an accelerated ratio. The number of sheep, though again on the increase, was still in 1884 nearly three millions less than in 1879. The demand for agricultural labour must have diminished. The injury to land done by a succession of bad seasons and by want of due cultivation is cumulative. It costs a great deal to bring into order a farm which has for years been neglected.

In all these ways the agricultural classes have suffered and continue to suffer. The loss of crops by bad seasons, by diminution in stock, and by deterioration of land, is an economical loss to the country generally; and so also is the loss of employment when the labourer is not, from want of versatility or for other reasons, able to find other employment. The rise and fall of rent or wages, and the low price of foreign corn are not, as pointed out in the last chapter, an economical loss to the country generally, but they cause suffering and inconvenience to particular classes, whilst benefiting others, and thus aggravate the general feeling of distress. What is the pecuniary amount of loss sustained by the agricultural classes, and how much of it is an absolute loss to the nation, it is impossible to estimate with certainty, but it is, no doubt, a real and efficient cause of temporary depression. Of one thing we may be sure, viz., that if we should again have good seasons, and if the land should again bring forth its full and fair produce, the other causes of agricultural distress, whatever their social or political effect, will not, under the Free Trade *régime*, be an economical loss to the country.

It must also be remembered that agricultural depression does not apply to the whole of the United Kingdom, but to the corn districts exclusively, or at any rate, specially. The grazing districts have not suffered, or at any rate, not in like proportion.

Care must also be taken not to confound agricultural distress with distress of the landed interest. A great and increasing part of the land of England is used for mining, manufacturing and residential purposes. Its value increases with the growing wealth of the country, and is not affected by the failure of harvests. The losses of the landed classes, and the silence and dignity with which they have been borne, should not prevent us from remembering what are the limitations of those losses.

## 2. *Depression in Shipping.*

A second cause of depression is to be found in the "boom" in shipping which culminated in 1883 and collapsed in 1884. I have elsewhere (p. 161) referred to the particulars of the collapse. At a period when the interest of money was falling, and when investors had difficulty in placing their funds, came an unprecedented demand for freights for corn, iron, and other commodities. Investors rushed madly into shipping, and the result has been a collapse of the trade here and throughout the world, accompanied by the most serious catalogue of losses by shipwreck we have ever experienced, which, though falling primarily on insurers, are nevertheless borne in the end by the nation.

*Causes of depression at present moment. 2. Boom and subsequent collapse in shipping*

## 3. *American Railways.*

In the third place there has been a similar "boom" in American railways, as I have shown below (p. 146), and a similar collapse.

*3. Boom and collapse in United States' railways.*

## 4. *Boom and Collapse in Iron.*

In the fourth place, these two "booms" in English shipping and in American railways have told upon the great iron and steel industry of this country. An exceptional and excessive demand has been followed by an excessive supply, a cessation of demand, and a glut, which still continues. The following is from the *Economist* of the 10th of January, 1885 :—

*4. Consequent revival and subsequent depression in iron trade.*

"Looking back at the history of the iron trade during the past few years, it is abundantly evident that the present troubles are traceable to the 'spurt' of 1879 and 1880. The evils begotten of the 'boom' of 1872–4 were, in one respect, less than those following in 1879–80. In the former period, there was scarcely any increase in the production of the world, whilst in 1880 and succeeding years the increase was quite remarkable, as the following figures will show :—

Production of Pig-iron throughout the World in thousands of Tons.

| 1883. | | 1882. | | 1881. | | 1880. |
|---|---|---|---|---|---|---|
| 20,239 | .. | 20,075 | .. | 18,966 | .. | 17,185 |
| 1879. | | 1877. | | 1874. | | 1872. |
| 13,768 | .. | 13,430 | .. | 13,057 | .. | 13,906 |

The great inflation in prices which took place during the years 1871–5, coupled as it was with a corresponding rise in wages,

Causes of
depression
at present
moment.
4. Iron.

led to some relaxation in the energy of the British workman, and so the evil of over-production was restrained. It took till 1879 to bring prices back to something like their normal condition, and had it not been for the breaking out of the American demand at the close of that year, we would have likely witnessed that 'natural' revival which seems to follow in recurring cycles. Instead of this, everything was thrown out of the natural order, and we are now passing through the period of reaction necessary to put matters right again. The development caused by the spurt of 1879–80 may be the better understood from the following figures, showing the extension of trade in rails, shipbuilding, &c.

*Production of Rails in the United Kingdom.*

| 1883. Tons. | 1882. Tons. | 1881. Tons. | 1880. Tons. | 1879. Tons. |
| --- | --- | --- | --- | --- |
| 1,037,194 | 1,235,785 | 1,023,740 | 739,910 | 519,718 |

*Total Tonnage of Ships built in the United Kingdom.*

| 1883. Tons | 1882. Tons. | 1881. Tons. | 1880. Tons. | 1879. Tons. |
| --- | --- | --- | --- | --- |
| 1,329,604 | 1,240,824 | 1,013,208 | 796,221 | 569,462 |

We estimate the total production of 1884 at 7,600,000 tons, against 6,009,434 tons in 1879. The fact here revealed explains one of the causes of the present depression.

" Large though the volume of trade was in 1884, it was very considerably under that of former years. The exports of iron and steel were over 500,000 tons less than in 1883, and 800,000 tons less than in 1882. At home the greatest depression was experienced in connection with shipbuilding and engineering. It is estimated that the tonnage launched was at least 500,000 tons less than in 1883. This would represent at least 300,000 or 350,000 tons less iron and steel consumed. These figures, taken in connection with some depression in other branches, would represent a reduction of at least 900,000 tons in the trade of 1884, when compared with the year preceding."

It is probable that the substitution of steel for iron is one cause of the boom, and of the subsequent reaction. The demand for the new article, steel, gave a great stimulus to the manufacture. That demand has been supplied, and the new article is much more durable than the old. Hence a falling off in the demand,

### 5. *Glut of Corn.*

Fifthly, there has been a glut of corn. Not that more corn has been produced than is needed, but more corn than could be paid for at prices sufficient to remunerate the growers, who have suffered, and are suffering, accordingly.

*Causes of depression at present moment.
5. Glut of Corn.*

### 6. *Wars and Tariffs.*

Sixthly and lastly, human stupidity and human passions have had something to answer for—partly in wars and rumours of war; partly in the protectionist remedies which many countries are adopting—remedies which can only aggravate the disease. The evil to be cured is, not that there is more of anything in the world, especially of food, than people want, but that it is in the wrong place or in the wrong hands. One would have thought that, so far as men are able to cure this evil by law, they would try to do so by removing all legal impediments which prevent a transfer to the right place or to the right hands of things which are in the wrong place or in the wrong hands. But instead of this, many nations are multiplying these impediments, and our Fair Trade friends would fain have us follow their mad examples.

*Wars and Protective Tariffs.*

These causes seem to me amply sufficient to account for the present depression in this country. But we should not exaggerate it, more especially as there seems to be some reason for thinking that the worst is at an end, and that a more hopeful feeling is beginning to prevail.

The following statistics for the last six years show that the depression in this country has not hitherto been of an extreme kind :—

*Extent of depression. Statistics— 1879 to 1884. Trade.*

*Value of Imports and Exports.*

| | Total net Imports in millions of pounds. | | Total net Exports of British produce in millions of pounds. |
|---|---|---|---|
| 1879 | .. .. .. | 306 | .. .. .. 192 |
| 1880 | .. .. .. | 348 | .. .. .. 223 |
| 1881 | .. .. .. | 334 | .. .. .. 234 |
| 1882 | .. .. .. | 348 | .. .. .. 241 |
| 1883 | .. .. .. | 361 | .. .. .. 240 |
| 1884 | .. .. .. | 327 | .. .. .. 233 |

In considering these figures it must be remembered that they denote value, not quantity; that prices have fallen; and

Extent of depression at present moment.

that, though money values may be less, the amount of useful commodities may be as great as before.

Entries and clearances of shipping.

*Entries and Clearances at Ports in the United Kingdom in millions of tons.*

|      | Total. | Sailing. | Steam. |
|------|--------|----------|--------|
| 1879 | 53     | 20       | 33     |
| 1880 | 59     | 22       | 37     |
| 1881 | 58     | 19       | 39     |
| 1882 | 61     | 18       | 43     |
| 1883 | 65     | 17       | 48     |
| 1884 | 64     | 14½      | 49½    |

Railways.

*Receipts from Railways in millions of pounds.*

|      | Goods. | Passengers. | Total. | 3rd Class Passengers only. |
|------|--------|-------------|--------|----------------------------|
| 1879 | £33    | 26          | 59     | 14                         |
| 1880 | 36     | 27          | 63     | 15                         |
| 1881 | 37     | 28          | 65     | 15                         |
| 1882 | 38     | 29          | 67     | 16                         |
| 1883 | 39     | 29          | 68     | 17                         |
| 1884 | 37     | 30          | 67     | 17                         |

Coal and iron.

*Coal and Iron produced in thousands of tons.*

|      | Coal.   | Pig Iron. |
|------|---------|-----------|
| 1879 | 133,808 | 5,995     |
| 1880 | 146,819 | 7,749     |
| 1881 | 154,184 | 8,144     |
| 1882 | 156,500 | 8,587     |
| 1883 | 163,737 | 8,529     |
| 1884 | 160,758 | 7,812     |

Cotton

*Cotton.*

|      | Raw Cotton used in millions of pounds. | Yards of piece goods exported in millions of yards. |
|------|----------------------------------------|-----------------------------------------------------|
| 1879 | 1,173                                  | 3,725                                               |
| 1880 | 1,373                                  | 4,496                                               |
| 1881 | 1,439                                  | 4,777                                               |
| 1882 | 1,461                                  | 4,349                                               |
| 1883 | 1,498                                  | 4,539                                               |
| 1884 | 1,487                                  | 4,417                                               |

Wool

*Raw Wool used in millions of pounds.*

| 1879 | 321 | 1882 | 357 |
|------|-----|------|-----|
| 1880 | 370 | 1883 | 340 |
| 1881 | 320 | 1884 | 381 |

*Consumption per head of certain articles.*

Extent of depression at present moment. Consumption of sugar, tea, &c.

|      | Sugar.[*] lbs. | Tea. lbs. | Coffee. lbs. | Tobacco. lbs. | Spirits. gallons. |
| --- | --- | --- | --- | --- | --- |
| 1879 | 66.24 | 4·70 | 1·00 | 1·41 | 1·11 |
| 1880 | 63·68 | 4·59 | 0·92 | 1·43 | 1·09 |
| 1881 | 67·36 | 4·58 | 0·89 | 1·41 | 1·08 |
| 1882 | 70·48 | 4·67 | 0·88 | 1·42 | 1·07 |
| 1883 | 71·74 | 4·80 | 0·89 | 1·42 | 1·06 |
| 1884 | 72·31 | 4·87 | 0·92 | 1·45 | 1·00 |

[*] Sugar is used in manufacture of jams, biscuits, &c., as well as in direct consumption.

*Average number of Paupers in receipt of relief in England and Wales in each year, ending Lady Day.*

Pauperism.

|      | Average Numbers. | Numbers per 1000 of population. |
| --- | --- | --- |
| 1879 | 765,455 | 30 |
| 1880 | 808,030 | 32 |
| 1881 | 790,937 | 31 |
| 1882 | 788,289 | 30 |
| 1883 | 782,422 | 30 |
| 1884 | 765,914 | 29 |

The particulars for the year ending Lady Day, 1885, are not published; but it appears from the monthly returns that the average numbers of in-door and out-door paupers relieved during the calendar years 1883 and 1884 were as follows—

| 1883 | 709,779 | Exclusive of about 45,000 lunatics |
| --- | --- | --- |
| 1884 | 700,745 | and 4,000 vagrants. |

The corresponding figures for the months of January and February, 1885, compared with the same months of 1884, are as follows—

|      | January. | February. | |
| --- | --- | --- | --- |
| 1884 | 720,498 | 727,189 | Exclusive of lunatics and |
| 1885 | 735,596 | 742,555 | vagrants, as above. |

*Deposits in Savings Banks in millions of pounds.*

Savings Banks.

|      | Post Office Banks. | Trustees. | Total. |
| --- | --- | --- | --- |
| 1879 | 32 | 44 | 76 |
| 1880 | 34 | 44 | 78 |
| 1881 | 36 | 44 | 80 |
| 1882 | 39 | 45 | 84 |
| 1883 | 42 | 45 | 87 |
| 1884 | 45 | 46 | 91 |

The Savings Banks also held the following amounts of Government stock for depositors :—

| 1883 | 1½ | ¼ | 1¾ |
| --- | --- | --- | --- |
| 1884 | 2 | ½ | 2½ |

The statistics of bankruptcy and of emigration I do not give here, as I have referred to them in the following chapter.

---

## CHAPTER XXXIII.

### DEPRESSION AT THE PRESENT MOMENT IN THE UNITED STATES, COMPARED.

Depression in the United States.

I HAVE said elsewhere that the causes of depression are so many and so various that it would be erroneous in the extreme to draw absolute conclusions from particular instances without a full knowledge of all the conditions. To attribute the prosperity of this country to Free Trade alone is a fallacy, which enables its opponents to turn the tables on us when that prosperity suffers a check. But if we can show that a country which has carried Protection further than any other, and which is at the same time our chief rival and customer—viz., the United States—suffers more from the present depression than we do, we may fairly conclude that our present evils are not due to Free Trade, and would not be removed by Protection. If we can further trace some connection between Protection and the principal evils from which the United States are suffering, we shall raise a further presumption in favour of a Free-Trade policy.

Mr. Forwood.

Now what is the condition of the United States at this moment. Mr. William B. Forwood, of Liverpool, a most competent witness, says, in a letter to the *Standard* of the 16th December, 1884—" It is not merely that the depression is intense; there are towns where not a single factory has worked for months past, and tens of thousands of working men are literally starving, but there is no hope that things can be better —their only customers are their own people; the tariff practically prohibits exports, and it is said that there are sufficient cotton and woollen factories and ironworks to produce in six what they can consume in twelve months."

Mr. McCulloch's report on the glut in manufactures in

The following is the account of the condition of United States manufactures given by Mr. McCulloch, Secretary to the United States Treasury, in his annual report for 1884—

"What the manufacturers now need is a market for their surplus manufactures. . . . After the war, stimulus was found in railroad building, and in extravagant expenditures induced by superabundant currency, and the time has now come when the manufacturing industry of the United States is in dire distress from plethora of manufacturing goods. the United States.

"Some manufacturing companies have been forced into bankruptcy; others have closed their mills to escape it; few mills are running on full time, and, as a consequence, a very large number of operatives are either deprived of employment, or are working for wages hardly sufficient to enable them to live comfortably, or even decently.

"The all-important question that presses itself upon the public attention is—How shall the country be relieved from the plethora of manufactured goods, and how shall plethora hereafter be prevented?  It is obvious that our power to produce is much in excess of the present or any probable future demand for home consumption.  The existing iron, cotton, and woollen mills, if employed at their full capacity, could meet in six months—perhaps in a shorter time—the home demand for a year.  It is certain, therefore, that unless markets now practically closed against us are opened—unless we can share in the trade which is monopolised by European nations—the depression now so severely felt will continue, and may become more disastrous."

Again he tells us that the total value of the exports of domestic merchandise amounted to 725 millions of dollars as against 804 millions in the preceding year, showing a decrease of nearly 80 millions; and he points out that, as regards shipping, the United States have almost ceased to be a maritime power—only 17 per cent. of her trade being carried in her own vessels.  It is not often that a Minister can be found to give so unfavourable an account of the industrial conditions of his own country.  But, unfavourable as it is, it is borne out, and more than borne out, by details obtained from other sources.

### Farming in the United States.

No full inquiry has been made into the state of the agricultural interest of the United States, but there is general evidence that the American corn farmer is depressed no less than his English brother.  Thus we are told that wheat cannot be produced by American farmers at existing prices; that the area of wheat is much less than last year; that the farms in the West are highly mortgaged at a high rate of interest amounting Agriculture in the United States.

K

Depression in the United States.

to as much as 10 per cent. ; that these advances were made on the basis of 80 cents to the dollar per bushel : and that wheat is now selling at 16 to 40 cents, the expense of production being 40 cents per bushel.*

### *Railways in the United States.*

Railways in the United States.

Again, if we take United States railways, the fall in their value during 1884 is very remarkable. Nearly 40 companies, with an aggregate length of 11,000 miles, and £143,000,000 of capital and debt, have gone into the hands of receivers.† About 10 per cent. of the entire railway mileage and of the normal capital invested in railway stock and bonds of the United States have gone into liquidation. A still larger proportionate number have become insolvent in the first quarter of the present year. In solvent companies the "shrinkage" is very great. Mr. Atkinson ‡ estimates " that 7,000,000,000 dollars worth of railway property have apparently depreciated at least 1,500,000 dollars within the past year—or, in other words, that perhaps 1,000,000,000 dollars of water (nominal capital) has been squeezed out, and during the process the true value of the remainder has been temporarily depressed 500,000,000 dollars." He points out the obvious reason, viz., that whilst during the last four years the grain, hay, and meat crops of the United States, which constitute one-half the substances moved by railway, have not increased more than 10 per cent., the railway mileage has increased by 40 per cent., viz., from 86,497 miles to 121,543 miles.§ In a letter to *Bradstreet's Journal* of 7th of February, the same statistician says that in 1882 about 650,000 men, mostly labourers, were employed in the mere construction of railroads, and that in 1884 not more than 220,000 were occupied in this work—thus throwing out of this work above 430,000 men.

### *Bankruptcies in the United States.*

Bankruptcies in the United States.

Take, again, bankruptcies. The number of mercantile failures in the United States in 1884 was larger than had been ever known —even in the disastrous year 1878. The following is an extract from *Bradstreet's Journal* of the 27th of December, 1884 :—

---

* *Standard*, 29th December, 1884.
† *Economist*, 17th January and 16th May, 1885.
‡ " Distribution of Products," p. 263. Putnam, 1885.
§ *Ibid.*, pp. 235, 238, 240, 258.

"The rate at which the increase in mercantile mortality throughout the country, dependent in part, of course, on the increase in number of business ventures, may be gathered from the following extract from *Bradstreet's Journal*:— Depression in the United States.

"*Failures in the United States for Six Years.*

| Year. | Number of Failures. | Aggregate Assets. | Aggregate Liabilities. | P. c. Assets to Liabilities. |
|---|---|---|---|---|
| | | $ | $ | |
| 1879 | 6,652 | 48,906,000 | 99,636,000 | 49 |
| 1880 | 4,350 | 27,430,000 | 57,120,000 | 48 |
| 1881 | 5,929 | 35,964,000 | 76,091,000 | 47 |
| 1882 | 7,635 | 47,469,000 | 93,238,000 | 51 |
| 1883 | 10,299 | 90,804,000 | 175,968,000 | 52 |
| 1884* | 11,600 | 130,000,000 | 240,000,000 | 54 |

* Partly estimated.

"Here is a probable increase of over 12 per cent. in the total number of failures for 1884 as against 1883, a probable gain of 44 per cent. in assets and of 37 per cent. in liabilities. The totals for 1884, furthermore, promise to exceed any previously recorded annual total, the largest heretofore having been given as 10,500 failures in 1878, with 234,000,000 dollars liabilities. If a comparison may be instituted between 1884 and 1878, with these totals, we find that the current year is likely to have 1,100 more failures than that in which the greatest commercial depression was experienced prior to the revival of trade in 1879, and that the total liabilities of failing trades in 1884 promise to be about 6,000,000 dollars greater."

Nor did the increase end with 1884. The same journal of 21st March, 1885, gives the following figures for the first two months and a half of the past four years:—

| | | | | |
|---|---|---|---|---|
| January 1st to March 14th ... ... | 1882 | 1883 | 1884 | 1885 |
| No. of failures in the United States ... | 1797 | 2691 | 2787 | 3349 |

Compare these figures with those of bankruptcies in England, for which the official figures are as follows:— And in England.

*Number of Bankruptcies proper, Liquidations, Schemes of Arrangement, and Compositions.*

| | No. |
|---|---|
| 1881 .. .. .. .. .. .. | 9,727 |
| 1882 .. .. .. .. .. .. | 9,041 |
| 1883 .. .. .. .. .. .. | 8,555 |
| 1884 .. .. .. .. .. .. | 4,205 |

Depression in the United States.

Considering the effect of the Bankruptcy Act of 1883, it would, of course, not be fair to take these English figures as absolute tests of the comparative commercial solvency of the trading classes in the several years referred to. The Act of 1883 has probably had the effect of preventing official insolvencies, and also of increasing private arrangements, though whether this has been the case to any great extent is very uncertain. But it may at any rate be concluded from the above figures, that there has been no special unsoundness in the trade of England during the year 1884, such as is shown by the insolvencies in the United States.

### Clearing House Business in the United States.

Clearing house business in the United States and in England.

Take again the amounts cleared at the London Bankers' Clearing House, and in New York, in each of the years from 1878 to 1884 inclusive.

IN THOUSANDS OF £'s.

| Years. | AT THE LONDON BANKERS' CLEARING HOUSE. | | | IN NEW YORK. | | |
|---|---|---|---|---|---|---|
| | Total amounts cleared. | Increase or decrease in each year compared with the previous year. | | Total amounts cleared. | Increase or decrease in each year compared with the previous year. | |
| | | Amount. | Per cent. | | Amount. | Per cent. |
| | 000 £'s | 000 £'s | | 000 £'s | 000 £'s | |
| 1878 | 4,992,000 | —50,000 | —1·0 | 3,238,367 | ( ? ) | —3·3 |
| 1879 | 4,886,000 | —106,000 | —2·1 | 4,367,153 | +1,128,786 | +34·9 |
| 1880 | 5,794,000 | +908,000 | +18·6 | 5,203,381 | +836,228 | +19·1 |
| 1881 | 6,357,000 | +563,000 | +9·7 | 6,871,226 | +1,667,845 | +32·1 |
| 1882 | 6,221,000 | —136,000 | —2·1 | 6,570,436 | —300,790 | —4·4 |
| 1883 | 5,929,000 | —292,000 | —4·7 | 5,190,142 | —1,380,294 | —21·0 |
| 1884 | 5,799,000 | —130,000 | —2·2 | 3,980,604 | —1,209,538 | —23·3 |

NOTE.—The business revived in both countries in 1880-1, in the United States more than in England; and fell off in both countries in 1883-4, but in the United States far more than in England.

### Emigration to the United States.

Emigration to the United States.

Emigration, properly understood, is another test of comparative depression. The principles which govern emigration between this country and the United States, as shown in Mr. Giffen's annual reports, appear to be as follows :—*

* See Mr. Giffen's Report on Emigration, Parliamentary Paper, No. 52, of 1883, and preceding reports.

Immigration has to be taken into account as well as Emigration, and there is at times a considerable immigration into this country from the United States, so that it is the balance of emigrants over immigrants to which we must look. In the present state of land and labour in the two countries the prevailing attraction is with the United States, which has the larger quantity of unoccupied land; and the great current of emigration flows, therefore, from England to the United States. But not only so. The attraction in each country fluctuates with the state of trade—it is greater in each country when trade is good, and less when trade is bad. The fluctuations of trade in the United States are greater than they are in England, partly in consequence of their Protective system, but also in consequence of other and more important causes.* The attraction of the United States for labour is consequently, at a period of good trade, not only positively, but proportionately, stronger than that of this country. If we could have a time when trade in the United States was very good, and trade in England very bad, we should have the maximum of attraction in the United States, and the largest amount of emigration from this country. But the two countries are so connected in business that trade is generally good in the one country at or about the same time at which it is good in the other, and *vice versa*. Under these conditions, when trade is good, or fairly good, in both countries, the attractions of the United States are, as we have seen, not only positively, but proportionately greater than at other times, and consequently at such times the balance of emigration to the United States increases. This accounts for the fact that emigration is often greatest when times are good in this country, a fact which has been perverted by the Fair Traders into a suggestion that emigration is the real reason why pauperism diminishes!† When the times become less good in both countries, the comparative attraction of the United States becomes less powerful, a return tide of immigration sets in, and the balance of emigration from this country becomes less. This is what has happened lately. The figures for recent years are as follow :—

---

* See Mr. Giffen's Essays on Finance, No. iv., page 137, on the depression of trade in raw material producing countries.

† Fair Trade position explained, p 64.

*Total arrivals in, and departures from, the United States from and to all countries.*

| | Arrivals. | | Departures. | | Excess of arrivals over departures. |
|---|---|---|---|---|---|
| 1879 | .. 253,210 | .. | 117,385 | .. | 135,825 |
| 1880 | .. 534,465 | .. | 109,007 | .. | 425,458 |
| 1881 | .. 743,712 | .. | 112,072 | .. | 631,640 |
| 1882 | .. 869,144 | .. | 133,496 | .. | 735,648 |
| 1883 | .. 712,515 | .. | 157,954 | .. | 554,561 |
| 1884 | .. 649,491 | .. | 187,706 | .. | 461,785 |

*Emigration to, and immigration from, the United States, from and to the United Kingdom, of persons of British and Irish origin only, each year from 1879 to 1884, and in the first four months of the year 1885:—*

| Period. | Emigration to United States from United Kingdom. | Immigration from United States to United Kingdom. |
|---|---|---|
| Year 1879 | 91,806 | 20,048 |
| ,, 1880 | 166,570 | 26,518 |
| ,, 1881 | 176,104 | 29,781 |
| ,, 1882 | 181,903 | 28,468 |
| ,, 1883 | 191,573 | 46,703 |
| ,, 1884 | 155,280 | 61,466 |
| Four months ended 30th April, 1885. | 40,174 | 11,981 |

There was a revival of trade in 1880 which went on till 1882-1883, and the balance of emigration from this country and into the United States went on increasing. About that time depression commenced in both countries, and has since increased. The balance of emigration following this depression has decreased also, and is still decreasing, showing that the comparative attractions of the United States for the labour of this country are decreasing, or in other words, that the United States have been having a very bad time.

### *Employment of Labour in the United States.*



Take, again, the most important feature of all—the employment of labour. Our own newspapers have been full of reports of the depressed state of labour in the United States.* But the most important evidence is to be found in *Bradstreet's*

* See, for instance, *Times*, Feb. 4th, 1885; *Economist*, Jan. 3rd, 1885, &c., &c.

*Journal.* This newspaper, at the end of last year, instituted a careful inquiry into the state of the leading manufacturing industries in the twenty-two Northern States of the Union. The results are stated as follows—" There has been a general reduction in wages varying from 20 to 25 and in some cases to 30 per cent., taking the year through. The reduced forces (*i.e.*, number of men) at work range from 33 per cent. to 12 per cent., not including reductions in clerical staff. . . . The total number reported out of work, due to shutting down of establishments, to enforced reduction of forces, or to strikes, is 316,000, or 13 per cent. of the whole number busy in 1880. Of these, the number out of work by strikes is not more than 5·3 per cent. ' There are no less than 55,000 industrial workers idle in New York, exclusive of clerks and salesmen.' ' In Philadelphia not less than 33,000.' ' At Pittsburgh, nearly 11,000,'" and so on.* The aggregate number of manufacturing operatives thrown out of work is estimated at not less than 350,000. How many of these men have found other employment or where is not known, but 350,000 fewer are reported to be employed on these industries than were so employed two years ago, and there is very great distress and want of employment. Further inquiries into the rates of wages have furnished the following results,† which are sufficiently important to be quoted *in extenso.*

" RATES OF REDUCTION SINCE JULY, 1882."

" *Lines in which Lower Wages and Fewer Employés are Conspicuous.*

"In December, 1884, *Bradstreet's* undertook to report the extent to which industrial workers had been thrown out of employment in the United States during two and one half years last past. The investigation was one unique in journalism, and was met by fairly satisfactory results, the showing being that about 350,000 fewer operatives were then employed than in 1882, or about 14 per cent. In the present instance it has undertaken to get the necessary data to determine the extent to which industrial workers' wages have been reduced during the same period.

"The inquiry embraces the leading manufacturing industries in the United States—those in which the value of the goods annually produced is equal to or in excess of 30,000,000

* *Bradstreet's*, 20th Dec., 1885.      † *Ibid.*, 14th March, 1885.

Depression in the United States. General reduction in wages

dols. It was manifestly impracticable to extend the investigation at this time to every city and town at which these industries are prominent.

"In order to furnish a fair and sufficiently comprehensive
exhibit of the rates of wages paid and received weekly, inquiries
were extended, in each case, to the leading establishments in
each industry at seven cities or towns. The cities were selected
on the basis of the amount of capital invested and value of
products in each line, and are given in order under appropriate
classifications by industries.

"In the lines of industry covered there were, in 1880,
194,500 establishments in the United States out of a total of
all manufacturing concerns amounting to 253,800 nearly 77
per cent. of the whole. The number of hands employed was
2,005,000 out of 2,732,595, or 73 per cent. The total wages
paid by them annually amounted to 688,361,961 dols., out of a
grand total of 947,953,795 dols., or 72 per cent. The annual
value of materials used was 2,654,702,809 dols., out of an
aggregate of 3,396,823.549 dols., or 77 per cent., and the annual
total value of products was 4,101,889,676 dols., out of a grand
aggregate in all industrial lines amounting to 5,369,579,191 dols.,
or 76 per cent. The industrial wages investigated represent,
therefore, those at seven cities in order of prominence, and
may be regarded as fairly typical of the rates paid to three-
quarters of the industrial workers of the country. The
investigation has been conducted at 60 cities, from which over
250 separate reports have been received, involving, at least,
1,500 special inquiries by correspondents of *Bradstreet's*
This does not include instances where information was refused,
or where it was furnished, but appeared to be faulty or likely
to mislead.

"There are three primary facts to be taken into account in
studying the classified tables of wages presented below :—

"1. With the restricted call for products, and in the effort
to maintain wages—under pressure from workers to have them
maintained—marked reductions in the number of employés
have been made since 1882, as pointed out in *Bradstreet's*,
December 20, 1884. As will be recalled, it was then shown—
that the enforced reductions in the number of employés, those
thrown out by shutting down of factories and mills, and by
strikes and lockouts (since 1882), amounted (as reported) to
316,000 in 21 States, where 90 per cent. of the total of indus-

trial workers were employed; that the grand total was probably nearer 350,000 than 316,000, or say 14 per cent. of the total engaged in 1882; that at least 80,000 fewer iron and steel, machinery and foundry, workers were employed—or 23 per cent. of the total dispensed with; that 35,000 fewer clothing operatives (east of Ohio), or 10 per cent.; 20,000 fewer cotton goods operatives, about 6 per cent.; 24,000 fewer woollen fabric operatives, or 7 per cent.; about 13,000 fewer tobacco operatives, or less than 4 per cent.; and about 4,700 glass workers, or say 1·3 per cent. of the 350,000 displaced—had been thrown out. This has been one element in helping to maintain the rate of wages of those remaining at work. The total displaced, as enumerated, number nearly 177,000, or about 51 per cent. of those whose services had been done away with.

"2. Work has been restricted at various establishments, hours having been shortened, or work furnished fewer days in the week.

"3. Employés have been given piece work in place of a stated sum per day, week, or month, the quantities furnished being limited in many cases.

"In addition to these, strong trades unions among iron and steel, glass workers, building trades, boots and shoes, tobacco and textile operatives, and in other lines, have brought a pressure to bear to prevent reductions of wages, frequently to gain an advance.

"The reductions in *rates* of wages in most all instances are less than the gross reductions in *amounts received* within two and one half years. The percentages of rate reductions calculated indicated, therefore, the apparent cut; in some cases (generally specified) it is actual, but the losses due to restricted time, or to a limited quantity of piece work, are not always a determinate factor.

"Several features of the exhibit are nevertheless more striking than any late developments regarding our manufacturing industries.

"*Six highly protected industries, iron and steel (also foundries and machine shops, etc.), clothing, cotton, woollen, tobacco, and glass manufactures, which employed 34 per cent. of all industrial workers (as reported in 1880), have thrown out one half of the total number of workers since 1882, 177,700 in number, as reported by "Bradstreet's" in December, 1884.*

Depression
n the
United
States.
Employ-
ment of
labour.

"*All of these lines have run nearly, if not quite, as much on short time as any others named.*

"*They, with other textile establishments, have practically had a monopoly of the larger strikes of the past year or two, with the exceptions of those in the coal regions.*

"*And, as exhibited with sufficient detail for generalisation in the wages report given below, they have suffered, on the average, a* GREATER *reduction in rates of wages paid.*

Steel and
iron have
suffered
most of all

"Iron and steel workers and coal miners have suffered by far the greatest reduction in wages from all causes, and are followed by operatives in textiles. Glassmakers, thus far, have suffered less, proportionately, than the above, and then only in certain departments of labour. Excepting tobacco and cigars from food products and the latter have suffered least of all. Wages rates in the building trades and woodworking industries have been only moderately depressed. Workers in leather have not found their wages cut severely, and paper mill employés and printers have escaped with but a moderate reduction. The average reduction in rates of wages paid and received in the various lines covered have been classified as follows :—

### "FOOD PRODUCTS.

| | Av. per ct. reduction wages. |
|---|---|
| Flour mill ... ... ... ... ... ... | None |
| Bakery ... ... ... ... ... ... | None |
| Slaughterhouse ... ... ... ... ... | — |
| Sugar refining (in rates paid) ... ... ... | None |
| Liquors, malt... ... ... ... ... ... | None |
| Liquors, distilled ... .. ... ... ... | 10 to 12 |
| Tobacco, cigars ... ... ... ... ... | 10 to 15 |
| Tobacco, chewing and smoking ... ... ... | 10 to 20 |

### TEXTILE PRODUCTS.

| | |
|---|---|
| Woollen goods, cloths (based on short time) ... | 25 to 30 |
| Woollen goods, clothing (men's) ... ... ... | 10 to 15 |
| Woollen goods, clothing (women's) ... ... | 10 to 15 |
| Cotton goods (cuts and short time)... ... ... | 25 to 30 |
| Silk goods (Paterson) ... ... ... | 15 to 25 |

### METAL PRODUCTS.

| | |
|---|---|
| Blast furnaces (eastern) ... ... ... | 11 |
| Blast furnaces (southern) ... ... ... | 20 |
| Blast furnaces (western) ... ... ... | 12 |
| Iron mills (eastern) ... ... ... ... | 15 to 22 |
| Iron mills (western) ... ... .. .. | 15 to 22 |

| METAL PRODUCTS (*continued*). | Av. per ct. reduc-tion wages | |
|---|---|---|
| Steel rail (western) ... ... ... | 30 | Depression in the United States. |
| Steel rail (eastern) ... ... ... | 20 | |
| Nail mill (western) (in rates paid) ... | None | Employment of labour |
| Tinware ... ... ... ... | 10 | |
| Agricultural implements ... ... | Little | |
| Foundry and machinery .. .. | 10 to 15 | |

LUMBER AND MANUFACTURES.

| | |
|---|---|
| Lumber, sawed and planed ... | Little |
| Sash, doors and blinds ... | 8 to 10 |
| Coopers ... ... ... | 10 to 15 |
| Furniture makers ... ... | 10 to 15 |

BUILDING TRADES.

| | |
|---|---|
| Carpenters ... ... | Little |
| Stone and marble cutters | Little |
| Brickmakers ... ... | Little |

LEATHER AND MANUFACTURES.

| | |
|---|---|
| Tanned and curried workers | Little |
| Harness and saddlery workers | 10 |
| Boot and shoe workers ... | 10 |
| Paper makers... ... ... | Little |
| Compositors ... ... ... | Little |
| Glass makers— | |
|    One class ... ... ... | Inc. 10 |
|    Another class ... ... | Dec. 18 |
|    Others ... ... ... | Same |
| Shipbuilding ... ... ... | — |
| Coal miners ... ... ... | 20 to 40 |

These figures from *Bradstreet's* report seem to deserve special attention; and it may be added that, whilst I am revising the proofs of these sheets, it is reported that the whole of the iron and steel industry west of the Alleghanies, employing, it is said, 75,000 hands, is out of work.

I have elsewhere * given details concerning certain special manufactures in the United States, viz., of clocks, woollens, copper, and steel rails, all pointing to the same conclusions, viz., that the manufacturing industries of the United States are much more depressed at the present moment, and are in a less healthy condition than our own; and, further, that the industries which are the least healthy and most suffering are those which have been most protected, viz., shipping, iron and steel, and

These facts illustrate the effect of Protection

* Pages 167 to 175.

Depression in the United States.

It illustrates the effect of Protection.

textiles. The case is extremely interesting, for it illustrates very forcibly the doctrines of political economists on the subject of Protection. The first and immediate effect of Protection in a country is to raise prices to the consumer. Whilst this lasts importation goes on ; the duty actually received on imported articles goes into the public exchequer ; whilst the increase of price of home-made articles goes into the pocket of the native producers. The profit thus made gives an unnatural stimulus to production. Capital is improperly and unhealthily attracted to the protected trade ; and the home competition becomes at last so severe as to reduce the price of the home-trade article almost to the level of the foreign article. Protection, then, ceases to raise the price, though it keeps out the foreign article. Then comes a plethora of home-trade goods ; the trade ceases to be profitable ; manufactories are shut up ; and workmen are turned off, or have to take very low wages. Exportation may take place for the moment, but it cannot last or be profitable, because Protection has so raised the cost of manufactures as to make it impossible to compete with foreign manufacturers in neutral markets. All this is just what has happened and is happening in the United States.

So long as seasons and climates vary, so long as men are subject to hopes and fears, commerce and industry will be subject to some of those ebbs and flows which cause so much uncertainty and so much human suffering. To what is inevitable we must submit. But it is sad to think that these ebbs and flows are aggravated by the folly of Governments which, by intercepting the gifts of Providence in one direction, and by applying an unnatural stimulus in another, check natural production, and stimulate unhealthy industries into unnatural activity, to be followed by equally unnatural and unnecessary prostration.

---

# CHAPTER XXXIV.

## SHIPPING.

Shipping of the United Kingdom.

So much has been said about shipping that I am almost afraid of referring to it, but it is so striking an instance of the advantages of freedom and the impotency and mischief of protection, that I must state the figures again. Most of the following are taken from the Appendix to Mr. Chamberlain's speech, as published by the Cobden Club.

*Statement of the Percentage of the Foreign Trade of the United Kingdom carried on in British Ships compared (in thousands of tons).*

| Average of Three Years. | Total Foreign Trade (Thousands of Tons). | Total carried in British Ships (Thousands of Tons). | Proportion of Total Trade carried on in British Ships (Per cent.). |
|---|---|---|---|
| 1854-6 | 19,582 | 11,537 | 59 |
| 1857-9 | 22,798 | 13,299 | 58 |
| 1860-2 | 25,940 | 15,094 | 58 |
| 1863-5 | 27,613 | 18,193 | 66 |
| 1866-8 | 32,566 | 22,095 | 68 |
| 1869-71 | 37,699 | 25,632 | 68 |
| 1872-4 | 44,123 | 29,485 | 67 |
| 1875-7 | 49,531 | 33,051 | 67 |
| 1878-80 | 54,349 | 38,025 | 70 |
| 1881-83 | 61,468 | 44,084 | 72 |

*Statement showing the Proportion of the Tonnage of the United Kingdom to the Tonnage of certain Foreign Countries at different Dates, multiplying steam tonnage by FOUR to reduce it to a common denominator with sailing tonnage (in thousands of tons).*

| Year. | United Kingdom. | | Foreign Countries. | | Total (Thousands of Tons). |
|---|---|---|---|---|---|
| | Thousands of Tons. | Per cent. of Total. | Thousands of Tons. | Per cent. of Total. | |
| 1860 | 5,942 | 42 | 8,143 | 58 | 14,085 |
| 1870 | 8,950 | 49 | 9,231 | 51 | 18,181 |
| 1880 | 14,679 | 57 | 11,182 | 43 | 25,861 |
| 1883 | 18,371 | 59 | 12,906 | 41 | 31,277 |

The foreign countries included are :—France, Germany, Holland, Belgium, Austria, Hungary, Italy, Sweden and Norway, Denmark, Greece, and the United States (oversea tonnage).

## TONNAGE BELONGING TO THE UNITED KINGDOM.
### (In Thousands of Tons.)

1850 (The Date of the Repeal of the Navigation Laws) { 3,397 Sailing. / 168 Steam. / 3,565 Total. }

| Years. | Sailing. | Steam. | Total. | Years. | Sailing. | Steam. | Total. |
|---|---|---|---|---|---|---|---|
| 1869 | 4,765 | 948 | 5,713 | 1877 | 4.261 | 2,139 | 6,400 |
| 1870 | 4,578 | 1,113 | 5,691 | 1878 | 4,239 | 2,316 | 6,555 |
| 1871 | 4,374 | 1,320 | 5,694 | 1879 | 4,069 | 2,511 | 6,580 |
| 1872 | 4,213 | 1,538 | 5,751 | 1880 | 3,851 | 2,723 | 6,574 |
| 1873 | 4,091 | 1,714 | 5,805 | 1881 | 3,688 | 3,004 | 6,692 |
| 1874 | 4,108 | 1,871 | 5,979 | 1882 | 3,622 | 3,335 | 6,957 |
| 1875 | 4,207 | 1,945 | 6,152 | 1883 | 3,514 | 3,728 | 7,242 |
| 1876 | 4,258 | 2,005 | 6,263 | | | | |

NOTE.— It seems important to notice that while the aggregate of sailing and steam tonnage has increased, the increase is exclusively in steam tonnage, which is more effective than sailing tonnage as three or four to one.



## TONNAGE BELONGING TO FRANCE.
### (In Thousands of Tons.)

| Years. | Sailing. | Steam. | Total. |
|---|---|---|---|
| 1840 | 653 | 9 | 662 |
| 1850 | 674 | 14 | 688 |
| 1860 | 928 | 68 | 996 |
| 1870 | 918 | 154 | 1,072 |
| 1879 | 676 | 256 | 932 |
| 1880 | 641 | 278 | 919 |
| 1881 | 602 | 312 | 914 |
| 1882 | 567 | 416 | 983 |



## OVER-SEA TONNAGE BELONGING TO THE UNITED STATES.
### (In Thousands of Tons.)

| Years. | Sailing. | Steam. | Total. |
|---|---|---|---|
| 1840 | 896 | 4 | 900 |
| 1850 | 1,541 | 45 | 1,586 |
| 1860 | 2,449 | 97 | 2,546 |
| 1870 | 1,324 | 193 | 1,517 |
| 1880 | 1,206 | 147 | 1,353 |
| 1881 | 1,182 | 153 | 1,335 |
| 1882 | 1,137 | 155 | 1,292 |
| 1883 | 1,130 | 172 | 1,302 |

*Total Trade of the United States carried in United States and Foreign Vessels respectively, with the Percentage carried by each (in thousands of dollars).* * Shipping.

| Years. | In American Vessels. | In Foreign Vessels. | Percentage in American Vessels. |
|---|---|---|---|
| 1840 | 198,424 | 40,802 | 82·9 |
| 1850 | 239,272 | 90,764 | 72·5 |
| 1860 | 507,247 | 255,040 | 66·5 |
| 1870 | 352,969 | 638,927 | 35·6 |
| 1881 | 268,080 | 1,378,556 | 16·0 |
| 1882 | 242,850 | 1,284,488 | 15·5 |
| 1883 | 261,718] | 1,290,030 | 16·3 |
| 1884 | 264,722 | 1,194,118 | 17·5 |

*Total Tonnage Entered and Cleared in the United States, in each of the years 1850, 1860, 1870, 1880, 1881, 1882, 1883, and 1884 (years ended 30th June), distinguishing American, British, and other Foreign Vessels* (in thousands of tons).*

| Years ended 30th June. | TONNAGE. | | | | PERCENTAGE. | | | |
|---|---|---|---|---|---|---|---|---|
| | American. | British. | Other Countries. | Total. | American. | British. | Other Countries. | Total. |
| | Tons. | Tons. | Tons. | Tons. | Per cent. | Per cent. | Per cent. | Per cent. |
| 1850 | 5,206 | 2,845 | 659 | 8,710 | 59·77 | 32·67 | 7·56 | 100 |
| 1860 | 12,087 | 4,068 | 910 | 17,065 | 70·83 | 23·84 | 5·33 | 100 |
| 1870 | 6,993 | 9,246 | 2,085 | 18,324 | 38·16 | 50·46 | 11·38 | 100 |
| 1880 | 6,834 | 20,697 | 8,523 | 36,054 | 18·95 | 57·41 | 23·64 | 100 |
| 1881 | 6,629 | 21,651 | 8,509 | 36,789 | 18·02 | 58·85 | 23·13 | 100 |
| 1882 | 6,658 | 20,583 | 8,116 | 35,357 | 18·83 | 58·22 | 22·95 | 100 |
| 1883 | 6,563 | 18,828 | 7,532 | 32,923 | 19·93 | 57·19 | 22·88 | 100 |
| 1884 | 6,439 | 17,125 | 6,709 | 30,273 | 21·27 | 56·57 | 22·16 | 100 |

Our success, it is to be observed, has taken place since we Early promise of United States Shipping. repealed our Navigation Laws, and deprived our shipowners of every privilege, whilst we have also given them free access to every market for their materials. In Europe we might have expected to remain supreme, but, within my own recollection, the United States were formidable rivals. When I was a boy

* From the United States statistics. The returns are inclusive of the Lake Trade between the United States and Canada.

Shipping.

American liners were the pride of Liverpool, and careful observers prophesied that United States shipowners must become the carriers of the world. The following passage from De Tocqueville's " Democracy in America " (vol. ii., chap. x.) is curious enough to deserve quotation.

De Tocqueville's Prophecy.

" From the Bay of Fundy to the Gulf of Mexico the coast of the United States extends for nearly 900 leagues. These shores form a single, uninterrupted line; they are all under the same rule. There is no nation in the world which can offer to commerce ports with greater depth, greater width, and greater safety. . . . . . Europe is, then, the market of America, as America is the market of Europe; and maritime trade is as necessary to the inhabitants of the United States, to bring their agricultural produce to our ports, as to take our manufactures to them. The Anglo-Americans have at all times shown a decided taste for the sea. Their independence, in breaking the commercial links which bound them to England, gave a new and powerful impulse to their maritime genius. Since that time the number of the ships belonging to the Union has increased nearly as fast as the number of its inhabitants. At this day it is the Americans themselves who carry to their homes nine-tenths of the imports from Europe. It is the Americans, too, who carry to the consumers of Europe three-quarters of the exports of the New World.* The ships of the United States fill the ports of Havre and Liverpool. One sees but few English or French ships in the port of New York. Thus, not only does the American merchant brave competition on his own soil; he competes successfully with foreigners on theirs. . . . . . I think that nations, like men, almost always show from their youth the powerful features of their destiny. When I see the spirit with which Anglo-Americans carry on trade, the facilities they possess for doing it, the success which they attain in it, I cannot help believing that they will one day become the first maritime power of the globe. They are impelled to take possession of the sea as the Romans were to conquer the world."

Such was De Tocqueville's prophecy in 1835. And now the ships of the United States are not one-fourth or, if steam is taken into account, not one-seventh of those of England!

* At this day, 1881, according to the statistics of the United States, 16 per cent. in value of their trade is carried in United States ships, and 84 per cent. in foreign ships, of which more than two-thirds are British.

And whilst American ships carry less than one-fifth of the whole trade of the United States, British ships carry much more than one-half of that trade. Shipping.

England has 50 per cent. of the ocean tonnage and carrying trade of the entire world, and America is nowhere. If England has special advantages from Nature, other nations have the same. As De Tocqueville truly remarks,—in seaports, in harbours, in human skill and industry, and in natural aptitude for the sea, America is not inferior to ourselves; of coal and iron she has an ample store; her geographical position is as good as ours. Every port in the world, our own included, is as free to American ships as to ours, whilst the Union closes her trade between her Atlantic and Pacific ports to our ships. But whilst we leave our shipowner to buy his materials and build and buy his ships where and how he pleases, America refuses to place a foreign-built ship upon her register, and imposes a duty of 40 per cent. on the materials of shipbuilding. At the same time, whilst she thus protects her shipowners out of existence, she leaves her capital and energy free to devote themselves to the production of food in her boundless realms of virgin soil, and the consequence is that, whilst she is developing with extraordinary rapidity those natural resources of soil and climate, with which her laws have not directly interfered, she has surrendered to us the field in which Nature allows us to compete, and which, at one time, she seemed destined to win also. Present state of American as compared with British Shipping.

We are accustomed to think our railway interest an important interest, and so it is. But in current expenditure on skilled labour our shipping interest is still more important. The fixed capital of the railways is nearly 800 millions; the fixed capital in ships is probably not a fourth or fifth of that amount. But the working expenses of the railways in 1880 were $33\frac{1}{2}$ millions, whilst the outgoings on shipping, which give employment and remuneration to a great variety of forms of skilled labour, probably amount to nearly double that sum. The gross income of the railways in 1880 was $65\frac{1}{2}$ millions. What the gross income of shipping was we have no means of estimating exactly; but it must have been very large indeed, probably much more than that sum. Our shipping interest is one of which the nation may well be proud. Shipping as compared with Railway Interest.

I have left the above as it was written in 1880. Since then, as every one knows, shipping has suffered severe de- Present depression.

L

pression.   The great prosperity of the trade down to the year 1883 had, as is too often the case, the effect of tempting capital into the trade, and of producing an over-supply.

I cannot give the facts better than in the words of Mr. Williamson, M.P.*

"In 1875 the sailing tonnage of the United Kingdom amounted to ...   ...   ...   ...   ...   4,144,504 tons.
The steam tonnage to ...   ...   ...   1,943,197   ,,

Together   6,087,701   ,,

"In 1883 the sailing tonnage was   ...   3,471,172   ,,
The steam tonnage had risen to   ...   3,725,229   ,,

Together   ...   7,196,401   ,,

"But that is only a partial and misleading view of the real state of the case, for, seeing that steam vessels do three times the work of sailing ships, it would appear that, in eight years, the carrying capacity of the mere increase in our steam tonnage since 1875 is more than equal to the entire carrying capacity of our mercantile navy of sailing ships at the present time.   The real increase in the capacity for work of our tonnage since 1875 would more accurately be represented by the following figures :—

1875—Sailing ships   ...   ...   ...   4,144,504 tons.
Steam, 1,943,197 tons, multiplied
by 3 to compare with sailing
ship tonnage ...   ...   ...   5,829,591   ,,

Joint capacity for work   ...   9,974,095   ,,

1883 – Sailing ships   . .   ...   ...   3,471,173   ,,
Steam, 3,725,229 tons, multiplied
by 3 to compare with sailing
ship tonnage ...   ...   ...   11,175,687   ,,

Joint capacity for work   ...   14,646,860   ,,

"Such an increase has been altogether wild and unjustifi-

* Article in *Fortnightly*, of January, 1885.

able, seeing our import and export trade has not grown of late Shipping. Present depression. years to any appreciable extent, and that our foreign commerce has for the present lost its former elasticity. The member for Birkenhead, who is a shipowner, chooses to pour out his sorrows on the floor of the House of Commons, and entreats Parliament to find a remedy. It would be more becoming that shipowners should seek some secluded spot and shed penitential tears over mistakes and miscalculations, which it is utterly beyond the power of the House of Commons to remedy. We shipowners (for I must myself speak as an erring member of the body) have seen the enormous yearly increase in our tonnage, and we gave no heed to the lesson till adversity has shown us our folly. As an instance of folly, I may state that one steamship company, which has come into existence within the last few years, and which has had to create trades for its vessels, has floated about two miles in consecutive length of steamships within a very short space of time. Not only has ill-advised enterprise of this description been most unprofitable to those concerned, but it has spread dismay among all the other companies with which its necessities have compelled it to enter into competition."

It may be added that this unhealthy competition has had also the effect of leading persons who had no knowledge of the business to invest money in it, too often imprudently and incautiously, and has thus been one amongst other causes of the state of things which has led to the present Royal Commission on Unseaworthy Ships, Loss of Life at Sea. In this place it may not be amiss to refer to one infringement of Free Trade principles which had the effect of aggravating the evil, viz., the French bounties on shipping, which induced an unnatural activity in English shipbuilding yards, for the purpose of supplying French owners with English-built ships, before the period at which protection to French-built ships should come into complete operation.

It need scarcely be added that the depression in question is, of course, fully shared by foreign shipping. Indeed, the proportion of British shipping employed in our own carrying trade has increased during the year 1884. The shipping built in the year has decreased from 892,000 tons in 1883 to 588,000 in 1884. A diminution in supply and a continued increase in demand will, no doubt, in course of time remedy the present suffering. Meanwhile we more than hold our own with other nations

L 2

# CHAPTER XXXV.

SPECIAL INSTANCES OF THE EFFECTS OF FREE TRADE AND
OF PROTECTIVE DUTIES ON PRODUCTION—LEATHER, SALT,
SILK, CLOCKS, WOOLLENS, STEEL RAILS, COPPER, BISCUITS,
WIRE.

THERE are one or two special illustrations of the benefit of free
tariffs in forwarding production, which it may be worth while
to mention specially.

### *Leather.*

Leather,
Increase of
Manufac-
tures of.

At the recent Leather Exhibition in this country it appeared
that the exportation of boots and shoes from this country was
largely increasing, whilst the importations from France and
other countries were decreasing, and at the same time the
importation of tanned and dressed hides into this country
was largely increasing. The following is the statement in
the report in the *Times* of the 27th September, 1881 :—

"The increase in the number of exhibits this year as compared with last is, roughly speaking, proportional to the improvement which has in the interval taken place in the trade of our
boot and shoe manufacturers, the Board of Trade returns for
the seven months ending July 31st, this year, showing that we
exported 3,277,740 pairs of boots and shoes in that period
against 2,800,992 in the corresponding period of 1880, and
3,071,424 in 1879. Our Australian colonies took 1,309,752
pairs. The imports of boots and shoes, on the contrary, showed a
decline. While 1,041,624 pairs were imported from France and
other countries in the first seven months of 1879, only 711,420
pairs were imported in 1880, and but 572,232 pairs in the corresponding period this year."

" From these figures it is argued that our English manufacturers are rapidly improving the quality and finish of their
goods, and are so enabled to compete successfully with Continental makers. Of materials, on the other hand, importations
show an increase. In the first seven months of 1879 we

imported 21,144,765 pounds weight of tanned and dressed hides; in 1880 the quantity had risen to 26,516,269 lbs., and in 1881 to 28,686,360 lbs." Special illustrations.

It further appeared from the speech of Mr. Jackson, M.P., that we import tanned leather to the value of three millions a year, that much of this leather comes from America, and that live cattle come here from America, that they are killed here, that their skins are sent back to America to be tanned, and that they are then sent back here to be used in manufacture. The reason, as I am informed, is not that we do not tan hides as well as the Americans; but that they, adopting newer and rougher methods, do the first part of the process more quickly and cheaply than we do, so that it is worth while to commence tanning in America, and then send back the hides to be completely tanned, and then used, in England. If so, it is a remarkable instance of modern division of labour, and of the advantage of free, cheap, and speedy communication. Free Importation of Foreign Hides.

It would, no doubt, save labour and expense if we could do the whole of the process of tanning as cheaply as the Americans, and it is to be hoped we may learn to do so. But our present system gives us both the finer process of tanning and the manufacture for export as well as for home consumption of cheap boots and shoes; whereas, if we imposed a tax on tanned hides for the supposed benefit of our tanners, we should probably destroy all prospect of improvement in our own tanning, and we should still more probably ruin our manufactures of boots and shoes, and divert it to our foreign rivals. Leather, Tanning and Manufactures of.

In turning to the returns, in which attempts have been made to discriminate between raw materials and manufactures, I find tanned hides inserted among manufactures. And in turning to the tariffs of foreign countries, I find that tanned leather is subject to a duty in France, Germany, Russia, Denmark, Sweden, Norway, Austria, Italy, and the United States. They would become more formidable competitors if they would give to their skilful and ingenious workers in leather the benefit of untaxed hides; but this they dare not do, for fear of their agriculturists.

From the most recent reports, it appears that this branch of English trade continues to be prosperous. The exports of manufactured leather grew very largely until 1882, and have

Special il-
lustrations. since remained large. The imports of raw materials, in the
shape of hides, continue to increase; and though the exports
of boots, shoes, and other manufactured articles were not quite
so large in 1884 as in some previous years, they maintained a
high figure, and appear, by the most recent returns, to be on
the increase.*

### *Salt.*

Salt,
French
duty on. Take, again, salt. Salt enters largely into manufacture.
It is a chief material of alkali, and alkali of glass. France
imposes a heavy duty on salt. In this country it is free and
cheap. We export a large and increasing quantity of alkali
(nearly 7,000,000 cwts. in quantity, and £2,400,000 in value,
in 1880; and somewhat more in quantity, though less in value,
in 1883), and a large and increasing quantity of glass
(£1,000,000 in value in 1880, and more, both in quantity and
value, in 1883), whilst neither alkali nor glass appear among
the principal articles of French export. Chemicals in the
French list may possibly include "alkali," but, if so, I find
that the export of French chemicals increased little, if at all,
in the 10 years ending with 1880, and was then only 56,700,000
francs, whilst the export of English chemicals increased from
£733,422 in 1866 to £2,384,021 in 1880. In this case we
can probably produce salt more cheaply than France, owing to
our geological formations. But she enhances her natural
difficulties by an artificial one.

### *Silk.*

Silk:
French
duty on
Cotton
Yarns. Again, if we take silk, which is a special French manufacture, it appears that France exported to us silk goods,
the produce of her own manufacture, to the amount of $6\frac{1}{4}$
millions sterling in 1860 before the French treaty came
into operation, and to the amount of $10\frac{1}{2}$ millions in 1866,
whilst the amount she exported to us in 1884 was only $3\frac{3}{4}$
millions; and I am informed that this diminution is due to the
protective duty she levies on cotton yarns, which are wanted to
mix with the silk, and which her manufacturers have consequently to pay dear for, whilst her successful rivals in Switzerland get their cotton yarns duty free. This subject has been

* See report in money article of *Times* of 19th January, 1885, and Board of
Trade returns for March, 1885.

lately much mooted in France. The following is an extract from the *Standard* of 31st December, 1884:—"The Lyons silk weavers maintained that many of the yarns could not be obtained elsewhere than in England, and that the competition of their industry with the silk industries of other countries was rendered absolutely impossible owing to the high customs to be paid on this their raw material. The cotton spinners of the northern districts, fancying their interests menaced, lost no time in protesting against the conclusions of the Lyons delegation, and contended that the distress among the weavers of Lyons was as nothing compared with that prevailing in the cotton districts." The remedy suggested by the President of the Lille Chamber of Commerce is very curious. It is to raise the duties on agricultural products, to make food dearer to all classes, and to restrict foreign trade, in order that by this means French agriculturists may grow rich, and become better purchasers of French manufactured goods! In a French official report,* I find that at St. Etienne, where silk ribands are the great manufacture, and where cotton yarns are used as one of the principal materials of the mixed fabrics now in fashion, the value produced has decreased in a few years from 93 to 43 millions of francs; the population has decreased in two years by 25,000; 10,000 hands are out of work; and 30,000 deprived of means of livelihood. In Lyons and its neighbourhood things are little better. Upwards of 100,000 hands are hard hit from the same cause. The exports of silk goods from France, which were worth nearly 500 millions of francs in 1874, were worth less than 300 millions in 1883, and the imports had increased in the same time. Many causes are alleged for this depression in the French silk trade, amongst others the heavy *octroi* duties on articles of consumption, and the heavy national taxation. But the chief permanent cause alleged is the duty on cotton yarns, which is imposed for the purpose of protecting the French cotton spinners of the North. And the remedy proposed is to lower these duties; and also to give a bounty on the export of French ribands! Meanwhile, I find that the exports of silk manufactures from England, which had dropped from a million and a half in 1860 to a million in 1867, rose in 1880 to two millions, and in subsequent years to two millions and a half.

Special illustrations.

* No. 3446 of 1884. Report by M. Laniessant, presented to Chamber of Deputies.

## *Clocks.*

Special illustrations.

Clocks in England and United States.

Take, again, clocks. The American clock manufacturers have for a great many years been the only makers who supplied the rest of the world with ordinary mantel clocks. A large business has been done, especially in those countries, such as England and the British Colonies, whose mantelpieces are used. Until a few years ago they had the field to themselves, when the same goods began to be made in England and Germany. Clocks thus made are gradually pushing the American goods out of the market. The difference in price to day is so large that it is possible to day to deliver some of these goods in America, with the 30 per cent. duty and freight, cheaper than the American goods. This is due to the great expense of American labour, and also of the fine materials of which clocks are made, and which has to pay the enormous American duty. Under these circumstances, American makers are losing the power of exporting, and are even out-sold at home, as is shown by the following figures :—

| Years. | Import of clocks from the United States into the United Kingdom. | Export of clocks and watches (of British produce) from the United Kingdom to the United States. |
|---|---|---|
| | Value.<br>£ | Value.<br>£ |
| 1880 | 153,815 | 29,979 |
| 1881 | 126,466 | 44,431 |
| 1882 | 129,159 | 73,142 |
| 1883 | 112,175 | 83,273 |
| 1884 | 106,914 | Not stated. |

## *Wool and Woollen Goods.*

Woollens in United States.

Take, again, the wool and woollen goods. On them there were in the United States small protective duties before the Civil War. These duties were largely increased during the war, and were so arranged as to give manufacturers of woollen goods compensating duties for the duties on wool; compensating duties for other internal taxation—since repealed; and protective duties in addition. These duties were, at the instance of wool growers and manufacturers, altered in 1867, so as to raise both the compensative and protective duty, and they now amount to from 50 to 100 per cent. on manufactured goods. The following is the practical result, extracted from Taussig's " History of the United States Tariff " ;—

"The most remarkable fact in the history of this piece of  legislation was its failure to secure the object which its supporters had in mind. Notwithstanding the very great degree of protection which the manufacturers got, the production of woollen goods proved to be one of the most unsatisfactory and unprofitable of manufacturing occupations. As a rule, a strong protective measure causes domestic producers to obtain, at least for a time, high profits; though under the ordinary circumstances of free competition profits are sooner or later brought down to the normal level. But in the woollen manufacture even this temporary gain was not secured by the home producers after the Act of 1867. A few branches, such as the production of carpets, of blankets, of certain worsted goods, were highly profitable for some years. These were the branches in which the compensating duties were most excessive, and the prominent manufacturers engaged in them had done most to secure the passage of the Act of 1867. Profits in these branches were, in course of time, brought down to the usual level, and in many instances below the usual level, by the increase of domestic production and domestic competition. The manufacture of the great mass of woollen goods, however, was depressed and unprofitable, even during the years immediately following the Act, notwithstanding the speculative activity and superficial prosperity of that time. Not only then, but throughout the period between 1867 and the present, there can be no doubt that the manufacturers have been steadily complaining, and have steadily found it difficult to make even average profits on their goods. One great cause of this undoubtedly has been that the tariff of 1867 gave particularly high protection on the cheaper and commoner grades of goods, and that domestic producers have been tempted to devote themselves too exclusively to making such goods. The high duty on wool, and the consequent hampering of the manufacturer in the choice of his material, have tended in the same direction. The majority of finer woollen goods are at present imported, and the manufacture in this country is confined chiefly to cheaper grades. The competition in the latter has been keen, and the production greater than the market can easily absorb. The entire absence of foreign competition has at the same time caused the machinery and methods of production in many mills to be backward and inefficient.

"Moreover, the unprosperous state of the manufacture has

Special illustrations.  had a depressing effect on the prices of wool, and on the wool growers. It is often said that the artificial condition of the tariff, in causing the manufacturers to confine themselves chiefly to cheap goods, has prevented the wool growers from obtaining any benefit whatever from the high duties on their material. However this may be, it is certain that the expectations of the wool growers, founded on the Act of 1867, were greatly disappointed. The final result of the existing system has been an increase of cost to consumers, without any permanent benefit to producers." *

Woollen goods.  The exports of woollen manufactures from the United States have been as follows :—

| | Aggregate values exported. | | To the United Kingdom. | | | Aggregate values exported. | | To the United Kingdom. |
|---|---|---|---|---|---|---|---|---|
| 1879 | ... | £72,292 | ... | £2,083 | 1882 | ... | £85,000 | ... | £3,125 |
| 1880 | ... | 45,208 | ... | 2,708 | 1883 | ... | 76,250 | ... | 1,666 |
| 1881 | ... | 68,958 | ... | 3,125 | 1884 | ... | 146,666 | ... | 28,125 |

In *Bradstreet's Journal*, of the 30th December, 1882, I find the following statement : "The New England mills may be said to employ 12,000 fewer hands than in 1882. The woollen industry has suffered for a year or two more than cotton."

Compare with this the account of the English woollen industry, which is neither hampered nor fostered by tariff arrangements.

A competent observer says—

" It is consolatory to be able to turn from the consideration of distressed industries to some which are, upon the whole, prosperous, and in which artisans and operatives are fully employed. One such is the worsted and woollen trade of Yorkshire—more especially of Bradford. It is most gratifying to find in that centre of industry, which was filled with gloom and anxious forebodings a couple of years ago, that the population is now fully employed, and that some machinery is actually standing idle from want of a sufficient supply of skilled operatives to keep it going." +

*         *         *         *         *

This is borne out by the following official returns of exports.

---

* Taussig's " History of the Existing Tariff," chap. iii. p. 65. Putnam, 1885.
† Article by Mr. Williamson, M.P., on Agricultural and Commercial Depression, in the *Fortnightly Review* for January, 1885, p. 77.

<table>
<tr><td rowspan="3">Years.</td><td rowspan="3">Aggregate value exported from the United Kingdom.</td><td colspan="2">Exported to the United States.</td></tr>
<tr><td>Quantity.</td><td>Value.</td></tr>
<tr><td>£</td><td>Yards.</td></tr>
<tr><td>1879</td><td>15,861,166</td><td>33,040,300</td><td>1,572,210</td></tr>
<tr><td>1880</td><td>17,265,177</td><td>40,646,800</td><td>2,530,700</td></tr>
<tr><td>1881</td><td>18,128,756</td><td>32,948,200</td><td>2,227,542</td></tr>
<tr><td>1882</td><td>18,768,634</td><td>42,412,900</td><td>2,859,311</td></tr>
<tr><td>1883</td><td>18,315,575</td><td>44,508,500</td><td>3,015,269</td></tr>
<tr><td>1884</td><td>20,131,252</td><td>41,656,800</td><td>3,144,611</td></tr>
</table>

*Woollen Manufactures Exported from the United Kingdom, 1879—1884, in the aggregate, and to the United States.*

Special illustrations.

### Steel Rails.

Take, again, the case of steel rails. The following is an extract from the same authority as I have quoted above :—*

"During the great demand for railroad materials which began on the revival of business in 1879, and continued for several years thereafter, the prices of steel rails were advanced so high that English rails were imported into the United States even though paying the duty of one hundred per cent. During this time the price in England was on the average, in 1880, about 36 dols. per ton, and in 1881 about 31 dols. per ton. In the United States, during the same years, the price averaged 67 dols. and 61 dols. per ton. That is, consumers in the United States were compelled to pay twice as much for steel rails as they paid in England. Anything which increases the cost of railroad building tends to increase the cost of transportation, and a tax of this kind eventually comes out of the pockets of the people in the shape of higher railroad charges for carrying freight and passengers. The domestic producers of steel rails secured enormous profits of one hundred per cent. and more on their capital during these years. These profits, as is always the case, caused a great extension of production. The men who had made so much money out of Bessemer steel in 1879—1881 put this money very largely into establishments for making more steel. New works were erected in all parts of the country. At the same time the demand fell off in consequence of the check to railroad building, and the increased supply, joined to the small demand, caused prices here to fall almost to the English rates. But during the years

Steel rails in United States.

* Taussig's "History of the United States Tariff," p. 69.

Special il-
lustrations.
Steel rails.

of speculation and railroad building, the tariff had yielded
great gains to makers of steel rails, and popular feeling against
this state of things was so strong that, in 1883, Congress felt
compelled to make a considerable reduction in the duty *—a
reduction, however, which has no practical effect, because the
unnatural increase in production in the United States owing to
the protective duty, and the subsequent decrease in demand,
have lowered the price of steel rails in the United States so
much that the reduced duty is still prohibitory."

The following table shows that the people of the United
States have had to pay to their steel rail manufacturers prices
varying from 30 to 50 per cent. more than has been paid in
England.

*Product, Imports, and Foreign and Domestic Prices in Dollars of
Bessemer Steel Rails.*

| Year. | Product in United States.[1] | Imports into United States.[1] | Average Price in United States.[2] | Average Price in England.[2] | Average Difference in Price. |
|---|---|---|---|---|---|
| 1871 | 38,300 | Not given. | 91·70 | 57·70 | 34·00 |
| 1872 | 94,000 | 150,000 | 99·70 | 67·30 | 32·40 |
| 1873 | 129,000 | 160,000 | 95·90 | 74·40 | 21·50 |
| 1874 | 145,000 | 101,000 | 84·70 | 57·50 | 27·20 |
| 1875 | 291,000 | 18,000 | 59·70 | 44·10 | 15·60 |
| 1876 | 412,000 | none. | 53·10 | 37·70 | 15·40 |
| 1877 | 432,000 | ,, | 43·50 | 31·90 | 11·60 |
| 1878 | 550,000 | ,, | 41·70 | 27·20 | 14·50 |
| 1879 | 684,000 | 25,000 | 48·20 | 24·70 | 23·50 |
| 1880 | 954,000 | 158,000 | 67·50 | 36·00 | 31·50 |
| 1881 | 1,330,000 | 249,000 | 61·10 | 31·20 | 29·90 |
| 1882 | 1,438,000 | 182,000 | 48·50 | 30·00 | 18·50 |
| 1883 | 1,286,000 | 38,220 | 37·75 | 25·40 | 12·35 |
| 1884 (Jan.) | — | — | 34·00 | 21·80 | 12·20 |

[1] In net tons of 2,000 lbs.　　　　[2] Price per gross ton of 2,240 lbs.†

The exports of steel rails from the United States are very
small, varying in values from £1,000 to £24,000 a year.

### Copper.

Copper in
United
States.

Take again the case of copper.

The following is a further extract from Taussig's "History
of the United States Tariff" :—

* Taussig, chap. iii. pp. 69, 70　　　　† *Ibid.*, p. 107.

"Before 1869 the duty on copper ore had been 5 per cent.; that on copper in bars and ingots had been two and a half cents per pound. Under the very low duty on copper ore, a large industry had grown up in Boston and Baltimore. Ore was imported from Chili, and was smelted and refined in these cities. But during the years immediately preceding 1869 the great copper mines of Lake Superior had begun to be worked on a considerable scale. These mines are probably the richest sources of copper in the world, and, under normal circumstances, would supply the United States with this metal more cheaply and abundantly than any other country; yet, through our Tariff policy, these very mines have caused us for many years to pay more for our copper than any other country. The increased production from these mines, with other circumstances, had caused copper to fall in price in 1867 and 1868, and their owners came before Congress and asked for an increase of duties. Copper ore was to pay three cents for each pound of pure copper, equal to twenty-five or thirty per cent., in place of the previous duty of five per cent., and ingot copper was to pay five cents per pound instead of two and a half cents. A more open use of legislation for the benefit of private individuals has probably never been made. The effect of the Act was, in the first place, to destroy the smelting establishments which had treated the Chilian ores. In the second place, it enabled the copper producers at home to combine, and to settle the price of their product without being checked by any possible foreign competition. It is a well-known fact that the mining companies of Lake Superior, which controlled, until within a year or two, almost the entire pro-duction of copper in the United States, have maintained for many years a combination for fixing the price of copper. Their price has been steadily higher than the price of copper abroad, and when they have found it impossible to dispose of all their product at home at the combination price, large quantities have been sent abroad, and sold there at lower prices, in order to relieve the home market. Several of these companies have paid for a series of years enormous profits—profits due in part, no doubt, to the unsurpassed richness of their mines, but in part also to the Copper Act of 1869." *

Compare with this account an account of the copper trade

* Taussig's "History of the Existing Tariff," ch. iii. p. 65.

in England, by the same competent authority I have referred to before *—

"The copper trade all through the late period of depression has been well maintained. If copper smelters have not been exceedingly prosperous—owing, perhaps, to the rapid and steady decline in the price of copper—their works and their men have at least been fully occupied, and their industry has grown of late by leaps and bounds. It may be of interest to give a few figures relating to the copper trade. The following have been the deliveries to smelters and others of foreign copper, consisting of copper ores, half smelted copper, and bars, at the ports of London, Swansea, and Liverpool, stated in tons of pure copper—

| 1880 | ... | ... | 64,451 tons. | 1882 | ... | ... | 67,382 tons. |
|------|-----|-----|--------------|------|-----|-----|--------------|
| 1881 | ... | ... | 63,397 ,, | 1883 | ... | ... | 73,394 ,, |

1884, up to 15th December, 84,441 tons, which may be taken *pro rata* for the twelve months as 88,112 ,,

"The supply from the Cornish mines has fallen off very markedly during the last quarter of a century, and must ere long become extinct, not from failure of the ores, but because the mines cannot be worked in competition with rich copper mines abroad. The following *data* may be interesting. In the year 1800 the produce of British mines forming the entire supply was 11,500 tons pure copper. In 1832, the year before any foreign copper was imported, the total had only risen to 11,941 tons pure copper. In 1833, foreign ores from Cuba and Chili were imported to a limited extent, but smelters had to give bond to re-export the copper product within six months, and were on that account often forced to sell for France at £5, or even £10, per ton under the price which they were getting in Birmingham. These fetters and restrictions were swept away with the Navigation Laws, and ever since the copper trade has increased rapidly, and continues to grow marvellously. The Cornwall and other British copper mines attained their maximum importance in 1856, when they yielded 13,275 tons of pure copper. In 1862 the production had fallen to 11,268 tons; 1875 production gave only 3,370 tons, 1880 gave only 2,783 tons, 1883 gave 2,526 tons, and 1884 only 2,410 tons. It results, therefore, that our copper industry, which half a century ago was fed entirely by the

---

* Article by Mr. Williamson, *Fortnightly*, Jan., 1885.

produce of our own mines, and which was established solely to  utilise that produce, came, through the operation of unrestricted commerce, to be fed in 1884 as follows, viz.—

" From the home sources of supply with    ...    2,416 tons.
From foreign sources with..    ...    ...    ...    88,112    „

" Who can doubt but that the operation of our unrestricted commercial policy has been, in regard to this great industry, of the most beneficent character? Yet the ruined British copper miners might have called out in past years as lustily as some British landowners are now doing for inquiries in order to make good a demand for protective duties. Had such a demand been granted to the copper miners of Cornwall, the copper trade might have been strangled, and the development of this important industry in England might never have obtained the pre-eminence it enjoys."

The exports of British copper amount in value to three millions and a half, and are increasing. The following Table, extracted from Taussig's " History of the United States Tariff," shows that during the last ten years the British consumer has had the benefit of the Free Tariff in a price of copper varying from one-third to one-seventh less than the price charged to the consumers of the United States by their privileged manufacturers.

*Production of Copper in the United States, and Foreign and Domestic Price.*

(Quantities in gross tons.)

| Year. | Domestic Production. | Price per lb. in Cents. | | Difference in Price. |
| --- | --- | --- | --- | --- |
| | | New York Lake Copper. | London Chili Bars. | |
| 1875 | 18,000 | 23·0 | 18·0 | 5·0 |
| 1876 | 19,000 | 21·5 | 16·5 | 5·0 |
| 1877 | 21,000 | 19·0 | 14·6 | 4·4 |
| 1878 | 21,500 | 16·5 | 13·5 | 3·0 |
| 1879 | 23,000 | 17·5 | 12·2 | 5·3 |
| 1880 | 27,000 | 20·0 | 13·5 | 6·5 |
| 1881 | 32,000 | 18·5 | 13·3 | 5·2 |
| 1882 | 41,000 | 18·7 | 14·4 | 4·3 |
| 1883 | 52,000 | 16·1 | 13·7 | 2·4 |
| 1884 | 6 mos. | 14·5 | 12·1 | 2·4 |

Considering the great advantages the United States possess in their copper mines, this is a very striking instance of the way in which freedom operates to produce a healthy trade to the producer and low price to the consumer, whilst protection has an opposite effect.

### *Biscuits.*



In the following chapter I have dealt at length with the subject of sugar. But two recent incidents may here be mentioned. France, as is well known, has recently imposed duties on corn and flour. In the course of the discussions on the measure, the manufacturers of biscuits and semolina complained that they would be injured by the tax on their raw material. French made semolina and biscuits were therefore protected by a considerable duty. French consumers will have to eat dear biscuits, and French biscuit makers will be unable to export.

Again, in the recent discussions on the Belgian sugar duties, the Belgian makers of jam, confectionery and biscuits sought for a drawback of the taxes which the Government were imposing on sugar, but were refused. England admits flour and sugar free. Her manufacture of jams and preserves is becoming an important trade, and she is supplying the world with biscuits.

### *Wire.*



Again, there have been loud complaints amongst our wire makers of the successful competition of foreign wire, and it has been said to be due to the excessive charges of English railways on the article when used at home. Thinking there must be some other reason, I applied to one of the telegraph construction companies, and learned from them that they bought German wire because it was better and cheaper; but that German competition had stimulated our own manufactures; that English made telegraph wire was much improved; and that they now give large orders to English makers. There is now a considerable export of telegraph wire. Telegraph construction is an important new branch of English manufacture; and if we had protected English made wire by a customs duty on foreign wire, we should probably have driven this manufacture to Germany.

# CHAPTER XXXVI.

## SUGAR.

Sugar claims a chapter to itself. From the time when the word, thrice uttered by the imperious voice of the first Pitt, cowed a tittering House of Commons into silence, it has occupied a prominent place in politics. It has been an important factor in the development of our Colonial Empire, in the struggles for the abolition of slavery, and in the controversies which have established and crowned Free Trade. Even at this moment, it attracts much attention from financiers and economists. The accident of bounties on foreign sugar, themselves an undoubted outrage on economic laws, give to the Protectionists an opportunity of masquerading as Free Traders in assailing bounties, and under this guise they seek, whilst advocating retaliation, to betray an outpost of Free Trade where they dare not attack the citadel. We are told that our present free admission of beet sugar is ruining the future of our own market ; that it is destroying cane sugar ; that it is alienating our colonies ; committees of the House of Commons advise retaliation ; statesmen seek for inquiry ; and agitators tell English workmen that they are deprived by foreign countries of 15 millions a year in work and wages. These suggestions and statements are for the most part not only not true ; they are the reverse of the truth. But it is worth while to examine the whole subject as carefully as my limits will allow, for the purpose of seeing, not only what modicum of truth there is in some of them, but what light the case throws on the economical laws we have been discussing.

Independently of the great political and social questions with which sugar has been connected, it possesses an economical and social importance of its own which it is difficult to exaggerate. The total production and consumption of the world is enormous ; though exact figures cannot be given. There are some countries in which the quantity is not precisely known, but is known to be very large. India, for instance, which exports little, has been estimated to pro-

M

Sugar.

duce and consume 2,000,000 tons or upwards. But omitting these countries, and taking those only whose production is accurately known, the present annual production of the world is estimated at more than 4,000,000 tons, which at £20 a ton would be worth £80,000,000. It also increases very largely. In 1855 the production of these same countries was less than 1,500,000 tons.* Further, the increase has taken place in cane

The supply is both of cane and beet sugar

sugar as well as in beet sugar. Thus the known total of cane sugar has increased from about 1,200,000 tons in 1853–1856 to upwards of 2,000,000 tons in 1882, whilst that of beet sugar increased in the same time from 200,000 tons to 1,780,000 tons.

Raised in all countries and climates.

This crop is raised in every quarter of the world, in every climate, and almost every country grows an increasing quantity. France, Germany, Austria, Hungary, Holland, Belgium, and Russia, Egypt, India, China, the Dutch and Spanish East Indies, Australia, Mauritius, the United States, the West Indies, and South America, all contribute to the enormous total. Between cane and beet there are few climates or soils which do not and cannot produce sugar. If ever there was an article of which the producing market is an open one, a market which cannot be closed or contracted by any ring or combination, it is sugar.

England's share as compared with other countries.

Of the supplies thus produced (again excluding India, China, and other countries of which the production is not known), England, though producing none herself, consumes the largest proportion. In 1883, the last year for which complete and final statistics are published, after deducting nearly 100,000 tons of re-exported sugar, of which more than half was refined in this country, her whole share was 1,083,000 tons, or about 68 lbs. per head of the population. This at £30 a ton, which, after taking into account expenses of manufacture and distribution, is probably not too high a figure, represents an annual expenditure of £30,000,000, or about half the sum which the people of the United Kingdom pay for wheat,† when wheat is at or under 40s. a quarter. At the same time the price has much diminished. In 1841 the average consumption per head of the population was 16·99 lbs., at an average price per cwt. of 63s. 5¾d., the wholesale value of the 16·99 lbs. per head; being therefore

* See *Produce Markets Review*, 28th June, 1884, and Parl. Paper, No. 325, of 1884.

† Parl. Paper 325, 1884, p. 9.

9s. 7½d.* In 1883 the estimated consumption per head was 68·1 lbs., at an average cost per head of 12s. 10d., or nearly four times the quantity to each person at only one-third more cost. In 1884 the quantities were about the same, but the price was about one-fifth less, making the cost per head in 1884 about 10s. 4d., against 9s. 7½d. for one-fourth of the quantity consumed in 1841.

It is worth while to observe in passing, that this result has been attained in a period in the course of which slavery has been abolished. This enormous increase in production and reduction of price is a consequent on the employment of labour which is free, and which, measured by the rate of wages, is comparatively costly.

Other countries have, of course, benefited, but far less than England. The United States is the next largest consumer. Her total consumption is 1,076,000 tons, or 50 lbs. per head of the population, and the price her people pay for it is estimated at 80 per cent. of the price they pay for their wheat, out of which price more than one-fourth is paid in the form of a protective duty, thus raising the price to the consumer by more than a third over that paid in England. During the last year, an Englishman has been paying about 2d., or 4 cents for a pound of good sugar, whilst, as we are told, a citizen of the United States has been paying 7 cents, or 3½d. France is estimated to consume 28 lbs. per head, and Germany 15 lbs. per head of her population,† both of these being countries which produce good beet sugar at the cheapest possible rates, but which, by their fiscal systems, prevent their own people from using it freely. What the exact prices to the retail purchaser in each country may be it is very difficult to tell, for there are sugars and sugars, and prices as well as qualities vary infinitely, according to circumstances. But it is quite certain that in each country the price to the consumer is raised by the whole amount of the duty, and probably by more. An investigation into the quality and price of the sugar retailed in Germany appears to show that where the English people pay 2d., 2½d., and 3d. a lb. for good sugar, the Germans pay nearly twice those sums for sugars of an inferior quality. The German housekeeper who wishes to sweeten her tea or to cook the sweet dishes in which Germans excel, has to pay at least twice as much for an

*Sugar*

*Share of the United States, France, and Germany.*

* Porter's Progress of the Nation.
† *Bradstreet's*, 28th March, 1885.   Parl. Paper 325, 1884. p. 41.

M 2

Sugar.

inferior article as her English sister.*  Germany is the country which shows the greatest skill in the production of sugar, which has advanced its manufacture to the highest point, adds comforts and luxuries to the life of the English workman, but does not allow its own poor and industrious people to enjoy the fruits of their own industry.  "Sic vos non vobis mellificatis apes!"  How this comes to pass we shall see presently.

It is food.

Considering that sugar has become an article of food, or of luxury, if you will, in which the poor share, not unequally, with the rich; which makes other food palatable and wholesome; and which women and children enjoy no less than men, the advantage of such a result as I have described to the toiling millions of the United Kingdom is no small matter.  But this result is not all.  The enormously increased supply of sugar has brought to them also increased employment and wages.

It gives employment.

The actual trade in the increase of quantity consumed has itself added large and profitable employment to our ships, to our railways, to our merchants and their clerks, to our refiners, and to our shopkeepers.  The amount thus expended on English labour in 1883 on the increased quantity of sugar used in that year, over and above the amount expended on similar labour in 1863, has been estimated by the authority mentioned below at £5,500,000.†

It is also raw material.

Nor is this all.  The whole of the sugar imported does not go into direct consumption, but becomes the raw material of various manufactures.  There is, of course, the refining, an increasing trade, of which I shall say more below.  But besides refining, there are a number of subsidiary manufactures depending on sugar, which are largely on the increase, and which are more important than refining.  Of these the largest is probably the manufacture of jams and confectionery, which is dependent on a cheap supply of refined sugar, and for which certain descriptions of *foreign refined* sugar are specially suitable.  We know that in London about 45,000 tons are used in the jam and confectionery business, employing from 5,000 to 6,000 persons; and the returns of this manufacture in Scotland show not much less.  More than 100,000 tons are employed in the United Kingdom in this business alone, and more than 12,000 hands,

---

* *Produce Markets Review*, p. 376, 28th June, 1884.
† For details see *Produce Markets Review*, 15th March, 1884.

which is more than twice the number of hands employed in sugar refining. This, it is to be remembered, is a manufacture which supplies a cheap and wholesome luxury to the poor, and which calls into existence other industries, such as fruit growing, which are themselves of great importance to the country. Other industries, such as the making of biscuits, with which we supply the world, and of mineral waters, brewing, and cattle feeding, also depend largely on sugar. Cheap and good sugar is a very important raw material.*

The importance to the nation of our cheap and plentiful supply of sugar it is therefore difficult to exaggerate. How have we managed to obtain it? The answer is very simple, viz., by opening our ports and receiving freely what our neighbours have offered us. But as our Protectionist friends wish us to reverse this policy, it is worth while to consider the point a little more carefully.

Sugar, considered as an article of general consumption, and, also, though the word is misleading, as an article of luxury, has been a favourite object of taxation; the more so, perhaps, because originally it was an article produced in foreign and distant countries. But even then much of it was refined in Europe, and this raised a difficulty. It has always been the practice where any article has paid duty, and has undergone a process of manufacture, to give back the duty on its being re-exported, under the name of "drawback." When the article exported can be recognised as the same article which has paid duty, this is a simple thing to do. But when the article has undergone a change since it paid duty, a calculation is necessary in order that the amount actually paid, no more and no less, may be restored as drawback. Thus an import duty was paid on raw sugar; it was refined in the country of import; and some of the refined sugar was re-exported. It became then a problem for the Governments of Europe to discover what was the relation of a given quantity of refined sugar to the raw sugar from which it was made, so as to determine what was the amount of duty to be repaid. This proved to be a very difficult problem, and the difficulty was much increased when European nations began to make sugar from beet, and when the problem was to determine not only the relation of raw sugar to refined sugar, but the relation of sugar,

* See *Produce Markets Review*, 26th July, 1884. Parl. Paper 325, 1884, p. 12, and Appendix thereto.

*Sugar.*

raw or refined, to the original material of which it was made. The Governments were in a dilemma. If they gave as drawback on the manufactured article less than had been paid on the raw material, they were burdening their manufacturers with a tax which discouraged exportation. If they gave more, they were giving a bounty on exportation, and were thus artificially raising the price to their own citizens, and lowering it to foreigners, by means of money drawn from the pockets of their own taxpayers. Beset by these embarrassments, the Governments of Europe, our own among the rest, floundered on for years. By conference after conference, by measure after measure, they endeavoured to hit the right mean; and generally speaking, the special trade, as is usual in such cases, got the better of the public, and secured to itself some bounty in the way of drawback. This was the state of things in 1863, and in this country a graduated scale of duties and drawbacks was established and sanctioned by International Convention in

*Reduction and final repeal in England of sugar duties.*

1864. At last, after the duties had been twice halved by successive Governments, they were wholly abolished in 1874. The results are as follow :—The consumption of the country was 473,000 tons in 1863 ; it was 1,083,000 tons in 1883. The exports had doubled also. The average cost of sugar to the

*Results.*

grocers was 41s. per cwt. in 1863 ; it was 23s. 3d. in 1883. This reduction consisted of the duty, which was 12s. 6d., and in addition of 5s. 1½d., or more than ½d. a lb. saved by increased demand and improved supply.* According to the official statistics, we paid for sugar imported, including duty, 18½ millions in 1863, whilst in 1883 we paid about 25 millions, and in 1884 we paid about 20 millions for twice the quantity, Sir Stafford Northcote removed a very troublesome tax, which brought into the revenue less than 6½ millions in 1863, and only about 3¼ millions in 1873, and in so doing he has saved the country from 12 to 17 millions in the price of sugar, as imported, and much more on sugar as retailed ; and he has vastly increased and improved the food of the people, besides encouraging many native industries.

Other nations have not been wise or rich enough to follow the same course. They all levy a considerable duty on sugar ; most of them make these duties differential in favour of their own manufacturers or colonists ; and many of them have so

---

* From the *Produce Markets Review*, 15th of March 1884.

arranged their drawbacks as to give their own manufacturers or Sugar. refiners a bounty on exported sugar. To give the history or details of these duties, "surtaxes," and bounties, or drawbacks, in detail, would be impossible, and they may be found in the various Parliamentary Papers.* But the following few facts are worth notice.

Germany imposes a tax of 12 marks per centner (about a cwt.) on raw sugar imported.† She also imposes a tax on the beet used in manufactures, estimated to be equal to ten marks per centner on the manufactured raw sugar; and a drawback, formerly of 9·40 marks, but now of 9 marks, is repaid on each centner of exported raw sugar. But by improvements in the growth of beet, and in the process of manufacture, much more sugar is produced from the given quantity of beet than the quantity it was estimated to produce, and the manufacturer, consequently, on exporting sugar, receives upon the excess a drawback or bounty which he has never paid as duty on the beet. What the amount of this bounty may be it is impossible to say with accuracy, for it varies with the skill and success of the grower and manufacturer. The average bounty has been variously estimated—from one shilling, or less, per cwt., to two or three times that amount; but the recent German Committee estimated the maximum at 1·40 marks per centner, or about 1s. 5d. per cwt. Under this system the German production has increased five-fold since 1871, and was, in 1883, 835,164,600 kilos. Of this, three-fifths was exported and two-fifths only consumed in the country. Of the total exports, amounting to 472,551,400 kilos., between three-fifths and four-fifths were exported to Great Britain. The Government have, in paying this bounty, lost what is estimated to amount to upwards of a million sterling of revenue which they would have received if the drawback had been equivalent, and not more than equivalent, to the duty. The German Government, alive to the loss, appointed last year a Committee of Experts to inquire into the subject, who found that the drawback was too large, and recommended a reduction; and a Bill was introduced for this purpose, but has not been pressed owing to the prevalent distress among German beet growers and sugar manufacturers. The effect of this system is very curious. That the Germans,

*marginal note:* German Tax and Drawback.

---

* See especially 317 and 422 of 1881, 325 of 1884, and 30 of 1885.
† Parl. Paper 39, December, 1884, p. 37, Report by Mr. Scott, Secretary to the German Embassy, on German Bounties.

Sugar.
German
tax and
drawback.

as taxpayers, lose, is clear; the Germans, as sugar consumers, do not gain, for the wholesale German price is regulated by the English market, and is exactly what the Englishman pays, with the whole drawback added. Where the English wholesale purchaser pays 12 marks per cwt. the German pays 21, an addition which is probably doubled before the sugar reaches the actual consumer; and we have already seen how comparatively dear and poor is his supply. But mark the further result: the German beet grower and sugar manufacturer, who probably gained much at first, is now at least as much distressed as our own refiners. Mr. Scott tells us that present prices admit of no profit; and that many manufacturers are working at a loss in hopes of a rise. The critical position of many of the German factories is notorious; but the best evidence of the distress is that the frugal German Government, though really anxious to abolish bounties, dare not at this moment proceed with the measure which their experts have recommended. In fact there has been a glut in the sugar trade, much aggravated by the foolish system of bounties, and whilst English consumers have benefited by the low price, none have, in the end, suffered more than the class of manufacturers whom it seemed *primâ facie* to benefit.

It should be added that the German exports of refined sugar have not increased in the same proportion as those of raw sugar. In 1882 they were 17·6 per cent. of her total exports of sugar, and in 1883 only 15·7 per cent. Her refiners, Mr. Scott's report tells us, cannot compete successfully with our own.*

Austro-
Hungary.

Austro-Hungary levies her duties on an estimate of the quantity of sugar contained in the vessels used in manufacture. A few years since, this estimate was so much too large as to give a large bounty on exportation, and Austria led the way in the race of ruin. She has since revised her estimate, and has fallen far behind Germany in exports. But not the less have her manufactures felt the recent glut and the reaction from the unnatural stimulus; and bankruptcies and failures among Austrian sugar makers have been notorious during the past year.

France.

France revised her system some years since, with the view of putting an end to bounties, and, though her production has increased rapidly, her exports have diminished. Frightened by

* Parl. Paper 39 of 1885, pp. 43 and 44.

the progress of Germany, and by the distress of her beet Sugar
growers and sugar makers, France last year revised her
sugar taxation. She raised her duty on home-grown sugar;
she increased the differential duties on foreign sugars; she
adopted the system of taxing beet as the raw material; and
purposely gave a heavy drawback on export. It is too
early to say what the actual result is, but it may be confidently
predicted that her measures will, if they have the effect contemplated, throw an additional burden on her exhausted
exchequer, and raise the price of sugar to her own consumers
and manufacturers.

Belgium, which has largely increased her exportation in late Belgium
years, has been also perplexed by the distress of her sugar
interest, and, after an inquiry into her mode of taxation, has
proposed a new law. She disapproves of bounties, and will not
extend them; nor will she substitute for her present system of
taxing the juice expressed from beet the German plan of taxing
the root itself. But she is imposing an increased differential
duty on foreign sugar. It deserves notice that the Belgian
makers of jams, confectionery, and biscuits, whose English
rivals have, as we have seen, profited so largely by the cheap
sugar of England, have petitioned their Government, but in vain,
for a drawback on exportation of the taxed sugar they use in
their manufacture.

Holland, which taxes her sugar by a process of sac- Holland.
charimetry, or chemical measurement of the quantity of sugar
contained in the juice, has recently revised her method. She
is said to give a considerable bounty, and has largely increased
her exports.

Nor are European countries alone in giving artificial protec- United
tion to sugar. The United States levy a protective duty of States.
from 12s. 10d. to 14s. per cwt. on foreign sugars. Brazil Brazil.
guarantees a high rate of interest on the capital employed in
sugar making, with the result that at present prices ruin is
impending over her sugar factories.*

The legislature of one of our most flourishing colonies— New
New Zealand—has recently passed an Act granting a professed Zealand.
bounty of one halfpenny per pound on the first thousand tons
of beetroot or sorghum sugar produced in the colony, besides
providing that no excise duty on sugar shall be levied so long

* Parl Paper 39, 1884, p. 29.

*Sugar.*

as the existing import duty of one halfpenny per pound continues in force ; and that if that duty be at any time increased, the excise duty leviable shall always be one halfpenny per pound less. Further, should the import duty be reduced, a sum per pound produced equal to the amount of the reduction is to be paid to home producers who may be tempted, by this Act, to embark in the industry.

*General action of Foreign Governments.*

For further details upon the action of Foreign Governments in the matter of sugar, I must refer to the Parliamentary Papers, 325, 1884, and 39, 1885. One or two points are clear from what I have stated. Foreign governments are all floundering in the difficulties from which we, by abandoning all taxation of sugar, have happily emerged. Most of them have imposed intentionally protective duties on foreign sugars; many give bounties on export; which, however, except in the case of France, are unintentional. All of them raise the price of sugar to their own consumers ; and those which give bounties cheapen it to foreigners. Above all, in all these countries, however much manufacture and export may have increased, there is great distress among the protected classes. Protection and bounties have produced their usual results, viz., an unnatural stimulus, and large immediate profits, followed by a glut, collapse, and ruin.

*Imports of sugar from, and exports of manufactures to Germany, Holland and Belgium.*

One other point deserves notice. If there are any countries of whose bounty-fed competition our sugar refiners and West Indian interests have complained, they are Germany, Holland, and Belgium. It is these countries, if any, which have displaced the labour of the English workman. We have already seen, in the account above given of the trades set in action by our increased sugar supply, how absurd this assertion is. But there is another answer, and, if not a mere coincidence, it is a curious illustration of the Free Trade maxim, "Take care of the imports, and the exports will take care of themselves." Our imports of sugar from Germany, Holland, and Belgium have been as follows :—

|  |  |  |  |  |  | Value. |
|---|---|---|---|---|---|---|
| 1880 | .. | .. | .. | .. | .. | £7,264,000 |
| 1881 | .. | .. | .. | .. | .. | 8,369,000 |
| 1882 | .. | .. | .. | .. | .. | 7,295,000 |
| 1883 | .. | .. | .. | .. | .. | 10,412,000 |

Showing an increase of about three millions. Our total exports of British and Irish produce to these countries have been as follows :—

|  |  |  |  |  |  | Value. | Sugar |
|---|---|---|---|---|---|---|---|
| 1880 | .. | .. | .. | .. | .. | .. £31,986,000 |  |
| 1881 | .. | .. | .. | .. | .. | .. 33,406,000 |  |
| 1882 | .. | .. | .. | .. | .. | .. 35,978,000 |  |
| 1883 | .. | .. | .. | .. | .. | .. 36,622,000 |  |

Showing an increase of about four millions and a half. Thus the increased import of sugar has been more than balanced by a proportionate export of our own manufactures, which must have given employment to an increased number of our own workmen employed on those manufactures.

So far as we have gone, there is certainly nothing in the present state of the sugar trade which should make us desire to imitate the systems of other nations. We are nevertheless asked to do so by two very importunate interests, viz., the sugar refiners of this country, and the English owners of West India sugar estates. Their cases are inconsistent, for it is the interest of the refiners to have cheap raw sugar, and it is the interest of the West India planters that raw sugar should be dear. But they unite in urging retaliation against foreign sugar bounties. Let us see first what their wrongs are, and then what are their proposed remedies.

First, as to the refiners. It is alleged that the foreign bounties are destroying this important trade; and agitators circulate the preposterous assertion that the British workman is thus deprived of 15 millions annually in wages. Now what are the facts. It was shown in 1881* that since 1864 the refining trade of this country had lost about 50,000 tons of loaf sugar; but had gained 30,000 tons of other sorts of hard sugar, and 300,000 of moist sugar.† The quantity of sugar refined at home has increased since 1880 from 653,000 tons to 816,000 tons; and the number of men employed in it has also increased considerably. The importation of foreign refined sugar did not increase between 1877 and 1883, being 171,000 tons in 1877, 152,000 tons in 1880, and 162,000 tons in 1883; in 1884 it was 210,000 tons. The exports of refined sugar from the United Kingdom have increased, being 56,000 tons in 1877, 48,000 tons in 1880, 58,000 in 1883, and 65,000 tons in 1884. These are not figures of a declining trade. But it is at the best a comparatively small trade, and the capital employed in it does not probably attain £3,000,000. It is, whether as regards capital or workmen employed, a trade of far less

Importuni-
ties of sugar
refiners and
West
Indian
planters.

Refiner's
case.

---

* Parl. Paper 317 and 422, of 1881.   † Parl. Paper 325, of 1884.

Sugar.

importance than the subsidiary trades mentioned above which cheap refined sugar has called into existence, and for some of which foreign refined sugar has special advantages.    In addition, there are, as we have seen, larger exports of other British produce called into existence in order to pay for the imported sugar.    Looking to the interest of the workman considered as a producer only, and putting aside his still more important interest as a consumer of sugar, it would be simple madness to exclude foreign refined sugar in the supposed interest of British refiners.

Case of West Indian planters.

The case of the West India sugar planters is one deserving of more sympathy.    They have no doubt been deprived, by the competition of beet sugar, of the proportion of the market of the United Kingdom which without such competition they might have expected to enjoy, and some part of this competition is no doubt due to foreign bounties.    But their statements are grossly exaggerated.    It is alleged, for instance, that the increase of beet sugar is entirely due to the bounty system.

Causes of growth of beet sugar.

This is contrary to the evidence which has been taken abroad, and which shows that the growth of beet is largely due to agricultural improvement in France and Germany, as well as to energy and skill in manufacture, and that it is intimately connected with improvements in the growth and feeding of cattle. It is, moreover, inconsistent with existing facts, as shown by the official statistics.    Only a part of the beet sugar produced is bounty-fed.    In some countries, *e.g.*, in France there has in late years been no bounty, and yet the production increases rapidly.    It is only on the sugar exported that a bounty can possibly be paid, and this is only 700,000 tons out of a total of beet sugar production of about 2,000,000 tons.

Restriction of the market impossible.

Another allegation is that bounty-fed sugar will, when it has driven all other sugar out of the market, become a virtual monopoly, that it will then rise in price, and that consumers will accordingly then suffer all the inconveniences of a restricted market.    The allegation scarcely needs refutation.    Much of the supply of beet sugar, as shown above, is not bounty-fed ; and cane sugar, as shown below, is not being driven out of the market.    Moreover, with such diversified area of production as I have shown to exist, there is probably no article in the world, not even wheat, in which it would be equally impossible to create any kind of monopoly or to raise prices unduly.

Another allegation is that cane sugar is being supplanted by beet—an allegation which is utterly untrue. British cane sugar has increased from 261,000 tons per annum in 1853-5, to 419,000 tons per annum in 1880-2 and in the same time foreign cane sugar has increased from 972,000 to 1,500,000 tons, though beet sugar has increased in a much larger proportion. British cane sugar has ever since 1868 maintained its proportion of the total supply of sugar—viz., 12 per cent. Comparing 1877-9 with 1880-2, the increase of West Indian sugar has been from 210,000 to 230,000 tons annually. The proportion of cane sugar imported into the United Kingdom has largely declined, and the actual amount of British cane sugar so imported has somewhat decreased; but the increased supply of that sugar has been diverted to North American and Australian markets.

Nor is there any reason to despair of the future of cane sugar. Skill and industry have done their utmost in growth and manufacture of beet, whilst much remains to be done to extract completely the much larger quantity of sugar contained in the cane. This, at least, is the opinion of many experienced persons, and among them of Mr. Baden Powell, and of Mr. Newton, President of the Chamber of Agriculture in the Mauritius, a colony second only to the West Indies in the production of cane sugar. In a remarkable paper, which has just been laid before Parliament, he exhorts his countrymen, who, in common with other sugar producers, are suffering from present low prices, to abandon all hope of Protective remedies, and to trust cheerfully to improved production.*

The case and prospects of the West India planters are therefore not so bad as has been stated; not worse, probably, at the present moment, than those of protected sugar producers in Foreign countries. There has been a general glut, and they, in common with others, have suffered. If they can retain their share of the North American market; and if, above all, as much skill and energy can be put into their manufacture as is put into the manufacture of beet sugar by France and Germany, there is no reason why they should not have a prosperous future. At the moment when I write the price of sugar is rising.†

But the case of the West Indian planters is open to one or two further observations.

Sugar.<br>Is cane being supplanted by beet?

---

* Parl. Paper c. 4455 of 1883.     † See *Times* of 28th May, 1883.

Sugar.
Planters interest and Colonial interest not identical.

It would be a mistake, at any rate as regards Jamaica, to treat the sugar interest as identical with that of the whole people. The interest is rather that of English capital. The black population have other employments and other interests.

West India sugar a comparatively small interest

In the second place, the West India sugar interest is a small interest compared with that of the consuming classes in England. The annual value of the whole of the sugar produced in the West Indies is probably under £5,000,000, as compared with £25,000,000 which was the declared value of the sugar imported into the United Kingdom in 1883. According to the representations of the West India sugar interest (which are no doubt exaggerations), the reduction in price of the sugar consumed in the United Kingdom due to foreign bounties is over £5,000,000. So that for the purpose of a small increase in their revenue, they ask us to sacrifice a sum which is more than equal to the whole of their production.

They have no case for change of our fiscal system.

Under these circumstances, whilst admitting that the West India sugar interests are suffering from the fiscal systems of other countries, though to a much less extent than has been supposed, they have no case for any remedy which would injuriously affect the much larger interests of consumers in the United Kingdom.

Remedies suggested by them.

It remains to consider very shortly the remedies suggested by the refiners and the West India interests. These consist in retaliation by means of duties to be imposed on bounty-fed sugars. It might be sufficient to refer to what has been said above as to retaliatory duties in general. All the arguments against retaliation in the case of protective duties apply to retaliation against bounties. Protective duties are even more injurious to the interests of this country than bounties, since they operate no less than bounties to the disadvantage of our producers; whilst, unlike bounties, they confer no benefit on our consumers. Both alike limit our means of selling; but foreign bounties give us the means of buying cheap, which foreign duties do not.

But there are some special considerations affecting retaliation against bounties, and against these bounties in particular.

What are bounties?

If we begin by retaliating against bounties, we must ask what is meant by the term. Canada and all new countries make grants of land to emigrants. Is this a bounty on corn growing? The Indian Government subsidize railways. Is this as some of our agriculturists are now alleging, a bounty on Indian wheat?   Brazil guarantees interest on capital invested in sugar factories, and New Zealand gives them special encouragement.   Are all these bounties, and are they to be assailed by retaliatory duties?   If so, what are the retaliatory duties to be, and where are they to stop? Sugar.

In the next place, what is the exact amount of the duty to be?   It is intended to neutralize the bounty, neither more nor less.   If it does more, it is plain Protection; if less, it does not answer its purpose.   But no one has the least conception what the bounty in any case is.   It differs in every country; on every parcel of sugar.   No two opinions agree about it in any one case.   To determine the amount of such a duty baffles all the experts.   It is an impossible task. What are the retaliatory duties to be?

Again; any such countervailing duty would be contrary to the most important clause in our commercial treaties, viz., that by which we give and receive "most favoured nation treatment." Most favoured nation clause.

Again; it is very improbable that retaliatory duties would produce the desired effect on Foreign Governments.   Most of them, for financial reasons, now dislike bounties, and know that they are taxing their subjects to give us cheap sugar.   If we retaliate, it will show that we think the bounties beneficial to the country which proposes them, and injurious to ourselves, and this will lend strength to the interests which desire to retain them. Bad effect of retaliation abroad.

Lastly, the effect of any countervailing duty would be to raise the price of a necessary article to all the people of the United Kingdom, and it would raise it by much more than the amount of the duty.   Assuming the duty to be 2s. 6d. per cwt., which is apparently not much more than half what the West Indian Committee thinks necessary, the amount of the tax, with a consumption of over a million of tons, would represent an additional tax of two and a half millions, and the actual burden of the tax would probably not be far short of five millions, or the equivalent of an income tax of from 2d. to 3d. in the pound, which would be paid chiefly by the working classes. Effect of duty on price.

The case against reversing our Financial policy by retaliation of any kind, in the case of any article whatever, seems to me to be overwhelming.   But that any impartial person should be found willing to reverse it in the case of sugar would be simply astounding. Conclusion as to sugar.

Sugar.

I have dwelt thus at length on this subject of sugar, in the first place because of the great and growing importance of the article ; in the second place because it illustrates the operation of bounties as well as of Protective duties ; and lastly, because the financial history of sugar in this and in other countries illustrates admirably the value of the principle of Free imports, which is advocated in this book.

----

# CHAPTER XXXVII.

## CONSEQUENCES OF RETALIATION, IF PRACTICABLE.

WE have seen that retaliation would be an impotent weapon in our hands : that to retaliate on articles of food, or of raw material, is out of the question ; and that to retaliate on manufactures, as proposed by the Fair Trade League, or on luxuries, as proposed by Lord Salisbury, would have no effect except that of exposing us to a far more dangerous retaliation in return.  We have also seen that our position as Free Traders in the midst of Protectionist countries is not such as to call for a change in our policy.  But, assuming that all these things were unproved ; supposing that a fundamental change is necessary ; and supposing that a retaliatory policy were possible for us, it is worth while to consider what its consequences would be.

Englishmen must buy dearer and worse Goods.

1. One effect of retaliation would be to deprive English people of the goods they can buy better and cheaper abroad.  This, if confined to luxuries, would, perhaps, be the least of the evils caused by it.  If the only effect of a high tariff were to limit the sums expended on the hothouse, the shrubbery, the game preserve, the hunting stable, the race-course, or the ball-room, there would be comparatively little objection to it.  The national loss would be small, but the effect, whether for fiscal or economical purposes, would be small also.  If retaliatory duties are to have any real effect, they must touch things which a great many people want and use ; and in this case the comfort and convenience of a large number of people would be seriously affected.

2. A second effect of retaliation would be to diminish the

sale and manufacture of English goods. Goods of foreign make bought for our use at home are *ex hypothesi* better and cheaper than similar goods of native manufacture. Goods of English make bought for use by foreigners abroad are *ex hypothesi* better and cheaper than similar goods of foreign manufacture. If English people are prevented from buying abroad, and foreigners from buying here, there will be less produced, less profit made, and less to spend in return on both sides. The Frenchman who sells his silk to us makes more profit, and buys directly or indirectly more of our goods in return than the English silk merchant would do if we were to compel English people against their will to use English silk instead of French silk.

3. We should cripple our own trade by depriving it of materials. Many, if not most, articles are made for further use in manufacture. What is a manufactured article in retrospect is raw material in prospect, as I have shown in the case of sugar, dressed hides, and numerous other articles.

4. We should also stunt and cripple our manufactures, by bestowing the fatal gift of Protection upon them, and depriving them of the stimulus of foreign competition. At this moment our leather trade suffers by American competition, because the Americans tan hides cheaper than we do. Our Bradford fabrics have been suffering, because our wives and daughters have found French or German woollens pleasanter or prettier than Yorkshire goods. They are now recovering their custom. If we were to exclude American leather, or French woollens, we should exclude the stimulus requisite for improvement in the tanneries and woollen mills of England, and very likely stop the improvement in these particular manufactures which is at this very moment in progress.

5. A further and a most serious evil has not been sufficiently considered. We are not now arguing with Protectionists, who wish to keep out foreign goods altogether; we are arguing with people who wish to exclude foreign goods only in order to make foreigners admit English goods. Now what will be the position of our unhappy protected interests when retaliation has effected its purpose, and when the foreign nation against whom it is directed offers us a free tariff on the condition of our repealing our protective duties? We shall have nursed up a miserable interest, feeble for purposes of production, as protected interests always are, but powerful in the lobbies, and

N

Conse-
quences of
Retaliation.

clinging with tenacity to its protective duties, which will then be seen to stand in the way of other and more important interests. This unhappy interest will either maintain itself to their detriment, or it will be sacrificed for their benefit, and its last state will be worse than its first. The ribbon-weavers of Coventry have time out of mind been complaining of bad trade and foreign competition. Since the French Treaty they have, at any rate, known their fate, and Coventry has other manufactures and other prospects of prosperity. It would be the height of cruelty to tempt capital and labour back into the ribbon trade by the prospect of a protection against French ribbons, to be withdrawn as soon as the French people become alive to their own true interests, and repeal their duties on English iron and cotton.

Confusion
at the
Custom
House.

6. A sixth evil of retaliation peculiarly evident to the official mind, but not the less a great public evil, is that it would lead to all the confusions and difficulties which arise from duties differing according to the nationality of the goods, and all the mischiefs and frauds attendant on certificates of origin. A generation has passed away since the reforms of the tariff swept this troublesome rubbish into the official waste-paper basket. Those who were at work then can remember what a relief that reform was. But the mischiefs formerly caused to trade in its then contracted state were as nothing compared to the evils which such a system would now inflict on trade, considering the infinitely greater number of commercial dealings which now take place, and the infinitely greater speed with which they must be conducted.

Expenses
of Collec-
tion.

7. A seventh evil would be an increase in the cost of the Customs staff, and in the general expenses and trouble of collection, which would run away with a large part of any duties that might be imposed.

Political
degrada-
tion.

8. Another, and most formidable evil is that which American writers have pointed out* as actually happening in the United States, viz., the lobbying and jobbery of all the different special interests seeking protection, tending, as has been stated above, not only to economical mischief, but to political degradation.

* See page 201

# CHAPTER XXXVIII.

## RETALIATION ON FRENCH SILKS AND FRENCH WINES.

LET us see how Retaliation would work in an actual and not improbable case. Proposals to tax French silk have been made and are not unlikely to be made again. Silk is, comparatively speaking, a luxury, and it is an important French manufacture. According to our own statistics, we imported silk to the value of about 10 millions sterling from France in 1880. There is some reason to doubt these figures, as the exports from France to England, according to French statistics, were only 6½ millions, of which 3¾ millions were French manufacture; but it is certainly an important article of French manufacture and export. We also make and export a large quantity of silk manufactures, amounting in 1883 to about two millions and a half. Let us see what would be the consequence of a high protective duty on French silk imported into England.

*Retaliation in the case of Silk.*

1. English people would get their silk goods less good and less cheap. This, it may be said, is a trifle. Silk is a luxury, and people can do very well without it. I will admit that it is not the most important of articles; but is it a trifle to make the handkerchief, the ribbon, the Sunday gown dearer and uglier? Is it a trifle to take from our people one of the few articles which add grace and beauty to our somewhat sombre and dreary life? Speaking in the interest of those who can spend little upon mere beauty and ornament, I cannot come to any such conclusion.

*Silk would be worse and dearer in England.*

2. It will diminish the quantity of English goods which are now sent, directly or indirectly, to France in return for French silk. This is beyond doubt. Whatever France sends us we pay for, and we pay for it in something we can make better than she does; we shall lose a certain quantity of French custom, directly or indirectly. But it will be said, "The money now spent by English people on French silk must be spent on something else; that something will probably be silk made in England, and so English labour and capital will be employed

*Fewer English Goods will be made and sold in Exchange.*

N 2

as much and as profitably as if they were employed to pay the French for their silk."

The rejoinder is clear : they will be employed, but not as much or as profitably. *Ex hypothesi* the French make the silk they send us better and cheaper than we do ; they can make more profit out of it, and can therefore spend more on other goods of ours in return. On the other hand, it is equally clear that the English capital and labour which we are going to divert into the silk business is now employed on something which pays better than silk, or they would be employed in making silk. Consequently, by diverting this labour and capital to silk-making we are making it less profitable than it was before the tax. There will be a loss all round.

Silk manufacture in England will not be stimulated by competition.

3. It will deprive our own silk manufacturers of the stimulus for improvement now arising from French competition ; and this, considering the value of French taste and ingenuity in improving the beauty of manufactures, is no small consideration.

A weak manufacture will be fostered.

4. It will call into existence a protected manufacture, weak and sickly as such manufactures always are. Who that remembers the constant distress of the Spitalfields weavers in the days of Protection can desire to see English money and English workmen again tempted by protective duties into such a business?

And this weak interest will hereafter be deserted.

5. It will not only coax a miserable trade into existence, but if Retaliation answers the purpose of its promoters, and the French are induced by our refusal of their silks to offer to take our cottons and wool and iron on reasonable terms, we shall be forced to abandon this protected trade to the tender mercies of French competition. We shall have indulged it and pampered it only to betray and desert it. We shall have educated a body of skilled workpeople to a special branch of work only to be left helpless and useless when it comes to an end.

The Custom House will have to distinguish the Country of origin of all imported Silk.

6. In the meantime we shall have to distinguish at the Custom House between French-made silk and all other silks ; for it is an essential part of the policy of Retaliation and Reciprocity that we are not to place these duties on the goods of countries which take our goods free. Switzerland, for instance, and probably Italy, send their silk goods to us through France. French goods may be sent to us through Belgium or Holland. We must therefore ascertain, before we allow any bale of silk goods to be landed in England, whether they have been

made in France or in some other country. Conceive the confusion, difficulty, and delay which such official obstructions would cause. They would injure trade more than the tax itself.

In silk I have taken a manufacture which is carried on both in France and England, and in which, therefore, Retaliation involves Protection to English manufacture. This would not be the case with wines, to which X. (the writer in the *Pall Mall Gazette*, to whom I have referred above) points as an article on which we might properly lay a retaliatory duty. If our hands are freed from treaty obligations, and if either fiscal or social reasons lead us to desire to alter our wine duties, by all means let it be done ; but if they are to be purely retaliatory—that is, if we impose duties which we know to be injurious to ourselves for the purpose of injuring France, and thereby compelling her to reduce some of her duties on our goods—then they would be open to all the objections I have pointed out in the case of silk. They would, it is true, not protect our manufactures of wine, as we have none, but they would protect the wine-growers of Spain, Italy, and Germany, which it is certainly not our object to do. In all other respects such duties would be followed by every one of the evil consequences I have pointed out as the consequences of a retaliatory duty on silk.

Retaliation on Wine.

---

## CHAPTER XXXIX.

### PROTECTION FOR THE PURPOSE OF CHECKING A TOO EXCLUSIVE DEVELOPMENT OF AGRICULTURE.

THERE is one attitude of young Protectionist countries towards trade which remains to be considered, viz., that of those who admit that they are incurring economical loss by their policy, but who, notwithstanding, resolutely exclude foreign manufactures, on the ground that the cultivation of the soil and the export of raw produce are not by themselves industries sufficient to promote national progress ; and that it is the interest and business of the State to foster other forms of industry, in order the sooner and the better to form a completely developed society. These views are probably wrong ; for two reasons.

Retaliation where Protection is adopted to check exclusive Agriculture.

Protection in young countries.

First, because in a growing agricultural society, left to itself, trade and manufacture necessarily grow up as the wants of the society develop. The local baker, butcher, carpenter, blacksmith, are soon wanted to supply the wants of the successful tiller of the ground; and other and more developed manufactures follow in due course, healthy and vigorous, because natural and necessary. Secondly, because, as all experience shows, protection breeds protection, and, once established, is most difficult to get rid of. Protection to one industry is an injury to another; that industry claims protection in its turn; and so on, till all society is bound up in a vicious circle in which each industry has, or thinks it has, an interest opposed to the interests of the whole, and though, perhaps, well able to stand alone, resolutely refuses to be the first to give up its established privilege.

Right or wrong, however, the views to which I have referred deserve more attention than they commonly receive from us, and are less easy to answer than the ordinary Protectionist fallacies. But, right or wrong, Retaliation against this class of Protectionists is still more foolish than against others. Retaliation plays their game exactly; it is their professed object to force their own labour and capital out of its natural channel—the tilling of the soil—and to turn it artificially into the channels of manufacture. By refusing to take their raw produce we help them in effecting this object; for we make their natural productions less valuable. So far from fearing Retaliation as an injury, they will accept it as a friend and an ally; so far from being frightened into opening their ports to our manufactures by the refusal of their raw produce, they will hail that refusal as the complement of their own policy.

---

# CHAPTER XI.

## RETALIATION DOES NOT ONLY NOT EFFECT ITS OBJECT, BUT HAS A CONTRARY EFFECT.

Retaliation will provoke Retaliation.

ALMOST any one of the objections above noticed appears to me to be fatal to the principle of Retaliation; but there is still another objection, which has as great weight as any of them.

Retaliation is not calculated to effect its object; it is calculated to effect the very opposite. It grows upon itself. It provokes additional Retaliation, until the nations are hopelessly alienated. A little consideration will show how natural this is, and how little reason we have to expect a favourable result from it.

In the first place, we lead Protectionists to think that we do not believe in our own principles. "See," they will say, "what England is doing. She professes to believe that the lowering of import duties is a good thing in itself, and yet she is taking the first opportunity to raise her own. We will follow her example rather than her precepts."

In the second place, a natural feeling of antagonism is aroused; and feeling is often stronger than self-interest. "We are giving so much, and you give so little; we will punish you by giving less." Canning's well-known despatch involves a political, if not an economical truth:—

> " In matters of commerce the fault of the Dutch
> Is giving too little and asking too much;
> With equal advantage the French are content,
> So we'll clap on Dutch bottoms twenty per cent."

It needs no thought to feel angry at an over-reaching bargainer; it needs much thought to see that the over-reacher over-reaches himself more than he over-reaches us—that we are the greatest gainers by what we have given him.

But this is not all. The strength of Protection lies in the power of concentrated protected interests. They spend money, time, and trouble in defence of their privileges; they intrigue behind the throne; they crowd the lobbies; and are ready to take the best advantage of the popular indignation caused by an unsuccessful negotiation. The French Emperor was either unable or unwilling to sacrifice his French ironmasters, though cheap iron was one of the first necessities of France. M. Tirard quakes before Rouen and Roubaix. The ironfounders of Pennsylvania are more urgent in the Senate House at Washington than all the western prairies. It needed a most unusual conjunction of political philosophy, public interest, wealthy manufacturers, distress among the working classes, and heroic leaders, to repeal our own Corn Laws. Our shipowners have scarcely yet forgiven the repeal of the Navigation Laws, though freedom of trade has given them the command of the seas. The recent growls from Preston, from Bradford, from

Retaliation produces Retaliation. Lincolnshire, the farming interest and from the sugar interest, show how soon and how easily, even in this country, partial and self-seeking interests could mislead the multitude and excite a jealous and angry cry, not only for Fair Trade but for absolute Protection to every special interest. Once embarked in a war of tariffs, and we are much more likely to arrive at Prohibition than at Free Trade.

Recent French duties on animals and corn. France is, perhaps, the country which at the present moment is making the most retrograde steps, and it is interesting to see how one Protective measure is leading to others. She protects the yarns which her silk manufacturers need, so she is asked to give a bounty on the export of silk. She protects her own sugar growers, so she must also protect her Colonial sugar growers and her refiners. To remedy agricultural distress, which appears to be greater in France than in England, the French legislature has imposed Protective duties on imported oxen of £1 a head, and on imported corn of 5s. a quarter. The tax on corn has led to a still higher duty on Foreign semolina and similar stuffs in order to protect the French makers of those articles; and to a very high Protective duty on Foreign flour in order to protect French millers. But the remarkable thing in reading the discussions on these measures is that the most common and most successful argument for protection to agriculture was that French manufactures were already protected at the expense of French agriculturists, and that it was therefore only fair to French agriculturists that they should be protected in turn, at whatever cost to French manufacturers. One bad step involves another. Each class seeks to be protected in turn; and they form in the end a ring of jobbing interests which unite in opposition to the public interest, because, though all suffer by it, each is afraid to be the first or only one to lose its privileges.

Experience in the United States The history of Protection in the United States is also very instructive. A moderate Protective system existed before the Civil War. During the war everything was taxed, whether imported or produced at home. Protective duties were largely increased in order to compensate for internal duties on the same articles, or for import duties on the raw material. After the war internal duties were taken off, but the compensating duties on imports were continued. They have even been increased, and such has been the influence of the Protected interest on each change in the tariff that measures intended to

give some relief to the consumer have been so manipulated as
to give more protection to the manufacturer. The Americans
have now, probably, the worst tariff in the world; and, whilst
they injure other nations, they are themselves the greatest
sufferers by it. Nor are the evils which result from it economical only. Mr. Taussig says:—*

"Contributions to the party chest are the form in which
money payments by the protected interest are likely to have
been made, so far as such payments were made at all. But the
general laxity of thought on public trusts undoubtedly made
possible the manipulation of the tariff in the interest of private
individuals. The tone of political life—as indeed that of commercial life—was lowered by the abnormal economic conditions
that followed the war, and the general demoralisation enabled
the Protected interests and their champions to rush through
Congress measures which, in a more healthy state of public
affairs, would have been reprobated and rejected."

Those who are anxious to re-introduce Protection in this
country should be warned by the example of the United States,
that if this game of favouritism to special interests were once
begun, it is not likely to stop without endangering public
morality, and causing evils which are even worse in their social
and political than in their economical aspect.

But, to return to the economical effect of Protection,
what are the teachings of experience? We have some Protectionist and some half-Protectionist countries. Do they get
better terms from each other than the Free-trading countries?
Does the United States get better terms from France or Germany or Canada than England or Holland? Are the Protectionist countries ready to fly into each other's arms? We
know very well that this is not the case. The very reason
for the adoption of the commercial policy which we pursued
from 1840 to 1860 was that negotiations for commercial
treaties had been tried and had failed signally. They had
been tried by the ablest negotiators, by Sir R. Peel and Mr.
Gladstone, and by the Minister who preceded them. They
had been tried with the best possible materials for negotiation,
with Protective duties on our part such as Lord Salisbury in his
wildest dreams can never hope to get; duties, too, which our own
Minister wished for our own sakes to reduce or repeal. When

* " History of the present Tariff," p. 75

Retaliation
produces
Retaliation

Mr. Ricardo brought forward his celebrated motion for reduction of duties in 1843 and 1844,* his first and strongest point was that negotiations for commercial treaties with Brazil, Portugal, Spain, and France had all been pending and had all come to an end, not only without any favourable result, but with the result of leaving our relations with those countries worse than they had previously been.  This no doubt was one principal reason why, though Mr. Ricardo's motion was rejected at the time as too abstract and absolute, Sir R. Peel and Mr. Gladstone subsequently adopted its policy.†

The conclusion of Mr. Ricardo's speech consisted of an apt quotation from Dr. Franklin, which may be almost taken as a prophecy.

Dr.
Franklin.

"Suppose X to be a country having three manufactures, cloth, silk, and iron, furnishing those manufactures to three countries, A, B, C ; and that X, to improve the cloth manufacture, should lay a duty amounting to prohibition on all the cloth coming from A ; that A, to retaliate, should lay a prohibitory duty on silk coming from X.  The silk-workers would begin to complain, and X, to protect them, should lay a prohibitory duty on the silk coming from B ; B, to retaliate, should put a prohibitory duty on iron coming from X.  The iron manufacturers would complain, and then X, to protect them, should lay a prohibitory duty on iron coming from C ; whilst C, to retaliate, should lay a duty on the cloth coming from X.  And Dr. Franklin asked, what benefit these four countries would gain by these prohibitions, while all four would have curtailed the sources of their comforts and the conveniences of life ?"

United
States and
Canada.
Reciprocity
Treaty.

Our experience is not confined to this side the Atlantic. Dr. Franklin's supposed case represents exactly the present relation between his own country and Canada.  The United States and Canada are meant by nature to do business freely with one another.  An artificial barrier between them is to the eyes of common sense, as of political philosophy, absurd and unnatural ; and yet it exists, and has grown into formidable dimensions within the last 25 years.  This is no doubt partly due to extraneous circumstances, such as the dispute about the Fisheries and Fenian raids ; but in the main it has been the natural result of endeavours to arrive at Free Trade by the road of Retaliation.  In 1854, as I have mentioned above, a

* "Hansard," vol. 73, p. 1271.
† See Sir R. Peel's speech, July 6, 1849.  "Hansard," vol. 106, p. 1429.

commercial treaty was made between Canada and the United Retaliation produces Retaliation.
States to the mutual advantage of both, under which certain
products of each country were admitted into the other duty
free, liberty to tax other products being still reserved. In 1865
the United States denounced that treaty. What were the reasons they gave for it? Those reasons were contained in an
elaborate report of the Committee of the House of Representa-
tives, which was laid before our Parliament.* The Committee
admit and assert, in the strongest terms, the importance to
Canada and to the United States of the most unrestricted intercourse, and indeed advocate, as the best if not the only method
of effecting it, a complete Zollverein, or Customs' Union on the
German plan, including all British North America, within the
limits of which no Customs' duties whatever should be levied.
The same Committee condemn the then existing treaty in
terms which remind one of our Fair Traders, because, as they
say, it was one-sided; in other words, because the people of the
United States obtained under it Canadian corn, and fish, and
timber duty free, whilst the Canadians were compelled by their
own import duties to pay an extra and unnecessary price for the
sugar, cotton, silk, iron, and wool of the United States. The
Committee made special, and apparently not ill-founded, complaints that Canada had ever since the treaty constantly
increased her duties on these articles until her conduct had
provoked severe observations from the English Colonial Minister, which again provoked unpleasant recrimination in the
Canadian Parliament. What induced Canada thus to increase
her duties, I do not know; but that she should do so in the
hope of obtaining still better terms from the United States was
a natural result of the bargaining system. At any rate, the
result was that the United States, instead of taking a step in the
direction of freedom, said, "If you give us such bad terms, we
will give you worse;" and they consequently withdrew from the
treaty, and left Canadian goods subject to their oppressive
tariff. The attempts at a bargain went on more or less until
1879, when Canada, finding herself worsted, determined to retaliate with greater vigour, and adopted the Protective tariff of
1879, of which we have heard so much, and which, whatever
Mr. Goldwin Smith may say, was distinctly Protectionist in
character, and was expressed and intended to be a commercial

* See Despatch from Lord Lyons, North America, No. 10, 1862.

Retaliation produces Retaliation.

blow to the United States. What will be the next step no on can say. Sooner or later both parties will probably come to their senses; but in the meantime, we may well ask, with Dr. Franklin, "what benefit those two countries have gained by their prohibitions, whilst each has curtailed the sources of their comforts and the conveniences of life?" But such is the natural result of the use of those dangerous weapons Retaliation and Reciprocity; and to such an end we may be very sure Retaliation would soon come in this country, especially if it were wielded by the hands of those who cannot see the fundamental truth that every separate restriction on commerce, whether imposed by ourselves or others, is a separate and independent evil to ourselves as well as to our neighbours, and that every removal of every restriction is a separate and independent gain to ourselves as well as to our neighbours.

# CHAPTER XLI.

### THE FRENCH TREATY OF 1860.

Cobden's Treaty gives no countenance to Retaliation.

To Retaliation, whatever Lord Salisbury may say, the French treaty of 1860, properly understood, gives no real countenance. In that treaty we neither imposed nor threatened to impose duties either on French or on any other goods; on the contrary, we took duties off French goods, and at the same time off similar goods the produce of all other countries.

We did nothing we should not have done without a Treaty.

In doing this, we were doing what was strictly for our own interest, independently of the action of France. In deference to the weakness of France, we put what we did into the form of a bargain—*Do ut des;* but we were giving nothing we should have wished to keep. What we did was, with one doubtful exception, what we should have done, and ought to have done, had France made no relaxation of her duties. This is the distinction which Lord Salisbury fails to see. There is a world-wide difference between taking advantage of the accident that what we do for our own sakes is looked on by a foreign nation as a concession, and doing something which for our own sakes we should avoid, in order to have a concession to make. The fact that the form of the French treaty has misled Lord Salisbury and others into overlooking this distinction, is, to my mind, the greatest objection to it.

The single exception to which I have referred, if indeed it is an exception, is the wine duty. Strong reasons, founded on considerations affecting the health of the people and the safety of the revenue, were given for the particular duties fixed in 1860-62. So far as these reasons support those duties, there can be no possible objection to them. But there can be no doubt that in fixing these duties the interests of France had also some influence, and there can be no doubt that these duties do give some advantage to French wine over the wines of other countries. Further investigation and experience have led to a doubt whether these duties were properly settled. The Committee of the House of Commons which sat upon this subject in 1879 came to the conclusion that the fiscal and social reasons given for these duties were insufficient, and the Spanish and Portuguese Governments have strongly and repeatedly remonstrated against them, as creating differential charges on the wines of Spain and Portugal. Spain has even gone so far as to retaliate by differential duties on English goods. Our own colonies have complained, as mentioned above. We have just now been proposing to alter our wine duties in order to admit the stronger wines of Spain, and we expected to obtain from Spain a reduction of her exorbitant charges on our goods. In reducing the wine duties we should be doing what is for our own interest ; and this is our real justification. The true policy for us to adopt is to have regard only to what we should do if no French or Spanish tariff existed : to admit low-priced French wines at a lower rate of duty ; to reduce the present duty on Spanish and Portuguese wines ; or to increase the wine duties altogether, and repeal some other tax, such as the tea duty ; whichever may be most advantageous to us, with a simple regard to the interests of our revenue and the benefits to be derived by our people from light or strong wines or from tea. If we simply admit Spanish and Portuguese wines because it is our interest to get those wines cheap, and to encourage trade with Spain and Portugal, it will be well. And if the present Spanish Minister wishes to make such a reduction the condition of reducing his own tariff, we properly get the benefit of his action. But if we tie our hands by a treaty, we may embarrass ourselves financially ; and if our arrangements

French Treaty.

were such as to place a differential and vindictive duty on the wines of France, we should undoubtedly be committing a great economical as well as political mistake, and be starting on a course of policy towards France which would have a bad effect, not only on the trade between the two countries, but on relations which are still more important than trade.

Cobden's Treaty not to be judged by economical results alone.

It is not, however, by the balance of economical results, past, present, or future, that the value of the French Treaty can be rightly judged. Its effect at the time in putting a stop to that alienation of the two nations which was then threatening to break out into war, and the kindly personal intercourse which has since been brought about between Frenchmen and Englishmen, are results of still greater importance than increase of trade. One thing, however, may be said of the French treaty, which, considering the danger of all negotiations of the kind, is perhaps not its least merit, viz., that it cannot be a precedent; for, by abolishing all or nearly all the duties we can spare, it has left us little or no means to strike further bargains.

In speaking as I have done of the French treaty of 1860, I am quite aware of the value of the system, well described in the following passage from Mr. Morley's "Life of Cobden."

" Most favoured Nation " clause.

" In these treaties, and in the treaty made afterwards by England with Austria, Sir Louis Mallet reminded its opponents in later years that each of them had a double operation. Not only does each treaty open the market of another country to foreign industry; it immediately affects the markets that are already opened. For every recent treaty recognised the 'most favoured nation' principle, the sheet-anchor of Free Trade, as it has been called. By means of this principle, each new point gained in any one negotiation becomes a part of the common commercial system of the European confederation. ' By means of this network,' it has been excellently said by a distinguished member of the English diplomatic service, ' of which few Englishmen seem to be aware, while fewer still know to whom they owe it, all the great trading and industrial communities of Europe— *i.e.*, England, France, Holland, Belgium, the Zollverein (1870), Austria, and Italy—constitute a compact international body, from which the principle of monopoly and exclusive privilege has once for all been eliminated, and not one member of which can take off a single duty without all the other members at once partaking in the increased trading facilities thereby

created. By the self-registering action of the "most favoured <sup></sup> French Treaty.
nation" clause, common to this network of treaties, the tariff
level of the whole body is being continually lowered, and the
road being paved towards the final embodiment of the Free
Trade principle, in the international engagement to abolish all
duties other than those levied for revenue purposes.'"

But it must be remembered that some of the nations have _Actual consequences of the Treaties._
drawn back from these treaties ; that Germany, Austria, Italy, and
France have recently raised their duties ; and that if it is a great
advantage to have duties reduced for us behind our back, and
without effort on our part, by the operation of the "most favoured
nation" clause, there is some inconvenience in having them
raised behind our back by action on the part of two foreign
nations with which we have nothing to do. It may also be some
drawback to the value of this generally excellent clause if one
nation—France, for instance—should be prevented from reducing her tariff in our favour, because if she did so, she would
be compelled by the "most favoured nation" clause to give
the same privilege to another nation—say Germany.

In short, if the separate action followed by us from 1840 to _Result of Treaties on action of Foreign Nations not altogether successful._
1860 was not successful in making other nations reduce their
duties, I think we must admit that neither has the treaty system
adopted in 1860 been followed by unalloyed success, whilst it
has certainly set men's minds in a wrong direction.

In making this reference to the French Treaty of 1860, I do
not wish to be understood as saying that the balance of results,
even in an economical point of view, have not been good. I
only say that there have been large drawbacks.

It may seem ungenerous and out of place, in a paper _Cobden's Views._
published by the Cobden Club, to say a word which seems to
throw doubt upon the great work of Cobden's later years. But
Cobden is beyond any such criticism. His greatness consisted
in the way in which he kept his great object in view, aided but
not fettered by formulas. When Freedom of Trade could be
promoted by separate action, he was for separate action ; when
he thought it could be promoted by joint action with France,
he was for joint action. If that joint action had been shown to
him to have consequences dangerous to Free Trade, he would
have been the first to abandon it. If I hesitate about the
policy and effect of the commercial treaties, it is certainly not
" because they do not sound in tune with the verbal jingle of an
abstract dogma." My doubts are very practical and concrete.

French
Treaty.
Real objec-
tion to the
Treaties,
that they
lead to
Retalia-
tion.

I am afraid of being led into Retaliation. If it is true, as some of the thorough-going advocates of the treaty appear to think, that it is useless for us to abolish our duties on imports, unless foreign nations at the same time abolish their duties on our exports, Lord Salisbury's conclusion is inevitable—we must reimpose our own import duties, until we can get foreign nations to take off theirs. To controvert this conclusion is one of the principal objects of this work.

CONCLUSIONS OF PART II. AS TO RETALIATION.

To sum up : the conclusions to which the above reasoning
leads us on the subject of Retaliation are as follow :—

1. Retaliation is an impotent weapon in our hands.

2. To lower foreign tariffs was not the sole or principal
object of the authors of our present policy.  They would have
adopted that policy had they known that no foreign tariff would
be lowered.

3. All duties are impediments to trade ; the fewer duties,
the fewer impediments.  We can remove our own duties ; we
cannot remove our neighbours'.

4. No tariff is an absolute barrier ; and a free country has
such advantages in production that it can compete with a
Protectionist country, even for the home market of the latter.

5. Exports involve imports ; all Protectionist countries desire to export, and must therefore import.  Where a Protectionist country exports to another country, the second country
must pay in goods, if not directly to the Protectionist country,
indirectly through some third country.

6. There are many free and many neutral markets, and
all of them a Free-trading country has advantages over a
Protectionist rival.

7. Protection has not, so far as we can judge, advanced
trade and manufacture in France, Germany, or the United
States, but the reverse.

8. The trade of a country depends on many things besides
Free Trade.  Free Trade only removes impediments.  What
can be claimed for Free Trade is that a country is better with
it than without it.  The prosperity of the United States does
not affect the question.

9. For the above reasons, there is no fear of our losin  our
market, and the case for Retaliation fails.

O

3. Mischievous.

10. Retaliation must, in its immediate consequences, be injurious to ourselves.

11. Retaliation is calculated to defeat its own object, and to provoke further Retaliation.

12. The Cobden treaty affords no ground whatever for Reciprocity or Retaliation.

Summary of Free Trade doctrine.

The simplicity of the Free Trade position is obscured by the vastness and complexity of modern business. But it is in truth simple in the extreme. This book and much else which has been written on the subject is only an expansion of the following elementary truths :—

Each man knows how to buy and sell better than his Government. Every one who buys sells at the same time.

1. Every man knows better what he wants to buy and sell than his Government can possibly know for him. He will buy and sell to the best advantage, if left free to buy and sell as he chooses.

2. Every one who buys, sells at the same time. His purchase is really an exchange. The money he pays for the goods which he buys is really an order given to the seller for other goods. The more buying the more selling.

Buying and selling between different countries do not differ from buying and selling at home.

3. As regards dealings between inhabitants of the same street, the same village, the same town, the same country, no one thinks of disputing these truths. But they are just as true as regards dealings between inhabitants of different countries.

No one who is master of these simple and obvious truths will be misled by Protectionist sophisms.

# FINAL CONCLUSIONS.

The proposals of the Fair Trade League, worthless as they may be in themselves, have afforded an opportunity for discussing points of some real interest, and for answering some questions which deserve an answer.

On the Colonial question it is impossible not to feel sympathy with the desire to draw closer the commercial bonds between ourselves and those growing communities of our own lineage and habits which it is England's greatest pride to have brought into existence. It has been the object of the first part of this paper to show that all the proposals which have been made for effecting this object by legislative means involve either restrictions on our trade with other countries, or restrictions on colonial self-government ; and that any such restrictions would tend to disruption, and not to closer union. *[New Colonial policy. Object may be good : Means are bad.]*

The great fact is that Governments cannot create trade ; they can only impede and injure it. They cannot divert it without diminishing it. When people talk of its being the duty of the Government to find markets for their people, what they mean is that the Government shall deprive their people of the markets which they find for themselves. *[Governments can check but not create Trade.]*

On the second great question which I have treated—viz., Retaliation—there can be no such sympathy. Retaliation appears to me to be the natural offspring of a state of mind which regards our gain as others loss—a state of mind which is the hot-bed of Chauvinism, Imperialism, and Protection. A wave of feeling springing out of this state of mind has lately swept over us and over the world : and it is not surprising that it should bring with it a moderate revival of Protection in countries where protected interests rule the State, and a feeble attempt to revive it in our own. But the great tide sweeps on its course, and this is but an eddy in the stream. Time and circumstances are in its favour, and its main course is in one direction. Steam and telegraph have brought the *[Retaliation bad in spirit as in effect.]* *[Hopeful Tendencies.]*

O 2

nations of the world together ; Prohibition has been succeeded by Protection, and Protection in many cases by Freedom; the limits of petty States have been enlarged into Customs Unions and Federations, which embrace whole continents.   Men are being brought more and more together, and in so doing they help one another more and more.   It is the misfortune of the state of mind to which I have referred that it fails to apprehend and appreciate that moral element in trade which gives to it its greatest value and significance—that element, namely, by virtue of which each act of trade is a good to both the parties to it, and each removal of a national restriction on trade is a good to all the nations concerned.   It is twice blessed. It blesseth him that gives and him that takes.   It reconciles self-interest with morality—our duty to ourselves with our duty to our neighbour ; and it thus brings the nations a little nearer to the distant ideal of the Christian moralist.

I cannot end this discussion better than with Cobden's own words :—

"I do not think the nations of the earth will have a chance of advancing morally in their domestic concerns to the degree of excellence which we sigh for until the international relations of the world are put upon a different footing.   The present system corrupts society, exhausts its wealth, raises up false gods for hero-worship, and fixes before the eyes of the rising generation a spurious if a glittering standard of glory.   It is because I believe that the principle of Free Trade is calculated to alter the relations of the world for the better, in a moral point of view, that I bless God I have been allowed to take a prominent part in its advocacy."

## TABLE I.

*Statement of the Value of the Exports of British and Irish Produce from the United Kingdom, and of the Amounts and Proportion Exported to Foreign Countries and British Possessions respectively, in each of the Years from 1856 to 1883 inclusive; in thousands of pounds, i.e., 100 = 100,000.*

| Years. | Total Value of Exports of British and Irish Produce. | Exported to Foreign Countries only. | | Exported to British Possessions only. | |
|---|---|---|---|---|---|
| | | Amount. | Per Cent. of Total. | Amount. | Per Cent. of Total. |
| | £ | £ | | £ | |
| 1856 | 115,827 | 82,527 | 71·2 | 33,300 | 28·8 |
| 1857 | 122,066 | 84,911 | 69·6 | 37,155 | 30·4 |
| 1858 | 116,609 | 76,386 | 65·5 | 40,223 | 34·5 |
| 1859 | 130,412 | 84,268 | 64·6 | 46,144 | 35·4 |
| 1860 | 135,891 | 92,226 | 67·9 | 43,665 | 32·1 |
| 1861 | 125,103 | 82,858 | 66·2 | 42,245 | 33·8 |
| 1862 | 123,992 | 82,097 | 66·2 | 41,895 | 33·8 |
| 1863 | 146,602 | 95,723 | 65·3 | 50,879 | 34·7 |
| 1864 | 160,449 | 108,735 | 67·8 | 51,714 | 32·2 |
| 1865 | 165,836 | 117,629 | 70·9 | 48,207 | 29·1 |
| 1866 | 188,917 | 135,198 | 71·6 | 53,719 | 28·4 |
| 1867 | 180,062 | 131,162 | 72·5 | 49,800 | 27·5 |
| 1868 | 179,678 | 129,813 | 72·2 | 49,865 | 27·8 |
| 1869 | 189,954 | 141,881 | 74·7 | 48,073 | 25·3 |
| 1870 | 199,587 | 147,773 | 74·0 | 51,814 | 26·0 |
| 1871 | 223,066 | 171,816 | 77·0 | 51,250 | 23·0 |
| 1872 | 256,257 | 195,701 | 76·4 | 60,556 | 23·6 |
| 1873 | 255,165 | 188,836 | 74·0 | 66,329 | 26·0 |
| 1874 | 239,558 | 167,278 | 69·8 | 72,280 | 30·2 |
| 1875 | 223,466 | 152,374 | 68·2 | 71,092 | 31·8 |
| 1876 | 200,639 | 135,780 | 67·7 | 64,859 | 32·3 |
| 1877 | 198,893 | 128,970 | 64·8 | 69,923 | 35·2 |
| 1878 | 192,849 | 126,611 | 65·7 | 66,238 | 34·3 |
| 1879 | 191,532 | 130,530 | 68·2 | 61,002 | 31·8 |
| 1880 | 223,060 | 147,806 | 66·3 | 75,254 | 33·7 |
| 1881 | 234,023 | 154,658 | 66·1 | 79,365 | 33·9 |
| 1882 | 241,467 | 156,641 | 64·9 | 84,826 | 35·1 |
| 1883 | 239,799 | 156,322 | 65·2 | 83,477 | 34·8 |

## TABLE II.

*Statement of the Value of the Total Exports of British and Irish, and Foreign and Colonial Produce from the United Kingdom, and of the Amounts and Proportion Exported to Foreign Countries and British Possessions respectively, in each of the Years from 1856 to 1883 inclusive; in thousands of pounds, i.e., 100 = 100,000.*

| Years. | Total Value of Exports. | Exported to Foreign Countries only. | | Exported to British Possessions only. | |
|---|---|---|---|---|---|
| | | Amount. | Per Cent. of Total. | Amount. | Per Cent. of Total. |
| | £ | £ | | £ | |
| 1856 | 139,221 | 102,525 | 73·6 | 36,696 | 26·4 |
| 1857 | 146,174 | 105,738 | 72·3 | 40,436 | 27·7 |
| 1858 | 139,783 | 96,570 | 69·1 | 43,213 | 30·9 |
| 1859 | 155,693 | 106,042 | 68·1 | 49,651 | 31·9 |
| 1860 | 164,521 | 117,988 | 71·7 | 46,533 | 28·3 |
| 1861 | 159,632 | 114,493 | 71·7 | 45,139 | 28·3 |
| 1862 | 166,168 | 120,744 | 72·7 | 45,424 | 27·3 |
| 1863 | 196,902 | 141,932 | 72·1 | 54,970 | 27·9 |
| 1864 | 212,588 | 156,892 | 73·8 | 55,696 | 26·2 |
| 1865 | 218,832 | 167,285 | 76·4 | 51,547 | 23·6 |
| 1866 | 238,906 | 181,738 | 76·1 | 57,168 | 23·9 |
| 1867 | 225,802 | 172,440 | 76·4 | 53,362 | 23·6 |
| 1868 | 227,779 | 174,061 | 76·4 | 53,718 | 23·6 |
| 1869 | 237,015 | 185,123 | 78·1 | 51,892 | 21·9 |
| 1870 | 244,080 | 188,689 | 77·3 | 55,391 | 22·7 |
| 1871 | 283,575 | 228,014 | 80·4 | 55,561 | 19·6 |
| 1872 | 314,589 | 248,980 | 79·1 | 65,609 | 20·9 |
| 1873 | 311,005 | 239,857 | 77·1 | 71,148 | 22·9 |
| 1874 | 297,650 | 219,740 | 73·8 | 77,910 | 26·2 |
| 1875 | 281,612 | 204,957 | 72·8 | 76,655 | 27·2 |
| 1876 | 256,777 | 186,627 | 72·7 | 70,150 | 27·3 |
| 1877 | 252,346 | 176,594 | 70·0 | 75,752 | 30·0 |
| 1878 | 245,484 | 173,491 | 70·7 | 71,993 | 29·3 |
| 1879 | 248,783 | 182,274 | 73·3 | 66,509 | 26·7 |
| 1880 | 286,415 | 204,887 | 71·5 | 81,528 | 28·5 |
| 1881 | 297,083 | 210,402 | 70·8 | 86,681 | 29·2 |
| 1882 | 306,661 | 214,323 | 69·9 | 92,338 | 30·1 |
| 1883 | 305,437 | 215,036 | 70·4 | 90,401 | 29·6 |

## TABLE III.

*Statement of the Value of the Imports of Merchandise into the United Kingdom, and of the Amounts and Proportion from Foreign Countries and British Possessions respectively, in each of the Years from 1856 to 1883 inclusive; in thousands of pounds, i.e., 100 = 100,000.*

| Years. | Total Value of Imports. | Imported from Foreign Countries only. | | Imported from British Possessions only. | |
|---|---|---|---|---|---|
| | | Amount. | Per Cent. of Total. | Amount. | Per Cent. of Total. |
| | £ | £ | | £ | |
| 1856 | 172,544 | 129,517 | 75·1 | 43,027 | 24·9 |
| 1857 | 187,844 | 141,661 | 75·4 | 46,183 | 24·6 |
| 1858 | 164,584 | 125,970 | 76·5 | 38,614 | 23·5 |
| 1859 | 179,182 | 139,707 | 78·0 | 39,475 | 22·0 |
| 1860 | 210,531 | 167,571 | 79·6 | 42,960 | 20·4 |
| 1861 | 217,485 | 164,809 | 75·8 | 52,676 | 24·2 |
| 1862 | 225,717 | 160,434 | 71·1 | 65,283 | 28·9 |
| 1863 | 248,919 | 164,235 | 66·0 | 84,684 | 34·0 |
| 1864 | 274,952 | 181,208 | 65·9 | 93,744 | 34·1 |
| 1865 | 271,072 | 198,231 | 73·1 | 72,841 | 26·9 |
| 1866 | 295,290 | 223,084 | 75·5 | 72,206 | 24·5 |
| 1867 | 275,183 | 214,449 | 77·9 | 60,734 | 22·1 |
| 1868 | 294,694 | 227,700 | 77·3 | 66,994 | 22·7 |
| 1869 | 295,460 | 225,044 | 76·2 | 70,416 | 23·8 |
| 1870 | 303,257 | 238,425 | 78·6 | 64,832 | 21·4 |
| 1871 | 331,015 | 258,071 | 78·0 | 72,944 | 22·0 |
| 1872 | 354,694 | 275,321 | 77·6 | 79,373 | 22·4 |
| 1873 | 371,287 | 290,277 | 78·2 | 81,010 | 21·8 |
| 1874 | 370,083 | 287,920 | 77·8 | 82,163 | 22·2 |
| 1875 | 373,940 | 289,516 | 77·4 | 84,424 | 22·6 |
| 1876 | 375,155 | 290,822 | 77·5 | 84,333 | 22·5 |
| 1877 | 394,420 | 304,866 | 77·3 | 89,554 | 22·7 |
| 1878 | 368,771 | 290,835 | 78·9 | 77,936 | 21·1 |
| 1879 | 362,992 | 284,049 | 78·3 | 78,943 | 21·7 |
| 1880 | 411,230 | 318,711 | 77·5 | 92,519 | 22·5 |
| 1881 | 397,023 | 305,483 | 76·9 | 91,540 | 23·1 |
| 1882 | 413,020 | 313,589 | 75·9 | 99,431 | 24·1 |
| 1883 | 426,892 | 328,210 | 76·9 | 98,682 | 23·1 |

# TABLE IV.

*Statement of the Total Value of Imports and Exports of Merchandise into and from the United Kingdom, and of the Amounts and Proportion from and to Foreign Countries and British Possessions, in each of the Years from 1856 to 1883 inclusive; in thousands of pounds, i.e. 100 = 100,000.*

| Years. | Total Value of Imports and Exports. | Total Value Imported from, and Exported to, Foreign Countries only. | | Total Value Imported from, and Exported to, British Possessions only. | |
|---|---|---|---|---|---|
| | | Amount. | Per Cent. of Total. | Amount. | Per Cent. of Total. |
| | £ | £ | | £ | |
| 1856 | 311,765 | 232,042 | 74·4 | 79,723 | 25·6 |
| 1857 | 334,018 | 247,399 | 74·1 | 86,619 | 25·9 |
| 1858 | 304,367 | 222,540 | 73·1 | 81,827 | 26·9 |
| 1859 | 334,875 | 245,749 | 73·4 | 89,126 | 26·6 |
| 1860 | 375,052 | 285,559 | 76·1 | 89,493 | 23·9 |
| 1861 | 377,117 | 279,302 | 74·1 | 97,815 | 25·9 |
| 1862 | 391,885 | 281,178 | 71·8 | 110,707 | 28·2 |
| 1863 | 445,821 | 306,167 | 68·7 | 139,654 | 31·3 |
| 1864 | 487,540 | 338,100 | 69·3 | 149,440 | 30·7 |
| 1865 | 489,904 | 365,516 | 74·6 | 124,388 | 25·4 |
| 1866 | 534,196 | 404,822 | 75·8 | 129,374 | 24·2 |
| 1867 | 500,985 | 386,889 | 77·2 | 114,096 | 22·8 |
| 1868 | 522,473 | 401,761 | 76·9 | 120,712 | 23·1 |
| 1869 | 532,475 | 410,167 | 77·0 | 122,308 | 23·0 |
| 1870 | 547,337 | 427,114 | 78·0 | 120,223 | 22·0 |
| 1871 | 614,590 | 486,085 | 79·1 | 128,505 | 20·9 |
| 1872 | 669,283 | 524,301 | 78·3 | 144,982 | 21·7 |
| 1873 | 682,292 | 530,134 | 77·7 | 152,158 | 22·3 |
| 1874 | 667,733 | 507,660 | 76·0 | 160,073 | 24·0 |
| 1875 | 655,552 | 494,473 | 75·4 | 161,079 | 24·6 |
| 1876 | 631,932 | 477,449 | 75·6 | 154,483 | 24·4 |
| 1877 | 646,766 | 481,460 | 74·4 | 165,306 | 25·6 |
| 1878 | 614,255 | 464,326 | 75·6 | 149,929 | 24·4 |
| 1879 | 611,775 | 466,323 | 76·2 | 145,452 | 23·8 |
| 1880 | 697,645 | 523,598 | 75·1 | 174,047 | 24·9 |
| 1881 | 694,106 | 515,885 | 74·3 | 178,221 | 25·7 |
| 1882 | 719,681 | 527,912 | 73·3 | 191,769 | 26·7 |
| 1883 | 732,329 | 543,246 | 74·2 | 189,083 | 25·8 |

# TABLE V.

*Statement in detail of the Total Exports of Merchandise from the United Kingdom to each of certain Foreign Countries and British Possessions, in each Year and Period of Five Years, since 1866, with the Proportions that the Amounts for each Country and Possession bear to the whole Exports in each Year and Period; the amounts being stated in thousands of pounds, i.e., 100 = 100,000.*

## A.—FOREIGN COUNTRIES.

| | RUSSIA. | | | | GERMANY. | | | | HOLLAND. | | | | BELGIUM | | | |
|---|---|---|---|---|---|---|---|---|---|---|---|---|---|---|---|---|
| | Exports of Foreign and Colonial Produce. | Exports of British Produce. | Total. Amount | Total. Per cent. of Total. | Exports of Foreign and Colonial Produce | Exports of British Produce | Total. Amount | Total. Per cent. of Total | Exports of Foreign and Colonial Produce. | Exports of British Produce | Total. Amount | Total. Per cent. of Total. | Exports of Foreign and Colonial Produce | Exports of British Produce. | Total. Amount | Total. Per cent. of Total. |
| | £ | £ | £ | | £ | £ | £ | | £ | £ | £ | | £ | £ | £ | |
| 1866 | 3,739 | 3,177 | 6,916 | 2·9 | 9,337 | 15,768 | 25,105 | 10·5 | 5,878 | 9,000 | 14,878 | 6·2 | 3,921 | 2,362 | 6,783 | 2·8 |
| 1867 | 3,307 | 3,944 | 7,251 | 3·2 | 9,325 | 20,543 | 29,868 | 13·2 | 5,526 | 9,423 | 14,949 | 6·6 | 4,565 | 2,816 | 7,381 | 3·3 |
| 1868 | 2,957 | 4,250 | 7,207 | 3·2 | 9,536 | 22,774 | 32,310 | 14·2 | 6,304 | 10,395 | 16,699 | 7·3 | 5,246 | 3,150 | 8,396 | 3·7 |
| 1869 | 3,189 | 6,465 | 9,654 | 4·1 | 9,230 | 22,842 | 32,072 | 13·5 | 6,623 | 10,760 | 17,383 | 7·3 | 4,909 | 4,004 | 8,913 | 3·8 |
| 1870 | 3,079 | 6,992 | 10,071 | 4·1 | 7,650 | 20,416 | 28,066 | 11·5 | 6,083 | 11,221 | 17,304 | 7·1 | 4,468 | 4,481 | 8,949 | 3·7 |
| Total for the Five Years | 16,271 | 24,628 | 41,099 | 3·5 | 45,078 | 102,343 | 147,421 | 12·6 | 30,414 | 50,799 | 81,213 | 6·9 | 23,109 | 17,313 | 40,422 | 3·4 |
| 1871 | 3,348 | 6,584 | 9,932 | 3·5 | 11,060 | 27,434 | 38,494 | 13·6 | 7,995 | 14,104 | 22,099 | 7·8 | 6,599 | 6,217 | 12,816 | 4·5 |
| 1872 | 2,860 | 6,609 | 9,469 | 3·0 | 11,531 | 31,619 | 43,150 | 13·7 | 8,124 | 16,212 | 24,336 | 7·7 | 6,601 | 6,499 | 13,100 | 4·2 |
| 1873 | 2,547 | 8,998 | 11,545 | 3·7 | 9,439 | 27,270 | 36,709 | 11·8 | 7,832 | 16,746 | 24,578 | 7·9 | 7,030 | 7,201 | 14,231 | 4·6 |
| 1874 | 3,088 | 8,777 | 11,865 | 4·0 | 10,328 | 24,800 | 35,128 | 11·8 | 6,863 | 14,427 | 21,290 | 7·2 | 6,825 | 5,828 | 12,653 | 4·3 |
| 1875 | 3,286 | 8,060 | 11,346 | 4·0 | 10,834 | 23,288 | 34,122 | 12·1 | 6,995 | 13,119 | 20,114 | 7·1 | 8,013 | 5,782 | 13,795 | 4·9 |
| Total for the Five Years | 15,129 | 39,028 | 54,157 | 3·6 | 53,192 | 134,411 | 187,603 | 12·6 | 37,809 | 74,608 | 112,417 | 7·6 | 35,068 | 31,527 | 66,595 | 4·5 |
| 1876 | 2,453 | 6,183 | 8,636 | 3·4 | 9,653 | 20,082 | 29,735 | 11·6 | 6,931 | 11,777 | 18,708 | 7·3 | 6,961 | 5,875 | 12,836 | 5·0 |
| 1877 | 2,065 | 4,179 | 6,244 | 2·5 | 9,308 | 19,642 | 28,950 | 11·5 | 6,419 | 9,614 | 16,033 | 6· | 6,456 | 5,304 | 11,760 | 4·7 |
| 1878 | 2,900 | 6,559 | 9,459 | 3·9 | 9,713 | 19,457 | 29,170 | 11·9 | 5,373 | 9,303 | 14,676 | 6·0 | 5,829 | 5,526 | 11,355 | 4·6 |
| 1879 | 2,962 | 7,645 | 10,607 | 4·3 | 11,032 | 18,592 | 29,624 | 11·9 | 6,100 | 9,353 | 15,453 | 6·2 | 6,781 | 5,106 | 11,887 | 4·8 |
| 1880 | 3,016 | 7,952 | 10,968 | 3·8 | 12,112 | 16,944 | 29,056 | 10·1 | 6,407 | 9,247 | 15,654 | 5·5 | 7,191 | 5,796 | 12,987 | 4·5 |
| Total for the Five Years | 13,396 | 32,518 | 45,914 | 3·6 | 51,818 | 94,717 | 146,535 | 11·4 | 31,230 | 49,294 | 80,524 | 6·2 | 33,218 | 27,607 | 60,825 | 4·7 |
| 1881 | 3,112 | 6,165 | 9,277 | 3·1 | 11,845 | 17,431 | 29,276 | 9·9 | 6,373 | 8,900 | 15,273 | 5·1 | 6,462 | 7,075 | 13,537 | 4·6 |
| 1882 | 2,866 | 5,772 | 8,638 | 2·8 | 12,007 | 18,518 | 30,525 | 10·0 | 6,872 | 9,380 | 16,252 | 5·3 | 7,037 | 8,080 | 15,117 | 4·9 |
| 1883 | 2,593 | 5,037 | 7,630 | 2·5 | 12,994 | 18,788 | 31,782 | 10·4 | 6,366 | 9,506 | 15,872 | 5·2 | 6,427 | 8,328 | 14,755 | 4·8 |
| Grand Total | 53,367 | 113,348 | 166,715 | 3·4 | 186,934 | 386,208 | 573,142 | 11·8 | 119,064 | 202,487 | 321,551 | 6·6 | 111,321 | 99,930 | 211,251 | 4·4 |

## TABLE V. (*continued*).

### A.—Foreign Countries (*continued*).

| — | France: Exports of Foreign and Colonial Produce. | France: Exports of British Produce. | France: Total: Amount. | France: Total: Per cent. of Total. | Italy: Exports of Foreign and Colonial Produce. | Italy: Exports of British Produce. | Italy: Total: Amount. | Italy: Total: Per cent. of Total. | Turkey.*: Exports of Foreign and Colonial Produce. | Turkey.*: Exports of British Produce. | Turkey.*: Total: Amount. | Turkey.*: Total: Per cent. of Total. | Egypt.†: Exports of Foreign and Colonial Produce. | Egypt.†: Exports of British Produce. | Egypt.†: Total: Amount. | Egypt.†: Total: Per cent. of Total. |
|---|---|---|---|---|---|---|---|---|---|---|---|---|---|---|---|---|
| | £ | £ | £ | | £ | £ | £ | | £ | £ | £ | | £ | £ | £ | |
| 1866 | 14,897 | 11,700 | 26,597 | 11.1 | 1,088 | 5,833 | 6,921 | 2.9 | 170 | 7,905 | 8,075 | 3.4 | 103 | 7,556 | 7,659 | 3.2 |
| 1867 | 10,901 | 12,121 | 23,022 | 10.2 | 1,014 | 4,881 | 5,895 | 2.6 | 267 | 6,626 | 6,893 | 3.1 | 173 | 8,198 | 8,371 | 3.7 |
| 1868 | 12,861 | 10,653 | 23,514 | 10.3 | 952 | 5,017 | 5,969 | 2.6 | 296 | 7,557 | 7,853 | 3.4 | 108 | 6,056 | 6,164 | 2.7 |
| 1869 | 11,839 | 11,438 | 23,277 | 9.8 | 1,078 | 6,162 | 7,240 | 3.1 | 360 | 6,938 | 7,298 | 3.1 | 90 | 7,983 | 8,073 | 3.4 |
| 1870 | 10,340 | 11,643 | 21,983 | 9.0 | 1,021 | 5,272 | 6,293 | 2.6 | 389 | 7,088 | 7,477 | 3.1 | 102 | 8,727 | 8,829 | 3.6 |
| Total for the Five Years | 60,838 | 57,555 | 118,393 | 10.1 | 5,153 | 27,165 | 32,318 | 2.8 | 1,482 | 36,114 | 37,596 | 3.2 | 576 | 38,520 | 39,096 | 3.3 |
| 1871 | 15,182 | 18,206 | 33,388 | 11.8 | 1,371 | 6,295 | 7,666 | 2.7 | 448 | 5,997 | 6,445 | 2.3 | 86 | 7,039 | 7,125 | 2.5 |
| 1872 | 11,023 | 17,269 | 28,292 | 9.0 | 1,158 | 6,558 | 7,716 | 2.5 | 531 | 7,639 | 8,170 | 2.6 | 95 | 7,213 | 7,308 | 2.3 |
| 1873 | 12,904 | 17,292 | 30,196 | 9.7 | 1,128 | 7,444 | 8,572 | 2.8 | 387 | 7,733 | 8,120 | 2.6 | 101 | 6,222 | 6,323 | 2.0 |
| 1874 | 13,019 | 16,370 | 29,389 | 9.9 | 1,394 | 6,370 | 7,764 | 2.6 | 459 | 7,038 | 7,497 | 2.5 | 89 | 3,585 | 3,674 | 1.2 |
| 1875 | 11,935 | 15,357 | 27,292 | 9.7 | 1,403 | 6,767 | 8,170 | 2.9 | 457 | 5,890 | 6,347 | 2.3 | 90 | 2,946 | 3,036 | 1.1 |
| Total for the Five Years | 64,063 | 84,494 | 148,557 | 10.0 | 6,454 | 33,434 | 39,888 | 2.7 | 2,282 | 34,297 | 36,579 | 2.5 | 461 | 27,005 | 27,466 | 1.8 |
| 1876 | 12,914 | 16,086 | 29,000 | 11.3 | 1,440 | 6,689 | 8,129 | 3.2 | 457 | 5,923 | 6,380 | 2.5 | 57 | 2,630 | 2,687 | 1.0 |
| 1877 | 11,431 | 14,233 | 25,664 | 10.2 | 1,131 | 6,219 | 7,350 | 2.9 | 380 | 5,625 | 6,005 | 2.4 | 54 | 2,273 | 2,327 | 0.9 |
| 1878 | 11,771 | 14,825 | 26,596 | 10.8 | 1,081 | 5,364 | 6,445 | 2.6 | 554 | 7,748 | 8,302 | 3.4 | 70 | 2,194 | 2,264 | 0.9 |
| 1879 | 11,569 | 14,989 | 26,558 | 10.7 | 1,056 | 4,984 | 6,040 | 2.4 | 498 | 7,208 | 7,706 | 3.1 | 64 | 2,144 | 2,208 | 0.9 |
| 1880 | 12,397 | 15,594 | 27,991 | 9.8 | 900 | 5,433 | 6,333 | 2.2 | 474 | 6,766 | 7,240 | 2.5 | 114 | 3,061 | 3,175 | 1.1 |
| Total for the Five Years | 60,082 | 75,727 | 135,809 | 10.5 | 5,608 | 28,689 | 34,297 | 2.7 | 2,363 | 33,270 | 35,633 | 2.8 | 359 | 12,302 | 12,661 | 1.0 |
| 1881 | 13,116 | 16,970 | 30,086 | 10.1 | 887 | 6,631 | 7,518 | 2.5 | 510 | 6,879 | 7,389 | 2.5 | 172 | 3,168 | 3,340 | 1.1 |
| 1882 | 12,337 | 17,421 | 29,758 | 9.7 | 986 | 6,480 | 7,466 | 2.4 | 548 | 6,423 | 6,971 | 2.3 | 170 | 2,451 | 2,021 | 0.9 |
| 1883 | 11,842 | 17,568 | 29,410 | 9.6 | 1,073 | 7,122 | 8,195 | 2.7 | 720 | 6,690 | 7,410 | 2.4 | 134 | 3,367 | 3,501 | 1.2 |
| Grand Total | 222,278 | 269,735 | 492,013 | 10.1 | 20,161 | 109,521 | 129,682 | 2.7 | 7,905 | 123,673 | 131,578 | 2.7 | 1,872 | 86,813 | 88,685 | 1.8 |

* Including Asiatic Turkey.

† Since the opening of the Suez Canal, some of the articles formerly entered as exported to Egypt have been entered as exported to the countries to which they were sent.

## TABLE V. (*continued*).

*Statement in detail of the Total Exports of Merchandise from the United Kingdom to each of certain Foreign Countries and British Possessions, in each Year and Period of Five Years, since 1866, with the Proportions that the Amounts for each Country and Possession bear to the whole Exports in each Year and Period ; the amounts being stated in thousands of pounds, i.e., 100 = 100,000.*

### A.—FOREIGN COUNTRIES (*continued*).

*(All amounts in £ thousands.)*

| — | UNITED STATES | | | | BRAZIL | | | | CHILI | | | | PERU | | | |
|---|---|---|---|---|---|---|---|---|---|---|---|---|---|---|---|---|
| | Exports of Foreign and Colonial Produce | Exports of British Produce | Total — Amount | Total — Per cent of Total | Exports of Foreign and Colonial Produce | Exports of British Produce | Total — Amount | Total — Per cent of Total | Exports of Foreign and Colonial Produce | Exports of British Produce | Total — Amount | Total — Per cent of Total | Exports of Foreign and Colonial Produce | Exports of British Produce | Total — Amount | Total — Per cent of Total |
| 1866 | 3,315 | 28,400 | 31,844 | 13·3 | 133 | 7,225 | 7,358 | 3·1 | 26 | 1,853 | 1,879 | 0·3 | 38 | 1,356 | 1,394 | 0·6 |
| 1867 | 2,591 | 21,520 | 24,120 | 10·7 | 128 | 5,803 | 5,931 | 2·9 | 59 | 2,524 | 2,583 | 1·1 | 62 | 1,422 | 1,484 | 0·7 |
| 1868 | 2,370 | 21,432 | 23,802 | 10·4 | 137 | 5,352 | 5,489 | 2·4 | 60 | 1,963 | 2,023 | 0·9 | 53 | 1,132 | 1,185 | 0·5 |
| 1869 | 2,164 | 24,624 | 26,788 | 11·3 | 156 | 6,965 | 7,121 | 3·0 | 54 | 1,990 | 2,044 | 0·9 | 48 | 1,382 | 1,430 | 0·6 |
| 1870 | 2,971 | 28,335 | 31,390 | 12·3 | 177 | 5,367 | 5,544 | 2·3 | 93 | 2,674 | 2,767 | 1·1 | 93 | 1,761 | 1,854 | 0·8 |
| Total for the Five Years | 13,144 | 124,710 | 137,800 | 11·7 | 731 | 30,604 | 31,335 | 2·7 | 292 | 11,004 | 11,296 | 1·0 | 294 | 7,053 | 7,347 | 0·6 |
| 1871 | 4,465 | 34,228 | 38,693 | 13·6 | 263 | 6,274 | 6,537 | 2·3 | 139 | 2,010 | 2,149 | 0·3 | 216 | 2,160 | 2,376 | 0·8 |
| 1872 | 5,171 | 40,737 | 45,908 | 14·6 | 262 | 7,520 | 7,782 | 2·5 | 221 | 3,148 | 3,369 | 1·1 | 473 | 2,870 | 3,343 | 1·1 |
| 1873 | 3,124 | 33,575 | 36,699 | 11·8 | 332 | 7,543 | 7,877 | 2·5 | 145 | 3,165 | 3,310 | 1·1 | 217 | 2,524 | 2,741 | 0·9 |
| 1874 | 3,996 | 28,242 | 32,238 | 10·8 | 308 | 7,678 | 8,046 | 2·7 | 141 | 2,751 | 2,892 | 1·0 | 237 | 1,593 | 1,830 | 0·6 |
| 1875 | 3,194 | 21,868 | 25,062 | 8·9 | 303 | 6,869 | 7,172 | 2·5 | 137 | 2,207 | 2,344 | 0·8 | 223 | 1,595 | 1,818 | 0·6 |
| Total for the Five Years | 19,950 | 158,650 | 178,600 | 12·0 | 1,528 | 35,530 | 37,414 | 2·5 | 783 | 13,281 | 14,064 | 0·9 | 1,366 | 10,742 | 12,108 | 0·8 |
| 1876 | 3,393 | 16,834 | 20,227 | 7·9 | 316 | 5,920 | 6,236 | 2·4 | 119 | 1,916 | 2,035 | 0·8 | 178 | 991 | 1,169 | 0·5 |
| 1877 | 3,509 | 16,377 | 19,886 | 7·9 | 447 | 5,959 | 6,406 | 2·5 | 109 | 1,502 | 1,611 | 0·6 | 155 | 1,266 | 1,421 | 0·6 |
| 1878 | 2,980 | 14,552 | 17,532 | 7·1 | 621 | 5,578 | 6,199 | 2·5 | 102 | 1,191 | 1,293 | 0·5 | 221 | 1,370 | 1,591 | 0·6 |
| 1879 | 5,197 | 20,322 | 25,519 | 10·3 | 301 | 5,685 | 5,986 | 2·4 | 99 | 950 | 1,049 | 0·4 | 162 | 747 | 909 | 0·4 |
| 1880 | 7,098 | 30,850 | 37,954 | 13·3 | 233 | 6,682 | 6,915 | 2·4 | 247 | 1,919 | 2,166 | 0·8 | 67 | 313 | 380 | 0·1 |
| Total for the Five Years | 22,177 | 98,941 | 121,118 | 9·4 | 1,918 | 29,824 | 31,742 | 2·5 | 676 | 7,508 | 8,184 | 0·6 | 783 | 4,687 | 5,470 | 0·4 |
| 1881 | 6,987 | 29,796 | 36,783 | 12·4 | 258 | 6,656 | 6,914 | 2·3 | 166 | 2,521 | 2,687 | 0·9 | 136 | 809 | 945 | 0·3 |
| 1882 | 7,738 | 30,970 | 38,708 | 12·6 | 450 | 6,876 | 7,326 | 2·4 | 152 | 3,000 | 3,152 | 1·0 | 184 | 985 | 1,160 | 0·4 |
| 1883 | 9,360 | 27,373 | 36,733 | 12·0 | 367 | 6,648 | 7,015 | 2·3 | 129 | 2,060 | 2,189 | 0·7 | 153 | 735 | 888 | 0·3 |
| Grand Total | 79,356 | 470,446 | 549,802 | 11·3 | 5,252 | 116,494 | 121,746 | 2·5 | 2,198 | 39,374 | 41,572 | 0·9 | 2,916 | 25,011 | 27,927 | 0·6 |

# TABLE V. (*continued*).
## A —FOREIGN COUNTRIES (*continued*).

| | CHINA.* | | JAPAN. | | | | OTHER FOREIGN COUNTRIES. | | | | TOTAL FOREIGN COUNTRIES. | | | |
|---|---|---|---|---|---|---|---|---|---|---|---|---|---|---|
| Ports share. | Total Amount. | Per cent of Total. | Exports of Foreign and Colonial Produce. | Exports of British Produce. | Total Amount. | Per cent of Total. | Exports of Foreign and Colonial Produce. | Exports of British Produce. | Total Amount. | Per cent of Total. | Exports of Foreign and Colonial Produce. | Exports of British Produce. | Total Amount. | Per cent of Total. |
| | £ | | £ | £ | £ | | £ | £ | £ | | £ | £ | £ | |
| 90 | 5,208 | 2·2 | 116 | 1,444 | 1,560 | 0·7 | 3,631 | 25,930 | 29,561 | 12·4 | 46,540 | 135,198 | 181,738 | 76·1 |
| 96 | 5,110 | 2·3 | 149 | 1,545 | 1,694 | 0·8 | 3,394 | 24,602 | 27,606 | 12·3 | 41,278 | 131,162 | 172,440 | 76·4 |
| 12 | 6,422 | 2·8 | 106 | 1,113 | 1,219 | 0·5 | 3,152 | 22,657 | 25,809 | 11·5 | 44,248 | 129,813 | 174,061 | 76·4 |
| 43 | 6,986 | 2·9 | 154 | 1,442 | 1,596 | 0·7 | 3,205 | 22,043 | 25,248 | 10·6 | 43,242 | 141,881 | 185,123 | 78·1 |
| 40 | 6,363 | 2·6 | 168 | 1,609 | 1,777 | 0·7 | 4,060 | 26,046 | 30,106 | 12·3 | 40,917 | 147,772 | 188,689 | 77·3 |
| 81 | 30,089 | 2·6 | 693 | 7,153 | 7,846 | 0·7 | 17,442 | 121,278 | 138,720 | 11·8 | 216,225 | 685,826 | 962,051 | 76·9 |
| 28 | 6,796 | 2·4 | 162 | 1,584 | 1,746 | 0·6 | 4,695 | 27,056 | 31,751 | 11·2 | 56,197 | 171,816 | 228,013 | 80·4 |
| 24 | 6,870 | 2·2 | 186 | 1,961 | 2,147 | 0·7 | 4,796 | 33,224 | 38,020 | 11·9 | 53,278 | 195,702 | 248,980 | 79·1 |
| 83 | 5,017 | 1·6 | 204 | 1,680 | 1,884 | 0·6 | 5,497 | 36,558 | 42,055 | 13·5 | 51,021 | 188,836 | 239,857 | 77·1 |
| 51 | 4,853 | 1·6 | 81 | 1,283 | 1,364 | 0·5 | 5,472 | 33,785 | 39,257 | 13·1 | 52,462 | 167,278 | 219,740 | 73·8 |
| 28 | 5,097 | 1·8 | 134 | 2,460 | 2,594 | 0·9 | 5,410 | 31,238 | 36,648 | 13·2 | 52,583 | 152,374 | 204,957 | 72·8 |
| 14 | 28,633 | 1·9 | 767 | 8,908 | 9,735 | 0·7 | 25,870 | 161,861 | 187,731 | 12·6 | 265,541 | 876,006 | 1,141,547 | 76·7 |
| 11 | 4,719 | 1·3 | 159 | 2,033 | 2,192 | 0·9 | 5,708 | 28,200 | 33,908 | 13·1 | 50,847 | 135,780 | 186,627 | 72·7 |
| 05 | 4,611 | 1·8 | 257 | 2,203 | 2,459 | 1·0 | 5,697 | 30,169 | 35,866 | 14·1 | 47,624 | 125,070 | 175,594 | 70·0 |
| 38 | 3,950 | 1·6 | 290 | 2,616 | 2,906 | 1·2 | 5,163 | 26,590 | 31,753 | 13·1 | 45,286 | 126,611 | 173,491 | 70·7 |
| 50 | 5,140 | 2·1 | 359 | 2,638 | 2,997 | 1·2 | 5,075 | 25,510 | 30,591 | 12·2 | 51,745 | 130,529 | 182,274 | 73·3 |
| 54 | 5,515 | 1·9 | 522 | 3,091 | 3,613 | 1·3 | 5,832 | 28,838 | 34,740 | 12·2 | 57,081 | 147,808 | 204,887 | 71·5 |
| 58 | 23,935 | 1·9 | 1,587 | 12,781 | 14,368 | 1·1 | 27,495 | 139,363 | 166,858 | 12·8 | 254,177 | 660,696 | 973,873 | 71·6 |
| 55 | 6,234 | 2·1 | 328 | 2,825 | 3,153 | 1·1 | 5,123 | 32,867 | 37,990 | 12·8 | 55,744 | 154,658 | 210,402 | 70·8 |
| 13 | 4,892 | 1·6 | 289 | 2,119 | 2,408 | 0·8 | 5,767 | 33,553 | 39,320 | 12·8 | 57,682 | 156,641 | 214,[illegible] | 69·9 |
| 25 | 4,528 | 1·5 | 325 | 2,277 | 2,602 | 0·9 | 5,928 | 36,598 | 42,526 | 13·9 | 58,714 | 156,322 | 215,[illegible] | 70·4 |
| 56 | 98,311 | 2·0 | 3,089 | 36,123 | 40,112 | 0·8 | 87,625 | 525,520 | 613,145 | 12·6 | 908,083 | 2,699,140 | 3,607,232 | 74·2 |

* Exclusive of Hong Kong and Macão.

## TABLE V. (continued).

Statement in detail of the Total Exports of Merchandise from the United Kingdom to each of certain Foreign Countries and British Possessions, in each Year and period of Five Years, since 1866, with the Proportions that the Amounts for each Country and Possession bear to the whole Exports in each Year and Period; the amounts being stated in thousands of pounds, i.e., 100 = 100,000.

### B.—BRITISH POSSESSIONS AND TOTALS.

| | BRITISH NORTH AMERICA. | | | | BRITISH WEST INDIES AND BRITISH GUIANA. | | | | AUSTRALIA AND NEW ZEALAND. | | | | BRITISH INDIA | | | |
|---|---|---|---|---|---|---|---|---|---|---|---|---|---|---|---|---|
| — | Exports of Foreign and Colonial Produce. | Exports of British Produce. | Total. Amount. | Total. Per cent. of Total. | Exports of Foreign and Colonial Produce | Exports of British Produce. | Total. Amount. | Total. Per cent. of Total. | Exports of Foreign and Colonial Produce. | Exports of British Produce. | Total. Amount. | Total. Per cent. of Total. | Exports of Foreign and Colonial Produce. | Exports of British Produce. | Total. Amount. | Total. Per cent. of Total. |
| | £ | £ | £ | | £ | £ | £ | | £ | £ | £ | | £ | £ | £ | |
| 1866 | 877 | 6,825 | 7,702 | 3·2 | 231 | 2,686 | 2,917 | 1·2 | 978 | 13,643 | 14,621 | 6·1 | 662 | 20,010 | 20,672 | 8·7 |
| 1867 | 868 | 5,862 | 6,730 | 3·0 | 228 | 2,293 | 2,521 | 1·1 | 744 | 9,614 | 10,358 | 4·6 | 1,042 | 21,805 | 22,847 | 10·1 |
| 1868 | 724 | 4,848 | 5,572 | 2·5 | 306 | 2,459 | 2,765 | 1·2 | 987 | 12,076 | 13,063 | 5·7 | 1,018 | 21,252 | 22,270 | 9·8 |
| 1869 | 750 | 5,159 | 5,909 | 2·5 | 304 | 2,488 | 2,792 | 1·2 | 970 | 13,412 | 14,382 | 6·1 | 951 | 17,560 | 18,511 | 7·8 |
| 1870 | 800 | 6,784 | 7,584 | 3·1 | 275 | 3,309 | 3,584 | 1·5 | 837 | 9,899 | 10,736 | 4·4 | 790 | 19,304 | 20,094 | 8·2 |
| Total for the Five Years | 4,019 | 29,478 | 33,497 | 2·9 | 1,344 | 13,235 | 14,579 | 1·2 | 4,516 | 58,644 | 63,160 | 5·4 | 4,463 | 99,931 | 104,394 | 8·9 |
| 1871 | 855 | 8,257 | 9,112 | 3·2 | 354 | 2,943 | 3,297 | 1·2 | 1,062 | 10,052 | 11,114 | 3·9 | 959 | 18,054 | 19,013 | 6·7 |
| 1872 | 1,131 | 10,193 | 11,324 | 3·6 | 357 | 3,325 | 3,682 | 1·2 | 1,341 | 14,142 | 15,483 | 4·9 | 1,015 | 18,471 | 19,486 | 6·2 |
| 1873 | 754 | 8,620 | 9,374 | 3·0 | 303 | 3,273 | 3,576 | 1·2 | 1,615 | 17,611 | 19,226 | 6·2 | 960 | 21,354 | 22,314 | 7·2 |
| 1874 | 879 | 9,332 | 10,211 | 3·4 | 302 | 3,228 | 3,530 | 1·2 | 1,606 | 19,063 | 20,669 | 6·9 | 1,354 | 24,081 | 25,435 | 8·6 |
| 1875 | 646 | 9,037 | 9,683 | 3·4 | 340 | 2,935 | 3,275 | 1·2 | 1,733 | 19,491 | 21,224 | 7·5 | 1,349 | 24,246 | 25,595 | 9·1 |
| Total for the Five Years | 4,265 | 45,439 | 49,704 | 3·3 | 1,656 | 15,704 | 17,360 | 1·2 | 7,357 | 80,359 | 87,716 | 5·9 | 5,637 | 106,206 | 111,843 | 7·5 |
| 1876 | 668 | 7,358 | 8,026 | 3·1 | 329 | 2,873 | 3,202 | 1·3 | 1,788 | 17,682 | 19,470 | 7·6 | 1,272 | 22,405 | 23,677 | 9·2 |
| 1877 | 643 | 7,613 | 8,256 | 3·3 | 306 | 2,832 | 3,138 | 1·2 | 2,218 | 19,286 | 21,504 | 8·5 | 1,281 | 25,338 | 26,619 | 10·6 |
| 1878 | 597 | 6,437 | 7,034 | 2·9 | 287 | 2,604 | 2,891 | 1·2 | 1,952 | 19,574 | 21,526 | 8·8 | 1,382 | 23,277 | 24,659 | 10·0 |
| 1879 | 674 | 5,445 | 6,119 | 2·5 | 276 | 2,671 | 2,947 | 1·2 | 1,689 | 16,271 | 17,960 | 7·2 | 1,340 | 21,375 | 22,715 | 9·1 |
| 1880 | 807 | 7,709 | 8,516 | 3·0 | 388 | 2,861 | 3,249 | 1·1 | 1,817 | 16,931 | 18,748 | 6·5 | 1,577 | 30,451 | 32,028 | 11·2 |
| Total for the Five Years | 3,389 | 34,562 | 37,951 | 2·9 | 1,586 | 13,841 | 15,427 | 1·2 | 9,464 | 89,744 | 99,208 | 7·7 | 6,852 | 122,846 | 129,698 | 10·1 |
| 1881 | 897 | 8,411 | 9,308 | 3·1 | 321 | 2,579 | 2,900 | 1·0 | 2,604 | 21,378 | 23,982 | 8·1 | 1,809 | 29,244 | 31,053 | 10·4 |
| 1882 | 983 | 9,700 | 10,683 | 3·5 | 300 | 3,167 | 3,467 | 1·1 | 3,086 | 25,365 | 28,451 | 9·3 | 1,523 | 29,059 | 30,582 | 10·0 |
| 1883 | 954 | 9,156 | 10,110 | 3·3 | 352 | 3,401 | 3,753 | 1·2 | 2,623 | 24,216 | 26,839 | 8·8 | 1,509 | 31,874 | 33,383 | 10·9 |
| Grand Total | 14,527 | 136,746 | 151,253 | 3·1 | 5,559 | 51,927 | 57,486 | 1·2 | 29,650 | 299,706 | 329,356 | 6·8 | 21,793 | 419,160 | 440,953 | 9·1 |

| — | Cape of Good Hope and Natal. | | | | Other British Possessions. | | | | Total British Possessions. | | | | Total Foreign Countries and British Possessions. | | | |
|---|---|---|---|---|---|---|---|---|---|---|---|---|---|---|---|---|
| | Exports of Foreign and Colonial Produce. | Exports of British Produce. | Total Amount. | Total Per cent. of Total. | Exports of Foreign and Colonial Produce. | Exports of British Produce. | Total Amount. | Total Per cent. of Total. | Exports of Foreign and Colonial Produce. | Exports of British Produce. | Total Amount. | Total Per cent. of Total. | Exports of Foreign and Colonial Produce. | Exports of British Produce. | Total Amount. | Total Per cent. of Total. |
| | £ | £ | £ | | £ | £ | £ | | £ | £ | £ | | £ | £ | £ | |
| 1866 | 61 | 1,399 | 1,460 | 0·6 | 639 | 9,157 | 9,796 | 4·1 | 3,448 | 53,720 | 57,168 | 23·9 | 49,928 | 188,918 | 238,906 | 100 |
| 1867 | 74 | 1,893 | 1,907 | 0·8 | 607 | 8,333 | 8,940 | 4·0 | 3,563 | 49,800 | 53,363 | 23·6 | 44,841 | 180,962 | 225,803 | 100 |
| 1868 | 69 | 1,591 | 1,660 | 0·7 | 749 | 7,639 | 8,388 | 3·7 | 3,853 | 49,865 | 53,718 | 23·6 | 48,101 | 179,678 | 227,779 | 100 |
| 1869 | 70 | 1,572 | 1,642 | 0·7 | 774 | 7,882 | 8,656 | 3·6 | 3,819 | 48,073 | 51,892 | 21·9 | 47,061 | 189,954 | 237,015 | 100 |
| 1870 | 104 | 1,859 | 1,963 | 0·8 | 771 | 10,660 | 11,431 | 4·7 | 3,577 | 51,815 | 55,392 | 22·7 | 44,494 | 199,587 | 244,081 | 100 |
| Total for the five Years | 378 | 8,314 | 8,692 | 0·7 | 3,540 | 43,671 | 47,211 | 4·0 | 18,260 | 253,273 | 271,533 | 23·1 | 234,485 | 939,099 | 1,173,584 | 100 |
| 1871 | 117 | 2,198 | 2,315 | 0·8 | 965 | 9,746 | 10,711 | 3·8 | 4,312 | 51,250 | 55,562 | 19·6 | 60,509 | 223,066 | 283,575 | 100 |
| 1872 | 288 | 3,706 | 3,994 | 1·3 | 922 | 10,718 | 11,640 | 3·7 | 5,054 | 60,555 | 65,609 | 20·9 | 58,332 | 256,257 | 314,589 | 100 |
| 1873 | 311 | 4,335 | 4,646 | 1·5 | 876 | 11,136 | 12,012 | 3·8 | 4,819 | 66,329 | 71,148 | 22·9 | 55,840 | 255,165 | 311,005 | 100 |
| 1874 | 400 | 4,302 | 4,702 | 1·6 | 1,089 | 12,274 | 13,363 | 4·5 | 5,630 | 72,280 | 77,910 | 26·2 | 58,092 | 239,558 | 297,650 | 100 |
| 1875 | 441 | 4,910 | 5,351 | 1·9 | 1,054 | 10,473 | 11,527 | 4·1 | 5,563 | 71,092 | 76,655 | 27·2 | 58,146 | 223,460 | 281,612 | 100 |
| Total for the five Years | 1,557 | 19,451 | 21,008 | 1·4 | 4,906 | 54,347 | 59,253 | 4·0 | 25,378 | 321,506 | 346,884 | 23·3 | 290,919 | 1,197,512 | 1,488,431 | 100 |
| 1876 | 315 | 4,369 | 4,684 | 1·8 | 919 | 10,172 | 11,091 | 4·3 | 5,291 | 64,859 | 70,150 | 27·3 | 56,138 | 200,639 | 256,777 | 100 |
| 1877 | 387 | 4,116 | 4,503 | 1·8 | 994 | 10,738 | 11,732 | 4·6 | 5,829 | 69,923 | 75,752 | 30·0 | 53,453 | 198,893 | 252,346 | 100 |
| 1878 | 546 | 4,913 | 5,459 | 2·2 | 991 | 9,433 | 10,424 | 4·2 | 5,755 | 66,238 | 71,993 | 29·3 | 52,635 | 192,849 | 245,484 | 100 |
| 1879 | 517 | 5,853 | 6,370 | 2·6 | 1,010 | 9,388 | 10,398 | 4·1 | 5,506 | 61,003 | 66,509 | 26·7 | 57,251 | 191,532 | 248,783 | 100 |
| 1880 | 570 | 6,630 | 7,206 | 2·5 | 1,108 | 10,672 | 11,780 | 4·2 | 6,273 | 75,254 | 81,527 | 28·5 | 63,354 | 223,060 | 286,414 | 100 |
| Total for the five Years | 2,341 | 25,881 | 28,222 | 2·2 | 5,022 | 50,403 | 55,425 | 4·3 | 28,054 | 337,277 | 365,931 | 28·4 | 282,831 | 1,006,973 | 1,289,804 | 100 |
| 1881 | 619 | 7,021 | 7,692 | 2·6 | 1,066 | 10,680 | 11,740 | 4·0 | 7,316 | 79,366 | 86,681 | 29·2 | 63,066 | 234,023 | 297,083 | 100 |
| 1882 | 582 | 7,490 | 8,078 | 2·6 | 1,030 | 10,379 | 11,077 | 3·0 | 7,513 | 84,980 | 92,338 | 30·1 | 63,194 | 241,417 | 300,001 | 100 |
| 1883 | 443 | 4,557 | 5,000 | 1·7 | 1,043 | 10,273 | 11,316 | 3·7 | 6,924 | 83,477 | 90,401 | 29·0 | 63,038 | 232,740 | 295,437 | 100 |
| Grand Total | 5,920 | 72,772 | 78,692 | 1·6 | 16,615 | 179,415 | 190,028 | 4·0 | 94,044 | 1,159,724 | 1,253,768 | 25·8 | 1,002,127 | 3,855,763 | 4,861,000 | 100 |

## TABLE VI.

Statement in detail of the Imports of Merchandise into the United Kingdom from each of certain Foreign Countries and British Possessions, in each Year and period of Five Years, since 1866, with the Proportions that the Amounts from each Country and Possession bear to the whole Imports in each Year and Period; the amount being stated in thousands of pounds—i.e., 100 = 100,000.

### A.—FOREIGN COUNTRIES.

| | RUSSIA. | | GERMANY. | | HOLLAND. | | BELGIUM. | | FRANCE. | | ITALY. | | TURKEY.* | | EGYPT.† | |
|---|---|---|---|---|---|---|---|---|---|---|---|---|---|---|---|---|
| | Amount. | Per cent. of Total. | Amount. | Per cent. of Total. | Amount. | Per cent. of Total. | Amount. | Per cent. of Total. | Amount. | Per cent. of Total. | Amount. | Per cent. of Total. | Amount. | Per cent. of Total. | Amount. | Per cent. of Total. |
| | £ | | £ | | £ | | £ | | £ | | £ | | £ | | £ | |
| 1866 | 19,625 | 6·6 | [illegible] | 6·5 | 11,7[illegible] | 4·0 | 7,[illegible] | 2·7 | 37,017 | 12·5 | [illegible]25 | 1·3 | 5,44[illegible] | 1·[illegible] | 15,[illegible] | 5·3 |
| 1867 | 22,287 | 6·1 | 1[illegible],807 | 6·[illegible] | 1[illegible],82[illegible] | 3·9 | 7,555 | 2·8 | [illegible],735 | 12·[illegible] | [illegible]107 | 1·1 | 4,[illegible]37 | 1·3 | 15,49[illegible] | 5·[illegible] |
| 1868 | 20,082 | 6·3 | 1[illegible],17[illegible] | 6·2 | 1[illegible],391 | 3·9 | [illegible]55 | 2·8 | 3[illegible],840 | 11·5 | 4,[illegible]4 | 1·4 | 6,2[illegible]7 | 2·1 | 17,505 | 6·0 |
| 1869 | 16,675 | 5·6 | 1[illegible],[illegible]84 | 6·2 | 12,7[illegible] | 4·3 | [illegible]01 | 3·2 | 3[illegible],5[illegible]7 | 11·3 | [illegible] | 1·4 | 7,747 | 2·[illegible] | 19,7[illegible] | 5·7 |
| 1870 | 20,501 | 6·3 | 15,404 | 5·1 | 14,[illegible]10 | 4·7 | 11,[illegible]48 | 3·7 | 37,[illegible]07 | 12·4 | [illegible]44 | 1·3 | 6,037 | 2·2 | 14,117 | 4·7 |
| Total for the Five Years | 69,[illegible] | 6·3 | [illegible],807 | 6·1 | 61,047 | 4·[illegible] | 44,[illegible] | 3·0 | 175,7[illegible] | 12·[illegible] | 13,7[illegible] | 1·3 | 30,3[illegible] | 2·1 | 79,365 | 5·4 |
| 1871 | 2[illegible],721 | 7·2 | 1[illegible],[illegible] | 5·[illegible] | 13,970 | 4·2 | 13,573 | 4·1 | [illegible],940 | [illegible] | 4,624 | 1·4 | 7,029 | 2·1 | 16,387 | 5·0 |
| 1872 | 24,[illegible] | 6·9 | 1[illegible],[illegible]3[illegible] | 5·4 | 14,1[illegible] | 3·7 | 13,211 | 3·7 | 41,8[illegible]3 | 11·8 | 4,159 | 1·2 | 5,441 | 1·5 | 16,456 | 4·6 |
| 1873 | 21,1[illegible] | 5·7 | 1[illegible],9[illegible]7 | 5·4 | 14,272 | 3·6 | 13,075 | 3·5 | 4[illegible],[illegible]39 | 11·7 | 3,631 | 1·0 | 6,0[illegible] | 1·6 | 14,156 | 3·8 |
| 1874 | 2[illegible],07[illegible] | 5·7 | 16,947 | 5·4 | 14,464 | 3·9 | 15,040 | 4·1 | 4[illegible],519 | 12·5 | 3,[illegible]4 | 1·0 | 5,843 | 1·6 | 10,515 | 2·8 |
| 1875 | 20,70[illegible] | 5·5 | 21,836 | 5·[illegible] | 14,837 | 4·0 | 14,[illegible]2[illegible] | 4·0 | 46,72[illegible] | 12·5 | 4,633 | 1·2 | 6,556 | 1·8 | 10,805 | 2·9 |
| Total for the Five Years | 110,87[illegible] | 6·2 | 160,205 | 5·6 | 64,652 | 3·9 | 69,730 | 3·9 | 20[illegible],230 | 11·6 | 20,881 | 1·1 | 30,948 | 1·7 | 68,409 | 3·8 |
| 1876 | 17,575 | 4·7 | 21,115 | 5·6 | 16,602 | 4·4 | 13,848 | 3·7 | 45,305 | 12·1 | 4,152 | 1·1 | 7,444 | 2·0 | 11,482 | 3·1 |
| 1877 | 22,142 | 5·6 | 26,[illegible]7[illegible] | 6·7 | 10,861 | 5·0 | 12,[illegible]8[illegible] | 3·3 | 45,8[illegible]3 | 11·6 | 4,101 | 1·0 | 6,852 | 1·7 | 11,102 | 2·8 |
| 1878 | 17,804 | 4·8 | 2[illegible],571 | [illegible]·4 | 21,466 | 5·8 | 12,[illegible]87 | 3·4 | 41,37[illegible] | 11·2 | 3,252 | 0·9 | 4,779 | 1·3 | 6,145 | 1·7 |
| 1879 | 15,877 | 4·4 | 21,[illegible]05 | 6·0 | 21,959 | 6·0 | 10,7[illegible] | 3·0 | 38,45[illegible] | 10·6 | 3,234 | 0·9 | 3,473 | 1·0 | 8,860 | 2·4 |
| 1880 | 10,030 | 3·9 | 24,355 | 5·9 | 25,909 | 6·3 | 11,254 | 2·7 | 41,07[illegible] | 10·2 | 3,385 | 0·8 | 3,874 | 1·0 | 9,191 | 2·2 |
| Total for the Five Years | 84,42[illegible] | 4·7 | 116,016 | 6·1 | 105,797 | 5·5 | 61,104 | 3·2 | 212,936 | 11·1 | 18,124 | 0·9 | 26,422 | 1·4 | 46,810 | 2·4 |
| 1881 | 14,053 | 3·5 | 23,650 | 6·0 | 23,023 | 5·8 | 11,510 | 2·9 | 3[illegible],6[illegible]4 | 10·1 | 3,275 | 0·8 | 4,17[illegible] | 1·0 | 9,318 | 2·3 |
| 1882 | 21,048 | 5·1 | 25,[illegible]71 | 6·2 | 25,321 | 6·1 | 14,933 | 3·6 | 3[illegible],0[illegible]0 | 9·5 | 3,481 | 0·3 | 4,63[illegible] | 1·2 | 7,796 | 1·9 |
| 1883 | 20,976 | 4·9 | 27,908 | 6·5 | 25,116 | 5·9 | 16,178 | 3·8 | 38,63[illegible] | 9·1 | 3,39[illegible] | 0·8 | 5,405 | 1·3 | 10,009 | 2·3 |
| Grand Total | 355,577 | 5·5 | 384,177 | 6·0 | 300,946 | 4·8 | 217,811 | 3·4 | 714,658 | 11·1 | 67,951 | 1·1 | 102,137 | 1·6 | 221,707 | 3·5 |

* Including Asiatic Turkey.

† Since the opening of the Suez Canal some of the articles formerly entered as imported from Egypt have been entered as imported from the countries of production, principally silk from China.

## TABLE VI. (continued).

### A.—FOREIGN COUNTRIES (continued).

| | UNITED STATES | | BRAZIL. | | CHILI. | | PERU. | | CHINA.‡ | | JAPAN. | | OTHER FOREIGN COUNTRIES. | | TOTAL FROM FOREIGN COUNTRIES. | |
|---|---|---|---|---|---|---|---|---|---|---|---|---|---|---|---|---|
| | Amount. | Per cent. of Total. | Amount. | Per cent. of Total. | Amount. | Per cent. of Total. | Amount. | Per cent. of Total. | Amount. | Per cent. of Total. | Amount. | Per cent. of Total. | Amount. | Per cent. of Total. | Amount. | Per cent. of Total. |
| | £ | | £ | | £ | | £ | | £ | | £ | | £ | | £ | |
| 1866 | 46,854 | 15·9 | 7,238 | 2·5 | 2,943 | 1·0 | 3,022 | 1·0 | 10,620 | 3·6 | 274 | 0·1 | 32,090 | 10·8 | 223,084 | 75·5 |
| 1867 | 41,046 | 14·9 | 5,902 | 2·1 | 4,418 | 1·6 | 3,701 | 1·3 | 9,213 | 3·4 | 318 | 0·1 | 33,703 | 12·3 | 214,449 | 77·9 |
| 1868 | 43,062 | 14·6 | 7,456 | 2·5 | 4,367 | 1·5 | 3,400 | 1·2 | 11,217 | 3·3 | 181 | 0·1 | 38,404 | 12·9 | 227,700 | 77·3 |
| 1869 | 42,573 | 14·4 | 7,313 | 2·5 | 3,635 | 1·2 | 3,993 | 1·4 | 9,621 | 3·3 | 167 | 0·1 | 38,515 | 13·0 | 225,044 | 76·2 |
| 1870 | 49,805 | 16·4 | 6,127 | 2·0 | 3,828 | 1·3 | 4,861 | 1·6 | 9,482 | 3·1 | 96 | — | 40,472 | 13·3 | 238,425 | 78·6 |
| Total for the Five Years | 223,340 | 15·3 | 34,036 | 2·3 | 19,191 | 1·3 | 18,907 | 1·3 | 50,153 | 3·4 | 1,036 | 0·1 | 183,184 | 12·5 | 1,128,702 | 77·1 |
| 1871 | 61,135 | 18·5 | 6,694 | 2·0 | 3,798 | 1·1 | 3,972 | 1·2 | 11,830 | 3·5 | 109 | — | 42,107 | 12·8 | 258,071 | 78·0 |
| 1872 | 54,064 | 15·4 | 9,450 | 2·7 | 5,592 | 1·6 | 4,212 | 1·2 | 13,246 | 3·7 | 184 | 0·1 | 50,242 | 14·1 | 275,321 | 77·6 |
| 1873 | 71,472 | 19·2 | 7,100 | 2·0 | 4,764 | 1·3 | 5,220 | 1·4 | 12,454 | 3·4 | 561 | 0·2 | 53,548 | 14·4 | 290,277 | 78·2 |
| 1874 | 73,868 | 20·0 | 7,003 | 1·9 | 4,701 | 1·3 | 4,501 | 1·2 | 11,146 | 3·0 | 573 | 0·1 | 49,194 | 13·3 | 287,920 | 77·8 |
| 1875 | 69,500 | 18·6 | 7,419 | 2·0 | 4,196 | 1·1 | 4,884 | 1·3 | 13,608 | 3·6 | 378 | 0·1 | 48,433 | 13·0 | 289,516 | 77·4 |
| Total for the Five Years | 330,780 | 18·4 | 37,066 | 2·1 | 23,051 | 1·3 | 22,789 | 1·3 | 62,284 | 3·4 | 1,805 | 0·1 | 243,524 | 13·4 | 1,401,105 | 77·8 |
| 1876 | 75,899 | 20·2 | 5,178 | 1·4 | 3,565 | 1·0 | 5,631 | 1·5 | 14,921 | 4·0 | 657 | 0·2 | 47,428 | 12·5 | 290,822 | 77·5 |
| 1877 | 77,066 | 19·7 | 6,345 | 1·6 | 3,359 | 0·8 | 4,697 | 1·2 | 13,421 | 3·4 | 734 | 0·2 | 49,523 | 12·7 | 304,866 | 77·3 |
| 1878 | 89,146 | 24·2 | 4,931 | 1·3 | 2,157 | 0·6 | 5,232 | 1·4 | 13,601 | 3·7 | 629 | 0·2 | 44,504 | 12·0 | 290,835 | 78·9 |
| 1879 | 91,812 | 25·3 | 4,750 | 1·3 | 3,738 | 1·0 | 3,489 | 0·9 | 11,049 | 3·0 | 451 | 0·1 | 44,631 | 12·4 | 284,049 | 78·3 |
| 1880 | 107,081 | 26·0 | 5,261 | 1·3 | 3,457 | 0·8 | 2,653 | 0·7 | 11,820 | 2·9 | 532 | 0·1 | 51,933 | 12·7 | 318,711 | 77·5 |
| Total for the Five Years | 441,770 | 23·1 | 26,185 | 1·4 | 16,259 | 0·9 | 21,702 | 1·1 | 64,812 | 3·4 | 3,003 | 0·2 | 238,109 | 12·5 | 1,479,283 | 77·9 |
| 1881 | 103,208 | 26·0 | 6,340 | 1·6 | 2,731 | 0·7 | 2,189 | 0·5 | 10,702 | 2·7 | 676 | 0·2 | 50,654 | 12·8 | 305,453 | 76·9 |
| 1882 | 88,353 | 21·4 | 6,412 | 1·6 | 3,437 | 0·8 | 2,685 | 0·7 | 9,936 | 2·4 | 721 | 0·2 | 59,903 | 14·5 | 313,580 | 76·0 |
| 1883 | [illegible] | 23·3 | 6,139 | 1·4 | 3,440 | 0·8 | 2,250 | 0·5 | 10,118 | 2·4 | 663 | 0·2 | 56,071 | 13·7 | 328,210 | 76·9 |
| Grand Total | 1,336,669 | 20·1 | 117,148 | 1·6 | [illegible] | 1·1 | 70,512 | 1·1 | 208,031 | 3·2 | 7,904 | 0·1 | 834,045 | 13·0 | 4,966,372 | 77·4 |

‡ Exclusive of Hong Kong and Macao.

P 2

## TABLE VI. (*continued*).

*Statement in detail of the Imports of Merchandise into the United Kingdom from each of certain Foreign Countries and British Possessions, in each Year and period of Five Years, since 1866, with the Proportions that the Amounts from each Country and Possession bear to the whole Imports in each Year and Period; the amounts being stated in thousands of pounds, i.e., 100 = 10,000.*

### B.—BRITISH POSSESSIONS AND TOTALS.

| | BRITISH NORTH AMERICA. | | BRITISH WEST INDIES AND BRITISH GUIANA. | | AUSTRALIA AND NEW ZEALAND. | | BRITISH INDIA. | | CAPE OF GOOD HOPE AND NATAL. | | OTHER BRITISH POSSESSIONS. | | TOTAL FROM BRITISH POSSESSIONS. | | TOTAL IMPORTS FROM FOREIGN COUNTRIES AND BRITISH POSSESSIONS. | |
|---|---|---|---|---|---|---|---|---|---|---|---|---|---|---|---|---|
| | Amount. | Per cent. of Total. | Amount. | Per cent. of Total. | Amount. | Per cent. of Total. | Amount. | Per cent. of Total. | Amount. | Per cent. of Total. | Amount. | Per cent. of Total. | Amount. | Per cent. of Total. | Amount. | Per cent. of Total. |
| | £ | | £ | | £ | | £ | | £ | | £ | | £ | | £ | |
| 1866 | 6,868 | 2·3 | 6,332 | 2·1 | 11,423 | 3·9 | 30,902 | 12·5 | 2,720 | 0·9 | 7,064 | 2·3 | 72,206 | 24·5 | 295,220 | 100 |
| 1867 | 6,767 | 2·5 | 5,812 | 2·1 | 12,264 | 4·7 | 25,488 | 9·3 | 2,741 | 1·0 | 6,986 | 2·5 | 60,734 | 22·1 | 275,123 | 100 |
| 1868 | 6,772 | 2·3 | 6,566 | 2·2 | 12,572 | 4·3 | 30,072 | 10·2 | 2,715 | 0·9 | 8,297 | 2·3 | 66,094 | 22·7 | 294,094 | 100 |
| 1869 | 7,735 | 2·6 | 5,985 | 2·0 | 12,147 | 4·1 | 33,245 | 11·3 | 2,726 | 0·9 | 8,572 | 2·9 | 70,416 | 23·3 | 295,460 | 100 |
| 1870 | 8,515 | 2·8 | 5,940 | 2·0 | 14,075 | 4·6 | 25,090 | 8·3 | 2,874 | 0·9 | 8,438 | 2·3 | 64,832 | 21·4 | 303,257 | 100 |
| Total for the Five Years | 36,657 | 2·5 | 30,691 | 2·1 | 63,101 | 4·3 | 150,797 | 10·3 | 13,776 | 0·9 | 40,160 | 2·3 | 335,182 | 22·0 | 1,463,884 | 100 |
| 1871 | 9,292 | 2·8 | 6,080 | 2·1 | 14,520 | 4·4 | 30,737 | 9·3 | 2,858 | 0·9 | 8,557 | 2·5 | 72,944 | 22·0 | 331,015 | 100 |
| 1872 | 9,131 | 2·6 | 6,445 | 1·8 | 15,626 | 4·4 | 33,002 | 9·5 | 3,718 | 1·0 | 10,771 | 3·1 | 79,373 | 22·4 | 354,694 | 100 |
| 1873 | 11,728 | 3·2 | 6,475 | 1·7 | 17,262 | 4·0 | 29,801 | 8·1 | 4,121 | 1·1 | 11,532 | 3·1 | 81,010 | 21·8 | 371,287 | 100 |
| 1874 | 11,859 | 3·2 | 6,184 | 1·7 | 18,548 | 5·0 | 31,198 | 8·4 | 4,297 | 1·2 | 10,072 | 2·7 | 82,163 | 22·2 | 370,083 | 100 |
| 1875 | 10,213 | 2·7 | 7,326 | 2·0 | 20,550 | 5·5 | 30,137 | 8·1 | 4,479 | 1·2 | 11,710 | 3·1 | 84,424 | 22·6 | 373,940 | 100 |
| Total for the Five Years | 52,223 | 2·9 | 33,415 | 1·9 | 86,516 | 4·8 | 155,645 | 8·6 | 19,473 | 1·1 | 52,642 | 2·9 | 399,914 | 22·2 | 1,801,019 | 100 |
| 1876 | 11,024 | 2·9 | 6,894 | 1·8 | 21,062 | 5·9 | 30,025 | 8·0 | 4,193 | 1·1 | 10,235 | 2·8 | 84,333 | 22·5 | 375,155 | 100 |
| 1877 | 12,036 | 3·1 | 6,935 | 1·8 | 21,732 | 5·5 | 31,225 | 7·9 | 4,275 | 1·1 | 13,351 | 3·3 | 89,554 | 22·7 | 394,420 | 100 |
| 1878 | 9,531 | 2·6 | 6,150 | 1·7 | 20,855 | 5·7 | 27,470 | 7·4 | 4,381 | 1·2 | 9,549 | 2·5 | 77,936 | 21·1 | 368,771 | 100 |
| 1879 | 10,446 | 2·9 | 7,066 | 1·9 | 21,065 | 6·1 | 24,698 | 6·8 | 4,610 | 1·3 | 10,158 | 2·7 | 78,943 | 21·7 | 362,992 | 100 |
| 1880 | 13,389 | 3·3 | 6,571 | 1·6 | 25,663 | 6·2 | 30,118 | 7·3 | 5,639 | 1·4 | 11,139 | 2·7 | 92,519 | 22·5 | 411,230 | 100 |
| Total for the Five Years | 56,426 | 3·0 | 33,616 | 1·8 | 112,177 | 5·9 | 143,536 | 7·5 | 23,098 | 1·2 | 54,432 | 2·7 | 423,285 | 22·1 | 1,912,568 | 100 |
| 1881 | 11,301 | 2·9 | 5,696 | 1·4 | 26,075 | 6·3 | 32,629 | 8·2 | 5,413 | 1·4 | 9,526 | 2·4 | 91,540 | 23·1 | 397,023 | 100 |
| 1882 | 10,399 | 2·5 | 6,530 | 1·6 | 25,175 | 6·1 | 39,021 | 9·6 | 6,275 | 1·5 | 11,131 | 2·7 | 99,431 | 24·0 | 413,620 | 100 |
| 1883 | 12,284 | 2·9 | 4,888 | 1·1 | 25,936 | 6·1 | 38,883 | 9·1 | 5,896 | 1·4 | 10,795 | 2·5 | 98,682 | 23·1 | 426,892 | 100 |
| Grand Total | 179,200 | 2·8 | 114,536 | 1·8 | 339,880 | 5·3 | 561,411 | 8·7 | 73,031 | 1·2 | 178,686 | 2·8 | 1,448,034 | 22·6 | 6,414,406 | 100 |

## TABLE VII.

*Statement compiled from the two previous Tables, showing the Proportion of the Total Foreign Trade of the United Kingdom—Imports and Exports of Merchandise—carried on with each of the undermentioned Foreign Countries and British Possessions, in each Year and Period of Five Years since 1866.*

FOREIGN COUNTRIES.

| | Russia. | Germany. | Holland. | Belgium. | France. | Italy. | Turkey. | Egypt. | United States. | Brazil. | Chili. | Peru. |
|---|---|---|---|---|---|---|---|---|---|---|---|---|
| | Per cent. | Per cent. | Per cent. | Per cent. | Per cent. | Per cent. | Per cent. | Per cent. | Per cent. | Per cent. | Per cent. | Per cent. |
| 1866 | 5·0 | 8·3 | 5·0 | 2·7 | 11·9 | 2·0 | 2·5 | 4·3 | 14·7 | 2·7 | 0·9 | 0·8 |
| 1867 | 5·9 | 9·7 | 5·1 | 3·0 | 11·3 | 1·8 | 2·2 | 4·8 | 13·0 | 2·3 | 1·4 | 1·0 |
| 1868 | 5·2 | 9·7 | 5·4 | 3·2 | 11·0 | 1·9 | 2·7 | 4·5 | 12·8 | 2·5 | 1·2 | 0·9 |
| 1869 | 4·9 | 9·5 | 5·7 | 3·4 | 10·7 | 2·1 | 2·3 | 4·7 | 13·0 | 2·7 | 1·1 | 1·0 |
| 1870 | 5·6 | 7·9 | 5·8 | 3·7 | 10·9 | 1·9 | 2·6 | 4·2 | 14·8 | 2·1 | 1·2 | 1·2 |
| For the Five Years | 5·3 | 9·0 | 5·4 | 3·2 | 11·2 | 1·9 | 2·6 | 4·5 | 13·7 | 2·5 | 1·2 | 1·0 |
| 1871 | 5·5 | 9·4 | 5·9 | 4·3 | 10·3 | 2·0 | 2·2 | 3·3 | 16·2 | 2·2 | 1·0 | 1·0 |
| 1872 | 5·0 | 9·3 | 5·6 | 3·9 | 10·5 | 1·8 | 2·0 | 3·6 | 15·0 | 2·6 | 1·3 | 1·1 |
| 1873 | 4·8 | 8·3 | 5·5 | 4·0 | 10·8 | 1·8 | 2·1 | 3·0 | 15·9 | 2·2 | 1·2 | 1·2 |
| 1874 | 4·9 | 8·2 | 5·4 | 4·1 | 11·4 | 1·7 | 2·0 | 2·1 | 15·9 | 2·3 | 1·1 | 0·9 |
| 1875 | 4·9 | 8·5 | 5·3 | 4·4 | 11·3 | 2·0 | 2·0 | 2·1 | 14·4 | 2·2 | 1·0 | 1·0 |
| For the Five Years | 5·0 | 8·8 | 5·5 | 4·1 | 10·8 | 1·8 | 2·1 | 2·9 | 15·5 | 2·3 | 1·1 | 1·1 |
| 1876 | 4·1 | 8·0 | 5·6 | 4·2 | 11·8 | 1·9 | 2·2 | 2·2 | 15·2 | 1·3 | 0·9 | 1·1 |
| 1877 | 4·4 | 8·5 | 5·5 | 3·8 | 11·1 | 1·8 | 2·0 | 2·1 | 15·1 | 2·0 | 0·8 | 0·9 |
| 1878 | 4·4 | 8·6 | 5·9 | 3·9 | 11·1 | 1·6 | 2·1 | 1·4 | 17·4 | 1·8 | 0·6 | 1·1 |
| 1879 | 4·3 | 8·4 | 6·1 | 3·7 | 10·6 | 1·5 | 1·3 | 1·8 | 19·2 | 1·8 | 0·8 | 0·7 |
| 1880 | 3·9 | 7·7 | 6·0 | 3·5 | 10·0 | 1·4 | 1·6 | 1·3 | 20·3 | 1·7 | 0·5 | 0·4 |
| For the Five Years | 4·2 | 8·2 | 5·8 | 3·8 | 10·9 | 1·6 | 1·9 | 1·7 | 17·6 | 1·3 | 0·3 | 0·8 |
| 1881 | 3·3 | 7·6 | 5·5 | 3·6 | 10·1 | 1·6 | 1·7 | 1·2 | 20·2 | 1·9 | 0·3 | 0·5 |
| 1882 | 4·1 | 7·8 | 5·8 | 4·2 | 9·6 | 1·5 | 1·6 | 1·3 | 17·7 | 1·9 | 0·0 | 0·5 |
| 1883 | 3·9 | 8·2 | 5·6 | 4·2 | 9·3 | 1·6 | 1·3 | 1·3 | 15·6 | 1·8 | 0·2 | 0·4 |
| For the 18 Years | 4·6 | 8·5 | 5·6 | 3·8 | 10·7 | 1·8 | 2·1 | 2·3 | 16·3 | 2·1 | 1·0 | 0·9 |

## TABLE VII. (*continued*).

| | FOREIGN COUNTRIES (*continued*). | | | | BRITISH POSSESSIONS. | | | | | | | Grand Total. |
|---|---|---|---|---|---|---|---|---|---|---|---|---|
| | China. | Japan. | Other Foreign Countries. | Total Foreign Countries. | British North America. | British West Indies and Guiana. | Australia and New Zealand. | British India. | Cape of Good Hope and Natal. | Other British Possessions. | Total British Possessions. | |
| | Per cent. | Per cent. | Per cent. | Per cent. | Per cent. | Per cent. | Per cent. | Per cent. | Per cent. | Per cent. | Per cent. | Per cent. |
| 1866 | 3·0 | 0·3 | 11·7 | 75·8 | 2·7 | 1·7 | 4·9 | 10·8 | 0·8 | 3·3 | 24·2 | 100 |
| 1867 | 2·9 | 0·4 | 12·4 | 77·2 | 2·7 | 1·7 | 4·6 | 9·9 | 0·9 | 3·3 | 22·8 | 100 |
| 1868 | 3·4 | 0·3 | 12·2 | 76·9 | 2·4 | 1·8 | 4·9 | 10·0 | 0·2 | 3·2 | 23·1 | 100 |
| 1869 | 3·1 | 0·3 | 12·0 | 77·0 | 2·6 | 1·6 | 5·0 | 9·7 | 0·8 | 3·3 | 23·0 | 100 |
| 1870 | 2·9 | 0·3 | 12·9 | 73·0 | 2·9 | 1·7 | 4·5 | 8·3 | 0·9 | 3·7 | 22·0 | 100 |
| For the Five Years | 3·0 | 0·3 | 12·2 | 77·0 | 2·7 | 1·7 | 4·8 | 9·7 | 0·9 | 3·2 | 23·0 | 100 |
| 1871 | 3·0 | 0·3 | 12·0 | 79·1 | 3·0 | 1·7 | 4·2 | 8·1 | 0·3 | 3·1 | 20·9 | 100 |
| 1872 | 3·0 | 0·3 | 13·3 | 78·3 | 3·1 | 1·5 | 4·6 | 7·9 | 1·2 | 3·4 | 21·7 | 100 |
| 1873 | 2·0 | 0·4 | 12·9 | 77·7 | 3·1 | 1·5 | 5·3 | 7·7 | 1·3 | 3·4 | 22·3 | 100 |
| 1874 | 2·4 | 0·3 | 13·3 | 76·0 | 3·3 | 1·5 | 5·0 | 8·5 | 1·3 | 3·5 | 24·0 | 100 |
| 1875 | 2·9 | 0·5 | 12·9 | 75·4 | 3·0 | 1·6 | 6·4 | 8·5 | 1·5 | 3·0 | 24·6 | 100 |
| For the Five Years | 2·8 | 0·4 | 13·1 | 77·3 | 3·1 | 1·5 | 5·3 | 8·1 | 1·2 | 3·5 | 22·7 | 100 |
| 1876 | 3·1 | 0·4 | 13·1 | 75·6 | 3·0 | 1·6 | 6·6 | 8·5 | 1·4 | 3·3 | 24·4 | 100 |
| 1877 | 2·8 | 0·5 | 13·1 | 74·4 | 3·1 | 1·6 | 6·7 | 8·0 | 1·4 | 3·0 | 25·6 | 100 |
| 1878 | 2·9 | 0·6 | 12·2 | 75·6 | 2·7 | 1·5 | 6·0 | 8·5 | 1·0 | 3·2 | 24·4 | 100 |
| 1879 | 2·0 | 0·6 | 12·3 | 76·2 | 2·7 | 1·6 | 6·5 | 7·8 | 1·8 | 3·4 | 23·8 | 100 |
| 1880 | 2·5 | 0·6 | 12·4 | 75·1 | 3·1 | 1·4 | 6·4 | 8·9 | 1·8 | 3·3 | 24·9 | 100 |
| For the Five Years | 2·8 | 0·5 | 12·8 | 75·4 | 2·9 | 1·5 | 6·6 | 8·5 | 1·6 | 3·5 | 24·6 | 100 |
| 1881 | 2·4 | 0·5 | 12·8 | 74·3 | 3·0 | 1·2 | 7·3 | 9·2 | 1·9 | 3·1 | 25·7 | 100 |
| 1882 | 2·1 | 0·4 | 13·8 | 73·4 | 2·9 | 1·4 | 7·4 | 9·8 | 2·0 | 3·1 | 26·6 | 100 |
| 1883 | 2·0 | 0·4 | 13·8 | 74·2 | 3·0 | 1·2 | 7·2 | 9·9 | 1·5 | 3·0 | 25·8 | 100 |
| For the 18 Years | 2·7 | 0·4 | 12·8 | 76·1 | 2·9 | 1·5 | 5·9 | 8·9 | 1·4 | 3·3 | 23·9 | 100 |

# TABLE VIII.

*Statement showing the Value of Imports of Merchandise into Germany from the under-
mentioned Countries, and of Exports thereof from Germany to the same Countries in
the Years 1868 to 1877, made up from the Statistics of the different Countries named
(in the absence of official German statistics) by treating the Exports from them to
Germany as Imports into Germany, and the Imports from Germany into them as Exports
from Germany; in thousands of Francs and Pounds sterling—i.e., 100 = 100,000.*

| Years. | IMPORTS INTO GERMANY FROM | | | | | | | EXCESS OF IMPORTS. | |
| | France. | Belgium. | Gt. Britain and British India. | Switzer-land. | Italy. | United States.† | Total of Enumerated Countries. | In Thousands of Francs | In Thousands of Pounds Sterling. |
|---|---|---|---|---|---|---|---|---|---|
| | F. | F. | F. | | F. | F. | F. | F. | £ |
| 1868 | 215,000 | 107,647 | 808,654 | Cannot be given. | 5,316 | 110,099 | 1,246,716 | 299,160 | 11,606 |
| 1869 | 305,000 | 121,276 | 803,716 | | 3,022 | 139,133 | 1,372,147 | 399,488 | 15,979 |
| 1870 | 104,000 | 138,535 | 708,014 | | 4,774 | 174,390 | 1,129,713 | 365,617 | 14,624 |
| 1871 | 199,000 | 209,085 | 971,234 | | 8,171 | 158,079 | 1,545,569 | 529,397 | 21,175 |
| 1872 | 410,000 | 240,277 | 1,083,667 | | 7,600 | 185,101 | 1,926,645 | 662,755 | 26,510 |
| 1873 | 463,000 | 266,064 | 919,239 | | 13,815 | 271,864 | 1,933,982 | 609,705 | 24,388 |
| 1874 | 414,000 | 243,120 | 883,241 | | 18,569 | 286,315 | 1,845,245 | 607,866 | 24,315 |
| 1875 | 427,000 | 244,272 | 856,539 | | 23,634 | 226,558 | 1,778,003 | 464,312 | 18,572 |
| 1876 | 431,000 | 244,322 | 748,336 | | 20,599 | 224,247 | 1,668,504 | 331,881 | 13,275 |
| 1877 | 395,000 | 222,767 | 732,028 | | 16,615 | 276,639 | 1,643,049 | 203,647 | 8,146 |

| Years. | EXPORTS FROM GERMANY TO | | | | | | | EXCESS OF EXPORTS. | |
| | France. | Belgium. | Gt. Britain and British India. | Switzer-land. | Italy. | United States.† | Total of Enumerated Countries. | In Thousands of Francs | In Thousands of Pounds Sterling. |
|---|---|---|---|---|---|---|---|---|---|
| | F. | F. | F. | | F. | F. | F. | F. | £ |
| 1868 | 266,000 | 111,549 | 454,614 | Cannot be given. | 8,028 | 116,365 | 956,556 | — | — |
| 1869 | 256,000 | 116,160 | 459,930 | | 10,107 | 130,462 | 972,659 | — | |
| 1870 | 103,000 | 121,688 | 386,013 | | 12,917 | 140,478 | 764,096 | — | |
| 1871 | 160,000 | 230,244 | 482,421 | | 13,019 | 130,488 | 1,016,172 | — | |
| 1872 | 358,000 | 168,554 | 481,984 | | 14,884 | 240,468 | 1,263,890 | — | |
| 1873 | 311,000 | 171,530 | 498,747 | | 23,710 | 319,290 | 1,324,277 | | |
| 1874 | 315,000 | 166,852 | 499,266 | | 27,809 | 228,332 | 1,237,349 | — | |
| 1875 | 349,000 | 171,597 | 546,498 | | 37,312 | 209,284 | 1,313,691 | — | — |
| 1876 | 389,000 | 195,763 | 528,107 | | 40,089 | 183,664 | 1,336,623 | — | — |
| 1877 | 373,000 | 214,767 | 657,387 | | 25,202 | 169,046 | 1,439,402 | — | — |

* The values of the United States exports to Germany have been reduced from currency
to specie values.

† The returns for the United States are for years ending 30th June.

## TABLE IX.

*Statement showing the Total Value of Merchandise Imported into, and Exported from, France, in the Years 1868 to 1877, according to the French official Returns; in thousands of francs, i.e., 100 = 100,000.*

NOTE.—The figures are those of the French "Special" Trade, viz., Imports for Domestic Use and Manufacture, and Exports of Domestic Produce and Manufacture.

| Years. | Total Imports. | Total Exports. | Excess of Imports. In Thousands of Francs and Thousands of £ sterling. | Excess of Exports. In Thousands of Francs and Thousands of £ sterling. |
|---|---|---|---|---|
|  | Francs. | Francs. |  |  |
| 1868 | 3,303,700 | 2,789,900 | { F. 513,800 } { £ 20,552 } | — |
| 1869 | 3,153,100 | 3,074,900 | { F. 78,200 } { £ 3,128 } | — |
| 1870 | 2,781,400 | 2,802,100 | — | { F. 20,700 } { £ 828 } |
| 1871 | 3,566,700 | 2,872,500 | { F. 694,200 } { £ 27,768 } | — |
| 1872 | 3,570,300 | 3,761,600 | — | { F. 191,300 } { £ 7,652 } |
| 1873 | 3,554,800 | 3,787,300 | — | { F. 232,500 } { £ 9,300 } |
| 1874 | 3,507,700 | 3,701,100 | — | { F. 193,400 } { £ 7,736 } |
| 1875 | 3,536,700 | 3,872,600 | — | { F. 335,900 } { £ 13,436 } |
| 1876 | 3,988,400 | 3,575,600 | { F. 412,800 } { £ 16,512 } | — |
| 1877 | 3,669,800 | 3,436,300 | { F. 233,500 } { £ 9,340 } | — |

## TABLE X.

*Statement showing the Value of Imports of Merchandise into France from the under-mentioned Countries, and Exports thereof from France to the same Countries, according to the French official Returns, in the Years 1868 to 1877, covering the period of the payment of the Indemnity to Germany ; in thousands of francs, i.e., 100 = 100,000.*

| Years. | IMPORTS. | | | | | | | EXCESS OF IMPORTS. | |
| --- | --- | --- | --- | --- | --- | --- | --- | --- | --- |
| | Germany. | Belgium. | Gt. Britain and British India. | Switzerland. | Italy. | United States. | Total of Enumerated Countries. | In Thousands of Francs. | In Thousands of Pounds sterling. |
| | F. | F. | F. | F. | F. | F. | F. | F. | £ |
| 1868 | 266,000 | 354,000 | 679,000 | 141,000 | 327,000 | 156,000 | 1,923,000 | — | — |
| 1869 | 256,000 | 316,000 | 687,000 | 133,000 | 321,000 | 174,000 | 1,887,000 | — | — |
| 1870 | 103,000 | 272,000 | 646,000 | 102,000 | 235,000 | 218,000 | 1,576,000 | — | — |
| 1871 | 160,000 | 476,000 | 920,000 | 105,000 | 441,000 | 190,000 | 2,292,000 | 189,000 | 7,560 |
| 1872 | 358,000 | 440,000 | 764,000 | 97,000 | 375,000 | 205,000 | 2,239,000 | — | — |
| 1873 | 311,000 | 475,000 | 673,000 | 92,000 | 346,000 | 199,000 | 2,096,000 | - - | |
| 1874 | 315,000 | 409,000 | 697,000 | 96,000 | 289,000 | 241,000 | 2,047,000 | — | — |
| 1875 | 349,000 | 439,000 | 753,000 | 94,000 | 322,000 | 190,000 | 2,147,000 | — | — |
| 1876 | 389,000 | 404,000 | 789,000 | 110,000 | 415,000 | 265,000 | 2,372,000 | — | — |
| 1877 | 373,000 | 409,000 | 724,000 | 96,000 | 342,000 | 258,000 | 2,202,000 | — | — |

| Years. | EXPORTS. | | | | | | | EXCESS OF EXPORTS. | |
| --- | --- | --- | --- | --- | --- | --- | --- | --- | --- |
| | Germany. | Belgium. | Gt. Britain and British India. | Switzerland. | Italy. | United States. | Total of Enumerated Countries. | In Thousands of Francs. | In Thousands of Pounds sterling. |
| | F. | F. | F. | F. | F. | F. | F. | F. | £ |
| 1868 | 215,000 | 272,000 | 882,000 | 263,000 | 171,000 | 126,000 | 1,929,000 | 6,000 | 240 |
| 1869 | 305,000 | 295,000 | 914,000 | 261,000 | 230,000 | 193,000 | 2,198,000 | 311,000 | 12,440 |
| 1870 | 104,000 | 311,000 | 849,000 | 263,000 | 201,000 | 307,000 | 2,035,000 | 459,000 | 18,360 |
| 1871 | 199,000 | 410,000 | 823,000 | 205,000 | 153,000 | 313,000 | 2,103,000 | — | — |
| 1872 | 410,000 | 479,000 | 937,000 | 294,000 | 229,000 | 333,000 | 2,682,000 | 443,000 | 17,720 |
| 1873 | 463,000 | 470,000 | 926,000 | 337,000 | 230,000 | 291,000 | 2,717,000 | 621,000 | 24,840 |
| 1874 | 414,000 | 524,000 | 992,000 | 300,000 | 204,000 | 296,000 | 2,730,000 | 683,000 | 27,320 |
| 1875 | 427,000 | 527,000 | 1,075,000 | 315,000 | 219,000 | 264,000 | 2,827,000 | 680,000 | 27,200 |
| 1876 | 431,000 | 446,000 | 1,036,000 | 279,000 | 216,000 | 230,000 | 2,638,000 | 266,000 | 10,640 |
| 1877 | 395,000 | 446,000 | 1,067,000 | 237,000 | 185,000 | 217,000 | 2,547,000 | 345,000 | 13,800 |

## TABLE XI.

*Statement showing the Value of the Imports of Merchandise and Treasure, on Private and Government Account, into British India from the United Kingdom, and Value of the Exports of the same, from British India to the United Kingdom, in the Years ended 31st March, 1871 to 1880; compiled from the official Statistics of the Indian Government; in thousands of pounds, i.e., 100 = 100,000.*

| Years ended 31st March. | Imports. | Exports. | Excess of | |
| --- | --- | --- | --- | --- |
| | | | Imports. | Exports. |
| | £ | £ | £ | £ |
| 1871 | 29,905 | 32,084 | — | 2,179 |
| 1872 | 33,739 | 33,021 | 718 | — |
| 1873 | 28,887 | 28,667 | 220 | — |
| 1874 | 30,888 | 28,832 | 2,056 | — |
| 1875 | 35,494 | 27,972 | 7,522 | — |
| 1876 | 34,519 | 28,371 | 6,148 | — |
| 1877 | 39,555 | 29,315 | 10,240 | — |
| 1878 | 47,198 | 30,804 | 16,394 | — |
| 1879 | 33,140 | 28,400 | 4,740 | — |
| 1880 | 38,440 | 27,781 | 10,659 | — |
| Total for the 10 Years. | 351,765 | 295,247 | 56,518 | — |

## TABLE XII.

*Statement showing the Value of the Imports of Merchandise and Treasure, on Private and Government Account, into British India, from the undermentioned Countries; and the Value of the Exports of the same from British India to the same Countries, in the Years ended 31st March, 1871 to 1880; compiled from the official Statistics of the Indian Government; in thousands of pounds, i.e., 100 = 100,000.*

NOTE.—The figures for the Years 1871-73 in the case of the United States are estimates; and for 1871 in the case of Austria and Italy are also estimates.

IMPORTS.

| Years ended 31st March. | France. | Austria. | Italy. | United States. | China and Hong Kong. | Ceylon. | Total of enumerated Countries. | Excess of Imports. |
|---|---|---|---|---|---|---|---|---|
| | £ | £ | £ | £ | £ | £ | £ | £ |
| 1871 | 423 | 67 | 66 | 66 | 4,290 | 1,035 | 5,947 | |
| 1872 | 555 | 122 | 115 | 73 | 4,014 | 1,088 | 5,967 | — |
| 1873 | 378 | 127 | 147 | 62 | 2,377 | 903 | 3,994 | — |
| 1874 | 362 | 93 | 339 | 98 | 3,141 | 909 | 4,942 | |
| 1875 | 413 | 96 | 280 | 193 | 2,957 | 941 | 4,880 | |
| 1876 | 678 | 118 | 527 | 201 | 2,901 | 966 | 5,391 | |
| 1877 | 592 | 120 | 1,366 | 172 | 2,127 | 987 | 5,364 | |
| 1878 | 571 | 120 | 435 | 280 | 4,031 | 797 | 6,234 | — |
| 1879 | 454 | 122 | 393 | 349 | 4,039 | 907 | 6,264 | — |
| 1880 | 588 | 156 | 785 | 526 | 5,587 | 1,091 | 8,733 | — |
| Total for the 10 Years. | 5,014 | 1,141 | 4,453 | 2,020 | 35,464 | 9,624 | 57,716 | — |

EXPORTS.

| Years ended 31st March. | France. | Austria. | Italy. | United States. | China and Hong Kong. | Ceylon. | Total of enumerated Countries. | Excess of Exports. |
|---|---|---|---|---|---|---|---|---|
| | £ | £ | £ | £ | £ | £ | £ | £ |
| 1871 | 2,013 | 600 | 700 | 2,232 | 12,333 | 1,620 | 19,498 | 13,551 |
| 1872 | 4,175 | 1,057 | 1,134 | 2,079 | 13,944 | 2,082 | 24,471 | 18,504 |
| 1873 | 2,673 | 1,100 | 954 | 1,821 | 12,259 | 2,314 | 21,121 | 17,127 |
| 1874 | 3,134 | 939 | 1,320 | 1,643 | 11,507 | 2,823 | 21,366 | 16,424 |
| 1875 | 4,449 | 1,321 | 1,112 | 1,886 | 11,751 | 2,497 | 23,016 | 18,136 |
| 1876 | 4,603 | 1,410 | 1,224 | 1,778 | 11,520 | 2,695 | 23,230 | 17,839 |
| 1877 | 5,437 | 1,428 | 1,410 | 1,896 | 13,442 | 3,396 | 27,009 | 21,645 |
| 1878 | 6,026 | 1,466 | 1,870 | 1,933 | 12,791 | 2,840 | 26,926 | 20,692 |
| 1879 | 3,947 | 1,395 | 1,673 | 2,038 | 13,677 | 3,787 | 26,517 | 20,253 |
| 1880 | 4,870 | 1,860 | 2,215 | 3,286 | 15,732 | 2,606 | 30,659 | 21,926 |
| Total for the 10 Years. | 41,327 | 12,576 | 13,612 | 20,592 | 128,956 | 26,750 | 243,813 | 186,097 |

## TABLE

*Return of the Rates of Import duty levied in the principal European Countries, in the United Articles of British Produce or Manufacture: taken from the Parliamentary Returns, Nos. alterations.*

| Articles. | FOREIGN COUNTRIES. | | | | | | |
|---|---|---|---|---|---|---|---|
| | Germany. | Holland. | Belgium. | France. | Italy. | Austria. | United States. |
| | £ s. d. Per cwt. | | £ s. d. Per cwt. | £ s. d. Per cwt. | £ s. d. Per cwt. | £ s. d. Per cwt. | £ s. d. Per cwt. |
| **Cotton Yarn (single unbleached):** | | | | | | | |
|   Up to No. 12 | 0 6 1 | Free | 0 6 1 | 0 6 1 | 0 7 4 | 0 6 1 | 2 6 8 and 20 % ad val. |
|   Above 12 to 17 | | | | | 0 8 11 | | |
|   " 17 " 23 | 0 9 2 | | 0 8 2 | 0 8 2 | | 0 8 2 | |
|   " 23 " 30 | | | | | 0 10 7 | | |
|   " 30 " 35 | | | | | | | |
|   " 35 " 45 | | | | | | | |
|   " 45 " 47 | 0 12 2 | | 0 12 2 | 0 12 2 | 0 13 0 | | |
|   " 47 " 60 | | | | | 0 15 10 | | |
|   " 60 " 70 | 0 15 3 | | 0 16 3 | 0 16 3 | 0 19 6 | 0 12 2 | |
|   " 70 " 77 | | | | From 1 0 4 to 6 1 11 | 1 4 5 | | |
|   " 77 " 79 | 0 18 3 | | | | | | |
|   " 79 | | | 0 4 0½ | | | | |
| **Cotton Cloth (unbleached):** | | | | | | | |
|   Weighing 13 kilogrammes and above per 100 sq. mètres: | | | | | | | |
|     Of 27 threads or less per 5 sq. millimètres | 2 0 8 | 5 % ad val. | 1 0 4 | 1 0 4 | 1 3 2 | 1 12 6 | Exceeding 5 oz. to the sq. yard: 2½d. per sq. yard or 3d. per sq. yard, according to quality. |
|     Of 28 to 35 thds. | | | | | 1 6 0 | | |
|     Of 36 " 38 " | | | 1 12 6 | 1 12 6 | | | |
|     Over 38 " | | | | | | 2 10 10 | |
|   Weighing from 11 to 13 kilogs. exclusive per 100 sq. mètres: | | | | | | | |
|     Of 27 threads or less | | | 1 0 4 | 1 0 4 | 1 6 10 | 1 12 6 | |
|     Of 28 to 35 thds. | | | | | | | |
|     Of 36 " 38 " | | | 1 12 6 | 1 12 6 | 1 10 6 | | |
|     Over 38 " | | | | | | 2 10 10 | |
|   Weighing from 7 to 11 kilogs. exclusive per 100 sq. mètres | | | From 1 4 5 to 4 1 3 | From 1 4 5 to 4 1 3 | From 1 6 10 to 1 10 6 | 1 12 6 or 2 10 10 as above | Other unbleached cotton tissues 35 % ad val. |
|   Weighing less than 7 kilogs. per 100 sq. mètres | | | From 1 12 6 to 6 1 11 | From 1 12 6 to 6 1 11 | From 1 12 6 to 2 0 8 | | |
| **Linen Yarn (single unbleached):** | | | | | | | |
|   Up to No. 5 (Eng) | 0 1 6½ | Free. | Free. | | 0 6 1 | 0 1 6½ | 40 % ad val. |
|   5 to 8 | 0 2 6½ | | | | | | |
|   9 " 10 | 0 3 0½ | | | | 0 8 2 | | |
|   11 " 20 | | | | | | | |
|   21 " 35 | 0 4 6¾ | | | | 0 12 2 | | |
|   36 " 40 | | | | | | | |
|   41 " 60 | 0 1 | | | | 0 14 8 | | |
|   61 " 119 | | | | | 1 4 5 | | |
|   Above 119 | | | | | 2 0 8 | | |

## XIII.

*States, and in the principal Colonial Possessions of the United Kingdom, on the undermentioned 200 and 218 of 1879, and 333 of 1881. It has not been found practicable to insert more recent*

### COLONIAL POSSESSIONS OF THE UNITED KINGDOM.

| New South Wales. | Victoria. | South Australia. | Western Australia. | Tasmania. | New Zealand. | Queensland. | Canada. | Cape of Good Hope. |
|---|---|---|---|---|---|---|---|---|
| £ s. d. Per cwt. | £ s. d. Per cwt. | £ s. d. Per cwt. | | | £ s. d. Per cwt. | | £ s. d. Per cwt. | |
| } 0 2 0 | 0 11 3 | 0 3 0 | { 12½ % ad val. | 10 % ad val. } | 0 5 0 { | 5 % ad val. | Under 40's 0 9 4 and 15 % ad val. Other, 20 % ad val. | 10 % ad val. |
| } Free. | Free. | Free. | { 12½ % ad val. | 10 % ad val. | { Free by Law of 24 Sept., 1881. } | 5 % ad val. | { sq. yard, ½d. to 1d. and 15 % ad val. } | 10 % ad val. |
| } 0 2 0 | 0 11 3 | 0 3 0 | { 12½ % ad val. | 10 % ad val. } | 0 5 0 { | 5 % ad val. | 20 % ad val. | 10 % ad val. |

**TABLE XIII.**

*Return of the Rates of Import Duty levied in the principal European Countries, in the United*
*Articles of British*

| Articles | FOREIGN COUNTRIES (continued). | | | | | | United States |
|---|---|---|---|---|---|---|---|
| | Germany. | Holland. | Belgium. | France. | Italy. | Austria. | |
| | £ s. d. Per cwt. | | £ s. d. Per cwt. | £ s. d. Per cwt. | £ s. d. Per cwt. | £ s. d. Per cwt. | £ s. d. Per cwt. |
| **Linen Cloth (unbleached):** | | | | | | | |
| 5 threads or less per 5 millimètres | | Sail-cloth free. | | 0 2 0½ | 0 4 10½ | 0 2 0½ | |
| 6 to 8 threads | From | | | 0 11 5 | to | | |
| 9 „ 11 „ | 0 3 0½ | Other 5% ad val. | 10% ad val. | 1 2 4 | 0 9 5 | | From 35% to 40% ad val. |
| 12 „ | to | | | 1 6 5 | | 0 12 2 | |
| 13 „ 14 „ | 1 10 6 | | | 1 16 7 | 1 3 6 | | |
| 15 „ 17 „ | | | | 2 6 9 | | | |
| 18 „ 20 „ | | | | 3 9 1 | | | |
| 21 „ 23 „ | | | | 5 5 8 | | | |
| 24 thrds. and above | | | | 6 1 11 | | 4 1 3 | |
| **Woollen Yarns (single unbleached):** | | | | | | | |
| Measuring to the kilogramme less than 30,500 mètres | | | | 0 10 2 | | | |
| 30,500 to 40,500 „ | | | | 0 14 3 | | | From 4 13 4 |
| 40,500 „ 50,500 „ | | | | 0 18 3 | | 0 1 6¼ | to |
| 50,500 „ 60,500 „ | | | | 1 2 4 | | | 11 13 4 |
| 60,500 „ 70,500 „ | 0 4 0½ | Free. | 0 8 2 | 1 6 5 | 1 0 4 | to | and 35% ad val. |
| 70,500 „ 80,500 „ | | | | 1 10 6 | | 0 8 2 | |
| 80,500 „ 90,500 „ | | | | 1 14 7 | | | |
| 90,500 „ 100,500 „ | | | | 1 18 7 | | | |
| 100,500 mètres and above | | | | 2 0 8 | | | |
| **Woollen Cloth (unprinted):** | | | | | | | |
| With cotton warp: | | | | | | | |
| Above 600 grms. per sq. mètre | 3 8 7 | 5% ad val. | 10% ad val. | 10% ad val. | 2 0 8 | 2 0 8 | All cloths weighing 4 oz. and above, per sq. yard, |
| 300 to 600 grms. per sq. mètre | | | | | | 2 10 10 | 11 13 4 and 35% ad val. |
| Less than 300 grms. per sq. metre | | | | | | 4 1 3 | |
| Other kinds: | | | | | | | |
| Above 600 grms. per sq. mètre | | | | | 3 1 0 | 2 0 8 | |
| 450 to 600 grms. per sq. mètre | | | | | | 3 0 11 | |
| Less than 450 grms. per sq. metre | | | | | | 4 1 3 | |
| **Porcelain:** | | | | | | | |
| White | 0 7 1 | 5% ad val. | 10% ad val. | 10% ad val. | 0 4 10½ | 0 5 1 | 45% ad val. |
| **Glass and Glasswares:** | | | | | | | |
| Common bottles | 0 1 6¼ | 5% ad val. | 0 0 4¾ | 0 0 6¼ | 100 bottles. 0 2 4¾ | 0 1 6¼ | 35% ad val. |
| Window glass: Common | 0 3 0½ to 0 5 1 | | 10% ad val. | 0 1 5 | Per cwt. 0 3 3 | 0 4 0¾ | 0 7 0 to 0 14 0 |
| **Plate glass:** Polished | 0 12 2 | | 10% ad val. | sq. yard. 0 2 8½ | 0 8 2 | 0 8 2 | Up to 24 by 30 in. sq., 1¼d. to 4d. per sq. ft. Of larger size, 1s. 0¼d. to 2s. 1d. per sq. ft. |

*(continued).*

*States, and in the principal Colonial Possessions of the United Kingdom, on the undermentioned Produce or Manufacture.*

COLONIAL POSSESSIONS OF THE UNITED KINGDOM *(continued)*.

| New South Wales. | Victoria. | South Australia. | Western Australia. | Tasmania. | New Zealand. | Queensland. | Canada. | Cape of Good Hope. |
|---|---|---|---|---|---|---|---|---|
| £ s. d. Per cwt. | £ s. d. Per cwt. | £ s. d. Per cwt. | | | £ s. d. Per cwt. | | £ s. d. Per cwt. | |
| Free. | Free. | Free. | 12½ % ad val. | Sailcloth free. Other 10 % ad val. | Sailcloth free. Other 15 % ad val. | 5 % ad val. | Sailcloth 25 % ad val. Other 20 % ad val. | 10 % ad val. |
| 0 2 0 | 0 11 | 0 3 0 | 12½ ad val. | 10 % ad val. | 0 5 0 | 5 % ad val. | 1 15 0 and 20 % ad val. | 10 % ad val. |
| Free. | 7½ % ad val. to 15 % ad val. | 5 % ad val. | 12 % ad val. | 10 % ad val. | 15 % ad val. | 5 % ad val. | 1 15 0 and 20 % ad val. | 10 % ad val. |
| Free. | cub. ft. 0 2 6 | 10 % ad val. | 12½ % ad val. | 10 % ad val. | 15 % ad val. | 5 % ad val. | 25 % ad val. | 12 % ad val. |
| | cub. ft. 0 1 0 | | | Free. | Free. | | | |
| | Free. | | | 10 % ad val. | 100 sq. ft. 0 2 0 | | | |
| Free | Free. | 10 % ad val. | 12½ % ad val. | | | 5 % ad val. | 20 % ad val. | 10 % ad val. |
| | Free. | | | 10 % ad val. | 15 % ad val. | | | |

### TABLE XIII.

*Return of the Rates of Import Duty levied in the principal European Countries, in the United*
*Articles of British*

#### FOREIGN COUNTRIES (continued).

| Articles. | Germany. | Holland. | Belgium. | France. | Italy. | Austria. | United States. |
|---|---|---|---|---|---|---|---|
|  | £ s. d. Per cwt. | £ s. d. Per cwt. | £ s. d. Per cwt. | £ s. d. Per cwt. | £ s. d. Per cwt. | £ s. d. Per cwt. | £ s. d. Per cwt. |
| Iron: |  |  |  |  |  |  |  |
| Pig | 0 0 6 |  | 0 0 2½ | 0 0 9¼ | Free | 0 0 6 | 0 1 5½ { 0 4 8 and 0 7 0 according to size } |
| Bar | 0 1 3½ |  | 0 0 4¾ | 0 2 5½ | 0 1 10½ | 0 2 6½ |  |
| Rails for Railways Iron | 0 1 3½ | Free | 0 0 4¾ | 0 2 5½ | 0 1 2¾ | 0 2 6½ | 0 3 3 |
| Rails for Railways —Steel |  |  |  | 0 3 8 |  |  | Partly Steel 0 4 8 / Pure Steel 0 5 10 |
| Copper: |  |  |  |  |  |  |  |
| Ingots, Cakes, or Slabs | Free | Free | Free | Free | 0 1 7½ | Free | 1 3 4 |
| Hammered, in Bars | 0 6 1 | Free | 0 4 6¾ | 0 4 0¾ | 0 4 0¾ | 0 8 2 |  |
| Tanned Leather (unwrought): |  |  |  |  |  |  |  |
| Ox and Cow Hides | From 0 9 2 to | Free | 0 6 1 | 0 4 0¾ | From 0 10 2 to | 0 8 2 | 15% to 25% ad val. |
| Calf skins | 0 13 3 |  |  |  | 0 12 2 |  |  |
| Alkali: |  |  |  |  |  |  |  |
| Bicarbonate of Soda | 0 1 3½ |  |  | 0 1 8½ | 0 0 2½ | 0 3 0½ | 0 7 0 |
| Crystals of Soda | 0 0 9½ | Free | Free | 0 0 9½ | Not specified | Not specified | Not specified |
| Soda Caustic | 0 2 0½ |  |  | 0 2 7½ | Pure 0 2 0½ / Impure 0 0 2½ | 0 4 0½ | 0 7 0 |
| Paper: |  |  |  |  |  |  |  |
| For Writing | 0 5 1 | 5% ad val. | 0 1 7½ | 0 *3 3 | 0 4 0¾ | 0 3 0½ | 35% ad val. |
| For Printing |  |  |  |  |  | 0 2 0½ | 20% or 25% ad val. according as unsized or sized. |
| Seed Oils: |  |  |  |  |  |  | Gal. |
| Linseed | 0 2 0½ | 0 0 11¼ | Free | 0 2 5½ | 0 2 5½ | 0 1 6½ | 0 1 6 |
| Rape |  |  |  |  |  |  | 0 1 2 |
| Coals | Free | Free | Free | Ton 0 0 11¼ | Free | Free | Anthracite Free. Bituminous, Ton 0 3 1½ |
| Beer or Ale: |  | Gal. | Gal. | Gal. | Gal. |  | Gal. |
| In Casks | 0 2 0½ | 0 0 2¾ | 0 0 2¾ | 0 0 2½ | 0 0 10½ | 0 3 0½ | 0 1 0 |
| In Bottles |  |  | 0 0 3 |  | 0 11 7½ 100 Btls. | 0 8 2 | 0 1 9 |

* An additional excise duty on letter paper of 4s. 7½d. per cwt. An additional
† Excise duty in addition ;—At 16 degrees

*(continued).*

*States, and in the principal Colonial Possessions of the United Kingdom, on the undermentioned Produce or Manufacture (continued).*

COLONIAL POSSESSIONS OF THE UNITED KINGDOM (continued).

| New South Wales. | Victoria. | South Australia. | Western Australia. | Tasmania. | New Zealand. | Queensland. | Canada. | Cape of Good Hope. |
|---|---|---|---|---|---|---|---|---|
| £ s. d. Per cwt. | £ s. d. Per cwt. | £ s. d. Per cwt. | £ s. d. Per cwt. | £ s. d. Per cwt. | £ s. d. Per cwt. | £ s. d. Per cwt. | £ s. d. Per cwt. | £ s. d. |
| Free | Free | Free | 10 % ad val. | Free<br>10 % ad val. | Free | 5 % ad val. | 0 0 5<br>17½ % ad val.<br>15 ad val.<br>Free to 1883 | 10 ad val. |
| Free | 25 % ad val. | Free | 10 to 12½ % ad val. | Free | Free | 5 % ad val. | 10 ad val. | 10 ad val. |
| Free | 20 % ad val.<br>7½ % ad val. | 10 % ad val. | 12½ % ad val. | 10 % ad val. | From 0 9 4 to 0 14 0 | 5 % ad val. | 10 % ad val.<br>15 to 20 % ad val. | 10 ad val. |
| Free<br>0 1 0 | Free<br>0 2 0 | 0 1 0 | 12½ % ad val.<br>0 0 6 | 0 4 8<br>0 2 4 | 0 1 0 | Not specified<br>0 1 0 | 20 % ad val. | 10 ad val. |
| Free | Free | Free | 12½ % ad val. | Free | Free | Not specified | Free | |
| 0 9 4 | 0 18 8 | 10 % ad val. | 12½ % ad val. | 10 % ad val. | Uncut free. Cut 15 % ad val. | 5 % ad val. | 20 % ad val. | 10 % ad val. |
| Free | Free | Free | 10 % ad val. | | Free | | | |
| Gal.<br>0 0 6 | Free | Gal.<br>0 0 6 | 12½ % ad val. | Gal.<br>0 1 0 | Gal.<br>0 0 6 | Gal.<br>0 0 6<br>5 % ad val. | 25 ad val.<br>20 % ad val. | Gal.<br>0 0 6 |
| Free | Free | Free | Free | Ton<br>0 1 0 | Free | Ton<br>0 1 6 | Ton<br>Anthret. 0 2 4<br>Bituminous 0 2 9½ | Ton.<br>0 0 10 |
| Gal.<br>0 0 6<br>0 0 9 | Gal.<br>0 0 9 | Gal.<br>0 0 9 | Gal.<br>0 1 0 | Gal.<br>0 0 9<br>0 1 3 | Gal.<br>0 1 3<br>0 1 6 | Gal.<br>0 0 9<br>0 1 0 | Gal.<br>0 0 5<br>0 0 9 | Gal.<br>0 0 4 |

excise duty on other kinds from 2s. 1¾d. to 4s. 2¼d. per cwt.

# TABLE XIV.

*Return of the estimated or actual ad valorem Rates of Import Duty levied in the principal European Countries, in the United States, and in the principal Colonial Possessions of the United Kingdom on the undermentioned Articles of British Produce or Manufacture: compiled chiefly from the information contained in the previous table.*

| ARTICLES. | A.—FOREIGN COUNTRIES. | | | | | | United States. |
| --- | --- | --- | --- | --- | --- | --- | --- |
| | Germany. | Holland. | Belgium. | France. | Italy. | Austria. | |
| | Ad val. | Ad val. | Ad val. | Ad val. | Ad val. | Ad val. | Ad val. |
| Cotton Yarns:<br>Single, unbleached . | *10 % | Free | *10 %<br>Except on the finer sorts, which are only subject to a registration duty. | *10 %<br>Except on the finer sorts, upon which the duties appear to be prohibitive. | *11 % | *9 . | ‡56 . |
| Cotton Cloth:<br>Unbleached (average quality) . . | *20 to 30 % | †5 . | *15 % | *15 % | *15 | *15 to 24 % | †35 . |
| Linen Yarns:<br>Single, unbleached | *1½ to 3 % | Free | Free | *9 % | *3 . | *1¼ % | †40 % |
| Linen Cloth:<br>Unbleached, Packing-cloth . .<br>Unbleached, other . | *5 to 10 % | Sailcloth Free<br>Other †5 % | †10 % | *3 %<br>*10 to 14 % | *7 %<br>*10 % | *3 %<br>*7 to 10 % | †35 to 40 . |
| Woollen Yarns:<br>Single, unbleached . | *1 % | Free | *2 % | The average appears to be between *4 % and *7 % | *7 % | *½ to 2 % | ‡80 % |
| Woollen Cloth:<br>Plain, unprinted . | *15 % | †5 % | †10 % | †10 % | *12 | *10 to 15 % | ‡75 % |
| Porcelain:<br>White . . . | *9% | †5 % | †10 % | †10 % | *7 % | *7 % | †45 . |
| Glass and Glasswares:<br>Common Bottles .<br>Window-glass, common . . . | *15 %<br>*18 % | †5 % | *4 %<br>†10 . | *6 %<br>*9 % | *12 %<br>*18 % | *15 %<br>*20 % | †35 %<br>*50 to 70 % |
| Plate Glass, polished | *16 % | | | *13 % | *10 % | *10 % | Smaller sizes *20 to 25 % larger sizes *65 to 110 % |

* Estimated rate on average price in the United Kingdom.     † Tariff rate on market value at port of import.     ‡ Partly estimated.

# TABLE XIV. (continued).

| ARTICLES. | A.—FOREIGN COUNTRIES (continued). | | | | | | |
|---|---|---|---|---|---|---|---|
| | Germany. | Holland. | Belgium. | France. | Italy. | Austria. | United States. |
| | Ad val. | Ad val. | Ad val. | Ad val. | Ad val. | Ad val. | Ad val. |
| Iron: | | | | | | | |
| Pig | *15 % | Free | *7 % | *25 % | Free | *15 % | *45 % |
| Bar | *16 % | | *5 % | *30 % | *25 % | *32 % | *60 % and 90 % according to size |
| Rails for Railways | *17 % | | *5 % | *33 % | *17 % | *35 % | *45 % |
| Steel Rails | | | | *50 % | | | Partly steel, *65 %; Pure steel, *30 % |
| Copper: | | | | | | | |
| Ingots, cakes or slabs | Free | Free | Free | Free | *2½ % | Free | *34 % |
| Hammered in Bars | *8 % | | *5 % | *5 % | *5 % | *10 % | *30 % |
| Tanned Leather (unwrought): | | | | | | | |
| Ox and Cow Hides | *9 % | Free | *4 % | *2½ % | *7 % | *5 % | +15 % to |
| Calf Skins | | | | | | | +25 % |
| Alkali: | | | | | | | |
| Bicarbonate of Soda | *13 % | Free | Free | *17 % | *2 % | *30 % | *70 % |
| Crystals of Soda | *23 % | | | *23 % | Not specified | Not specified | Not specified |
| Caustic Soda | *20 % | | | *26 % | *Pure 20 % | *40 % | *70 % |
| Paper: | | | | | | | |
| For Writing | *9 % | +5 % | *3 % | *5½ % (and 13 additional excise duty) | *7 % | *5½ % | +35 / +20 % or 25 % according as unsized or sized |
| For Printing | *14 % | | *4 % | *9 % | *11 % | | |
| Seed Oils: | | | | | | | |
| Linseed | *8 % | *3½ % | Free | *o % | *o | *6 % | *72 |
| Rape | *7 % | | | *5 | *5 | *5 % | *48 |
| Coals: | Free | Free | Free | *10 % | Free | Free | Anthracite, Free. Bituminous, *33 % |
| Beer or Ale: | | | | | | | |
| In Casks | *10 % | *12 % | *12½ % | *11 | (and 20 additional excise duty) | *15 | *55 |
| In Bottles | | | *14 | | | *40 | *95 |

* Estimated rate on average price in the United Kingdom.     † Tariff rate on market value at port of import.

Q 2

## TABLE XIV. (continued).

*Return of the estimated or actual ad valorem Rates of Import Duty levied in the principal European Countries, in the United States, and in the principal Colonial Possessions of the United Kingdom on the undermentioned Articles of British Produce or Manufacture (continued).*

II.—COLONIAL POSSESSIONS OF THE UNITED KINGDOM.

| ARTICLES. | New South Wales. | Victoria. | South Australia. | Western Australia. | Tasmania. | New Zealand. | Queensland. | Canada. | Cape of Good Hope. |
|---|---|---|---|---|---|---|---|---|---|
| | Ad val. | Ad val. | Ad val. | Ad val. | Ad val. | Ad val. | Ad val. | Ad val. | Ad val. |
| Cotton Yarns: | | | | | | | | | |
| Single, unbleached. | *1¾ | *10 % | *2½ | ‡12½ % | †10 | *4 | ‡5 | ‡20 to §25 % | †10 % |
| Cotton Cloth: | | | | | | | | | |
| Unbleached (average quality) | Free | Free | Free | ‡12½ % | †10 % | Free by Law of 24 Sept., 1881 | ‡5 | §16 % | †10 |
| Linen Yarns: | | | | | | | | | |
| Single, unbleached. | *1¾ % | *3 % | *2 | ‡12½ % | †10 % | *3½ % | ‡5 % | ‡20 % | †10 % |
| Linen Cloth: | | | | | | | | | |
| Unbleached, Packing-cloth. | Free | Free | Free | ‡12½ % | Sailcloth Free | Sailcloth Free | ‡5 % | Sailcloth‡25 % | †10 % |
| Other | | | | | Other†10 % | Other 15 % | | Other ‡20 % | |
| Woollen Yarns: | | | | | | | | | |
| Single, unbleached. | *½ | *3 | *1 | ‡12½ % | †10 % | *1½ % | ‡5 | §30 % | †10 % |
| Woollen Cloth: | | | | | | | | | |
| Plain, unprinted | Free | †7½ to 15 % | +5 % | ‡12½ % | †10 % | 15 % | ‡5 % | §30 % | †10 % |
| Porcelain: | | | | | | | | | |
| White | Free | — | †10 % | ‡12½ % | †10 % | 15 % | ‡5 % | ‡25 % | †10 % |
| Glass and Glasswares: | | | | | | | | | |
| Common Bottles | | — | | | Free | Free | | | |
| Window-glass, common | Free | Free | †10 % | ‡12½ % | †10 % | — | ‡5 % | ‡20 % | †10 % |
| Plate Glass, polished | | | | | | 15 % | | | |
| Iron: | | | | | | | | | |
| Pig | Free | Free | Free | ‡10 % | Free | Free | Free | *13 % | |
| Bar | Free | Free | Free | ‡10 % | †10 % | Free | ‡5 % | ‡17½ % | †10 % |
| Rails for Railways | | | | | | | | ‡15 % | |
| Steel Rails | | | | | | | | Free to 1883 | |

* Estimated rate on average price in the United Kingdom.
‡ Tariff rate on average price in the United Kingdom.
† Tariff rate on average price in United Kingdom, plus about 10 %.
§ Partly estimated.

## TABLE XIV. (*continued*).

B.—COLONIAL POSSESSIONS OF THE UNITED KINGDOM (*continued*).

| ARTICLES. | New South Wales. | Victoria. | South Australia. | Western Australia. | Tasmania. | New Zealand. | Queensland. | Canada. | Cape of Good Hope. |
|---|---|---|---|---|---|---|---|---|---|
| | Ad val. | Ad val. | Ad val. | Ad val. | Ad val. | Ad val. | Ad val. | Ad val. | Ad val. |
| Copper: | | | | | | | | | |
| Ingots, cakes, or slabs / Hammered in Bars. | Free | †25 % | Free | ‡10 to ‡12½ % | Free | Free | ‡5 % | ‡10 % | †10 % |
| Tanned Leather (un-wrought): | | | | | | | | | |
| Ox and Cow Hides | Free | †20 % | †10 % | ‡12½ % | †10 % | *7½ % | ‡5 % | ‡10 % | †10 % |
| Calf Skins | | †7½ % | | | | | | ‡15 to 20 % | |
| Alkali: | | | | | | | | | |
| Bicarbonate of Soda | Free | Free | *10 % | ‡12½ % | *47 % | *10 % | Not specified | ‡20 % | †10 % |
| Crystals of Soda | *30 % | *60 % | *30 % | *15 % | *70 % | *30 % | *30 % | | |
| Caustic Soda | Free | Free | Free | ‡12½ % | Free | Free | Not specified | Free | |
| Paper: | | | | | | | | | |
| For Writing | *17 % | *33 % | †10 % | ‡12½ % | †10 % | Uncut, Free; Cut, 15 % | ‡5 % | ‡20 % | †10 % |
| For Printing | Free | Free | Free | ‡10 % | | Free | | | †10 % |
| Seed Oils: | | | | | | | | | |
| Linseed | *24 % | Free | *24 % | ‡12½ % | *48 % | *24 % | *24 % | ‡25 % | *24 % |
| Rape | *21 % | | *21 % | | *42 % | *21 % | ‡5 % | ‡20 % | *21 % |
| Coals: | Free | Free | Free | Free | *10 % | Free | *15 % | Anthracite, *23 %; Bituminous, *28 % | *8 % |
| Beer or Ale: | | | | | | | | | |
| In Casks | *27 % | *40 % | *40 % | *55 % | *40 % | *68 % | *40 % | *23 % | *18 % |
| In Bottles | *40 % | | | | *68 % | *80 % | *55 % | *40 % | |

* Estimated rate on average price in the United Kingdom.
‡ Tariff rate on average price in the United Kingdom.
† Tariff rate on average price in United Kingdom, plus about 10 %.

# TABLE XV.

*Statement showing in what Proportion, according to value, the principal Articles of Food, except Fruit, were imported into the United Kingdom from Foreign Countries and British Possessions in the Year 1883; with the Total Values of such Articles Imported from all Foreign Countries and British Possessions respectively.*

| PRINCIPAL ARTICLES. | A.—FOREIGN COUNTRIES. | | | | | | | | | | | | |
| --- | --- | --- | --- | --- | --- | --- | --- | --- | --- | --- | --- | --- | --- |
| | Russia. | Sweden. | Denmark | Germany. | Holland. | Belgium. | France. | Spain. | Portugal. | Roumania | China. | Foreign West India Islands. | United States. |
| | Per cent. | Per cent. | Per cent. | Per cent. | Per cent. | Per cent. | Per cent. | Per cent. | Per cent. | Per cent. | Per cent. | Per cent. | Per cent. |
| Animals, living: | | | | | | | | | | | | | |
|   Oxen, Bulls, Cows, and Calves | — | 5·1 | 24·1 | 6·4 | 2·7 | — | 0·9 | 4·7 | 5·0 | — | — | — | 37·9 |
|   Sheep and Lambs | — | 1·0 | 10·5 | 41·3 | 22·9 | 7·1 | — | — | — | — | — | — | 8·4 |
| Bacon and Hams | — | — | 1·7 | 14·3 | 0·3 | 0·1 | — | — | — | — | — | — | 78·7 |
| Butter | 0·3 | 4·7 | 18·3 | 6·9 | 35·7 | 2·2 | 24·0 | — | — | — | — | — | 4·8 |
| Cheese | 0·1 | 0·2 | 0·1 | 0·1 | 16·9 | 0·1 | 1·5 | — | — | — | — | — | 55·1 |
| Cocoa | — | — | — | 1·0 | 0·2 | 0·3 | 5·2 | 0·2 | 2·1 | — | — | 1·1 | 2·3 |
| Coffee* | — | — | — | 4·9 | 1·5 | 1·0 | 2·2 | — | 0·8 | — | 0·3 | 1·1 | 3·7 |
| Corn, Grain, and Flour: | | | | | | | | | | | | | |
|   Wheat | 20·0 | — | — | 4·6 | — | — | — | — | — | 0·6 | — | — | 42·6 |
|   Barley | 29·9 | 3·0 | 5·7 | 13·6 | 0·1 | — | 10·5 | — | — | 24·0 | — | — | 0·9 |
|   Oats | 57·0 | 33·2 | 2·2 | 4·3 | 1·5 | — | 0·2 | — | — | — | — | — | — |
|   Maize | 3·6 | — | — | 0·7 | — | — | — | — | — | 18·5 | — | — | 66·2 |
|   Wheat-meal and Flour | 0·4 | 0·5 | 2·7 | 11·4 | — | — | 1·0 | — | — | — | — | — | 66·7 |
| Eggs | 0·1 | 0·1 | 5·3 | 24·5 | 0·7 | 22·4 | 45·5 | 0·6 | 0·2 | — | — | — | — |
| Meat of all kinds (salted, fresh, or preserved) | 1·0 | — | 1·2 | 2·1 | 6·4 | 3·1 | 0·9 | — | — | — | — | — | 66·3 |
| Potatoes | — | — | 0·1 | 38·0 | 4·3 | 0·2 | 27·4 | 0·2 | 1·2 | — | — | — | — |
| Rice | — | — | — | 2·7 | 3·3 | — | 0·1 | — | — | — | 0·1 | — | — |
| Spices of all sorts, including Pepper | — | — | — | 0·2 | 4·1 | — | 0·4 | — | — | — | 4·0 | — | 0·2 |
| Spirits of all sorts | 0·5 | — | 0·2 | 5·6 | 6·2 | 0·4 | 55·8 | — | — | — | — | 0·5 | 2·3 |
| Sugar, refined | — | — | — | 17·5 | 30·4 | 3·3 | 44·4 | — | — | — | — | — | 4·0 |
| Sugar, unrefined | — | — | — | 30·9 | 1·6 | 7·2 | 1·4 | 0·1 | — | — | 0·7 | 1·9 | 0·1 |
| Tea | — | — | — | — | 0·9 | — | — | — | — | — | 64·4 | — | 0·1 |
| Tobacco, manufactured and unmanufacturd | — | — | — | 3·6 | 11·2 | 1·3 | 2·1 | 0·8 | — | — | 1·0 | 21·4 | 48·5 |
| Wine of all sorts | — | — | — | 1·2 | 4·7 | 0·2 | 49·5 | 22·1 | 18·0 | — | — | — | — |

* Only about one-fifth of the Coffee imported is retained for consumption.

## TABLE XV. (continued).

| PRINCIPAL ARTICLES. | A.—FOREIGN COUNTRIES (continued). | | | B.—BRITISH POSSESSIONS. | | | | | | | TOTAL. | |
|---|---|---|---|---|---|---|---|---|---|---|---|---|
| | Other Foreign Countries. | Total Foreign Countries. | | British India. | Australia & New Zealand. | British West Indies & British Guiana. | British North America. | Other British Possessions. | Total British Possessions. | | Amount. | Per ct. |
| | | Amount. | Per cent. of total. | | | | | | Amount. | Per cent. of total. | | |
| | Per cent. | £ | | Per cent. | Per cent. | Per cent. | Per cent. | Per cent. | £ | | £ | |
| Animals, living : | | | | | | | | | | | | |
| Oxen, Bulls, Cows, and Calves. | 0·2 | 8,126,037 | 87·0 | — | — | — | 12·3 | 0·7 | 1,206,205 | 13·0 | 9,332,242 | 100 |
| Sheep and Lambs . | 0·2 | 2,301,585 | 91·4 | — | — | — | 8·6 | — | 216,797 | 8·6 | 2,518,382 | 100 |
| Bacon and Hams . | — | 9,541,466 | 95·1 | — | — | — | 4·9 | — | 494,860 | 4·9 | 10,036,326 | 100 |
| Butter . | 0·8 | 11,503,649 | 97·7 | 0·3 | — | — | 2·2 | — | 270,284 | 2·3 | 11,773,933 | 100 |
| Cheese . | — | 3,624,704 | 74·1 | — | — | — | 25·9 | — | 1,265,696 | 25·9 | 4,890,400 | 100 |
| Cocoa . | 24·1 | 273,967 | 36·3 | — | — | 62·1 | — | 1·6 | 479,795 | 63·7 | 753,762 | 100 |
| Coffee . | 42·9 | 2,880,545 | 58·4 | 17·1 | — | 2·7 | — | 21·8 | 2,055,920 | 41·6 | *4,936,465 | 100 |
| Corn, Grain, and Flour : | | | | | | | | | | | | |
| Wheat . | 8·2 | 23,912,277 | 76·0 | 16·8 | 4·3 | — | 2·9 | — | 7,542,204 | 24·0 | 31,454,481 | 100 |
| Barley . | 12·0 | 5,722,147 | 99·7 | 0·1 | — | — | 0·2 | — | 19,648 | 0·3 | 5,741,795 | 100 |
| Oats . | 0·5 | 4,954,146 | 98·9 | — | 0·5 | — | 0·6 | — | 56,147 | 1·1 | 5,010,293 | 100 |
| Maize . | 4·8 | 9,723,688 | 93·8 | 0·1 | — | — | 6·1 | — | 646,386 | 6·2 | 10,370,074 | 100 |
| Wheat-meal and Flour | 13·9 | 11,921,298 | 96·6 | — | 0·4 | — | 3·0 | — | 423,480 | 3·4 | 12,344,778 | 100 |
| Eggs . | 0·1 | 2,718,322 | 99·5 | — | — | — | — | 0·5 | 13,733 | 0·5 | 2,732,055 | 100 |
| Meat of all kinds (salted, fresh, or preserved) | 2·0 | 5,163,957 | 83·0 | — | 13·5 | — | 3·5 | — | 1,054,631 | 17·0 | 6,218,630 | 100 |
| Potatoes . | 0·1 | 1,133,187 | 71·5 | — | — | — | — | 28·5 | 452,078 | 28·5 | 1,535,260 | 100 |
| Rice . | 1·3 | 237,304 | 7·5 | 92·0 | — | — | — | 0·5 | 2,938,122 | 92·5 | 3,175,426 | 100 |
| Spices of all sorts, including Pepper . | 7·6 | 254,321 | 16·5 | 12·1 | — | 7·6 | — | †63·8 | 1,262,381 | 83·5 | 1,536,702 | 100 |
| Spirits of all sorts . | 0·6 | 1,383,225 | 72·3 | 0·3 | 0·1 | 26·6 | — | 0·7 | 531,343 | 27·7 | 1,914,568 | 100 |
| Sugar, refined . | 0·2 | 4,459,695 | 99·8 | — | — | 0·2 | — | — | 8,922 | 0·2 | 4,468,617 | 100 |
| Sugar, unrefined . | ‡33·1 | 15,761,043 | 77·0 | 5·0 | — | 15·1 | — | 2·9 | 4,712,194 | 23·0 | 20,473,237 | 100 |
| Tea . | 0·3 | 7,641,849 | 66·2 | 32·2 | 0·4 | — | — | 1·2 | 3,901,082 | 33·8 | 11,542,931 | 100 |
| Tobacco, manufactured and unmanufactured | 7·9 | 2,796,961 | 97·8 | 1·6 | — | 0·1 | 0·1 | 0·4 | 63,866 | 2·2 | 2,860,827 | 100 |
| Wine of all sorts . | 3·1 | 5,385,825 | 98·8 | 0·2 | 0·4 | — | — | 0·6 | 66,128 | 1·2 | 5,451,953 | 100 |
| Total . | .. | 141,421,193 | | | | | | | 29,701,952 | | 171,123,145 | |

* Only about one-fifth of the coffee imported is retained for consumption.
† 54·1 per cent. of the total value of spices imported came from the Straits Settlements.
‡ 26·7 per cent. of the total value of the unrefined sugar imported came from Java, Peru, and Brazil.

## TABLE XVI.

*Statement showing the Proportion per cent. of the Total Value of the Articles of Food named in Table XV. imported into the United Kingdom from Foreign Countries and British Possessions, for the Year 1883.*

| COUNTRIES. | Per Centage of Total. |
|---|---|
| **A.—*Foreign Countries.*** | |
| Russia . . . | 6·7 |
| Sweden . . . | 1·7 |
| Denmark . . . . . . | 3·4 |
| Germany . . . . . . . | 9·9 |
| Holland . . . . . | 5·4 |
| Belgium . . . . . . | 1·8 |
| France . | 6·8 |
| Spain . . . | 1·0 |
| Portugal . . . | 0·9 |
| Roumania . . . | 2·0 |
| China . . . . . . . | 4·5 |
| Foreign West India Islands . . . | 0·6 |
| United States . . . . . | 28·9 |
| Other Foreign Countries . | 9·1 |
| Total of Foreign Countries . | 82·7 |
| **B.—*British Possessions.*** | |
| British India . | 8·2 |
| Australia . . . . . . . | 1·4 |
| British West Indies and British Guiana . | 2·5 |
| British North America . | 3·2 |
| Other British Possessions . | 2·0 |
| Total of British Possessions . . | 17·3 |
| Total of Foreign Countries and British Possessions . . . . . . | 100 |

## TABLE XVII.

*Statement showing the Value of the Exports of British and Irish Produce in each of the Years 1870, 1880, and 1883, classified as Articles of Food, Raw Materials, and Manufactured Goods; in thousands of pounds, i.e., 100 = 100,000.*

| ARTICLES EXPORTED. | 1870. | 1880. | 1883. |
|---|---|---|---|
| **(a) ARTICLES OF FOOD :—** | £ | £ | £ |
| Animals, living : | | | |
|   Oxen, bulls, cows, and calves | 41 | 60 | 193 |
|   Sheep and lambs | 26 | 35 | 43 |
|   Swine | 2 | 3 | 2 |
| Beer and ale | 1,882 | 1,734 | 1,820 |
| Biscuit and bread | 436 | 583 | 597 |
| Butter | 316 | 202 | 212 |
| Cheese | 110 | 51 | 59 |
| Corn, grain, meal, and flour : | | | |
|   Wheat | 544 | 348 | 23 |
|   Malt | 242 | 162 | 134 |
|   Oats | 160 | 99 | 38 |
|   Other kinds of grain | 30 | 24 | 19 |
|   Wheat-meal and flour | 163 | 74 | 60 |
|   Other kinds of meal and flour | 6 | 12 | 24 |
| Fish, fresh and cured : | | | |
|   Salmon | 45 | 42 | 47 |
|   Herrings | 723 | 1,422 | 1,427 |
|   Pilchards | 30 | 47 | 42 |
|   Cod and ling | 44 | 44 ⎫ | |
|   Oysters | 30 | 45 ⎬ | 367 |
|   Unenumerated | 44 | 179 ⎭ | |
| Hops | 93 | 53 | 90 |
| Pickles, vinegar, and sauces | 470 | 679 | *1,221 |
| Provisions, unenumerated | 926 | 1,035 | 822 |
| Spirits, British and Irish | 183 | 544 | 810 |
| Sugar, refined and candy | 934 | 1,127 | 1,237 |
|   ,,   molasses, treacle, and syrup | 35 | 186 | 246 |
| Tobacco and snuff, manufactured in the United Kingdom : | | | |
|   Snuff | 58 | 7 | 6 |
|   Other kinds of manufactured tobacco | 31 | 25 | 25 |
| Wine, British made | 3 | 3 | 10 |
|         Total | 7,607 | 8,825 | 9,575 |
| **(b) RAW MATERIALS :—** | | | |
| Clay, unmanufactured | 98 | 163 | 192 |
| Coals, cinders, &c. : | | | |
|   Coals | 5,290 | 7,837 | 9,971 |
|   Coke and cinders | 224 | 338 | 340 |
|   Products of coal, peat, or shale, including naphtha, paraffine and oil thereof, and petroleum, pitch, and tar | 331 | 492 | 1,018 |

* Includes confectionery—previously included with "Other Manufactured Goods" on page 254.

## TABLE XVII. (*continued*).

| ARTICLES EXPORTED. | 1870. | 1880. | 1883. |
|---|---|---|---|
| (*b*) RAW MATERIALS (*continued*) :— | £ | £ | £ |
| Copper, ore .. | 1 | 8 | 7 |
|   ,, unwrought, in ingots, cakes, or slabs | 796 | 1,054 | 1,143 |
| Flax and hemp, dressed and undressed .. | 183 | 111 | 174 |
| Grease, not otherwise described .. .. | 73 | 285 | 415 |
| Hides, raw .. .. .. .. .. | 77 | 194 | 146 |
| Iron: | | | |
|   Ore .. .. .. .. .. | 1 | 27 | 8 |
|   Old, for re-manufacture .. .. .. | 502 | 1,165 | 338 |
|   Pig and puddled .. .. .. .. | 2,229 | 5,219 | 4,077 |
| Lead, ore .. .. .. .. .. | 2 | 4 | 4 |
|   ,, pig .. .. .. .. .. | 760 | 357 | 312 |
| Rags (except woollen), and other materials for making paper .. | 390 | 673 | 503 |
| Seeds of all sorts .. .. .. .. | 137 | 231 | 268 |
| Skins and furs : | | | |
|   Sheep and lambs, undressed (without the wool) .. .. .. | 257 | 715 | 378 |
|   Foreign, dressed in the United Kingdom | 164 | 673 | 848 |
|   Unenumerated .. .. .. .. | 130 | 256 | 231 |
| Steel, cast in ingots.. .. .. .. | 12 | 187 | 93 |
| Tin, unwrought .. .. .. .. | 633 | 399 | 524 |
| Wood and timber, rough-hewn, sawn, or split .. .. .. .. | 43 | 55 | 39 |
| Wool, sheep and lambs, British .. .. | 581 | 1,187 | 1,030 |
|   ,, not being sheep and lambs, including foreign (dressed in the United Kingdom), and flocks and rag-wool .. .. .. .. | 166 | 547 | 517 |
| Zinc or spelter, ore .. .. .. .. | 4 | 2 | 9 |
|   ,, ,, crude, in cakes .. .. | 84 | 94 | 65 |
| Other articles, unmanufactured .. .. | 576 | 999 | 881 |
|      Total .. .. .. .. | 13,744 | 23,272 | 23,531 |
| (*c*) MANUFACTURED GOODS :— | | | |
| Alkali .. .. .. .. .. | 1,486 | 2,398 | 2,125 |
| Apparel and slops .. .. .. .. | 2,205 | 3,212 | 3,634 |
| Arms, ammunition, &c. : | | | |
|   Shot of iron, including shells .. .. | 9 | 41 | 30 |
|   Gunpowder .. .. .. .. | 427 | 373 | 385 |
|   Percussion caps .. .. .. .. | 54 | 73 | 68 |
|   Ordnance stores and ammunition, unenumerated .. .. .. | 485 | 530 | 577 |
|   Cannon and mortars .. .. .. | 106 | 92 | 132 |

### TABLE XVII. (*continued*).

| ARTICLES EXPORTED. | 1870. | 1880. | 1883. |
|---|---|---|---|
| (c) MANUFACTURED GOODS (*continued*):— | £ | £ | £ |
| Arms, ammunition, &c. (*continued*): | | | |
| Muskets .. .. .. .. .. | 98 | 61 | |
| Rifles .. .. .. .. .. | 655 | 95 | 355 |
| Fowling pieces .. .. .. .. | 95 | 133 | |
| Revolvers .. .. .. .. .. | 18 | 16 | 6 |
| Other firearms .. .. .. .. | 6 | 2 | 21 |
| Parts of firearms .. .. .. .. | 8 | 39 | |
| Swords, cutlasses, bayonets, and other arms, not being firearms .. | 14 | 4 | 3 |
| Bags and sacks, empty .. .. .. | 914 | 1,452 | 1,138 |
| Bleaching materials .. .. .. | 177 | 442 | 480 |
| Books, printed .. .. .. | 631 | 970 | 1,175 |
| Brass, manufactures of .. .. .. | 247 | 323 | 432 |
| Candles of all sorts .. .. .. .. | 133 | 143 | 148 |
| Caoutchouc manufactures .. .. .. | 693 | 834 | 1,070 |
| Carriages, carts, &c. : | | | |
| Railway carriages .. .. .. | 88 | 76 | 426 |
| ,,       waggons, trucks, &c. .. .. | 388 | 215 | 668 |
| Cement .. .. .. .. .. | 366 | 693 | 925 |
| Chemical products or preparations, unenumerated .. .. .. | 1,043 | 2,384 | 1,678 |
| Clay, manufactures thereof .. .. | 176 | 191 | 229 |
| Clocks, watches, and parts thereof .. | 146 | 157 | 311 |
| Coal, cinders, &c. : | | | |
| Fuel, manufactured .. .. .. | 124 | 197 | 336 |
| Copper, wrought or manufactured : | | | |
| Mixed, or yellow metal for sheathing .. | 796 | 1,022 | 1,182 |
| Unenumerated .. .. .. .. | 1,228 | 1,258 | 1,245 |
| Cordage cables, and ropes of hemp or like material .. .. .. | 354 | 296 | 436 |
| Cotton twist and yarn .. .. .. | 14,671 | 11,902 | 13,510 |
| Cotton Manufactures : | | | |
| Piece goods, plain .. .. .. | 33,831 | 34,755 | 34,151 |
| ,,       ,,   printed .. .. .. | 18,137 | 22,377 | 20,831 |
| ,,       ,,   of mixed materials .. | 339 | 546 | 552 |
| Lace and patent net .. .. .. | 839 | 1,974 | 2,708 |
| Hosiery, stockings and socks .. .. | 293 | 402 | 536 |
| ,,       of other sorts .. .. .. | 520 | 541 | 634 |
| Thread for sewing .. .. .. | 1,208 | 2,073 | 2,361 |
| Other manufactures, unenumerated .. | 1,578 | 994 | 1,163 |
| Earthen and china ware: | | | |
| Red pottery and brown stone ware .. | 56 | 87 | 135 |
| Earthenware, china ware, parian, and porcelain .. .. .. | 1,637 | 1,978 | 2,198 |
| Furniture (household), cabinet and upholstery wares .. .. .. | 231 | 481 | 706 |

## TABLE XVII. (*continued*).

| Articles Exported. | 1870. | 1880. | 1883. |
|---|---|---|---|
| (c) Manufactured Goods (*continued*):— | £ | £ | £ |
| Glass : | | | |
|   Plate, rough or silvered (including looking-glasses and mirrors) .. | 145 | 193 | 261 |
|   Flint, plain, cut, or ornamental (including bottles and phials of flint glass) .. .. .. .. | 254 | 249 | 339 |
|   Common bottles.. .. .. .. | 307 | 333 | 356 |
|   Other manufactures, unenumerated .. | 127 | 147 | 128 |
| Haberdashery and millinery (including embroidery and needlework) .. | 4,813 | 3,875 | 3,880 |
| Hardware and cutlery, unenumerated .. | 3,812 | 3,521 | 3,756 |
| Hats of felt .. .. .. .. .. | 344 | 558 | 699 |
|   ,,   straw .. .. .. .. | 142 | 395 | 398 |
|   ,,   other sorts .. .. .. .. | 41 | 53 | 41 |
| Implements and tools : | | | |
|   Agricultural .. .. .. .. | 249 | 263 | 353 |
|   Unenumerated .. .. .. .. | 77 | 115 | 500 |
| Iron : | | | |
|   Bar .. .. .. .. .. | 2,252 | 1,907 | 1,751 |
|   Angle .. .. .. .. .. | 62 | 76 } | 283 |
|   Bolt and rod .. .. .. .. | 301 | 393 } | |
|   Railroad : | | | |
|     Rails and tie rods .. .. .. | 7,136 | 4,212 | 4,593 |
|     Wheels and axles .. .. .. | 638 | 276 ( | 1,420 |
|     Unenumerated .. .. .. .. | 982 | 584 \ | |
|   Wire of iron or steel (except telegraph) | 366 | 828 | 927 |
|   Sheets, and boiler and armour plates .. | 977 | 1,229 | 1,480 |
|   Galvanised, other than wire .. .. | 454 | 1,361 | 1,749 |
|   Hoops .. .. .. .. .. | 688 | 793 | 671 |
|   Tin plates.. .. .. .. .. | 2,363 | 4,458 | 4,705 |
|   Anchors, grapnels, chains, and cables .. | 382 | 265 | 389 |
|   Tubes and pipes, wrought .. .. | 324 | 452 | 512 |
|   Nails, screws, and rivets .. .. | 332 | 374 | 406 |
|   Cast or wrought and all other manufactures, unenumerated .. | 2,369 | 2,700 | 3,309 |
|   Steel, bar, of all kinds .. .. .. | 985 | 987 | 1,089 |
|   ,,   sheets .. .. .. .. | 107 | 96 | 215 |
|   Manufactures of steel, or of steel and iron combined .. .. .. | 575 | 827 | *581 |
| Lead, rolled and sheet, piping and tubing | 186 | 226 | 241 |
| Leather, tanned, unwrought .. .. | 850 | 1,153 | 1,637 |
|   ,,   wrought, boots and shoes .. | 1,148 | 1,282 | 1,542 |
|   ,,   ,,   other articles, unenumerated .. .. .. .. | 300 | 375 | 422 |

* Exclusive of surgical and anatomical instruments, which are included with "other manufactured goods" for this year.

## TABLE XVII. (*continued*).

| Articles Exported. | 1870. | 1880. | 1883. |
|---|---|---|---|
| (*c*) MANUFACTURED GOODS (*continued*):— | £ | £ | £ |
| Linen and jute yarn | 2,434 | 1,212 | 1,327 |
| Linen and jute manufactures : | | | |
| Linen piece goods, plain, unbleached or bleached | 5,983 | 4,819 | 4,408 |
| Ditto, checked, printed, or dyed, and damasks and diapers | 421 | 150 | 214 |
| Sailcloth and sails | 193 | 166 | 172 |
| Thread for sewing | 283 | 372 | 293 |
| Linen manufactures, unenumerated | 369 | 328 | 352 |
| Jute manufactures | 790 | 2,255 | 2,518 |
| Lucifer and vesta matches | 169 | 145 | 151 |
| Machinery and millwork : | | | |
| Steam engines, or parts of, locomotive | 810 | 785 | 1,387 |
| Steam engines, or parts of, other descriptions | 1,188 | 2,001 | 2,911 |
| Not being steam engines, agricultural | 303 | 680 | 865 |
| ,, other descriptions | 2,993 | 5,797 | 8,272 |
| Manure, unenumerated | 415 | 1,128 | 2,162 |
| Medicines | 615 | 814 | 923 |
| Musical instruments and parts thereof | 146 | 200 | 255 |
| Oil, other than essential and medicinal : | | | |
| Seed | 1,286 | 1,621 | 1,864 |
| Other sorts, unenumerated | 119 | 351 | 364 |
| Oil and floor cloth (including india-rubber cloth) | 219 | 383 | 598 |
| Painters' colours and materials | 884 | 1,174 | 1,278 |
| Paper : | | | |
| Writing or printing, and envelopes | 428 | 856 | 1,026 |
| Hangings | 119 | 138 | 160 |
| Pasteboard, millboard, &c. (including playing cards) | 19 | 38 | 48 |
| Unenumerated (and articles of paper, except papier mâché) | 84 | 208 | 211 |
| Perfumery of all sorts | 102 | 108 | 142 |
| Pictures | 86 | 310 | 320 |
| Plate, gold and silver | 59 | 67 | 79 |
| Plated and gilt wares | 131 | 167 | 261 |
| Prints, engravings, drawings, &c. | 41 | 97 | 175 |
| Saddlery and harness | 327 | 436 | 429 |
| Saltpetre (British prepared) | 77 | 60 | 33 |
| Silk, thrown, twist, or yarn | 1,154 | 684 | 706 |
| Silk manufactures : | | | |
| Of silk only— | | | |
| Broad stuffs | 510 | 710 | 648 |
| Handkerchiefs, scarfs, and shawls | 149 | 409 | 357 |
| Ribbons of all kinds | 96 | 123 | 183 |

## TABLE XVII. (*continued*).

| Articles Exported. | 1870. | 1880. | 1883. |
|---|---|---|---|
| (*c*) Manufactured Goods (*continued*):— | £ | £ | £ |
| Of Silk only (*continued*): | | | |
| Lace | 81 | 110 | 194 |
| Unenumerated | 299 | 251 | 256 |
| Of silk and other materials— | | | |
| Broad stuffs | 231 | 302 | 607 |
| Other kinds | 85 | 125 | 181 |
| Soap | 218 | 440 | 450 |
| Stationery, other than paper | 489 | 724 | 883 |
| Stones and slates: | | | |
| Slate by tale | 141 | 177 | 192 |
| Grindstones, millstones, and other sorts of stone | 138 | 84 | 93 |
| Telegraph wires and apparatus | 2,523 | 1,301 | 1,238 |
| Umbrellas and parasols | 253 | 458 | 537 |
| Wood and timber, manufactured: | | | |
| Staves and empty casks | 157 | 113 | 117 |
| Unenumerated | 80 | 251 | 409 |
| Woollen and worsted yarn: | | | |
| Woollen yarn (carded) | 98 | 107 | 180 |
| Worsted yarn (combed) | 4,897 | 3,238 | 3,087 |
| Woollen and worsted manufactures: | | | |
| Coatings, duffels, &c., all wool | 3,086 | 2,920 | 7,351 |
| „ „ of wool mixed with other materials | 1,664 | 3,816 | |
| Worsted stuffs, all wool | 2,052 | 1,029 | 7,688 |
| „ „ of wool mixed with other materials | 11,736 | 6,213 | |
| Blankets and blanketing | 645 | 587 | 488 |
| Flannels | 366 | 310 | 349 |
| Carpets, not being rugs | 1,393 | 1,134 | 1,259 |
| Shawls | 117 | 158 | 158 |
| Rugs, coverlets, or wrappers | 151 | 361 | 343 |
| Hosiery | 266 | 320 | 397 |
| Small wares and manufactures of wool or worsted, unenumerated | 190 | 418 | 281 |
| Yarn, alpaca, mohair, and other sorts, unenumerated | 189 | 878 | 954 |
| Zinc or Spelter, manufactures of | 57 | 41 | 33 |
| Other Manufactured Goods | 3,034 | 5,917 | 6,543 |
| Total | 178,236 | 190,963 | 206,693 |

## SUMMARY OF FOREGOING TABLE.

| | 1870. | | 1880. | | 1883. | |
|---|---|---|---|---|---|---|
| | Amount. | Per cent of Total | Amount. | Per cent of Total | Amount. | Per cent of Total |
| | £ | | £ | | £ | |
| Articles of Food, Drink, and Tobacco | 7,607 | 4 | 8,825 | 4 | 9,575 | 4 |
| Raw Materials .. | 13,744 | 7 | 23,272 | 10 | 23,531 | 10 |
| Manufactured Goods | 178,236 | 89 | 190,963 | 86 | 206,693 | 86 |
| Total Exports of British and Irish Produce .. | 199,587 | 100 | 223,060 | 100 | 239,799 | 100 |

## TABLE XVIII.

*Statement showing the Proportion of Food, Raw Materials, and Manufactured Articles in the Domestic Exports of France, for each of the Years 1869 and 1879, compiled from the French official Returns; in thousands of pounds, i.e., 100 = 100,000.*

| ARTICLES EXPORTED. | 1869. | 1879 |
|---|---|---|
| (a) ARTICLES OF FOOD :— | £ | £ |
| Brandy, spirits, and liqueurs ... ... ... | 2,457 | 4,130 |
| Butter and cheese ... ... ... ... | 3,116 | 2,665 |
| Cattle, &c. .. ... ... ... ... | 1,351 | 893 |
| Eggs ... ... ... ... ... ... | 1,455 | 1,304 |
| Farinaceous substances not otherwise specified | 805 | 1,818 |
| Fish ... ... ... ... ... ... | 694 | 1,519 |
| Fruit, for the table ... .. ... ... | 1,086 | 998 |
| ,, oleaginous ... ... ... ... | 621 | 334 |
| Grain and meal : Wheat, spelt, meslin ... | 661 | 392 |
| Rye ... ... ... ... | 893 | 301 |
| Other kinds ... ... | 1,215 | 1,066 |
| Hops ... ... ... ... ... .. | 475 | 81 |
| Ice ... ... ... ... ... ... | 304 | 221 |
| Meat of all kinds ... ... ... ... | 398 | 445 |
| Oil, olive ... ... ... ... ... | 136 | 200 |
| Salt ... ... ... ... ... ... | 86 | 102 |
| Sugar, raw ... ... ... ... ... | 602 | 537 |
| ,, refined ... ... ... ... ... | 3,240 | 4,033 |
| Syrups, preserves, &c. ... ... ... ... | 174 | 195 |
| Tobacco, manufactured... ... ... ... | 45 | 70 |
| Truffles ... ... ... ... ... | 57 | 298 |
| Vegetables, green, salted, or preserved ... | 166 | 541 |
| Wines of all kinds ... ... ... ... | 13,447 | 10,308 |
| Other articles of food ... .. ... ... | 533 | 708 |
| Total of Food ... ... ... ... | 34,017 | 33,159 |

## TABLE XVIII. (*continued*).

| ARTICLES EXPORTED. | 1869. | 1879. |
|---|---|---|
| (*b*) RAW MATERIALS :— | £ | £ |
| Building materials (lime, bricks, slate, &c.) ... | 375 | 504 |
| Cards for carding machines ... ... ... | 84 | 75 |
| Coal and coke ... ... ... ... .. | 178 | 273 |
| Cotton, raw ... ... ... ... ... | 3,016 | 2,675 |
| Fat, oil ... ... ... ... ... ... | 66 | 252 |
| Feathers ... ... ... ... ... ... | 143 | 1,348 |
| Flax and hemp ... ... ... | 364 | 519 |
| Grease of all kinds ... ... ... | 689 | 1,053 |
| Hair of all kinds ... ... ... | 489 | 454 |
| Hemp fibre ... ... ... ... | 127 | 123 |
| Hides, raw ... ... ... .. | 971 | 2,110 |
| Horses, mules, &c. ... ... ... | 788 | 638 |
| Madder .. ... ... ... | 519 | 22 |
| Native resins ... ... ... ... | 228 | 137 |
| Ores of all kinds ... ... .. | 242 | 120 |
| Pitch and mineral tar ... ... ... | 62 | 110 |
| Rags for paper making... ... ... ... | 440 | 611 |
| Saffron ... ... ... ... ... ... | 176 | 158 |
| Silk, raw and waste ... ... ... ... | 6,245 | 6,344 |
| Silkworms' eggs... ... ... ... ... | 199 | 98 |
| Sowing seed ... ... ... .. ... | 823 | 646 |
| Stones, lithographic and other... ... ... | 178 | 263 |
| Wood, for building purposes ... ... ... | 1,292 | 869 |
| Wool, raw ... ... ... ... ... | 1,787 | 4,689 |
| Other raw materials ... ... ... ... | 2,001 | 1,119 |
| Total Raw Materials ... | 21,482 | 25,210 |
| (*c*) MANUFACTURED ARTICLES :— | | |
| Arms and ammunition ... ... ... ... | 164 | 256 |
| Artificial flowers, &c. ... ... ... ... | 1,240 | 1,205 |
| Basketwork of all kinds ... ... ... | 61 | 136 |
| Books, stationery, &c. ... ... ... ... | 825 | 956 |
| Candles ... ... ... ... ... ... | 306 | 81 |
| Caoutchouc manufactures ... ... ... | 166 | 187 |
| Carriages ... ... ... .. | 139 | 116 |
| Chemical products not otherwise specified ... | 1,424 | 1,500 |
| Clocks and watches ... ... ... ... | 452 | 627 |
| Colours ... ... ... ... ... ... | 489 | 449 |
| Copper, wrought ... ... ... ... | 346 | 182 |
| Cutlery ... ... ... ... ... ... | 59 | 105 |
| French fancy wares ... ... ... ... | 211 | 246 |
| Furniture, and other wood manufactures ... | 987 | 1,203 |
| Garancine (extract of madder)... ... ... | 557 | 14 |
| Glass, and glass wares ... ... ... ... | 911 | 790 |

## TABLE XVIII. (*continued*).

| Articles Exported. | 1869. | 1871. |
|---|---|---|
| (c) MANUFACTURED ARTICLES (*continued*) : – | £ | £ |
| Gold and silver wares | 954 | 2,316 |
| Grindstones | 142 | 283 |
| Haberdashery, &c. | 6,087 | 5,420 |
| Hats, of felt | 405 | 405 |
| ,, mats, and other manufactures of straw or bark | 398 | 664 |
| Instruments: optical, mathematical, surgical, &c. | 163 | 312 |
| ,, musical | 406 | 399 |
| Leather wares | 3,966 | 5,930 |
| Machinery | 595 | 921 |
| Medicines, compounded | 619 | 425 |
| Oil-cake | 564 | 416 |
| Paper and cardboard | 779 | 886 |
| Perfumery | 707 | 315 |
| Pottery and porcelain | 317 | 516 |
| Quinine, sulphate of | 90 | 224 |
| Skins and hides, dressed | 3,242 | 3,846 |
| Soap, other than scented | 421 | 362 |
| Tartrates... | 243 | 505 |
| Tissues: Cotton... | 2,959 | 2,535 |
| ,, Linen, hempen, and jute | 733 | 1,048 |
| ,, Silk | 17,894 | 9,070 |
| ,, Woollen | 10,732 | 12,371 |
| Umbrellas and parasols | 133 | 136 |
| Tools, and other metal wares | 1,510 | 2,711 |
| Wearing apparel | 3,349 | 2,710 |
| Works of art | 436 | 494 |
| Yarns : Cotton ... | 115 | 98 |
| ,, Linen, hempen, and jute | 339 | 366 |
| ,, Woollen | 1,112 | 1,748 |
| Other manufactured articles | 2,757 | 4,022 |
| Total of Manufactured Articles | 70,504 | 69,516 |

R

## SUMMARY OF FOREGOING TABLE.

|  | Amount. | | Percentage. | |
|---|---|---|---|---|
|  | 1869. | 1879. | 1869. | 1879. |
|  | £ | £ |  |  |
| Food ... ... ... | 34,017 | 33,159 | 27·0 | 26·0 |
| Raw Materials ... | 21,482 | 25,210 | 17·0 | 19·8 |
| Manufactures ... | 70,504 | 69,516 | 56·0 | 54·2 |
| Total ... ... | 126,003 | 127,885 | 100 | 100 |

## TABLE XIX.

*Statement showing the Proportion of Food, Raw Materials, and Manufactured Articles in the Domestic Exports of Germany, for each of the Years 1869 and 1879; compiled from the official Returns of Germany; in thousands of marks, i.e., 100 = 100,000.*

| ARTICLES EXPORTED. | 1869.* | 1879. |
|---|---|---|
| (a) FOOD :— | Marks. | Marks. |
| Animals, living— |  |  |
| Cattle ... ... ... ... | 32,800 | 45,350 |
| Sheep ... ... ... ... | 30,000 | 37,600 |
| Swine ... ... ... ... | 16,400 | 24,090 |
| Beer ... ... ... ... ... | 3,400 | 23,400 |
| Brandy ... ... ... ... | 20,700 | 14,800 |
| Butter ... ... ... ... ... | 26,800 | 22,000 |
| Fruit of all kinds ... ... ... | 52,000 | 77,700 |
| Grain— |  |  |
| Wheat ... ... ... ... ... | 149,000 | 127,000 |
| Barley ... ... ... ... ... | 17,200 | 40,600 |
| Oats ... ... ... ... ... | 15,900 | 15,500 |
| Other grain, and flour ... ... ... | 104,200 | 166,900 |
| Hops ... ... ... .. ... ... | 18,200 | 22,300 |
| Meat ... ... ... ... ... ... | 6,600 | 8,970 |
| Sugar, raw ... ... ... ... ... | 10,600 | 58,200 |
| „ refined ... ... ... ... | 4,500 | 21,390 |
| Syrup and molasses ... ... ... ... | 5,700 | 10,190 |
| Tobacco, manufactured ... ... ... | 11,800 | 6,760 |
| „ unmanufactured ... ... ... | 8,300 | 1,380 |
| Wine ... ... ... ... ... ... | 22,800 | 21,910 |
| Other articles of food ... ... ... | 10,226 | 12,930 |
| Total of Food ... { Marks | 567,126 | 758,970 |
| { £ | 28,356* | 37,948 |

* The values for 1869 are estimated only.

## TABLE XIX. (*continued*).

| ARTICLES EXPORTED. | 1869.* | 1872. |
|---|---|---|
| **(b) RAW MATERIALS :—** | Marks. | Marks. |
| Animal produce, &c.... | 36,500 | 90,680 |
| Cotton, raw ... | 61,865 | 65,000 |
| Flax, hemp, and jute | 23,208 | 40,250 |
| Fuel ... | 97,200 | 84,200 |
| Hides and skins, including leather— | | |
|    Cow hides ... | 18,470 | 22,800 |
|    Other kinds | 18,034 | 24,680 |
| Horses | 12,745 | 34,000 |
| Metals, crude— | | |
|    Pig iron ... | 12,814 | 25,610 |
|    Iron and steel, unmanufactured ... | 12,604 | 64,650 |
|    Other raw metals ... | 69,730 | 60,440 |
| Oil : Petroleum | 7,738 | 4,480 |
| Ores and minerals— | | |
|    Iron ore ... | 5,400 | 20,900 |
|    Other kinds | 84,480 | 73,200 |
| Rags for paper-making | 500 | 7,480 |
| Silk, raw | 17,630 | 48,300 |
| Wood of all kinds for further manufacture | 115,800 | 70,500 |
| Wool (sheep's) | 74,026 | 66,440 |
| Soap, oil and resins ... | 40,000 | 55,720 |
| Other unmanufactured articles | 58,896 | 86,330 |
| Total of Raw Materials ...   { Marks | 767,660 | 945,660 |
|       { £ | 38,383* | 47,283 |
| **(c MANUFACTURED ARTICLES :—** | | |
| Books, pamphlets, and other publications... | 23,000 | 22,200 |
| Chemical products, drugs, &c. | 48,931 | 120,780 |
| Dyewoods ... | 1,496 | 1,800 |
| Gunpowder ... | 811 | 3,920 |
| Glasswares and earthenware | 51,500 | 55,000 |
| Guano... | 2,600 | 1,890 |
| India-rubber manufactures ... | 18,780 | 15,000 |
| Iron and steel, manufactures of | 31,882 | 47,400 |
| Leather wares | 31,784 | 51,750 |
| Machinery | 21,212 | 39,010 |
| Manures (except guano) | 4,218 | 22,230 |
| Metal wares ... | 6,104 | 11,200 |
| Paper and paper-hangings ... | 17,000 | 26,100 |
| Rails for railways | 13,350 | 23,000 |
| Ships ... | 43,000 | 32,590 |

* The values for 1869 are estimated only.

R 2

## TABLE XIX. (*continued*).

| ARTICLES EXPORTED. | 1869.* | 1879. |
|---|---|---|
| (*c*) MANUFACTURED ARTICLES (*continued*):— | Marks. | Marks. |
| Tissues— | | |
|     Cotton ... ... ... ... ... | 73,945 | 95,260 |
|     Linen and hempen ... ... ... | 22,475 | 13,560 |
|     Silk ... ... .. ... ... ... | 86,418 | 66,690 |
|     Woollen ... ... ... ... ... | 161,502 | 142,100 |
|     Other kinds, and ready-made clothing ... | 75,407 | 98,590 |
| Wood wares and basket work ... ... | 14,974 | 43,100 |
| Works of art, ornaments, &c. ... ... | 74,000 | 54,900 |
| Yarns— | | |
|     Cotton ... ... ... ... | 10,692 | 24,700 |
|     Linen and hempen ... ... | 5,072 | 4,700 |
|     Woollen ... ... ... ... | 32,292 | 24,400 |
|     Other kinds ... ... ... | 62 | 3,700 |
| Other manufactured articles ... | 4,770 | 25,450 |
| Total of Manufactures    Marks | 877,277 | 1,071,020 |
| £ | 43,864* | 53,551 |

## SUMMARY OF FOREGOING TABLE.

| | Amount. | | | | Percentage. | |
|---|---|---|---|---|---|---|
| | 1869. | 1879. | 1869. | 1879. | 1869. | 1879. |
| | Marks. | Marks. | £ | £ | | |
| Food . . | 597,126 | 758,970 | 28,356 | 37,948 | 25·6 | 27·3 |
| Raw Materials | 767,660 | 945,660 | 38,383 | 47,283 | 34·7 | 34·0 |
| Manufactured Articles . | 877,277 | 1,071,020 | 43,864 | 53,551 | 39·7 | 38·7 |
| Total . . | 2,212,063* | 2,775,650 | 110,603* | 138,782 | 100 | 100 |

* The values for 1869 are estimated only.

## TABLE XX.

*Statement showing the Proportion of Food, Raw Materials, and Manufactured Articles in the Domestic Exports of the United States, for each of the Years 1870 and 1880. (Years ended 30th June), compiled from the official Returns of the United States; in thousands of dollars, i.e., 100 = 100,000.*

| ARTICLES EXPORTED. | Years ended 30th June. | |
|---|---|---|
| | 1870.† | 1880.† |
| **(a) FOOD :—** | Dollars. | Dollars. |
| Animals, living | 1,045 | 15,882 |
| Beer, ale, porter, and cider | 26 | 299 |
| Bread and breadstuffs : | | |
| Indian corn | 1,289 | 53,298 |
| Wheat | 47,171 | 190,546 |
| Wheat flour | 21,170 | 35,333 |
| Other breadstuffs | 2,621 | 8,860 |
| Fruits | 543 | 2,091 |
| Hops | 2,516 | 2,573 |
| Oil, Vegetable | 326 | 3,476 |
| Provisions : | | |
| Bacon and hams | 6,123 | 50,988 |
| Beef, fresh | } 1,940 { | 7,442 |
| ,, salted | | 2,881 |
| Butter | 592 | 6,691 |
| Cheese | 8,881 | 12,172 |
| Lard | 5,933 | 27,920 |
| Meats, preserved | 314 | 7,877 |
| Pork | 3,253 | 5,930 |
| Other | 2,140 | 5,142 |
| Spirits | 726 | 3,028 |
| Sugar, refined | 555 | 2,718 |
| ,, unrefined, and molasses | 91 | 541 |
| Tobacco, and manufactures of | 22,705 | 18,442 |
| Total of Food { Dollars | 129,960 | 464,130 |
| { £ | 21,660* | 96,694* |
| **(b) RAW MATERIALS:—** | | |
| Coal | 1,306 | 2,058 |
| Cotton, raw | 227,028 | 211,536 |
| Furs and furriers' wares | 1,941 | 5,404 |
| Ginseng | 455 | 533 |
| Raw hides and skins | 365 | 649 |

* In the year 1870 the conversions have been made at the currency rate of 3s. 4d. to the dollar, and in 1880 at the average rate of 4s. 2d.

† Exclusive of bullion and specie.

## TABLE XX. (*continued*).

| ARTICLES EXPORTED. | Years ended 30th June. | |
| --- | --- | --- |
| | 1870.† | 1880.† |
| **(b) RAW MATERIALS (*continued*):—** | Dollars. | Dollars. |
| Naval stores (resin, turpentine, tar, and pitch) | 1,920 | 2,453 |
| Oil, Mineral ... | 32,669 | 36,219 |
| ,, Animal (fat and fish) ... | 1,148 | 1,676 |
| Quicksilver ... | 512 | 1,360 |
| Seeds ... | 98 | 2,777 |
| Tallow ... | 3,815 | 7,689 |
| Wool, raw ... | 55 | 72 |
| All other unmanufactured articles ... | 2,285 | 2,128 |
| Total of Raw Materials ...  { Dollars | 273,597 | 274,554 |
| £ | 45,600* | 57,199* |
| **(c) MANUFACTURED ARTICLES:—** | | |
| Agricultural implements ... | 1,069 | 2,246 |
| Books, pamphlets, and other publications... | 341 | 627 |
| Carriages, railway cars, carts, and parts thereof ... | 977 | 1,407 |
| Clocks and watches ... | 589 | 1,453 |
| Copper, and manufactures of ... | 1,042 | 849 |
| Cotton, manufactures of ... | 3,787 | 9,981 |
| Drugs, chemicals, medicines, and dye stuffs (including acids) ... | 2,495 | 3,531 |
| Fancy articles, combs, perfumery, and toilet soap ... | 409 | 876 |
| Glass and glass wares ... | 531 | 750 |
| Hemp, and manufactures of, including cordage ... | 582 | 1,629 |
| Iron and steel, and manufactures of ... | 13,483 | 14,716 |
| Jewellery, and other manufactures of gold and silver ... | 60 | 232 |
| Leather, and manufactures of ... | 673 | 6,760 |
| Manures ... | 115 | 604 |
| Marble and stone, and manufactures of ... | 180 | 653 |
| Metals, and manufactures of, not elsewhere specified ... | 401 | 971 |
| Musical instruments ... | 267 | 811 |
| Oilcake ... | 3,419 | 6,260 |
| Ordnance stores ... | 1,229 | 777 |

---

* In the year 1870 the conversions have been made at the currency rate of 3s. 4d. to the dollar, and in 1880 at the average rate of 4s. 2d.

† Exclusive of bullion and specie.

## TABLE XX. *(continued)*.

| ARTICLES EXPORTED. | Years ended 30th June. | |
|---|---|---|
| | 1870.† | 1880.† |
| *(c)* MANUFACTURED ARTICLES *(continued)* :— | Dollars. | Dollars. |
| Paper and stationery ... ... ... | 515 | 1,183 |
| Soap, common ... ... ... ... | 623 | 690 |
| Starch ... ... ... ... ... | 107 | 448 |
| Turpentine, spirits of ... ... ... | 1,357 | 2,132 |
| Wearing apparel ... ... ... ... | 619 | 708 |
| Wood, and manufactures of... ... ... | 13,735 | 16,237 |
| Wool, manufactures of ... ... ... | 124 | 216 |
| All other manufactured articles ... ... | 2,922 | 8,515 |
| Total of Manufactures ...   { Dollars | 51,651 | 85,262 |
| { £ | 8,609* | 17,763* |

### SUMMARY.

| | †AMOUNT. | | | | PERCENTAGE. | |
|---|---|---|---|---|---|---|
| | 1870. | 1880. | 1870. | 1880. | 1870. | 1880. |
| | Dollars. | Dollars. | £ | £ | | |
| Food . . . | 129,960 | 464,130 | 21,660 | 96,694 | 28·6 | 56·3 |
| Raw Materials . | 273,597 | 274,554 | 45,600 | 57,199 | 60·1 | 33·3 |
| Manufactured Articles } . | 51,651 | 85,262 | 8,609 | 17,763 | 11·3 | 10·4 |
| Total . . | 455,208 | 823,946 | 75,869 | 171,656 | 100 | 100 |

* In the year 1870 the conversions have been made at the currency rate of 3s. 4d. to the dollar, and in 1880 at the average rate of 4s. 2d.

† Exclusive of bullion and specie.

## TABLE XXI.

*Comparative table showing the Population, Public Debt, Imports, and Exports of the Australian Colonies and New Zealand for each of the Eleven Years— 1873-83. (From the Victorian Year Book.)*

### VICTORIA (87,884 SQUARE MILES).

| Year. | Population on the 31st December. | Public Debt on the 31st December. | Imports. | Exports. |
|---|---|---|---|---|
|  |  | £ | £ | £ |
| 1873 | 772,039 | 12,445,722 | 16,533,856 | 15,302,454 |
| 1874 | 783,274 | 13,990,553 | 16,953,985 | 15,441,109 |
| 1875 | 791,399 | 13,995,093 | 16,685,874 | 14,766,974 |
| 1876 | 801,717 | 17,011,382 | 15,705,354 | 14,196,487 |
| 1877 | 815,494 | 17,018,913 | 16,362,304 | 15,157,687 |
| 1878 | 827,439 | 17,022,065 | 16,161,880 | 14,925,707 |
| 1879 | 840,620 | 20,050,753 | 15,035,538 | 12,454,170 |
| 1880 | 860,067 | 22,060,749 | 14,556,894 | 15,954,559 |
| 1881 | 882,232 | 22,426,502 | 16,718,521 | 16,252,103 |
| 1882 | 906,225 | 22,103,202 | 18,748,081 | 16,193,579 |
| 1883 | 931,790 | 24,308,175 | 17,743,846 | 16,398,863 |
| Total | .. | .. .. | 181,206,113 | 167,043,692 |

### NEW SOUTH WALES (309,175 SQUARE MILES).

| Year. | Population on the 31st December. | Public Debt on the 31st December. | Imports. | Exports. |
|---|---|---|---|---|
|  |  | £ | £ | £ |
| 1873 | 560,275 | 10,842,415 | 11,088,388 | 11,815,829 |
| 1874 | 584,278 | 10,516,371 | 11,293,739 | 12,345,603 |
| 1875 | 606,652 | 11,470,637 | 13,490,200 | 13,671,580 |
| 1876 | 629,776 | 11,759,519 | 13,672,776 | 13,003,941 |
| 1877 | 662,212 | 11,724,419 | 14,606,594 | 13,125,819 |
| 1878 | 693,743 | 11,688,119 | 14,768,873 | 12,965,879 |
| 1879 | 703,143 | 14,937,419 | 14,198,847 | 13,086,819 |
| 1880 | 739,385 | 14,903,919 | 13,950,075 | 15,525,138 |
| 1881 | 781,265 | 16,924,019 | 17,409,326 | 16,049,503 |
| 1882 | 817,468 | 18,721,219 | 21,281,130 | 16,716,961 |
| 1883 | 869,310 | 21,632,459 | 20,960,157 | 19,886,018 |
| Total | .. | .. .. | 166,720,105 | 158,193,090 |

## TABLE XXI. (*continued*).

### QUEENSLAND (668,224 SQUARE MILES).

| Year. | Population on the 31st December. | Public Debt on the 31st December. | Imports. | Exports. |
|---|---|---|---|---|
| | | £ | £ | £ |
| 1873 | 146,690 | 4,782,850 | 2,885,499 | 3,542,513 |
| 1874 | 163,517 | 5,249,350 | 2,962,439 | 4,106,462 |
| 1875 | 181,288 | 6,435,250 | 3,328,009 | 3,857,576 |
| 1876 | 187,100 | 6,435,250 | 3,126,559 | 3,875,581 |
| 1877 | 203,084 | 7,685,350 | 4,068,682 | 4,361,275 |
| 1878 | 210,510 | 8,935,350 | 3,436,077 | 3,190,419 |
| 1879 | 217,851 | 10,192,150 | 3,080,889 | 3,434,034 |
| 1880 | 226,077 | 12,192,150 | 3,087,296 | 3,448,160 |
| 1881 | 226,968 | 13,245,150 | 4,063,625 | 3,540,366 |
| 1882 | 248,255 | 13,125,350 | 6,318,463 | 3,534,452 |
| 1883 | 287,475 | 14,907,850 | 6,233,351 | 5,276,608 |
| Total | .. | .. .. | 42,590,889 | 42,167,446 |

### SOUTH AUSTRALIA (903,425 SQUARE MILES).

| Year. | Population on the 31st December. | Public Debt on the 31st December. | Imports. | Exports. |
|---|---|---|---|---|
| | | £ | £ | £ |
| 1873 | 198,075 | 2,174,900 | 3,841,100 | 4,587,859 |
| 1874 | 204,623 | 2,989,750 | 3,983,290 | 4,402,855 |
| 1875 | 210,442 | 3,320,600 | 4,203,802 | 4,805,051 |
| 1876 | 225,677 | 3,837,100 | 4,576,183 | 4,816,170 |
| 1877 | 236,864 | 4,737,200 | 4,625,511 | 4,626,531 |
| 1878 | 248,795 | 5,329,600 | 5,719,611 | 5,355,021 |
| 1879 | 259,460 | 6,605,750 | 5,014,150 | 4,762,727 |
| 1880 | 267,573 | 9,865,500 | 5,581,497 | 5,574,505 |
| 1881 | 286,324 | 11,196,800 | 5,244,064 | 4,407,757 |
| 1882 | 293,509 | 12,472,600 | 6,707,788 | 5,359,890 |
| 1883 | 304,515 | 13,891,900 | 6,310,055 | 4,883,461 |
| Total | .. | .. .. | 55,807,051 | 53,581,827 |

## TABLE XXI. (*continued*).

### WESTERN AUSTRALIA (975,920 SQUARE MILES).

| Year. | Population on the 31st December. | Public Debt on the 31st December. | Imports. | Exports. |
|---|---|---|---|---|
|  |  | £ | £ | £ |
| 1873 | 25,761 | 35,000 | 297,328 | 265,217 |
| 1874 | 26,209 | 119,000 | 364,263 | 428,837 |
| 1875 | 26,709 | 135,000 | 349,840 | 391,217 |
| 1876 | 27,321 | 135,000 | 386,037 | 397,293 |
| 1877 | 27,838 | 161,000 | 362,707 | 373,352 |
| 1878 | 28,166 | 184,556 | 379,050 | 428,491 |
| 1879 | 28,668 | 361,000 | 407,299 | 494,884 |
| 1880 | 29,019 | 361,000 | 353,669 | 499,183 |
| 1881 | 30,013 | 511,000 | 404,831 | 502,770 |
| 1882 | 30,766 | 511,000 | 508,755 | 583,056 |
| 1883 | 31,700 | 611,000 | 516,847 | 447,010 |
| Total | .. | .. .. | 4,330,626 | 4,811,310 |

### TASMANIA (26,375 SQUARE MILES).

| Year. | Population on the 31st December. | Public Debt on the 31st December. | Imports. | Exports. |
|---|---|---|---|---|
|  |  | £ | £ | £ |
| 1873 | 104,217 | 1,477,600 | 1,107,167 | 893,556 |
| 1874 | 104,176 | 1,476,700 | 1,257,785 | 925,325 |
| 1875 | 103,663 | 1,489,400 | 1,185,942 | 1,085,976 |
| 1876 | 105,484 | 1,520,500 | 1,133,003 | 1,130,983 |
| 1877 | 107,104 | 1,589,705 | 1,308,671 | 1,416,975 |
| 1878 | 109,947 | 1,747,400 | 1,324,812 | 1,315,695 |
| 1879 | 112,469 | 1,786,800 | 1,267,475 | 1,301,097 |
| 1880 | 114,762 | 1,943,700 | 1,369,223 | 1,511,931 |
| 1881 | 118,923 | 2,003,000 | 1,431,144 | 1,555,576 |
| 1882 | 122,479 | 2,050,600 | 1,670,872 | 1,587,389 |
| 1883 | 126,220 | 2,385,600 | 1,832,637 | 1,731,599 |
| Total | .. | .. .. | 14,888,731 | 14,456,102 |

## TABLE XXI. (*continued*).

### NEW ZEALAND (104,027 SQUARE MILES).

| Year. | Population on the 31st December. | Public Debt on the 31st December. | Imports. | Exports. |
|---|---|---|---|---|
| | | £ | £ | £ |
| 1873 | 295,946 | 10,913,936 | 6,464,687 | 5,610,371 |
| 1874 | 341,860 | 13,366,936 | 8,121,812 | 5,251,269 |
| 1875 | 375,856 | 17,400,031 | 8,029,172 | 5,828,627 |
| 1876 | 399,075 | 18,678,111 | 6,905,171 | 5,673,465 |
| 1877 | 417,622 | 20,691,111 | 6,973,418 | 6,327,472 |
| 1878 | 432,519 | 22,608,311 | 8,755,663 | 6,015,525 |
| 1879 | 463,729 | 23,958,311 | 8,374,585 | 5,743,126 |
| 1880 | 484,864 | 28,583,231 | 6,162,011 | 6,352,692 |
| 1881 | 500,910 | 29,659,111 | 7,457,045 | 6,060,876 |
| 1882 | 517,707 | 30,235,711 | 8,609,270 | 6,658,008 |
| 1883 | 540,877 | 31,385,411 | 7,974,038 | 7,095,999 |
| Total | .. | .. | 83,826,872 | 66,617,430 |

### DOMINION OF CANADA. (*From the Canadian Statistics.*)

*Number of Population, Amount of Public Debt, and Total Value of Imports and Exports, including Bullion and Specie, in each of the years 1873 to 1883.*

| Years ended 30th June. | Population. | Debt.† | Imports | Exports |
|---|---|---|---|---|
| | | £ | £ | £ |
| 1873 | 3,686,096* | 20,801,763 | 26,669,017 | 18,706,233 |
| 1874 | | 22,567,701 | 26,711,164 | 18,614,985 |
| 1875 | | 24,168,412 | 25,639,642 | 16,226,454 |
| 1876 | Cannot be given | 25,948,232 | 19,418,822 | 16,868,007 |
| 1877 | | 27,757,356 | 20,693,325 | 15,807,374 |
| 1878 | | 29,242,097 | 19,392,039 | 16,525,764 |
| 1879 | | 29,789,622 | 17,075,922 | 14,894,011 |
| 1880 | | 31,760,747 | 18,018,697 | 18,314,887 |
| 1881 | 4,324,810 | 32,374,121 | 21,943,925 | 20,477,254 |
| 1882 | Cannot be given | 32,012,844 | 24,879,062 | 21,278,584 |
| 1883 | | 33,013,899 | 27,552,921 | 20,434,543 |
| Total | .. | .. | 247,994,536 | 198,148,096 |

* Census of 1871.  † Total net liabilities of the Dominion and Provincial Governments.

NOTE.—In converting dollars into pounds sterling, the dollar is estimated at 4s. 2d.

| Vessels belo[nging to] the United [Kingdom] on 31st Dece[mber].<br>Sailing. | Letters delivered per head of Population in the United Kingdom. | YEARS. |
|---|---|---|
| In Thousands of Tons. | Number. | |
| — | — | 1884 |
| 3,465 | 37 | 1883 |
| 3,514 | 36 | 1882 |
| 3,622 | 35 | 1881 |
| 3,688 | 34 | 1880 |
| 3,851 | 33 | 1879 |
| 4,069 | 32 | 1878 |
| 4,239 | 32 | 1877 |
| 4,261 | 31 | 1876 |
| 4,258 | 31 | 1875 |
| 4,207 | 29 | 1874 |
| 4,108 | 28 | 1873 |
| 4,091 | 28 | 1872 |
| 4,213 | 28 | 1871 |
| 4,375 | 27 | 1870 |
| 4,578 | 27 | 1869 |
| 4,765 | 26 | 1868 |
| 4,878 | 26 | 1867 |
| 4,853 | 25 | 1866 |
| 4,904 | 24 | 1865 |
| 4,937 | 23 | 1864 |
| 4,930 | 22 | 1863 |
| 4,731 | 21 | 1862 |
| 4,397 | 20 | 1861 |
| 4,301 | 20 | 1860 |
| 4,204 | 19 | 1859 |
| 4,226 | — | 1858 |
| 4,205 | — | 1857 |
| 4,141 | — | 1856 |
| 3,980 | — | 1855 |
| 3,969 | — | 1854 |
| 3,943 | — | 1853 |
| 3,780 | — | 1852 |
| 3,550 | — | 1851 |
| 3,476 | — | 1850 |
| 3,397 | — | 1849 |
| 3,326 | — | 1848 |
| 3,249 | — | 1847 |
| 3,167 | — | 1846 |
| 3,069 | — | 1845 |
| 3,004 | — | 1844 |
| 2,931 | — | 1843 |
| 2,898 | — | 1842 |
| 2,933 | — | 1841 |
| 2,839 | — | 1840 |
| 2,680 | | |

(*a*) The receipts of local authorities include money borrowed, Government contributions, and receipts from sales of property, &c.

(*b*) The tax was not extended to Ireland until the year 1853.

(*c*) For ten months only.

(*d*) The nationality of emigrants was not distinguished before 1853.

(*e*) The number of vagrants relieved is not included.

(*f*) Imports were first entered by real values in 1854.

(*g*) Until 1873, vessels engaged in the coasting trade, carrying minerals, British timber, and British quarried stone, fresh meat, and fish, and a few other articles, were omitted from the coasting returns. The increase caused by including these vessels was about 4½ million tons.

(*h*) Vessels belonging to the Channel Islands and the Isle of Man are included.

(*i*) The Post Office Savings Banks were established in 1861. The accounts for these banks are made up to the 31st December, and for the Trustees' Savings Banks to the 20th November.

(*k*) The decrease is stated to be due to the relief which was given in 1880 being discontinued.

(*l*) The increase is stated to be due to food and clothing supplied at the schools through the Duchess of Marlborough, Mansion House, and *New York Herald* Committees.

(*m*) The decrease is stated to be due to exceptionally severe weather, and the prevalence of scarlatina and measles.

(*n*) The decrease is stated to be caused by the partial failure of the potato crop, and the prevalence of epidemics and distress.

(*o*) There is no definite explanation of the decrease, but 37 teachers are reported to have been arrested for complicity in Fenianism.

(*p*) The decrease is stated to be due to the severity of the weather.

(*q*) Sugar is now used as an article of manufacture as well as of personal consumption.

S

PRINTED BY CASSELL & COMPANY, LIMITED, LA BELLE SAUVAGE, LONDON, E.C.

# COBDEN CLUB LEAFLETS.

*Supplied in Packets of* 100, *price* 1s.   *Those marked* * 2s.

1. The Dog and the Shadow.
2. What does Reciprocity-Protection propose to do?
3. The Results of Protection in Germany.
4. The Rt. Hon. John Bright, M.P., on "Fair Trade."
5. Mr. Arthur Arnold, M.P., on "Fair Trade."
6. Bread Tax Once More. From "Punch."
7. A Catechism for "Fair Traders." By the Rt. Hon. W. E. Baxter, M.P.
8. Free Trade and the Working Men. By the Rt. Hon. W. E. Baxter, M.P.
9. *Fair Trade and Free Trade. By Sir B. Samuelson, Bart., M.P.
10. Free Trade: What it does for England, and How it does it. By George W. Medley.
11. Facts for Artisans. By George W. Medley.
12. Mr. Cobden on "Re-distribution of Seats."
13. *Protection in France.
14. *Facts for Labourers. By George W. Medley.
15. *The Farmers and Protection. By Charles Whitehead.
16. Facts for Farmers. No. I.—Depression in Agriculture. By George W. Medley.
17. The Effects of Protection in America. By Sir William Bower Forwood.
18. Would Protection remove the present Distress, and Benefit the Working Man? By Joseph Arch.
19. The Newcastle Weekly Chronicle on the Cobden Club Leaflets.
20. Memorial Verses on Richard Cobden, 1865.
21. Robbing a Thousand Peters to pay One Paul. By George Jacob Holyoake.
22. Less Free Trade or More: Which Shall it Be? By J. Hampden Jackson.
23. *Facts for Farmers. No. II.—Depression in Agriculture. By George W. Medley.
24. *Fair Trade: its Impossibility. By Sydney Buxton, M.P.
24. Reciprocity Explained. By George Jacob Holyoake.
26. *Words of Warning to Agricultural Labourers and other Working Men. By Alfred Simmons, the Leader of the Kent and Sussex Labourers.
27. How they Succeed in Canada. (From the *Agricultural Gazette*, January 5th, 1885.)
28. Free Trade and Fair Trade: What do the Words Mean? By James E. Thorold Rogers.
29. Free Trade *v.* Protection (*alias* "Reciprocity," *alias* "Fair Trade"). By John Noble.
30. The British Peasant on the Right Hon. J. Lowther's Proposition—that he should pay "a farthing a week" on his Bread, to benefit the Landed Interest.
31. The Farmer of Kent. From *The Suffolk Chronicle* of forty years ago.
32. Will a Five-Shilling Duty on Corn raise the price of Bread, or not?
33. United States Protection *v.* British Free Trade. By the Right Hon. W. E. Baxter, M.P.
34. The Right Hon. John Bright on "The Safety of the Ballot."
35. The Secrecy of the Ballot.

**The Early Days of Christianity.** By the Ven. Archdeacon FARRAR, D.D., F.R.S. *Popular Edition*, 1 Vol., cloth, 6s. ; Persian morocco, 10s. 6d. *Library Edition, Ninth Thousand,* Two Vols., demy 8vo, cloth, 24s. (*Can also be had in morocco binding.*)

**The Life of Christ.** By the Ven. Archdeacon FARRAR, D.D., F.R.S.
*Bijou Edition*, complete in Five Vols., in case, 10s. 6d. the set.
*Popular Edition*, in One Vol., cloth, 6s.; cloth gilt, gilt edges, 7s. 6d. ; Persian morocco, 10s. 6d. ; tree calf, 15s.
*Library Edition.* 31*st Edition.* Two Vols., cloth, 24s. ; morocco, £2 2s.
*Illustrated Edition.* With about 300 Illustrations. Extra crown 4to, cloth, gilt edges, 21s. ; calf or morocco, £2 2s.

**The Life and Work of St. Paul.** By the Ven. Archdeacon FARRAR, D.D., F.R.S. *Popular Edition*, One Vol., cloth, 6s. ; Persian morocco, 10s. 6d. *Library Edition.* (*19th Thousand.*) Two Vols., demy 8vo, cloth, 24s. ; morocco, £2 2s. *Illustrated Edition*, cloth, gilt edges, 21s.

**An Old Testament Commentary for English Readers.** By various Writers. Edited by the Right Rev. C. J. ELLICOTT, D.D Lord Bishop of Gloucester and Bristol. Complete in Five Vols., price 21s. each.
VOL. I. contains GENESIS to NUMBERS.
VOL. II. contains DEUTERONOMY to SAMUEL II.
VOL. III. contains KINGS I. to ESTHER.
VOL. IV. contains JOB to ISAIAH.
VOL. V. contains JEREMIAH to MALACHI.

**A New Testament Commentary for English Readers.** Edited by the Right Rev. C. J. ELLICOTT, D.D., Lord Bishop of Gloucester and Bristol. Three Vols., cloth, £3 3s. ; or in half-morocco, £4 14s. 6d.
VOL. I. contains the FOUR GOSPELS. £1 1s.
VOL. II. contains the ACTS to GALATIANS. £1 1s.
VOL. III. contains the EPHESIANS to the REVELATION. £1 1s.

**Sermons Preached at Westminster Abbey.** By ALFRED BARRY, D.D., D.C.L., Bishop of Sydney, Metropolitan of New South Wales, and Primate of Australia. Cloth, 5s.

**Geikie, Cunningham, D.D., Works by.** Hours with the Bible, Six Vols., 6s. each ; Entering on Life, 3s. 6d. ; The Precious Promises, 2s. 6d. ; The English Reformation, 5s. ; Old Testament Characters, 6s ; The Life and Words of Christ, Two Vols., large 8vo, cloth, 30s. ; *Student's Edition.* Two Vols., cloth, 16s.

**The Bible Educator.** Edited by the Very Rev. E. H. PLUMPTRE, D.D. Illustrated. Four Vols., 6s. each ; or Two Vols., 21s.